LECTURES

ON

ENGLISH HISTORY

AND

TRAGIC POETRY,

AS ILLUSTRATED BY SHAKSPEARE.

BY

HENRY REED,

LATE PROFESSOR IN THE UNIVERSITY OF PENNSYLVANIA.

"Dramatica est veluti Historia spectabilis; nam constituit imaginem rerum tanquam presentium: Historia, autem, tanquam præteritarum."—*Bacon, de Augm. Sc.* lib. ii. ch. xiii.

PHILADELPHIA:

CLAXTON, REMSEN & HAFFELFINGER,

819 & 821 MARKET STREET.

1869.

STEREOTYPED BY L. JOHNSON AND CO.
PHILADELPHIA.

INTRODUCTION.

THE success of the first series of Mr. Reed's Lectures on English Literature, has tempted me to a new experiment on the kindness of the public. This volume comprises two courses on kindred subjects—one delivered in 1846, on the Historical Plays of Shakspeare—from the dim legendary period, when scarcely the form of history is maintained, down to the edge of the poet's own day and generation, the reign of Henry the Eighth—the other, a very brief one on Tragic Poetry, in 1842. The first course was prepared for the smaller class of the College Chapel; and the second, which was by comparison very highly elaborated, for a more popular audience. With this latter course Mr. Reed took great pains, and had reason to be content with the result; for they were listened to with delight by a most intelligent audience, and added much to his local reputation. Both will, I am sure, be read with great pleasure, though of them, as of all these posthumous works, it is but fair to say that they are in want of the critical revision which the author alone could have given, and must be read, not as carefully-written essays, but as spoken discourses intended more for the ear than the eye. Practically, there 's good reason in

Sydney Smith's distinction, if not as to the greater care necessary, at least as to the greater care usually taken in what is written to be read than in what is written to be spoken. Mr. Reed wrote, not carelessly, but very rapidly. In one of his private letters (to many of which, by-the-by, I have referred in the notes to this volume) he thus describes not only his mode of composition, with its attendant embarrassments, but the feeling almost of enthusiasm which his theme often excited:—"Since you were here," he writes, "a very busy man have I been—perpetually haunted by the writing of one lecture a week, and usually not being able to finish it till about an hour before it was wanted. This has been a severity on one who likes to compose with a leisurely thoughtfulness. I have just got through the Shakspeare part of my course, with a lecture on Hamlet yesterday evening. I could scarcely have conceived how much my reverential admiration—wonder at the genius of the myriad-minded one—has deepened by this kind of study of his dramas—'in the lowest deep, a lower deep.' John Milton is before me in awful majesty for Monday next."

Thus he wrote and felt when poetical study occupied his mind; and, though this letter does not refer to these courses of lectures, but to one other more extended on the British Poets, which I yet hope to give to the public, I have quoted it in some measure to account for slight inaccuracies—the fruit of haste, and also as a revelation of the earnest and thoughtful spirit that influenced him throughout. His was the heart of a most devout poetical student.

Of the first course of lectures on English History as illustrated by Shakspeare, I need only say, in addition to the explanations of the Introductory Lecture, that this mode of historical writing is entirely new. With the exception of some fugitive essays in English magazines—the object of which was to show how wrong Shakspeare was—I am aware of nothing of the kind in the language. How the idea of using Shakspeare's plays, in Lord Bacon's phrase, as "Historia spectabilis," is developed, the indulgent reader must determine, bearing in mind throughout, that the drama is not used merely as a mode of illustrating historical records or lightening their gravity, not as a means of entertainment and relief, but as an instrument of deep philosophy in combining two great departments of human thought and knowledge too often dissociated. "I seek," to use Mr. Reed's words, "this combination, not so much as a means of relieving the severity of historical study and making it more attractive, as because I have a deep conviction that poetry has a precious power of its own for the preservation of historical truth; that it can so revivify the past—can put such life into it, as to make it imperishable." The attempt is now before the reading public.

In editing this volume I have added a few notes, and in them have, in several instances, availed myself of my brother's private correspondence. It is of so interesting a nature—so varied, and, as with every thing he wrote, so characteristic, and transparent to his pure tastes and gentle nature, that I am inclined to promise, at no very distant day, a memoir of his life and correspondence. I speak doubtfully; for, though among his family and intimate friends every hour of desolate separation, with its sad thoughts and memories, is less tolerable, (and I write these words at the distance of more than a year from the day of the sacrifice of the Arctic,) such a step must very much depend on the favour with which these volumes are received by the public.

Down to this point of time, as I have said, the publication of Mr. Reed's works has been eminently successful; the Lectures on English Literature having passed through several editions—three in this country, and at least one in a cheap form in Great Britain. Rarely has an unheralded book been more kindly received both at home and abroad. I have not seen the English edition, which I understand to be in the form of what is known as "Railway reading." It has, of course, been printed without regard to the American copyright, affording in a small but very striking way (for here, those who are wronged are the widow and orphan) an illustration of the discreditable condition of the law between the two countries, the responsibility for which, I am sorry to say, rests on my own countrymen. I am the more free to express this opinion, recollecting, as I do most distinctly, how strong were my brother's feelings—how intensely he felt, as a matter of American self-reproach, the want or the denial of international copyright.

In preparing this volume for the press, I am glad to make my acknowledgements for great assistance rendered to me by Professor George Allen—one of my brother's colleagues at the University of Pennsylvania. W. B. R.

OCTOBER 9, 1855.

CONTENTS.

LECTURES ON ENGLISH HISTORY.

LECTURE I.—INTRODUCTORY.

ON THE STUDY OF HISTORY.

LECTURE II.

THE LEGENDARY PERIOD OF BRITAIN: KING LEAR.

LECTURE III.

THE ROMAN AND SAXON PERIODS: CYMBELINE AND MACBETH.

LECTURE IV.

THE REIGN OF KING JOHN.

LECTURE V.

THE REIGN OF RICHARD THE SECOND.

LECTURE VI.

THE REIGN OF HENRY THE FOURTH.

LECTURE VII.

THE CHARACTER AND REIGN OF HENRY THE FIFTH.

LECTURE VIII.

THE REIGN OF HENRY THE SIXTH.

LECTURE IX.

THE WARS OF THE ROSES.

LECTURE X.

RICHARD THE THIRD—HENRY THE EIGHTH.

LECTURES ON TRAGIC POETRY.

LECTURE I.

LECTURE II.

LECTURE III.

LECTURE IV.

LECTURES

ON

ENGLISH HISTORY.

LECTURE I.—INTRODUCTORY.*

On the Study of History.

Shakspeare's Chronicle-Plays—Legendary history: King Lear—Roman and Saxon: Cymbeline and Macbeth—Nature of the subject generally—Imaginative history defined—Not historical romance—Power of Imagination in historical painting—Archbishop Whateley's analysis—Lord Bacon's idea of dramatic poetry—Milton's Vision of Greece, in Paradise Regained—Sense of reality—Famines as described in history and poetry—Genoa in 1799—Ghent in the fourteenth century—Philip Van Artavelde—Archdeacon Hare—Remote and obscure legends—Reality too distinct—Images and memories of the dead—Effect of travel in the Holy Land—Volney—Written historical painting—Charles Lamb—Belshazzar's Feast—Washington Allston—Poetical history of the Bible—The reputed philosophy of history—Lingard and Hume—Arnold—Tragic poetry—Sir Walter Scott—Funerals actual and picturesque—Hogarth—Hume's accidental theory—Outline of Shakspeare's histories—Novelty of the subject of this lecture.

It is my purpose to explain to you the nature of the course which I have announced, and to present some considerations respecting the study of history.

---

* Delivered in the College Hall of the University of Pennsylvania, December 8th, 1846.

The subject of these lectures is that portion of modern history which is illustrated by Shakspeare's historical drama. The earliest of the reigns thus illustrated is that of King John; the latest is that of Henry the Eighth: and between these, are Richard the Second, Henry the Fourth, the Fifth, the Sixth, and Richard the Third. This is a series, it will be observed, which carries us back into the agitated turmoil of the Middle Ages, and leads us on to the later form of social and political life in that period of history, which, to distinguish it from the mediæval, has been called the "modern of the modern." In these "Chronicle-Plays," as they are styled, there is comprehended the story of three eventful centuries—the thirteenth, fourteenth, and fifteenth—broken, indeed, by some considerable intervals of time. I will endeavour in the lectures partially to notice those intervals; and I propose to extend my subject into a more remote antiquity, by taking the tragedy of King Lear as illustrative of the legendary times, and Cymbeline and Macbeth, of the Roman and Saxon periods, respectively.

The nature of this subject renders these lectures literary as well as historical; and they must combine the study of those two high departments of human thought, —poetry and history. Now I desire to say, at the outset, that I have sought this combination, not so much as a means of relieving the severity of historical study and making it more attractive, as because I have a deep conviction, that Poetry has a precious power of its own for the preservation of historical truth; that it can so revivify the past—can put such life in it—as to make it imperishable. I have it greatly at heart to carry this deep conviction of mine into your minds, and hope to be able to show, if not by argument in this lecture, at least by actual evidence in those that follow, how a great poet may be, at the same time, a great historian.

Before going further with the subject of my lecture, let me take two or three minutes to prevent some misapprehensions, which might otherwise occur. While there may be a legitimate and valuable service of the faculty of imagination in the cause of history, there is certainly a great deal that is utterly spurious and deceptive, especially in the shape of historical novels, among which the few excellent stand distinguished from a multitude that are worthless. I have no occasion to refer to them, and wish to be understood as treating my subject altogether apart from them.

Again, when I state that the imagination may minister to the knowledge of history, I certainly do not mean to say, that the poetic or dramatic form is better than any other form of history, or, indeed, to make any kind of comparison between them. There is in each its own peculiar value; and so vast is the range of history, that it needs them all: it gives ample duty to every one who labours to save the memory of the past—whether it be he who zealously collects authentic documents, or pores over time-worn inscriptions, or gathers unwritten traditions—whether it be annalist, or chronicler, or biographer, or historian. I allude to these various functions, not in the way of comparison, but, on the contrary, to show that no disparagement of them is to be understood, when I assert the use of the imagination in the study of history.

Let me premise one other remark—that in employing the term "Imagination," I mean not such a faculty of the mind as gives birth to the common works of fiction, nor even such as is represented in the inadequate analysis that is met with in the usual systems of metaphysics, but that creative power which, whether it bear the name of imagination or no, is an element of every great mind, without which there may be acute intellect, there may be fine talents, but there cannot be that which is known as GENIUS. I mean that inventive wisdom, which brings the truth to life by the help of its own creative energy—the poetic element which is found, not only in the souls of mighty artists, whether their art be poetry, or painting, or sculpture, but also of great philosophers and historians.

I now may proceed in my endeavour to show, that this imaginative power does render important service in the acquisition of historical knowledge. In the first place, I ask your attention to this fact—that, whenever the imagination of a great artist, be he poet or be he painter, has touched any historic character or event, forthwith it acquires a lifelike reality, which other portions of history, on which no such light has fallen, do not possess. Why is it that we have so vivid a conception of that scriptural occasion—St. Paul at Athens—but because, in one of the grandest of the cartoons, Raffaelle has given to Christendom a vision of the apostle in that sublime attitude—

> "As if the expanded soul diffused itself,
> And carried to all spirits, with the act,
> Its affluent inspiration."*

* This illustration was, no doubt, suggested by a letter from Charles Lamb to Southey, 6th May, 1815. He says, referring to "Roderic," where these lines occur—"It struck me forcibly that the feeling of these lines might have been suggested to you by the cartoon of Paul at Athens." Final Memorials, vol. iv. p. 215. W. B. R.

Again, why is it that that splendid legend of early Roman history—the story of Coriolanus—is so fresh and familiar to us, except that Shakspeare has so impersonated the pride of that patrician soldier, as to make us feel that he was not a mere name on the page of history, but a human being with like passions as ourselves. I present to you this fact also as unquestionably true, that the portion of English history which Shakspeare has treated is more familiarly known, not only popularly, but in well-educated minds, and especially with reference to the characters of famous personages, than any other part of it. Why is it, that the first great civil conflict—the baronial war, in the reign of Henry the Third, with De Montfort at its head, —he who, when he fell, earned "a hero's honour and a martyr's name"—why is it known so much less than that other civil feud, the fury of which was quenched by the blood spilt on Bosworth Field?* Why is this, except that the latter period is seen in the light that is shed upon it by the imagination of Shakspeare? How the dramatic poet has so wrought upon those times as to inspire a life into them, I will not now stop to inquire. It is the fact I wish you to consider. From this, I pass to an authority on which much stress may be laid, because it comes from a writer remarkable for his logical and rather unimaginative habit of mind. It is a no less severe logician than Archbishop Whateley, who thus reasons, to show how imagination is needed in the study of history:—

"It has seldom or ever been noticed, how important, among the intellectual qualifications for the study of his-

* Sir Francis Palgrave.

tory, is a vivid imagination—a faculty which, consequently, a skilful narrator must himself possess, and to which he must be able to furnish excitement in others. Some may perhaps be startled at this remark, who have been accustomed to consider Imagination as having no other office than to feign and falsify. Every faculty is liable to abuse and misdirection, and Imagination among the rest; but it is a mistake, to suppose that it necessarily tends to pervert the truth of history, and to mislead the judgment. On the contrary, our view of any transaction, especially one that is remote in time or place, will necessarily be imperfect, generally incorrect, unless it embrace something more than a bare outline of the occurrences—unless we have before the mind a lively idea of the scenes in which the events took place, the habits of thought and of feeling of the actors, and all the circumstances connected with the transaction—unless, in short, we can, in a considerable degree, transport ourselves out of our own age, and country, and persons, and imagine ourselves the agents or spectators. It is from a consideration of all these circumstances, that we are enabled to form a right judgment as to the facts which history records, and to derive instruction from it. What we imagine, may, indeed, be wholly *imaginary*, *i.e.* unreal; but it may be what actually does or did exist. To say that Imagination, if not regulated by sound judgment and sufficient knowledge, may chance to convey to us false impressions of past events, is only to say that man is fallible. But such false impressions are even much the more likely to take possession of those whose imagination is feeble or uncultivated. They are apt to imagine the things, persons, times, countries, &c., which they read of, as much less different from what they see around them than is really the case."*

This may serve to correct a common misapprehension respecting the functions of the Imagination, and to show that, when disciplined and cultivated, it serves the cause of truth. This, too, is to be thought of, that the neglect of its culture does not extinguish it; for existing, as it does, though in very different degrees, in all minds, it will act in some way, perhaps feebly, and fitfully, and irregularly; and if it is not trained in the service of wisdom and truth, it certainly will be found in alliance with folly and falsehood.

I pass to another authority, immeasurably higher, when I quote a single sentence from Lord Bacon, who has said, that "Dramatic poetry is like history made visible, and is an image of actions past, as if they were present."† Now I stand upon this sentence as the text of my lectures, and on the authority of Bacon as sustaining the view I am anxious to present of the imaginative study of history. In truth, I need attempt no more than to evolve the wisdom that is wrapped in these few words of a great philosopher—one of the greatest the world has known.

When Lord Bacon speaks of dramatic poetry being history made visible, he could not have been thinking of mere scenic representations. Theatric art, in his day, was too rude and contracted for him to see in it aught but what was too mean to show the images of actions

* Whateley's Elements of Rhetoric, p. 176.

† "Dramatica est veluti Historia spectabilis: nam constituit imaginem rerum tanquam presentium: Historia, autem, tanquam præteritarum." De Augm. Sc. lib. ii. ch. xiii.

past, as if they were present; and, indeed, he speaks elsewhere of its low estate. He thought of no scenic representation—no mere bodily vision—no spectacle for the outward eye—but of that vision of the mind, that inward sight, which Imagination gives. The aspiring and far-reaching genius of Bacon felt that, while our sensuous nature is limited to the visible, the audible, the present, and the palpable, the spirituality of our being can comprehend the remote and the unseen. The heroes of antiquity rise up again in lifelike reality, and distant regions of the earth are made apparent; and, indeed, it may happen that the actual vision of the eyes may be most fitly told in words that speak only of the visions of the mind. When Milton visited the south of Europe, it was in his thoughts, after wandering in Valdarno, and by the leafy brooks of Vallambrosa, and amid the ruins of Rome, to cross from Italy over into Greece. But this cherished purpose was thwarted by tidings that came from his own afflicted country; and, deeming it the duty of England's sons to stand upon England's soil in her season of adversity, he speeded homeward. Greece was never seen by Milton—I mean by those bodily eyes, which afterward were quenched in blindness. But the spiritual power of his imagination, enriched as it was with classic lore, had borne him to the glorious promontory of Attica. He had seen the olive groves of Academe; he had heard the whispers of the waters of Ilissus—the industrious murmur of the bees; he had felt the pure air that was wafted from the waves of the bright Ægean Sea to mingle with the breath of the flowery Hymettus. The poet's splendid vision has been recorded; and when, a few years ago, a learned traveller visited

Greece, he lingered upon Hymettus; and, gazing over the country around Athens, he said:—"I cannot leave the spot—the scene now present to my eyes—without repeating the description given by one who was no eye-witness of it. To omit it would be injustice to Athens as well as to Milton;"—and that fine description in the fourth book of Paradise Regained, was aptly rehearsed amid the music of those natural sounds, which are yet heard upon the hills of Attica.*

Another and higher exercise of the Imagination is when it is employed to give us a sense of reality in the knowledge of the actions and the sufferings that history records. The mind may learn the facts of history, and the memory may, at need, recall them; and yet there may be, withal, a most inadequate conception of their truth and reality. How little sense, at best, is there of what the annals of the world tell, of suffering humanity! We read or hear, for instance, of a battle, and the numbers of those who have fallen in it; and, after a cold calculation, we think it a large or small proportion; and it makes about as much impression on us as any other statistics might. No sympathy is touched by these aggregates. The intellect calmly comprehends the facts, but the imagination is not astir to give them reality in our minds. It is comparatively a recent event in history—the dreadful famine in which thousands of the Genoese perished—when, in 1799, the French army

* Quoted in substance from "Greece, Pictorial, Descriptive, and Historical, by Christopher Wordsworth, DD., p. 31." Milton's words as he turned from this glorious promise were—"Turpe enim existimabam, dum mei cives de libertate dimicarent, me, animi causa, otiose peregrinari." W. B. R.

under Massena was besieged in their city, and a British fleet kept such unrelenting guard in that magnificent bay, that naught reached the sufferers, save the waves that

> "Dash their white foam against the palace walls
> Of Genoa—the superb."*

The inhabitants of that wealthy and luxurious city were reduced to all desperate extremities, and twenty thousand innocent persons—women, too, and children—perished by the slow misery of famine. History tells us of these things in its didactic form: it gives us the information, but it gives us no more. In the fourteenth century, the like calamity, with pestilence superadded to famine, desolated one of the opulent and populous Flemish towns, and it is thus described in the Chronicles of Froissart:—

"This whole winter of 1382, the Earl of Flanders had so much constrained Ghent, that nothing could enter the place by land or water: he had persuaded the Duke of Brabant and Duke Albert to shut up their countries so effectually, that no provisions could be exported thence, but secretly, and with a great risk to those who attempted it. It was thought by the most intelligent, that it could not be long before they perished through famine,—for all the storehouses of corn were empty, and the people could not obtain bread for money. When the bakers had baked any, it was necessary to guard their shops; for the populace, who were starving, would have broken them open. It was melancholy to hear these poor people (for men, women, and children of good substance were in this

---

* Wordsworth's Musings near Aquapendente. Works, p. 319.

miserable plight) make their daily complaints and cries to Philip Van Artavelde, their commander-in-chief."

So is the suffering city described in the simple style of the old chronicler, and with, indeed, rather more of animated narrative than history generally gives.

I now refer to the fine historical drama by a living poet,—the Philip Van Artavelde of Henry Taylor,—to show how the image of the past is there presented. We gain the vision, when we read the words with which Van Artavelde addresses his companions as they see the city of Ghent lying in its wretchedness beneath them:—

"Look round about on this once populous town!
Not one of these innumerous house-tops
But hides some spectral form of misery,
Some peevish, pining child, and moaning mother,
Some aged man, that in his dotage scolds,
Not knowing why he hungers,—some cold corse,
That lies unstraightened where the spirit left it."

A still deeper sense of reality is given by the imagination being carried into the interior of one of those afflicted dwellings. Van Artavelde, meeting his sister, after her return from the awful charity of a starving and pestilential city, questions her—

"Now render me account of what befel—
Where thou hast been to-day.
Clara. It is but little.
I paid a visit first to Ukenheim,
The man, who whilome saved our father's life,
When certain Clementists and ribald folk
Assailed him at Malines. He came last night,
And said he knew not if we owed him aught,
But if we did, a peck of oatmeal now
Would pay the debt, and save more lives than one.

I went. It seemed a wealthy man's abode;
The costly drapery and good house-gear
Had, in an ordinary time, betokened
That with the occupant the world went well.
By a low couch, curtained with cloth of frieze,
Sat Ukenheim, a famine-stricken man,
With either bony fist upon his knees,
And his long back upright. His eyes were fixed
And moved not, though some gentle words I spake:
Until a little urchin of a child,
That called him father, crept to where he sat,
And plucked him by the sleeve, and with its small
And skinny finger pointed: then he rose,
And with a low obeisance, and a smile
That looked like watery moonlight on his face,
So pale and weak a smile, he bade me welcome.
I told him that a lading of wheat-flour
Was on its way, whereat, to my surprise,
His countenance fell, and he had almost wept.

Art. Poor soul! and wherefore?

Clara. That I soon perceived.
He plucked aside the curtain of the couch,
And there two children's bodies lay composed.
They seemed like twins of some ten years of age,
And they had died so nearly both together
He scarce could say which first: and being dead,
He put them, for some fanciful affection,
Each with its arm about the other's neck,
So that a fairer sight I had not seen
Than those two children, with their little faces
So thin and wan, so calm, and sad, and sweet.
I looked upon them long, and for a while
I wished myself their sister, and to lie
With them in death, as they did with each other;
I thought that there was nothing in the world
I could have loved so much; and then I wept;
And when he saw I wept, his own tears fell,
And he was sorely shaken and convulsed,
Through weakness of his frame and his great grief.

Art. Much pity was it he so long deferred
To come to us for aid.
Clara. It was, indeed.
But whatsoe'er had been his former pride,
He seemed a humbled and heart-broken man.
He thanked me much for what I said was sent;
But I knew well his thanks were for my tears.
He looked again upon the children's couch,
And said, low down, they wanted nothing now.
So, to turn off his eyes,
I drew the small survivor of the three
Before him; and he snatched it up, and soon
Seemed quite forgetful and absorbed. With that
I stole away."

Now this is purely imaginary; and yet, how perfectly expressive is it of the truth! How much more truthful is it than mere lifeless narrative-accuracy; and how deeply into our hearts does it carry the sense of the reality! Consider how little was known a few years ago of this same Philip Van Artavelde, until, within our own day, the vision of a living English poet's imagination is turned to the comparatively obscure region of the annals of Flanders, and forthwith Van Artavelde becomes, what even Froissart had not succeeded in making him, a familiar historical personage.

In continuing this analysis of the employment of the Imagination in the study of history, there are still higher and more precious functions, than this power of presenting picture-like impressions, which I have been endeavouring to illustrate.

We are all of us, I dare say, apt to think of the composition and the study of history as a much simpler and easier thing than it really is. But if history were no more than a mere chronicle of facts,—a mere record of men, their deeds, and their dates,—reflect how soon there gather over these uncertainty, obscurity, and blank oblivion. It may be that the historian is toiling to recover the knowledge of some far remote age—that he strives to decipher the timeworn inscriptions of a lost language, or the mystery of hieroglyphics, or that he questions the awful silence of the Pyramids, which, almost as long, it might seem, as the earth has endured, have been pointing to the sun, or bearing on their huge bulk the darkness of the night. Or it may be that the historian's labour is not upon the scant materials of a dim antiquity, but upon the immense accumulation from which the history of a later time is to be extracted. Now, in either case, it is scarcely possible to estimate justly, much less to exaggerate, the magnitude of such labour, or the might of human genius, that is needed to achieve even an approach to it. This has been eloquently set forth by a thoughtful living author, in a sentence which reminds me of the magnificent structure of the prose of Milton or Jeremy Taylor:—"The field of operation is so vast and unsurveyable, so much lies wrapped up in thick, impenetrable darkness, while other portions are obscured by the mists which the passions of men have spread over them, and a spot, here and there, shines out dazzlingly, throwing the adjacent parts into the shade; the events are so inextricably intertwisted and conglomerated, sometimes thrown together in a heap,—often rushing onward and spreading out like the Rhine, until they lose themselves in a morass,—and now and then, after having disappeared, rising up again, as was fabled of the Alpheus, in a distant region, which they reach through an unseen channel; the peaks, which first meet our eyes, are mostly so barren, while the fertilizing waters flow secretly through the valleys; the statements of events are so perpetually at variance, and not seldom contradictory; the actors on the ever-shifting stage are so numerous and promiscuous; so many undistinguishable passions, so many tangled opinions, so many mazy prejudices are ever at work, rolling and tossing to and fro in a sleepless conflict, in which every man's hand and heart seem to be against his neighbour, and often against himself; it is so impossible to discern and separate the effects brought about by man's will and energy, from those which are the result of outward causes, of circumstances, of conjunctures, of all the mysterious agencies summed up under the name of chance; and it requires so much faith, as well as wisdom, to trace any thing like a pervading overruling law through the chaos of human affairs, and to perceive how the banner which God has set up, is still borne pauselessly onward, even while the multitudinous host seems to be struggling waywardly, busied in petty bickerings and personal squabbles;—that a perfect, consummate history of the world may not unreasonably be deemed the loftiest achievement that the mind of man can contemplate."* It is from the entangled and enormous mass, thus described, of memorials, and traditions, and records, that history is to be evolved. For the work, there is not a faculty of the human mind that is not needed, besides the great moral qualification—a love of truth, that shall be at once calm in its action, and passionate in its earnestness and its impatient hatred of falsehood. What concerns my present subject chiefly is,

* Hare's Guesses at Truth. First Series, p. 353.

that historic truth is gained, not only by the logical processes of the intellect, but by that inventive power which can discover the truth when argument alone could not have disclosed it; and it has been wisely said, that the union of the poet and the philosopher is essential to form the perfect historian. It is not, I think, possible to find, in the records of all literature, one great historian in the constitution of whose mind the imaginative faculty is not a large element—the ability, not simply to reason about historic testimony, but also to behold the past—to see it with the mind's eye; and this is essentially the same thing as poetic vision, by which the dead, the distant, are made living and present. It is only when this philosophic and poetic power combined looks upon the multitudinous facts of past times, that these facts are duly arrayed and harmonized into just order and proportion. Amid the actual occurrences, how much is there that is unmeaning and worthless—nay, worse than worthless, because often obtrusive, and standing between our minds and that which is significant and valuable. All such obstructions the genuine historian sweeps away in silence; and knowledge is acquired, not only by what is told, but by what is left untold. Men, and the deeds of men, are to be exhibited in the just subordination to the controlling agencies of their times. The simple chronicler may be content to make his record of events with no discrimination; but history is more than a chronological table, and the historian must idealize the actual; he must give it such a form, that we may see the causes of events, and the living, actuating principles that were at work in them. Now, when the philosophic or the imaginative eye of the historian—(I care not which it be called, for I believe all true philosophy is imaginative, and all genuine imagination is philosophical)—when the eye of the historian contemplates a period of history, after deep study, he sees all that is important, and influential, and permanent, and he sees it in all its essential character and reality, while a thousand insignificant circumstances have faded out of his thoughts. Thus it is that the actual is idealized into the highest and purest truth.

Reflect how often our sense of truth is impaired or impeded by the pressure on our minds of what is actual, and visible, and present. A faithful painter may, in the highest style of his art, portray a human face with all its characteristic expression and in all its true individuality; and yet the nearest relatives are not only the hardest to satisfy, but, by the very nature of their familiarity with the subject, will often be the worst judges of the likeness. Again, I believe we are all of us very apt to fail in appreciating the best and the noblest parts in the characters of those whom we know familiarly, for the thousand familiarities of common life interpose; and it is sad to think, that often it is not until Death hath hallowed and idealized the character, that we can do it justice. Then the eye can no longer see the familiar face, the ear no longer catch sounds of the familiar voice; but the soul, apart from the senses, is left to the solemn, solitary work, and beholds the strength and the purity of the spirit that has passed away, more truly than when it was incarnate in this life.

I use these illustrations to show how much that which is matter of fact, as it is called, often stands in the way of truth; and I cannot doubt, that one of the great moral purposes for which the Imagination has been implanted in us is, that it may enable us to triumph over the bondage of the senses, of which it may be said, as of the elements of fire and water, that they are good servants, but very bad masters. The soul must keep dominion over them, or else we are sure to be beset by the manifold mischiefs and miseries of materialism in some or other of its forms. The most elevated sense of truth in the spirit of a man may be grievously and disastrously disturbed by the presence of that which affects only the senses. It is said that Volney was made an infidel by his travels in Palestine; and though it is fearful to think of faith dying out of a Christian's soul in consequence of his eyes having before them the visible presence of the Holy Land, yet there is a natural process by which such a defection is conceivable.

When, at a distance, we think of Mount Sinai, or of the Mount of Olives, or of that other more awful eminence, they are more spiritual than material places of the earth. The "Delectable Mountains" in the Pilgrim's Progress are, to my mind, scarce more visionary; and with such feelings, the events that give a sanctity to those spots, are in perfect harmony. But when the traveller actually stands upon that ground,—when it is visible and tangible,—and when, feeling the very soil, the vegetation, and the stones, beneath his feet, he calls to mind Jehovah's presence on that selfsame place, or the Saviour's incarnate life, then the impression of the senses and the spiritual associations may come in conflict. In the heart of Volney it proved an irreconcilable conflict, and faith yielded to what was sensuous. It may well be believed, that any one who visits that land, not in the reverential spirit of the early Christian pilgrim, but with the thoughtless sight-seeing temper of the modern traveller, has need to pray that his faith be strengthened before his eyes rest on places, which, before, had only been apprehended by his imagination.

In the composition of history, and eminently in the historical drama, there must needs be this poetic process, by which the actual is subordinated to the ideal, that which is inconsiderable put out of sight, and such unity given to the subject as will best display its real truth. It is one of the chief functions of the Imagination to give unity and harmony to the materials of which it treats; and, perhaps, I may explain this more clearly by reference to an act kindred to historical poetry,—I mean, historical *painting*. In one of the most admirable of the Elia Essays, so full of a fine and humorous philosophy, Charles Lamb has observed that "not all that is optically possible to be seen is to be shown in every picture. By a wise falsification, the great masters of painting got at their true conclusions, by not showing the actual appearances that is, all that was to be seen at any given moment by an indifferent eye, but only what the eye might be supposed to see in the doing or suffering of some portentous action."* In this same essay, he shows, by a careful comparison, that it is in their barrenness of the imaginative faculty, that most modern works of art are so inferior to the paintings by the great masters, which, on this very account, were so much more impressive and truthful. He exemplifies this deficiency in Martin's historical paintings, which are familiar to us all by the help

* Essay on the Barrenness of the Imaginative Faculty in the Productions of Modern Art. Lamb's Prose Works, vol. iii. p. 176.

of the engravings; and in the Belshazzar's Feast of that artist, after noticing the alarm which has thrown the well-dressed lords and ladies in the Hall of Belus into such admired confusion, he justly asks,—"Is this an adequate exponent of supernatural terror? The way in which the finger of God writing judgments would have been met by a guilty conscience? There is a human fear, and a divine fear. The one is disturbed, restless, and bent upon escape. The other is bowed down, effortless, and passive."* This same scriptural subject has been treated by another modern artist—one whose genius was full of that imaginative power, which was the glory of the old masters—I mean our countryman, the late Washington Allston; and I wish that you had seen that great, but unfinished painting, were it only that I might now the better appeal to it as an illustration, to show how the imagination can worthily and triumphantly reproduce the events of history. On beholding it, one is made to feel that the supernatural writing was a transaction, so to speak, between God and that impious king—the prophet participating in divine power, while he is inspired to interpret the mysterious words. You see that it is upon Belshazzar that the awful terror has fallen with all its weight—that it is he—still gorgeous with barbaric pearl and gold, and just now so proud in his profanity—that it is he, and, perhaps, he alone that has beheld the fingers of a hand come forth and write upon the palace walls; and that it is his spirit which is withered by the prophet's interpretation—"God hath numbered thy kingdom and finished it. Thou art weighed in the balances

* Lamb's Prose Works, vol. iii, p. 173.

and art found wanting. Thy kingdom is divided, and given to the Medes and Persians." In the foreground of the picture are seen the queen, heart-stricken with terror, and awe, and grief—the group of the baffled soothsayers and astrologers—the captive Israelites reverentially bowing around their inspired countryman. In the middle distance are the tables of the impious feast, with Belshazzar's thousand lords—his wives and concubines; and afar off, methought I saw thousands of Babylonians thronging to the huge idol that towered in the distance—and yet all so controlled by the genius of a great historical painter, that there is ever present to your mind the leading truth of the history,—that it is Belshazzar's soul that God is dealing with, and that it is over his appalled spirit that is hanging the fulfilment which closes the story of him and his empire. "In that night was Belshazzar slain, and Darius the Mede took the kingdom." The creative power of a great artist, a poet-painter, has made that historical occasion visible. I am sure that I am thus made to feel the truth and the reality of that chapter of sacred history more deeply than I ever felt it before, and that I shall never think of it otherwise than as Allston has shown it to me.* So is it

* In the summer of 1842, my brother accompanied me on a visit to New England, and there he became personally acquainted with Mr. Allston. He saw "Belshazzar" afterward. In an address delivered before the Art Union of Philadelphia, he thus refers to this visit:—

"When Death suddenly, but with its gentlest stroke, closed the career of the most eminent painter our country has produced,—I mean the late Washington Allston,—the paint was left wet on that great scriptural painting, unhappily incomplete, to which he had devoted many of the best, and all the later, years of his life,—a life that the imagination of the genuine painter addresses itself to the imagination of the spectator; and, as history is wrought on by the genius of the artist, so it is by that of the historical poet: so, indeed, too,—in a somewhat different way,—by every great historian. All history of a high order must be animated by the vivifying spirit of the Imagination; and I give the highest possible authority for this opinion, when I remind you that inspired history abounds with it. That one chapter, for instance, which describes the event of which I have just been speaking, the downfall of the Babylonian Empire, is instinct with Imagination from the first verse to the last.

Having chanced to touch upon this train of thought, let me follow it a step further, for the sake of the authority. So large a space in the record of revelation is occupied by history and poetry, that one cannot help recognising and revering them as the appointed modes

---

and a name which I cannot mention without regretting that I must not stop to say what might be said of them, as showing the beauty and the dignity, the truth and the moral power, that dwell in the soul of a great Christian artist. With his high powers as a painter, there was united a most exquisite spirit of criticism, wherein it would have been hard to say which was the largest element,—a fine philosophy or tender Christian sympathy. I remember with what deep but tranquil emotion, in tones that were the very music of modesty and genius, he lamented, rather than rebuked, that injurious temper of criticism which seizes on the weak points of a painter's work, and shuts its vision to all that is genuine and great. He made the remark with reference to Haydon; and I could not but recall it, when, not a great while afterward, we heard the tragic story of that painter's death,—how, in the metropolis of Great Britain, he was driven by neglect and that wrong, which Allston had reproved, to a crazed brain and an awful suicide." W. B. R.

of divine instruction—as chosen instruments for the guidance of the human soul. You find there history, in its severe form of the Chronicles; you find poetry in its most sublime form; and, what is more applicable to my present subject, you find history and poetry combined in those marvellous proportions unattainable by the uninspired imagination of man. And what a dull, dreary, dismal Bible it would be, if all that was imaginative in it were quenched! If inspiration come direct—direct, I mean, from the throne of God—into the mind of man, it has utterance, for the most part, in some imaginative form—it may be a lyric chaunt, like that which burst from the lips of Moses and Miriam over the Egyptian warriors, Busiris and his Memphian chivalry,—"the horse and his rider cast into the sea;" and if the inspiration is given to tell, not of the past, but of the future, it finds voice in the lofty strains of *prophetic* poetry. And so when inspiration comes into the mind; as the constitutional endowment of poetic genius, it, too, seeks expression in some imaginative form, whether its plastic power be employed on the canvas, or on marble, or in words.

In the next place, a great impediment in the way of historical knowledge, as, indeed, of all knowledge, is that he who writes, and he who reads, history, is apt to bring with him prejudices and prepossessions; and accordingly, the study is carried on, not with the love of truth as the prime and master impulse, but to make out some theory, or to sanction some preconceived bias. The consequence of this is, that there are few histories to which the reader can intrust himself with believing, confiding docility; instead of which, he has to be perpetually on his guard, as if he were walking with a foe instead of a friend; and he is forced to seek truth by that painful, miserable process of balancing one extreme against another. Of all the histories of England, there is not one, I am safe in saying, which is not, in one way or other, a partisan history; and the historians who make the proudest boast of their philosophy and their liberality, are not seldom the most narrow-minded and treacherous; so that it has been well said that, what has been called "the philosophy of history, may be denominated the philosophy of romance; for by few writers has so much been done to pervert the truth of history, as by the so called 'philosophical historians.'"*

I have said there is not an impartial history of England, inasmuch as every writer of it has looked on his subject, not in the clear atmosphere of candour and of truth, but through the disturbing medium of some party opinions and feelings. Each historian has some point of vision to which he is bound by his prejudices; and only from that can he look back on past ages. Worse than all, the most familiar history of England, the classic history,—I mean Mr. Hume's,—is the product of a mind, that could look upon other times only through those deadly vapours that are perpetually rising from an infidel's heart. From the low and unhealthy region of a shallow, deistical philosophy, he never rose to the lofty stations of truth; and how could a dry, hard, sophistical,

* This remark will be found in the advertisement to the fourth volume of the quarto, and, I believe, first, edition of Lingard's History of England, p. vi. In the last edition, revised shortly before the author's death, he says:—"Nor do I hesitate to proclaim my belief that no writers have proved more successful in the perversion of historic truth than speculative and philosophical historians." W. B. R.

and unimaginative intellect, like his, have any feeling in common with the heroism and the piety of other ages? With an impassable gulf between his spirit and the spirit of those times, how could he be a faithful or a just historian of them?

Now, to bring these considerations to bear on my subject, when an historian, whether in prose or poetry, comes to his arduous work, a strong and well-disciplined imagination lifts him up from the atmosphere of prejudice and error into a pure region of truth. It is the precious moral agency of the Imagination to raise us out of a narrow-minded selfishness; it enables us to think and to feel with others, and thus to judge of them with candour and with charity, and therefore with truth. It puts it in the historian's power to look upon distant ages in the spirit of those ages, and thus to give a genuine knowledge of them. Instead of this, history is made controversial; it is tortured into the sanction or the subversion of some system; and it is seen only in such a light, or is placed only in such a light, that all the events of past ages shall seem to do homage to some narrow-minded and exclusive speculation of the historian. Political writers, for instance, treat the civil institutions, even of antiquity, in such a way, that the narrative shall make, respectively, in favour or against modern theories of liberalism or absolutism. The Protestant and the Roman Catholic historian will so shape their stories of the early and middle ages of the Church and of Europe, as to support or condemn the great movement of the Reformation; and thus, while writing the history of one century, they will, in reality, be thinking much more of another and a later one. Or an historian, like Hume, writing in the deistical temper of his own day, labours to make all history servile to the shallow skepticism of the eighteenth century; and though unable to conceal, that Christianity, or rather let me say more precisely, the Church of Christ, is the great distinguishing element of modern history, Hume never spares the pains to tempt the unwary reader to think, with him, that all religious feeling is either fraud or superstition, and that Christian earnestness is no more than a mockery or a delusion. But the dutiful culture of the Imagination, together with that of the practical understanding, saves us from many errors that else are apt to beset us in our narrow-mindedness. The historian, as he goes forth into the past ages of the world, needs all the comprehensive spirit which the philosophic imagination gives,—the ample feeling with which a true poet, on beholding, in another region of Christendom, religious rites different from the familiar ones of his own land, exclaims—

"Where'er we roam—along the brink
Of Rhine, or by the sweeping Po,
Through Alpine vale or champaign wide,
Whate'er we look on—at our side
Be Charity, to bid us think
And feel if we would know."*

This spirit of capacious charity, which is one of the characteristics of the imaginative mind, brings with it this great gain, that it leads the historian to do justice to the better side of human nature as it is displayed in history. He will habitually seek out all that is good

* Wordsworth's Lines composed in one of the Catholic Cantons. Works, p. 280.

and great in the annals of the world, and thus will feed the genial sense of admiration on which the health of our moral nature so much depends. It is with admirable feeling that Arnold says,—"If an historian be an unbeliever in all heroism—if he be a man who brings every thing down to the level of a common mediocrity, depend upon it the truth is not found in such a writer."* The best truth of history, let me add, is lost to that censorious, sneering, sarcastic temper, which is its own curse; for it can see only what is selfish, and mean, and vicious. There will, indeed, be found enough of evil passion and guilt upon the pages of history; but when sentence is pronounced, let it be with the tone of solemn judgment, and not of satire.† Clinging to the truth in all that is pure and elevated in our struggling human nature, we may do well to cherish the memory of the heroic deeds, the virtues, the self-devotion, and whatever else has given

---

* Lectures on Modern History, p. 301.

† I shall have occasion, at one part of this course, in connection with the career of Henry the Fifth, to see the tone of history alleviated by the inimitable comic element of the character of Falstaff; but, for the most part, we find that the historical drama carries us into the region of lofty passions—that its largest element is that of tragedy—that it is by suffering that the characters of men and nations are formed and disciplined—that it is in the school of adversity that high virtues are engendered; for,

"Oh, Life! without thy chequered scene
Of right and wrong, of weal and wo,
Success and failure, could a ground
For magnanimity be found;
For faith, 'mid ruined hopes, serene?
Or whence could virtue flow?"

Wordsworth, p. 280. H. R.

glory and dignity to the generations of mankind. This is the most permanent and the most precious portion of history, and it is that to which a well-cultivated imagination, and, indeed, the simplest good sense and good feeling, will turn instinctively. Remember how much it is a matter of choice and of habit with us, whether we will look upon things with a good or an evil eye; and remember, too, that the seat of the scoffer is not the seat of wisdom—that truth is vouchsafed to him who seeks it with a generous sympathy and a docile temper, and that it is denied to him who comes with suspicion, and pride, and a spirit of contempt.

Let me give a single illustration, to show how the self-same occasion may be presented under very different aspects, in one of which there may be present that which disturbs and distracts our impressions of the truth, while in the other the imaginative view may be much more faithful to them. In a passage in his private diary, Sir Walter Scott has expressed an aversion to funerals, because so much of what is seen and heard at them is painfully discordant with the genuine grief, the depth of which can neither be seen nor heard. "I hate funerals," he writes; "there is such a mixture of mummery with real grief—the actual mourner, perhaps, heart-broken, and all the rest making solemn faces, and whispering observations on the weather or public news, and here and there a greedy fellow enjoying the cake and wine. But," he adds, "the funeral at a distance,—the few mourners on horseback, with their plaids wrapped around them,—the father heading the procession as they enter the river, and pointing out the ford by which his darling is to be carried—none of the subordinate figures in discord with the general tone of the incident, but seeming just accessories and no more—the distant funeral is affecting."* The first of these scenes Scott saw with the keen, observing eye, with which he studied human nature in its weakness as well as its strength: the other he beheld with a poet's eye; and he gazed on it as it was idealized by the distance and by his own imagination. I ask you which of these views is the true one? It may be answered that each has a truth of its own. Well, then, which more truly expresses the real feeling of the occasion? If the purpose be to show the utter heartlessness of mourning, then Hogarth's picture of a funeral, at once comic and hideous, will best answer the purpose; but then, at best, it is only satire, and we feel the truth of that view which is harmonized by the imagination.†

---

* Lockhart's Scott, vol. viii. p. 322.

† Hogarth's Pictures, or rather the folio volume of engravings, was one of the picture-books of my boyhood; and now I am not ashamed to record the heresy, that no creation of art is in every way more repulsive to me. The fun is, to my eye, hideous. They may be historical pictures, (so Hazlitt dignifies them,) but they are historical of the most unpicturesque period of modern times—the first quarter or half of the eighteenth century—the early Georgian era. If Hogarth had illustrated such a ghastly book as Lord Hervey's Memoirs, what happy congeniality of art and letter-press it would have been!—and what man or woman of delicacy would care to open the volume!

W. B. R.

A friend, to whom I have shown this note, calls my attention to a passage from Goethe, on the same subject:

"The third work formed for itself quite another circle of readers. The interest devoted to *Lichtenberg's Hogarth* was, in reality, a factitious interest: for how could the German feel any real enjoyment of whims and oddities that rarely occurred in the circumstances of the

The poetic faculty enables the historian or the historical poet to accomplish another important result in our knowledge of historical occurrences and characters. In the preface to the tragedy of "Richelieu," Bulwer speaks of the historic drama as "the concentration of historic events;" and Coleridge has described it as "a collection of events borrowed from history, but connected together, in respect of cause and time, poetically and by dramatic fiction; and thus, while the unity from mere succession may be destroyed, it is supplied by a unity of a higher order, which connects the events by reference to the workers, gives a reason for them in the motives, and presents men in their causative character."* Now, this "unity of a higher order" which Coleridge speaks of, brings to view that moral meaning, which, while it is the chief value of history, is so difficult to discover in the multitude and perplexity of historical events. Facts, which seem to stand wholly apart, are shown to have some moral association: a blessing, which actually followed, perhaps, afar off and obscurely, is brought near to the happy influence which produced it, and retribution comes manifestly to guilt, which brings suffering not only to itself, but to the innocent, according to the dark

simple and pure life of his own countrymen? It was only the tradition, which made current upon the Continent a name glorified by the English—it was only the singularity of being able to possess all of these whimsical representations complete in one body, and the convenient circumstance that there was no need of bringing to the study and admiration of these works any knowledge or feeling of art, but only a bad disposition and contempt for mankind—that favoured, in a very peculiar way, this remarkable success." Goethe's Works, (1840,) vol. xxvii. p. 511. (Annalen, oder Tag-und Jahres-Hefte.)

* Literary Remains. Works, vol. viii. p. 29.

mystery of that law, by which misery is carried down to the third and fourth generations.

When Hume, in his history, reaches the end of a splendid era of English history, he closes it with this reflection—that "the study of the early institutions of the country is instructive, as showing that a mighty fabric of government is built up by a great deal of *accident*, with a very little human foresight and wisdom." In our meek hours of faith, we are taught that not a sparrow falls to the ground without God's providence; and then we turn to the infidel history to learn there how the "kingly commonwealth" of England, that has swayed the happiness of millions of human beings, and has sent forth this vast Republic of the West, grew up by *accident;* that, with all its influence on the human race, it was but the creature of chance. It is thus that history becomes atheism, from which we may gladly turn to the better philosophy of the poet-historian.* In

* My brother had a strong aversion (if such a word is admissible in matters of criticism) to Hume and his History; and, as is clear from many passages of these lectures, was at no pains to conceal it. He had no sympathy with the tolerance of error which praises Hume, adopts or recommends his history as a text-book, and contents itself with incidental corrections of errors and misrepresentations. (Smyth's Lectures, vol. i. lect. v.) He would as soon have taught from Paine as from Hume; for he believed that Hume's principles, enforced more perniciously in his History than anywhere else, were, as Lord Brougham admits them to be, "atheism, not skepticism." (Men of Letters, p. 177. Art. on Hume.) To Hume's skill as a rhetorician, he, perhaps, did injustice—though, with my brother, I incline to the belief that time and improving criticism are damaging this fame also. The passages from Hume cited by Lord Brougham as "magnificent," do not so impress me. Others, not quoted, such as his description of Charles the First's execution, are most graceful and picturesque.

Shakspeare's admirable description of poetic genius, one of its noblest attributes is, that it glances from earth to heaven. Nowhere has this been more finely exemplified than in his own "Chronicle-Plays." If the Greek drama was controlled by Destiny,—the despotism of a blind, inexorable Fate,—the Christian historical drama has a Providence for its leading idea. In the periods of history which I propose to examine and illustrate by the English historical plays of Shakspeare, it will be seen that, while he embodies a great variety of human character and passions, he shows it all as an agency in the providential government of the world. After disposing of the early history, I hope to be able to show to those who may accompany me in this course of lectures, how the guilt that hung over the usurpation of King John brought not only retribution on himself, but unmerited misery upon the innocent Arthur—how the giddy tyranny and the frailties of the second Richard found sad expiation in a tragic death. We may there trace the fortunes of the Lancastrian kings, from the elevation of Bolingbroke, onward, through the martial glories of his son's reign, to the disastrous civil wars of the Roses. In the last of these historical dramas, we shall see one of the noblest tragic representations of the mutability of earthly power; and we may contemplate the sublime, historical impartiality with which the poet has portrayed the splendid and haughty career of England's Great Cardinal.

As a *per contra* to Lord Brougham's excessive panegyric on Hume, the student is referred to an admirable article entitled "Hume and his Influence on History," in vol. lxxiii. p. 536, of the Quarterly Review. W. B. R.

In conclusion, let me say, that, apart altogether from the mode of treating it, I cannot, for one moment, distrust the intrinsic interest of the *subject* of this course of lectures. It is a subject of ample magnitude; and of this I have become more deeply sensible the more I have dwelt upon it since I first proposed it to my mind. It is, therefore, with no affectation of modesty that I assure you I have a strong feeling that these lectures must be very inadequate to a subject which grows in my thoughts as I work upon it. The subject is a new one, too—I mean, as to the mode of treating it; and it will demand much care and study to keep the historic and poetic elements in just proportions. In this, I have no authority or example to guide me.

I will endeavour to give the subject an interest and value in the minds of those who will accompany me in the course; but if I should not succeed in this, remember what I tell you now,—the fault is in me, and not in my subject.

LECTURE II.*

The Legendary Period of Britain: King Lear.

Legendary period prior to the Roman invasion—Julius Cæsar—Malone's comment—Fabulous antiquity of British kings—Brutus of Troy—Authentic ancient history limited to Southern Europe—Britain out of the path of the ancient world—Faber's idea of the Mediterranean—Milton's History of England—Faith in ancient legends—Claim of Edward the First to the sovereignty of Scotland—The Papal reference—Difference of British and classical legends—Grote on Greek legends—Minstrelsy and romance—Washington, in our sense, a legendary idea in America—Lives of the saints—Symbolical legends—Popular faith in legends—Identified with reverence for ancestry—Sir Robert Walpole's false idea of history—Niebuhr—Modern colonies—King Lear a dramatic legend—Filial relation—Illustrations appropriate to paganism—Lear's invocation of heathen gods—Charles Lamb's criticism on Lear.

In the examination of the period of history, which forms the subject of these lectures, I shall follow chronological order as the most natural arrangement. I am, therefore, now led back into that dim, or rather dark, region of historical knowledge, which may be fitly described as the *legendary period of British history*. Amid the multitude of stories or fables which belong to these times, one found its way to the heart of Shakspeare; and, by the wondrous alchemy of his genius, it was transmuted into, perhaps, the most impressive and

---

* December 15th, 1846.

awful tragedy in the whole range of dramatic literature. The obscure and neglected legend lives, by transmigration, in that imperishable drama, which shows us the royal and the parental misery of the breaking heart of King Lear.

The legendary period of British history is to be understood as embracing those ages, which, beginning in a distant and indefinite antiquity, end with the opening of authentic annals. That authentic history begins under the unfavourable circumstances of observation which is limited and prejudiced, for it is found in the military narrative of a Roman soldier, who met the Britons in bloody warfare. The scanty information to be derived from Julius Cæsar's memoirs of his campaigns is, at best, the description of an enemy and a Roman; and, in judging of the value of such testimony, it should be borne in mind, that, whatever were the virtues of the Roman character, and whatever praise there may be in calling a man, now-a-days, an "old Roman," there was found among that people little of veracity or magnanimity in their dealings with their enemies. Still, though the narrative by Cæsar is not entitled to entire confidence, it does give the first solid footing for English history to stand upon. We learn certain facts from it, distorted and coloured though they be by the medium through which they have come to us. We can believe that the great triumvir, after having led his legions in victory from one province of Gaul into another, found a new adversary, when the Britons crossed the narrow channel of the sea to help the kindred people who dwelt in Armorica—there where, at this present time, their descendants are found, I mean, that very peculiar race who occupy the north-western corner of France, the province of Brittany. When the subjugation of Gaul was completed, Cæsar, revolving, perhaps, his plans against the freedom of the republic, looked round and beheld on one side the dark and impenetrable forests of Germany, and on the other what appeared the more accessible and easy conquest of the almost unknown land of the Britons. He looked to the white cliffs of these shores, perhaps with a revengeful eye against the confederates of his Gallic enemy—perhaps impelled to continued war by the fire of that lust of conquest, which burned in the heart of Roman soldiers for eight centuries and more—burned until it was quenched, not only by exhaustion, but by the fulfilment of providential purposes. Whatever was the impulse—whether these, or the improbable and meaner one, which has been imputed to Cæsar by one of his own countrymen, the coveting of British pearls—the invasion of Britain added nothing to Roman power or pride.* The eagles were fluttered in their flight; and, when thanks were given at Rome to the gods, it may well be questioned, as Milton intimates in his History of England, whether it was for a conquest or an escape—whether it was for an exploit done or for a discovery made. At the end of the campaigns, the conqueror of Britain was not master of one foot of British ground; not a Roman colonist was left in the land; and Julius Cæsar, at his return to Rome, dedicated to the goddess Venus a corslet of these British pearls—a gift, which

* Tacitus, Vit. Agricolæ cap. xii. Cicero ad Att. iv. 16. Ad Fam. vii. 7. Lingard, ch. i. The authority alluded to in the text was, doubtless, Suetonius, C. Julius Cæsar s. 47:—"Britanniam petîsse, spe margaritarum, quarum amplitudinem conferentem, interdum suâ manû exegisse pondus" W. B. R.

was, perhaps, the more precious from the fact, that the Romans went home with no inclination to renew the search for that kind of jewels.

It is certain that, in the invasion of Britain, Cæsar encountered a foe who caused a dismay, from which even the discipline of his veteran legions with difficulty rallied; and I must confess that, while we applaud the heroism of the standard-bearer of the tenth legion, I have a deeper sympathy with the rude barbarians who gathered by thousands to defend their native shores. If it was true martial virtue for the Roman to leap into the waves and bid his hesitating fellow-soldiers follow him, there was a nobler spirit in those undaunted Britons, who rushed into the sea to strike the invader before his foot polluted their soil.

It is not my intention to dwell upon such familiar passages in history as the descent of Julius Cæsar on the British shore; but I could hardly say less in asking your attention to the manner in which the authentic history of Britain has its beginning, with that event, about fifty years before the birth of our Saviour. It is the practice of the later writers of English history to make no attempt to present any narrative of the earlier period, which is abandoned as purely legendary or hopelessly involved in fable or confused tradition. It should be understood, however, that, in doing so, they pursue a course very different from that of the early historians of England, who had no fear in looking into a very remote antiquity, and no difficulty in persuading themselves that they saw a great deal there. They dealt with their eras of a thousand years with a magnificent assurance, and marshalled kings and dynasties of kings in complete chronology and exact succession. They carried their elaborate genealogy so far beyond the Olympiads, that, by the side of it, Greek and Roman history seems a thing of yesterday. British antiquity is made to run parallel with Egypt's ancient lore, and with the prophets, and kings, and judges of Israel. It stops at the Deluge, and is every thing but antediluvian.

This confident chronology of the chroniclers startles us with its boldness and its minute accuracy; and, indeed, it seems fantastic, if not ludicrous, when we are gravely told of one British king flourishing in the time of Saul, and another being contemporary with Solomon; and that it was in the period of the prophet Isaiah that King Lear was ruler in the land. Yet this mythical chronology appears to have been for so long a time part of the popular literature of England, and to have taken such hold on the mind, that one of the commentators on Shakspeare thinks it worth while to remark, that the name of Nero is introduced in King Lear about three hundred years before he was born; and another commentator on the same passage, where Edgar says that "Nero was an angler in the lake of darkness," goes still more seriously to work in the way of correction, by remarking that "this is one of Shakspeare's most remarkable anachronisms; for that King Lear succeeded his father Bladud in the year of the world 3105, and Nero, in the year 4017, was sixteen years old when he married Octavia, Cæsar's daughter."* Surely, the fancies and fables of the

* Grote's History of Greece, vol. i. 642, Eng. ed.; 485, Am. ed. This whole subject is discussed by Mr. Grote, and thence the hints in the lecture were obviously taken. Mr. Grote's note is this:—"Dr.

romancers and chroniclers had as much of wisdom in them as there is in such commentary. Who, as he gives his heart up to the study of this grand tragedy, ever heeds or thinks of the chronology? In the course of this lecture I will endeavour to show, that the poetic truth is preserved, so far as the drama stands in relation to an age and a land of paganism; but, besides that, it mattered not in what particular century the story was cast, or whether it corresponded with the history of other countries. From the legends of Britain, Shakspeare culled the story as one which he felt the power of his imagination could make as universal, and as perpetual, as the human heart—that he could create a sympathy with it, which, growing out of the relation of father and child, must endure as long as the earth is peopled. What need the poet care for the violation of a fabulous chronology, when he was giving poetic reality to the sublime passion of Lear, and when, in the character of Cordelia, he was creating such a personification of all that is graceful and dutiful in womanly nature—a being, the very embodiment of filial piety, whom every parent, the wide world over, may bless, and every daughter reverence?

I have spoken of the authentic history of Britain be-

Zachary Grey has the following observations in his 'Notes on Shakspeare,' (London, 1754, vol. i. p. 112.) In commenting on the passage in King Lear—

'Nero is an angler in the lake of darkness,'

he says:—'This is one of Shakspeare's most remarkable anachronisms. King Lear succeeded his father Bladud A. M. 3105; and Nero, A. M. 4017, was sixteen years old when he married Octavia, Cæsar's daughter.'" W. B. R.

ginning only when the inhabitants of that country came in contact, or rather collision, with the Romans; and this may lead us to the consideration, that all the authentic history of the ancient world—its sacred and profane history—is almost entirely limited to the story of those races of men, who dwelt on the borders of the Mediterranean. The region of that great inland sea is the domain of ancient history. As you pass away from the sound of its waves, the voice of history dies away with it; and the countless generations, that lived and died at a distance from the shores of the midland sea, have hardly more place in our thoughts than if they had been the inhabitants of another planet. We read the history of the Israelites and of Egypt, the history of the Greeks and the history of the Romans, and this we call ancient history; and then we think we have read the history of all the ancient world: yet it is the story of only those who occupied a small belt of the earth's surface. The light of history seems to fade unless it is reflected from the glancing waters of the bright Mediterranean; and we scarce recognise the existence of mankind dwelling in the vast spaces of the North, and the East, and the South. The Celt and the Cambrian, the Briton and the German, are known only when Rome is waging war with them or is dismayed at their approach. We must come to the borders of the Adriatic and the Ægean shores, or to where the Nile pours its turbid current to the sea, to find the history of the Old World; for, elsewhere, it is either a desert vacancy of historical knowledge, or else what was once known has passed into dark oblivion. The tribes that moved on many a Northern plain have kept no kindred with the nations of history, and many a mighty empire has passed forever out of the memory of man.

> "Palmyra, central in the desert,"*

is no more than a name; and

> "Babylon,
> Learned and wise, hath perished utterly,
> Nor leaves her speech one word to aid the sigh
> That would lament her."†

Britain did not lie in the path of the ancient world. I am very sure that when we think of ancient history, we do not adequately or distinctly conceive what vast spaces of the earth are left untouched.

We have, I am inclined to think, a kind of ill-defined notion, that all the races of men had gathered either to the west of Asia, or the north of Africa, or to the sunny regions of Southern Europe. The great highway of the human race seems to us to have been the Mediterranean Sea alone; and certainly there is no spectacle on the earth which can call up so many historic memories—such throngs of thoughts associated with other ages. If each wild wave upon its surface were vocal, it might speak a history; for all that was glorious in profane story, and all that was holy in sacred, centred there. It is the natural expression of a thoughtful mind, when a modern traveller thus describes his first sight of the great and beautiful sea that touches the shores of three continents:—"I was looking upon the Mediterranean: it was the first time those haunted waters had met my gaze

---

* The Excursion, book viii, p. 626, Am. ed.

† Wordsworth's Sonnet on Missions and Travels, p. 352.

I pondered on the name—the Mediterranean—as if the very letters had folded in their little characters the secret of my joy. My inner eye roved in and out along the coasts of religious Spain, the land of an eternal crusade, where alone, and for that reason, the true religiousness of knighthood was ever realized; it overleaped the straits and followed the outline of St. Augustine's land, where Carthage was and rich Cyrene; onward it went to 'old hushed Egypt,' the symbol of spiritual darkness, and the mystical house of bondage; from thence to Jaffa, from Jaffa to Beyroot; the birthplace of the Morning, the land of the world's pilgrimage, where the Tomb is, lay stretched out like a line of light, and the nets were drying on the rocks of Tyre; onward still along that large projection of Asia, the field ploughed and sown by apostolic husbandmen; then came a rapid glance upon the little Ægean islands, and upward through the Hellespont; and, over the Sea of Marmora, St. Sophia's minaret sparkled like a star; the sea-surges were faint in the myriad bays of Greece, and that other peninsula, twice the throne of the world's masters, was beautiful in her peculiar twilight."*

* Faber's "Sights and Thoughts," p. 112. My brother had read this volume some years before, and was much delighted with it. Writing to a friend, in 1842, he says:—"I have been reading aloud to my one listener (Charles Lamb's idea of an audience) Faber's Sights and Thoughts in Foreign Churches and among Foreign Peoples. It is a remarkable production—very bold and very beautiful—one of the most imaginative and fanciful prose books I ever read—very, very Oxfordish in its fashion of sentiment and reflection—abounding in architectural spirit which would delight you, and Wordsworthian deeply, saving an occasional censoriousness which he ought to cure. But I found it one of those books which I delight in floating along

Britain was too remote from the region of the Mediterranean to have any place in ancient history; and all that was known of it was, that it must have been peopled at an early age of the world, and that it was occasionally visited by some of the maritime people of the South for purposes of traffic. This long tract of time is not, however, left wholly a blank, for the legendary story tells us, that the Britons were descended from Trojan ancestry, and take their name from Brutus, who came from Troy to the shores of a land called "Albion," and conquered the inhabitants. Such is the story of national origin given by all the early English chroniclers, who narrate also the succession of a long dynasty of kings—"sprung of old Anchises' line"—who ruled over Britain in times very long ago. It is the very witchcraft of history; and, as we read in these legendary annals the name of one king after another, they pass before the mind, visionary creations like the shadows of the kings that the weird sisters showed to Macbeth,—one "gold-bound brow is like the first, a third is like the former,"—and others more shadowy still, like the images of the many more reflected in the glass of the spectral Banquo. In the history of England written by Milton, he precisely enumerates this series of ancient sovereigns according to the traditions, which he recapitulates dutifully, though with something like impatience, when, in one part of his narrative, he has to speak of "twenty kings in a continued row, who either

---

the tide of, though, in this case, there are some ugly snags and sawyers in the stream. The volume abounds in deep and beautiful reflections clothed in prose most musical. In one or two places its beauty is marred by some John Bullish impudence about America." MS Letter, July 23, 1842. W. B. R.

did nothing or lived in ages that wrote nothing—a foul pretermission," he adds, "in the author of this, whether story or fable, himself weary, as seems, of his own tedious tale." These negative sovereigns are succeeded by one who is recorded to have excelled all before him in the art of music, whereupon Milton quaintly laments that he "did not leave us one song of his twenty predecessors' doings;" and, on reaching the confines of authentic history, he likens the change to the approach of "dawn to one who had set out on his way by night and travelled through a region of smooth or idle dreams."*

The very origin of this legendary British history is wrapped in obscurity. It was circulated chiefly by the chronicle of Geoffrey of Monmouth, a Welsh ecclesiastic, who flourished in the twelfth century; but, as the legend of the Trojan migration and settlement in Britain is traced back to still earlier writers, it is reasonable to believe, that the chronicle was either a translation from the British into the Latin language of an ancient history of Britain found in Armorica, or a compilation of all the stories and fables which had currency in the shape of Welsh songs and oral traditions among the descendants of the Britons. It would be a weary, and probably vain, inquiry to consider minutely the claims which such historical materials have on our belief; and so little is there attractive in the legends of British history, that I need not attempt to dwell upon any of the alleged facts. But I wish, before passing from this part of my subject, briefly to examine the curious tenacity with which the belief in this legendary literature was once held, and to

---

* History of Britain, pp. 36, 37.

show that it was not relinquished until a more critical standard of historic belief was adopted, and scientific investigation took the place of uninquiring and passive credulity. It has been said that no man, before the sixteenth century, presumed to doubt that the Britons were descended from Brutus the Trojan; and it is equally certain that no modern writer could presume confidently to assert it.

Let us turn to Milton's history of England; for, if it were only as a psychological speculation, it will be curious to observe how such a subject was regarded by a masculine and mighty mind, in which, too, there was a feeling very far removed from reverence for *monastic* legendary lore. I have already noticed his scarce-repressed impatience, as he rehearsed some passages in the history which he dismisses with these words:—"I neither oblige the belief of other persons, nor hastily subscribe my own. Nor have I stood with others computing or collating years and chronologies, lest I should be vainly curious about the time and circumstance of things whereof the substance is so much in doubt." When he introduces the subject, after having summarily disposed of the stories anterior to the Trojan legend, it is with these words, in which it is easy to trace a lingering respect for the time-honoured legends:—"Of Brutus and his line, with the whole progeny of kings to the entrance of Julius Cæsar, we cannot so easily be discharged—descents of ancestry long-continued, laws and exploits not plainly seeming to be borrowed or devised, which, on the common belief, have wrought no small impression, defended by many, denied utterly by few. For what though Brutus and the whole Trojan pretence were yielded up, (seeing tney who first devised to bring us from some noble ancestor were content at first with Brutus, the Consul, till better inventions, though not willing to forego the name, taught them to remove it higher into a more fabulous age; and, by the same remove, lighting on the Trojan tales, in affectation to make the Briton of one original with the Roman, pitched there,) yet those old and inborn names of successive kings never any to have been real persons, or done in their lives at least some part of what has been so long remembered, cannot be thought without too strict an incredulity. * * * For these and the causes above mentioned, that which has received approbation from so many I have chosen not to omit. Certain or uncertain,—be that upon the credit of those whom I must follow,—so far as keeps aloof from impossible and absurd, attested by ancient writers from books more ancient, I refuse not as the due and proper subject of story."*

It is not difficult to observe in this a conflict in the mind of Milton between his feelings and his judgment; on the one hand, a lingering respect for a long-continued and habitual popular belief, and, on the other, the sense of the destitution of historical testimony. And, indeed, with whatever superciliousness we may now look upon this old traditional history, it was no slight thing to sweep coldly and sternly away all that, for centuries, had found ready acceptance in the minds of men—the innocent superstitions of their country's annals. Milton shared in a measure the spirit of the English chroniclers who flourished before his day, and shows some sympathy

* History of Britain, pp. 10-37.

with the zeal with which they strove against a growing incredulity, which, by converting the legendary history into pure fable, would destroy with a breath whole dynasties of kings and the exploits and adventures of their forefathers during centuries. But they were striving against the progress of the science of history, in which the annalist and chronicler stand midway between romance or heroic legend, and genuine history.

It is most difficult for us, in these later days of higher standards of historic credibility, to form any thing like an adequate conception of the entire and unquestioning confidence, which was felt for the story of British origin and the race of ancient British kings. Of this feeling there is a curious proof in a transaction in the reign of Edward the First, when the sovereignty of Scotland was claimed by the English monarch. The Scots sought the interposition and protection of the Pope, alleging that the Scottish realm belonged of right to the See of Rome. Boniface the Eighth, a pontiff not backward in asserting the claims of the papacy, did interpose to check the English conquest, and was answered by an elaborate and respectful epistle from Edward, in which the English claim is most carefully and confidently derived from the conquest of the whole country by the Trojans in the times of Eli and Samuel—assuredly, a very respectable antiquity of some two thousand four hundred years. No Philadelphia estate could be more methodically traced back to the proprietary title of William Penn, than was this claim to Scotland up to Brutus, the exile from Troy. The names of the successors of Brutus, in a long lineage, are regularly stated, with various facts, which are asserted as having unquestionably existed from antiquity in the memory of men—"*procul dubio ab antiquo*"—and the Pope is respectfully entreated, at the same time, not to be deluded by cunningly devised and fantastical forgeries. Now, all this is set forth with the most imperturbable seriousness, and with an air of complete assurance of the truth. It appears, too, to have fully answered the purpose intended; and the Scots, finding that the papal antiquity was but a poor defence against such claims, and as if determined not to be outdone by the Southron, replied in a document asserting their independence by virtue of descent from Scota, one of the daughters of Pharaoh. The Pope seems to have been silenced in a conflict of ancestral authority, in which the succession of St. Peter seemed quite a modern affair, when overshadowed by such Trojan and Egyptian antiquity.*

Confidently as this early history of Britain was once believed, and reluctantly as it was gradually discredited, it cannot be said to possess, at least in its present condition, any historic value. But when we consider that in our own day a great historical mind like Niebuhr's has actually made discoveries of historic truth in what used to appear so inextricably fabulous as the early history of Rome; when such historical sagacity as his has been successfully employed, not to teach a sweeping skepticism, but a just discrimination between what was actual and what was fable; and when we see a mind so zealous after truth as Arnold's, carefully cherishing the Roman legends, not, indeed, as history, but as illustrative of it—we may venture a thought, that haply it may be reserved

---

* Lingard, vol. ii. pp. 564, 565.

for some historian in like manner to search out the truth that now is buried beneath the mass of the old British legends. There is, to be sure, this important difference between them and the legends of Greece and Rome, that the latter were native to the inhabitants of those lands, that they sprang up among them, and therefore were illustrative of the feelings and the mind of the nation in a far greater degree than can be claimed by the Welsh and British traditions. The most recent English historian of Greece, in speaking of that part of his work which he has devoted to the legendary period, uses this language:

"I describe the earlier times by themselves, as conceived by the faith and feeling of the first Greeks, and known only through their legends—without presuming to measure how much or how little of historical matter these legends may contain. If the reader blames me for not assisting him to determine this—if he ask me why I do not undraw the curtain and disclose the picture—I reply in the words of the painter Zeuxis, when the same question was addressed to him on exhibiting his masterpiece of imitative art—'The curtain *is* the picture!' What we now read as poetry and legend was once accredited history, and the only genuine history which the first Greeks could conceive or relish of their past time: the curtain conceals nothing behind, and cannot, by any ingenuity, be withdrawn."*

Now, to apply this to the legendary history of Britain, there is such uncertainty as to its origin—such doubt whether it was not of foreign instead of domestic growth,

* Preface to Grote's History of Greece, vol. i. p. xiii

that we cannot say in reference to it that "The curtain *is* the picture." The legend of the Trojan ancestry of the Britons has, indeed, great antiquity. Sir Francis Palgrave—a high authority—in his learned work on the English Commonwealth, speaks of it as a doubtful point, whether the stories on that subject existed before the arrival of the Romans, or whether the adventures of Brutus were invented by the bards, to propitiate the favour of those who also prided themselves on being the progeny of Æneas.

The legendary history of nations has filled so large a space in historical literature, that it has been truly pronounced an universal manifestation of the human mind, belonging to what is called the age of historical faith as distinguished from historical reason.* Now, why is it that legendary history is composed, and why is it so long believed? Those who look on humanity with an evil-eye, and speak of it with a satirical tongue, will say that it comes of man's propensity to falsehood. This is a solution more simple and superficial than satisfactory. It must be some deep and prevailing, but I hope better, feeling that gives birth to legendary lore. The heart of a nation, as it grows strong, craves for knowledge of its ancestry; and, if there be no historical records, if naught else be forthcoming, the heroic lay, the minstrel's song, romance or epic poem, are produced to fill the blank spaces of the past. Even when there are genuine materials of history, they are shaped and modified, and often made, as it were, legendary, by any strong and universal feeling in the heart of the people. To give a familiar

* Mr. Grote.

illustration of the controlling power of such sentiments, the profound and fervent reverence for the memory of Washington so sways the popular historical conception of the war of independence, as to identify it almost wholly with his character and services—making him the ONE great champion of the cause. While it is known that much was achieved by the wisdom and fortitude of others, and that there was much that Washington had no part in, who for one moment could desire to disparage, or even critically to measure, that large and uncalculating homage, the justice of which is best proved by the depth and fervour of it? And it is the highest evidence of the reality of his fame, that all nicer estimates are mastered by this judgment of the heart, which makes the history of the Revolution centre around him.

It has been ingeniously and truly said—"We all write legends. Who has not observed in himself, in his ordinary dealings with the facts of everyday life, with the sayings and doings of his acquaintances, in short, with every thing which comes before him as a *fact*, a disposition to forget the real order in which they appear, and to rearrange them according to his theory of how they ought to be? Do we hear of a generous, self-denying action,— In a short time the real doer and it are forgotten; it has become the property of the noblest person we know. So a jest we relate of the wittiest person; frivolity of the most frivolous; and so on. Each particular act we attribute to the person we conceive most likely to have been the author of it. And this does not arise from any wish to leave a false impression, scarcely from carelessness; but only because facts refuse to remain bare and isolated in our memory: they will arrange themselves under some law or other; they must illustrate something to us—some character, some principle—or else we forget them. Facts are thus perpetually, so to say, becoming unfixed and rearranged in a more conceptional order. In this way we find fragments of Jewish history in the legends of Greece; stories from Herodotus become naturalized in the tradition of early Rome; and the mythic exploits of the Northern heroes, adopted by the biographers of Saxon kings. So with the great objects of national interest. Alfred, 'England's darling,' the noblest of the Saxon kings, became mythic almost before his death; and, forthwith, every institution that Englishmen most value, of law or church, became appropriated to him. He divided England into shires—He established trial by jury—He destroyed wolves—and made the country so secure, that golden bracelets hung untouched in the open road. And when Oxford was founded, a century was added to its age, and it was discovered that Alfred had laid the first stone of the first college." Again, it is said,—"Time, in another way, plays strange tricks with facts, and is ever altering, shifting, and even changing their nature in our memory. Every man's past life is becoming mythic to him; we cannot call up again the feelings of our childhood; only we know that what then seemed to us the bitterest misfortunes, we have since learnt by change of character or circumstance to think very great blessings; and even when there is no change, and were they to recur again, they are such as we should equally repine at; yet, by mere lapse of time, sorrow is turned to pleasure, and the sharpest pang at present becomes the most alluring object of our retrospect. The sick bed, the school trial, loss of friends, pain and grief of every kind, become rounded off and assume a soft and beautiful grace. The harshest facts are smoothed and chastened off in the past like the rough mountains and jagged rocks in the distant horizon. And so it is with every other event of our lives; read a letter we wrote ten years ago, and how impossible we find it to recognise the writer in our altered selves. Incident after incident rises up and bides its day, and then sinks back into the landscape. It changes by distance, and we change by age. While it was present it meant one thing, now it means another; and to-morrow, perhaps, something else on the point of vision alters. Even old Nature, endlessly and patiently reproducing the same forms, the same beauties, cannot reproduce in us the same emotions we remember in our childhood. Then, all was Fairy-land; now, time and custom have deadened our sense, and

'The things which we have seen we now can see no more.'

This is the true reason why men people past ages with the superhuman and the marvellous. They feel their own past was, indeed, something miraculous, and they cannot adequately represent their feelings except by borrowing from another order of beings."*

This is also to be considered—that, doubtless, many an early narrative was composed, not with claim to literal belief, but as *legends* in the true sense of the term—productions intended to be read for example and instruction, given to simple, uncriticising folk, as moral apologues are to children. We judge them, therefore, perhaps by a wrong standard, and look on them with contempt because

* Lives of the English Saints, No. iv. pp. 75–78.

we lose sight of their moral purpose. Early history abounds with prodigies and portents, miraculous agencies and supernatural interpositions, stories that are sometimes impressive and often grotesque. Such things are acceptable to a certain condition of the human mind, and while they prevail there may be a great deal of stupid and superstitious credulity along with innocent docility of belief. Later ages grow beyond all this, but that growth is not necessarily all gain; for if irrational credulity be avoided, there is an opposite extreme—skepticism—infidelity—atheism. Now, wild and extravagant and absurd as were the stories of the olden time, they did lead men to the belief that there is another world beyond that which we see; that there are realities beyond the things which we can handle; and, still more, that there is a providential government of the world, and that, as the earth rolls on through the silent spaces of the firmament, God's hand is upon it, and that his eye is on the soul of each creature of the countless generations of men that rise up and sink into their graves. In the olden time men were, no doubt, very superstitious—very credulous—they believed a great deal that was monstrously absurd—they believed it simply because it was told to them—in short, they believed a great deal too much; but in that excess of belief was comprehended a faith in the invaluable truths which were just now referred to. Of such truths the early legends are symbolical; and, when my thoughts turn to a history like Hume's, I do not fear to say that it is also legendary in its own way, but the doctrine which it symbolizes is that there is no providence over nations or men. I do not mean that he teaches this merely by silence, but by assertion or insinuation, that the affairs of this world are governed by chance; and that whenever a religious feeling is manifest as an agency in human events, it is no divine impulse, but a delusion—a folly or a fraud, as if God in anger had cast this earth from him to roll onward with all its miserable freight of humanity beyond his sight and beyond his care. The early popular histories of England contained a large element of belief, and the later history in most general use contains, in an equally large proportion, the element of unbelief; and surely it is, at the least, as irrational to believe too little as to believe too much.

The popular faith in legendary history may be traced to a cause deep seated in human nature. With the progress of cultivation, men become conscious of the high privilege of humanity of connecting itself with times that are gone by; and they feel that there is no more dismal condition than when the past is wholly lost to it. I do not mean the mere pride of ancestry, but that feeling with which the heart searches for its dead kindred. It is an universal sentiment of civilized humanity; it is witnessed in an Old Mortality laboriously renewing the timeworn tombstones of the Covenanters, or in the great Orator of antiquity who knew the power of it, when, nearly two centuries after the great Athenian victory, he put at least a moment's fire into the hearts of his degenerate countrymen as he adjured them by the dead at Marathon.* Every people, as they rise in virtue and intelligence, crave a history of their own; and, for lack of that which is authentic, they welcome the imaginative legend and the rude chronicle. The genuine dignity of the nation

* Demosthenes de Corona, s. 208.

grows as its history gathers, and there is a moral power in the mere memory of an heroic age. The spirit of a people must be fed with its historic associations; its natural food is the story of the good and great men of their blood; deprived of that, it languishes and dies. If the legendary lore of the olden time appear to the severe judgment of later days to be puerile or fantastic, let it be remembered that it shows the aspiring spirit of the people, and that it is proof of that moral temper which, as has been well said, elevates the present by doing reverence to the past. The ready belief was given, not in weakness, but in strength, when men became conscious of that power in themselves, which is told of by Shakspeare in his simple and sublime description of man as a being "looking before and after." This power and the historic feeling that comes with it, do not exist when man is in a state of barbarism. What is the past to him,

> "If his chief good and market of his time
> Be but to sleep and feed?"

This historical feeling is so closely connected with man's moral nature, that I believe we might safely infer from the condition of it the state of civilization of a people. It has been said of individual character, that—

> "The man whose eye
> Is ever on himself, doth look on one
> The least of Nature's works,—one who might move
> The wise man to that scorn, which wisdom holds
> Unlawful ever."*

* Wordsworth's Lines left on a seat in a Yew-Tree, p. 33.

It is equally true of a generation of men; for when, in its self-sufficiency, it separates itself from all that have gone before, it does so to its own grievous degradation. It is better that legendary associations with the past should be created if historic associations cannot be found; for a nation stands on the highest moral station when, looking back, it can appropriate the poet's words—

> "The thought of our past years in me doth breed
> Perpetual benediction."*

The legendary history of Britain, which is now become so obsolete, did, in its own time, good service in helping to form the national character; and, doubtless, the people rightfully and worthily kept their faith in it as long as they did. It was far better than that vicious and sophisticated skepticism, which would beggar us of the accumulated inheritance of past ages by destroying belief in the evidence. Everybody, probably, has heard the story that is told of Sir Robert Walpole, who, when his son, Horace Walpole, was about to read to him some historical production, interrupted him by saying, "Oh, do not read history, for that I know must be false!" It was an appropriate sentiment; for it was uttered by one who, during a long and prosperous administration, did as much as any minister that ever lived to demoralize the government and the people, and who, no doubt, formed his estimate of history from the performances of the venal party-writers in his service; and whom, as Lord Mahon says in his history, "he hired as he hired the ditchers on

* Ode on Intimations of Immortality, p. 471.

his estate."* By the side of such a sentiment, observe how much nobler a spirit is in the words of Niebuhr, when, speaking of the phrensy of the French Revolution, he says that "Only once has the world beheld universal contempt invoked upon the whole of the past, and that, on the other hand, the lessons of all experience teach us, that a nation cannot possess a nobler treasure than the unbroken chain of a long and brilliant history. It is the want of this that makes all colonies so sickly. Those of the Greeks, indeed, seldom cut off their recollections altogether from the root of their mother city. Modern colonies have done so; and this unnatural outrage has, perhaps, operated still more than other circumstances to plunge them into a state of incorrigible depravity."†

---

* History of England, vol. ii. p. 240.

† Niebuhr's exact words are these: — "Notwithstanding this solemnity and the perpetual abolition of the name of King, the Romans were far from reflecting an indiscriminate hatred on the memory of the monarchical times. The statues of the kings, and among them, it appears, even that of the last Tarquinius, were preserved and probably multiplied. Their laws and institutions, in civil as well as religious matters, continued to exist in full efficacy. The change of the constitution originally affected only a single branch; and it never was the intention of the Romans to despoil themselves of a rich inheritance of laws and reminiscences. It is only in our own days that men have witnessed the consequences of that phrensy which, with a species of pride hitherto unparalleled, entailed upon itself humiliation and slavery, while it laid claim to unexampled perfection and boasted to form a new world from the chaos. Only once has the world seen (and we have seen) a general contempt of the past excited, and men priding themselves in the title of emancipated slaves. Something similar, indeed, and somewhat similar results, were experienced in the religious revolutions. The Protestant churches have thrown aside the Saints and Fathers, and suffered in

In quoting these words of Niebuhr's, I cannot forbear adding what may appear a slight digression, but is really in further illustration of my subject. It is, I think, in the freedom from this reproach on modern colonies that our own country had so much of moral strength in its transition from the colonial to the national condition. The British colonists in America never did cut off their recollections from the root of their mother country; and accordingly when resistance became necessary, they were fortified in it by the feeling that they were contending for no new-born freedom, but for ancient rights; and that thus they were keeping, and not breaking, covenant with the mighty dead. In England, Burke, at the outset, warned his countrymen what would be the character of the colonial resistance; because, he said, a favourite study with the colonists was *English* law. There never was an instance in which it was more momentous as a matter of education--and I use that word in its most comprehensive sense—to preserve and teach the history of a nation. The revolutionary period of our annals must be so presented to the reason and the imagination in the American mind as to make it—what there is ample materials for making it—an historical, and not a fabulous,

---

consequence. It is the same in science and literature. But, on the contrary, the experience of universal history attests that a nation can possess no wealth more splendid than a long and brilliant antiquity. All colonies languish under this defect. Those of the Greeks seldom wholly rent themselves in recollection from the stock of the parent state; modern colonies have done so, and have sunk by that unnatural abruption, perhaps still more than by any other circumstances, into incurable deterioration." Niebuhr's Rome, by Walter, vol I. p. 338. W. B. R.

heroic age. It must be cultivated, not only because it is the past, with which we are immediately connected, but because it does not stop there. No one can adequately comprehend the American Revolution, unless he goes far beyond it into a more distant past along the line of the progress of constitutional freedom—beyond the Great Charter—beyond the laws of Edward the Confessor—to the times of the saintly and heroic Alfred; for it is a precious truth, that the war of our independence was a wave of what a great poet has called—

> "The flood
> Of British freedom which, to the open sea
> Of the world's praise, from dark antiquity
> Hath flowed."*

Niebuhr's words may be applied in justification of the legendary history I have been considering; for that brought to those for whom it was written, as genuine history should bring to us—

> "Ennobling impulse from the past."

The generations of mankind are passing over the earth—swiftly, one wave of them after another, breaking on the shores of eternity; but it is not like the wild waves of the sea, that leave no more than a little foam and a few weeds on the barren sand. The generations of men fall rather like the leaves of the forest strewn by autumnal winds; but, as they perish, they leave behind them a fertilizing power on the soil, from which other trees grow to live in the light

* Wordsworth, p. 255. Sonnet.

of other summers, and to battle with the winds of other winters.

In considering the legendary period of Britain, I have only alluded to the sublime tragedy which Shakspeare has created out of one of the simple stories which form the mythology of that age. By attempting to say more than I have done of the tragedy of King Lear, I should have been making a vain effort to extract from it more of historical illustration than it gives, and which we cannot expect to find until we come to the tragedy of King John and the other, properly, "*Chronicle*-Plays." But I now proceed to what does belong to my present course, and add a few remarks on the historical relations of the tragedy of King Lear.

The extended and abiding interest in this drama is produced by the genius of the Poet appealing to the universal feeling connected with the relation of parent and child—the common and instinctive sense of the hideousness of filial ingratitude and of the beauty of filial piety. There would be deep pathos in the story of any aged father turned adrift by his ungrateful daughters, were the scene laid in any period of the world or in any condition of society—be it of yesterday or of a thousand years ago—be it in palace or in cottage: but in the hands of Shakspeare it was to be raised to the highest sublimity, and the sympathy was to be made to sink into the lowest depths of the human heart. To achieve this, the wondrous sagacity of the poet sought for a remote period of history, where royalty still wore something of its patriarchal state, so that filial ingratitude should, at the same time, be treason, and filial piety be identified with all that is noble and beautiful in loyalty and truth. The king, abdicating his throne and making partition of his realm, is, at the same time, the fond father making over in his lifetime the inheritance to his children; and on the ruins of parental authority there falls the fading splendour of sinking royalty. The cup of Lear's agony overflows with kingly and parental grief. Domestic discord is civil war; and when the natural and closest ties of blood are torn asunder by the inhuman daughters, the whole state of society is convulsed, and the realm is rent by crime and anarchy. The Poet knew, that it was only in an early social condition, and a simple patriarchal form of government, that his imagination could find ample space to show the uncontrolled misery which follows revolt against the laws of natural affection. In such a state of society there is nothing to counteract the appropriate consequences of such guilt.

The scene of such a drama is well laid, too, in a pagan age and country. We have, it seems to me, on this account a keener sense of the pitiable impotence of Lear, when we hear him in his moods of wrath or in his hours of misery swearing

> "By the sacred radiance of the sun,
> The mysteries of Hecate and the night,"

or invoking Nature for fierce retribution upon his own offspring. It would be harrowing—horrible, rather than tragic—to hear a *Christian* parent, even when so abused, imprecating curses on his children; it would be better for him to sink submissively under the burden of his wrongs. But the wild spirit of the *heathen* father's revenge is in harmony with his times; and appropriate to a mysterious and barbaric age is the sublime threatening of his vengeance—sublime from its very indistinctness—as if too vast to shape itself in thought or word—the most awful menace of revenge that ever burst from a father's heart in wrath upon the head of an impious child, when, in the agony of finding Goneril and Regan confederate against him, he exclaims to them—

> "I will do such things,—
> What they are, yet I know not; but they shall be
> The terrors of the earth."

Again, placed as the drama is in the darkness of paganism, the fury of the elements, when Lear is driven forth into the storm, acquires a wild significance, as if the lightning and the thunder were conscious powers of evil in mysterious alliance with the wicked hearts of his daughters; and when the passionate king swears by Jupiter and Apollo, what can his heathen gods do to save him from such a wicked confederacy? The might of the malice of his daughters, and not less the tyranny of the pitiless storm, we are made to feel; and we see no power in a pagan creed to interpose against them.* It is as coming from the lips of a heathen that we feel, too, what has been finely spoken of as Lear's sublime identification of his age with that of the "Heavens themselves," when, in his reproaches to them for conniving at the injustice of his children, he reminds them that they themselves are old.†

---

* Dr. Johnson's note on this passage is,—"Shakspeare makes his Lear too much of a mythologist; he had Hecate and Apollo before."
W. B. R.

† Lamb's Essay on Shakspeare's Tragedies. Prose Works, vol. i. p. 122.

Shakspeare has been reproached with a deviation from history in the catastrophe of this tragedy. "King Lear," as saith the story of the legend, "again after three years obtained the crown." The legend and the tragedy are each the production of imaginative art—the one of art in its rude form, and the other of art in its highest power. It was well enough in the simple fable to recompense the king for such wrongs and deprivations by giving him his sceptre and his crown again; but, after the intensity of suffering embodied in the tragedy—after the sublime accumulation of wrongs and of anguish—after that majestic madness, in which Lear's heart was chastened, as his intellect was broken, what could be the appropriate sequel but death? Indeed, in the words of Kent—that admirable personification of honour and humour and fidelity and manliness, the perfect gentleman in a barbaric age—in his words as he stood by his expiring sovereign—

> "He hates him
> That would, upon the rack of this tough world,
> Stretch him out longer."

The tragic poet cannot misrepresent the story of the life of our fallen and struggling human nature by the unnatural compensation of "a happy ending."* It is well said by a German critic that "Tragedy, in its full

* "A happy ending!" says Lamb; "as if the living martyrdom that Lear had gone through—the flaying of his feelings alive, did not make a fair dismissal from the stage of life the only decorous thing for him." W. B. R.

historical significance, was not made for tender, weak-nerved spirits. It requires strong shoulders to support the whole burden of the tragical which the life of humanity contains."*

---

* Ulrici's Shakspeare's Dramatic Art, p. 236. If the reader feel any disappointment at the brief comment of this lecture on the tragedy, I beg him to remember that these lectures are historico-critical merely, and to refer to the first of the series in this volume on Tragic Poetry, where King Lear is critically considered. W. B. R.

LECTURE III.*

The Roman and Saxon Periods: Cymbeline and Macbeth.

Legendary history continued—Artegal and Elidure—The Northern and Southern nations—Geographical divisions of Europe—Attempts of invasion frustrated—Rome sacked by the Gauls—Greece invaded and rescued—Defeat of Varus in the forest of Teutoburg—The memory of Arminius—Hermann—His unfinished monument—Decisive battles of the world—Professor Creasy's volumes—The fall of the Roman Empire—Effect of Roman subjugation of Britain—British kings—Cymbeline a British king—Imogen—Roman remains in Britain—Sir Walter Scott and Ritson—Diocletian's persecution—Arthur and Merlin—Ethelred—Paulinus—Alfred—Coleridge's estimate of his character—Difficulty of discussing historical questions—Polemics—Dunstan, an illustration—Sir Roger de Coverley—Saint Dunstan—Want of a poetic view of his character—The Danes—Canute the Great—Ballads—Edward the Confessor—Touching for the "king's evil"—Reference in Macbeth—The palace and the tombs of English kings.

In my last lecture I was engaged in considering that remote and uncertain period, during which the people of Britain dwelt apart from the rest of the known world—the purely legendary period of British history. In the fabulous chronicles of those ages there may, perhaps, be germs of truth; and, hereafter, historical science may bring to light more than our philosophy now dreams of.

---

* January 4th, 1847.

Before I turn away from the antiquity, in which Britain was morally and intellectually, as well as physically, an island in a northern sea, let me briefly notice one legend which, like that of King Lear, illustrates the simplicity of feeling belonging to such periods, when the social and family relations have the same kind of importance, as the great political combinations have in ages more advanced. Having to find whatever of good there is amid the fables of the simple annals of the very olden time, I would fain persuade you that they have at least this merit—they show us human beings, it may be only fabulous men and women, but still beings with human hearts, actuated by the passions and motives of humanity; whereas, in many a stately history of more authentic times, you find names of real personages indeed, but only names, without a principle of life in them; so that they do, in truth, become utterly unreal to us, and might be, for all the sympathy we can have, another order of created beings, and history might be the story of another planet. This is one grievous want in all histories, except those of a rare and high order—the want of that one touch of nature that "makes the whole world kin." National society is made to appear, not as if it were a community of thinking, sentient human beings, but like some vast and insensate machine swayed by the craft of courts, or urged by martial prowess. The chief part of what we know of the past is aggregate war; so that it has been said with lively truth, that "Many histories give you little else than a narrative of military affairs, marches and countermarches, skirmishes and battles; which, except during some great crisis of a truly national war, affords about as complete a picture of a nation's life as an account of the doses of physic a man may have taken, and the surgical operations he may have undergone, would of the life of an individual."*

In the tragedy of King Lear we saw that the national history was identified with a simple story of parental anguish and filial ingratitude, alleviated by the blessed influences of the filial piety of one virtuous daughter. Another portion of that early history is a simple story of *fraternal* affection, which gave to one of the ancient kings of Britain the title of the "pious Elidure." It is told how the good king Gorbonian reigned wisely and well—building temples to the gods, and giving to every man his due, and the people prospered; until, this just king dying, a son, unworthy of him, came to the throne—the tyrant Artegal. The impatient nobles and the vexed people drove him from his kingdom; and, while he was wandering in foreign lands, his brother Elidure is placed on the throne. After many wanderings, the exile came across the seas to live a hidden life in his native land, seeking there no more than water from the spring and the chance food an outlaw finds. The king, hunting in the forest of Calater, by chance meets his deposed and now humbled brother; and, in an instant, the prevailing power of fraternal love leaves no room for any lingering pride of royalty. The forlorn outcast is recognised by this gentle barbarian as not only his brother but his king; and, abased as he is by memory of his former years, and chastened by poverty and grief, he is bidden to take the sceptre again. Elidure intercedes for him with an offended nation; and, by such heroic affection, he puts away from himself a kingdom to reinstate a repentant

* Hare's Guesses at Truth. First Series, p. 358.

brother. A modern poet has given the legend in language appropriately unadorned, and thus it closes:

> "The story tells what courses were pursued,
> Until King Elidure, with full consent
> Of all his peers, before the multitude,
> Rose,—and, to consummate this just intent,
> Did place upon his brother's head the crown,
> Relinquished by his own;
> Then to his people cried, 'Receive your lord,
> Gorbonian's first-born son, your rightful king restored!'
> The people answered with a loud acclaim:
> Yet more;—heart-smitten by the heroic deed,
> The reinstated Artegal became
> Earth's noblest penitent; from bondage freed
> Of vice,—thenceforth unable to subvert
> Or shake his high desert.
> Long did he reign; and when he died, the tear
> Of universal grief bedewed his honoured bier.—
> Thus was a brother by a brother saved;
> With whom a crown (temptation that hath set
> Discord in hearts of men, till they have braved
> Their nearest kin with deadly purpose met)
> 'Gainst duty weighed, and faithful love, did seem
> A thing of no esteem;
> And, from this triumph of affection pure,
> He bore the lasting name of '*pious Elidure.*'"*

The legend of Artegal and Elidure, like that of King Lear, belongs to those times in which Britain was, at least as far as authentic history informs us, in its insular solitude. I proceed now to a period when there was intercourse between Britain and the South. It is in the early part of those times that Shakspeare has laid the scene of the play of "Cymbeline," in which we find him

* Wordsworth's Artegal and Elidure. Works, p. 93

transporting his characters from London to Rome, with a violation of one of the dramatic unities that shocks the French critics, and with a speed that outstrips even modern locomotion. The play affords very little historical illustration; which, indeed, we can hardly expect to find until, as I have said, we come to the period of the proper "Chronicle-Plays."

I have had occasion to direct your attention to a fact which, though quite obvious, is apt, I think, to escape reflection unless especially noticed,—I mean the fact that our ancient history is confined, almost entirely, to the region of the shores of the Mediterranean Sea. I wish now to proceed with the further consideration of the breaking down of those limits, and the expansion of history which is consequent on the intercommunion of the Mediterranean people with the nations of the North. They were kept apart until the time came when God's purposes in the providential government of the earth were to be fulfilled by blending them together. I say they were *kept apart;* and I mean, of course, by something more than human power. No theory of mere secondary historic causes is adequate to explain the long-continued separation of the Northern and Southern nations of Europe; and that there was a providence in it appears, too, from this,—that it is that very separation which has influenced the whole course of modern history, taking as it does so much of its character from the infusion of the fresh life of the people of the North.

In the reading of history, our minds do not look upon the nations of Northern and Southern Europe relatively to each other. In the history of Greece or of Rome, the occasional introduction of some Northern race is an episode in the story of the Greeks and Romans, and it is nothing more. But my present subject draws us to the general view of those nations as they stood in relation one to the other—the North to the South—for many long ages isolated, and then thrown into national communion of a certain kind. A great barrier divided them; and that it was to endure for a certain period of the world as an effectual separation, appears from this,—that the power on neither side was able prematurely to break it down. The North could not conquer the South on the soil of the South, nor could the South conquer the North on Northern ground. There was mutual strength for independence and mutual weakness for conquest. In God's good season, the great partition wall crumbled and fell as if by "the unimaginable touch of Time;" while, before that period, no power of the hosts of men had prevailed against it.*

If you look at the map of Europe, you cannot fail to observe, in connection with this subject, how much there is in geographical character that served at once to hem in the nations of the South, and hinder them and the nations of the North from reciprocal conquest. Between the western coast of the Euxine Sea and the Atlantic Ocean, there runs east and west a great mountain range, which, beginning with the chain of Mount Hæmus to the north of Macedon, continues westward with the Alpine range, and ends with the Pyrenees, thus forming a vast natural rampart to Greece, Italy, and Spain,—the regions of the Mediterranean. When they of the South

* "The unimaginable touch of Time." Wordsworth's Sonnet on Mutability, p. 368.

crossed this barrier in the search of new homes, their progress was arrested by other natural boundaries; for they stopped on the borders of the great rivers of central Europe. The great North was still a vast and unknown domain; for it has been well said that—"The Roman colonies, along the banks of the Rhine and the Danube, looked out on the country beyond those rivers as we look up to the stars, and see with our eyes a world of which we actually know nothing. The Romans knew that there was a vast portion of earth which they did not know; how vast it might be was a part of its mysteries."*

But that the Northern and Southern nations were providentially kept distinct is, to my mind, still more apparent by the whole tenor of ancient history; for, whenever these two races came in contact, or rather in conflict, there is something that looks like a vain and impious strife against a Divine decree. It is not the story of an ordinary invasion and repulse: it is something more—a dim intimation of more than human agency—the awfulness of Divine interposition making it manifest that there were great providential purposes, and that a signal retribution was to fall on every attempt to frustrate them. It is like a religious service, in which the rites of paganism assume a peculiar and unwonted solemnity.

Observe how it was when the Northern nations first came into connection with the civilized world in the fourth century before the birth of our Saviour. The Celts or Gauls came down by tens of thousands upon

* Arnold's Lectures on Modern History, Am. ed., p. 47.

the plains of Italy, and swept onward in savage and sanguinary triumph to the gates of Rome. Of the routed and slaughtered Roman army only a few fugitives had escaped. In dismay, the city was well-nigh abandoned; for the great mass of the Commons, with their wives and children, fled to other towns. The holy things of Roman worship were removed or buried. What could be more hopeless? But the young Patricians resolved to defend the citadel—that which was the sanctuary of the nation—the most sacred spot, the safety of which seemed to secure their national existence, though the rest of the city were given up to foreign pillage. The aged Senators, who could serve their country only by their deaths, assembled, clad in their most solemn vestments and in their triumphal robes; and, repeating the words after the high-priest for the redemption of their country, they devoted themselves, and the army of the Gauls with themselves, to the spirits of the dead and the Earth, the common grave of the living. It is a very familiar part of Roman story how they awaited in their curule chairs, in calm and awful silence, the approach of their destroyers, and how the fierce barbarians were, for a moment, awed by the sight. One of the soldiers stroked the long white beard of Marcus Papirius; but the old man, who had been a minister of the gods, was outraged by the touch of profane barbarian hands, and smote the Gaul with his ivory sceptre. The blow was the signal for unsparing slaughter;—they perished, but pestilence soon swept the invader from the land. I refer to such familiar events, because they are so plainly significant of the mutual repulsion of these races, and they show that hundreds of years were still to pass before the Gaul and the Roman could dwell together.

Again, when, in the third century, the North sought by conquest communion with the South, more than two hundred thousand of the Gauls broke through the frontiers of Macedon; and there occurred that sublime passage in Greek history when the Northern barbarians, like the Persians of yore, sought the plunder of the magnificent temple of the Delphic Apollo—the centre of all the religious emotions of Grecian idolatry. The immense host of the invader fled in confusion when the sanctuary, with all its accumulated treasures, was almost in their power for pillage; and the legend tells how the spirit of Apollo fell on them to bewilder and destroy. Amid the earthquake and the tempest, which came in that wondrous hour of battle, the priests rushed forth exclaiming that they had seen the god pass across the vault of the temple, and that they had heard the whistling of the arrows and the clanging of the lances of the armed deities of Greece. When the morrow's sun arose, the huge bulk of many a Northern warrior lay buried beneath the rocks of Delphi, while the survivors were fleeing away in panic from the sunny regions of the South. This showed that the Gaul and the Greek were not to dwell together.*

Once more, when, in the first century before the Christian era, the great Cimbric and Teutonic invasion of Italy was driven back by the stern Plebeian soldier, Caius Marius, nothing resulted in the way of permanent subjugation. It was simply invasion and repulse, as if some huge wave had rushed in, and, after doing its work of partial devastation, had rolled back again into its cus-

* B. C. 279. Smith's History of Greece, (Felton,) p. 528.

tomary channel. When the tide of invading conquest set in a different direction, and pressed upon the regions of the North, it soon, in like manner, found its limit. The legions of the first Roman emperor penetrated into the forests of Germany, but they penetrated to perish there. The soldiers of the South had crossed the borders of what seemed to be forbidden ground even to the victorious progress of Roman conquest, and the penalty was defeat and extermination. A nation rose,—mighty Germany—

"She of the Danube and of the Northern Sea;"*

and the great victory achieved by Hermann and his Teutonic soldiers was naught less than the total sacrifice of the Roman intruders. The palace of the Cæsars echoed with the imperial lamentations for the lost legions; and when, some years afterwards, Germanicus, with another Roman army, followed in the footsteps of Varus, never did Roman pride receive a sterner or more impressive rebuke than when, amid the silence and gloom of the forest of Teutoburg, they reached a spot where, for the first time, the fate of Varus and his legions was legible in the rusting fragments of Roman weapons, and the more awful characters of the bleaching bones of their slaughtered countrymen.† In commemoration of the achievement of the hero of the first war of German independence, a colossal statue of Hermann has been constructed, within, I believe, the last ten or fifteen years, upon the spot which

---

* Wordsworth's Sonnet, "A Prophecy," p. 258.

† Tacitus, Ann. i. 61, 62. Suetonius thus records imperial sorrow: "Adeo denique consternatum ferunt, ut, per continuos menses barbâ capilloque submisso, caput interdum foribus illideret, vociferans 'Quintili Vare, legiones redde!'" Augustus, c. 23. W. B. R.

has been classic in the national mind of Germany in all later ages. If, in such a tribute paid by filial piety after a lapse of eighteen hundred years, we may, on the one hand, see something rather grotesquely characteristic of German deliberation, we may also find in it a proof of the awakening sense of reverence for ancient times in the heart of this nineteenth century. It seems to me, let me add, one of the healthful symptoms of a better spirit of the times, that a people should now deem it not too late to commemorate an heroic act of eighteen hundred years ago: it is a change from that rash and revolutionary temper which was of late so rife—which looked upon the olden time with disdain, and with that insolence of self-sufficiency which vaunts, that

> "Of old things, all are over old:
> Of good things, none are good enough:
> We'll show that we can help to frame
> A world of other stuff."*

It is this victory of Hermann over the Romans that Arnold refers to when, during a tour in Germany, he says:—"Far before us lay the land of our Saxon and Teutonic forefathers—the land uncorrupted by Roman or any other mixture—the birthplace of the most moral races of men that the world has yet seen—of the soundest laws, the least violent passions, and the fairest domestic and civil virtues. I thought of that memorable defeat of Varus and his three legions, which forever confined the

* Wordsworth's "Rob Roy's Grave," p. 243. "It is something to see reviving that filial feeling towards the years which begot us, which delights to own gratitude for the benefits received from them, and to deal reverently even with their faults, rather than to insult them by a perpetual boast of our own superiority." Quarterly Review, 1841. Vol. lxix. p. 113. W. B. R.

Romans to the western side of the Rhine, and preserved the Teutonic nation—the regenerating element in modern Europe—safe and free."* It was this battle, and the defeat of the Moors by Charles Martel, that Arnold used to rank as the two most important battles in the world. The victory in the forest of Teutoburg saved Germany from Roman subjugation, as the battle of Tours stayed the course of Saracenic aggression upon Western Christendom, preserving European civilization from Asiatic conquest, as, in ancient times, the victory of Marathon—another of the critical battles in the world's history—had saved Greece from Persian power.†

---

* Life and Correspondence. App. C. p. 454.

† The idea of a series of critical or decisive battles in the world's history, originating, perhaps, in an incidental remark of Mr. Hallam, has been cleverly elaborated in a work with this title by Professor Creasy, of University College, London; and I am glad of the occasion, valueless as my testimony may be, to bear it not only to the attractiveness, but the value of these volumes. The series extend from Marathon to Waterloo, with, as it seems to me, but one material omission,—for Mr. Creasy's view extends to this side of the Atlantic,—the battle on the Plains of Abraham, in 1759, by which the French Colonial America was destroyed, and North America became English beyond peradventure. Surely, this was a decisive battle.

From this work, I am tempted to make an extract illustrative of what is alluded to in the text,—the memorial of Arminius's victory.—"Nearly eighteen centuries after the death of Arminius, the modern Germans conceived the idea of rendering tardy homage to their great hero; and, accordingly, some eight or ten years ago, a general subscription was organized in Germany, for the purpose of erecting, on the Osning, (a conical mountain, which forms the highest summit of the Teutoburger Wald, and is eighteen hundred feet above the level of the sea,) a colossal bronze statue of Arminius. The statue was designed by Bandel. The hero was to stand, uplifting a sword in his right hand, and looking towards the Rhine. The height of the statue

Now the general historical view which I wish to impress on your minds is this—that the nations of Northern and Southern Europe were providentially kept apart until a period when intercourse should produce very different results from what would have followed had they come together sooner. When the people of the North came into continued contact with the Romans, the Roman Empire—the fourth empire—had completed the mighty work which was assigned to it in the providential government of the earth. The office of the Roman Empire among nations, according to the well-known prophetical description in the book of Daniel, was to "devour," to "tread down," to "break in pieces;" and wonderfully did Rome fulfil her function; for, from the primal gathering upon the Palatine Hill, she went right onward for eight centuries, on a career of conquest as straight as her own great roads—the Emilian or the Appian highway. That which was typified in the prophet's vision as the fourth beast, "dreadful and terrible and strong exceedingly,"—the iron power of Rome,—achieved the work assigned

was to be eighty feet from the base to the point of the sword, and was to stand on a circular Gothic temple, ninety feet high, and supported by oak-trees as columns. The mountain, where it was to be erected, is wild and stern, and overlooks the scene of the battle. It was calculated that the statue would be clearly visible at a distance of sixty miles. The temple is nearly finished, and the statue itself has been cast at the copper-works of Lemago. But there, through want of funds to set it up, it has lain for some years, in disjointed fragments, exposed to the mutilating homage of relic-seeking travellers. The idea of honouring a hero who belongs to *all* Germany, is not one which the present rulers of that divided country have any wish to encourage; and the statue may long continue to lie there, and present too true a type of the condition of Germany herself." Creasy's Fifteen Decisive Battles of the World, vol. i. p. 250.

to it, by conquering the tribes and islands and nations, and absorbing them in her own vast unity—by converting an ancient dynasty like Egypt into a Roman province—or sweeping away the last remnant of Greek freedom and the fragments of the Macedonian Empire—or by annihilating a commercial realm like Carthage with its colonies.

Bringing this to bear immediately on my subject, Britain, too, came within the scope of Rome's destiny; for Roman warfare was carried there and Roman power established. But it was slow and feeble and imperfect conquest, as in the evening of a well-fought day, when the soldier fights faintly or is sinking down to sleep on his field of battle—or in old age, when the veteran's arm is not so strong nor his passions so fierce. The conquest of Britain seems to me very different from the early conquests made by Rome; it was not such subjugation as destroys the elements of nationality. The whole power did not pass into the hands of the Romans, but was shared by victors and vanquished.

The Roman supremacy was established, and the independence of the Britons was destroyed, except in the west of the island, where the mountains of Wales gave a home to British freedom; still, the conquest was not of such a nature as either to sweep the original inhabitants from the land, or to reduce them to abject servitude. It was certainly conquest, and, doubtless, accompanied with much of the misery of conquest; but it partook also of the nature of alliance, or what may be intimated by a term which has become familiar of late to our ears—a kind of *annexation*. The Britons were Romanized, but they did not cease to be the British people. It was not a revolution utterly destructive of national character or of religious and political institutions. The conquered race seemed to be more benefited than the conquerors. During the early period of Roman warfare in Britain, the evils of foreign invasion were cruelly inflicted; and we can easily credit the story of Boadicea—the slaughter of the Druids—the captivity of Caractacus, and the forced exile of many from their homes to make room for the soldiers of the Roman legions. But when the fierceness of the war was over, the Roman and the Briton dwelt together; and, while Roman law was introduced, much of subordinate authority was preserved in the hands of British rulers. Under the Roman Empire there were British kings, and thus the royal title was perpetuated in an imperial province. To anticipate a term of the feudal system, Britain was a kind of vassal nation of the Roman Empire; and, while it kept its own national identity, it received and appropriated to itself much that was beneficial in Roman government. Tacitus is referred to as expressing surprise, if not indignation, at the facility and eagerness with which the Britons adopted the customs, the arts, the garb, and the refinement of their conquerors.*

In the play of Cymbeline, Shakspeare has portrayed the two nations in such a relation as that which I have been endeavouring to present to your minds. He is careful to preserve a certain degree of British independence, while Roman influence or supremacy is also recognised; and, with regard to national character, he shows, in the Italian villain of the play, how thoroughly demoralized the Roman people had become—how much they had lost

* Tacitus, Vit. Agricolæ, c. xvi.

of the high and heroic part of their nature in the low and irreligious sensuality of Epicurean philosophy.* On the other hand, the poet has shown, in the Britons of the play, the good and the evil which appertain to an imperfect condition of civilization. He has elevated our thoughts of ancient Britain by adorning it with the character of Imogen—one of the loveliest of that matchless company of women who have their life and being in the drama of Shakspeare; and in the wild heroism of her two brothers,—the stolen sons of Cymbeline,—he has shown, what has been truly said, that—"When a rude people have lost somewhat of their ferocity, and have not yet acquired the vices of a later stage of civilization, their character really exhibits much that is noble and excellent; and, both in its good and bad points, it so captivates the imagination, that it has always been regarded by the writers of a more advanced state of society with an admiration even beyond its merits."

In the imperfect state of historical knowledge respecting the early period of British history, we are apt, I think, to form a false conception of the civilization of the Britons. Receiving the first impression of their rude barbarism, we not only trust the description too much, but we carry it too far, in their history; and, accordingly, the common notion of the ancient Briton is, that they were savages who sacrificed human victims, and painted their skins. The truth as to the condition of

---

* It was upon the trial of the queen that Mr. Brougham, speaking of the perjured Italian witness, quoted Iachimo's words:

"I have belied a lady,
The princess of the country; and the air on't
Revengingly enfeebles me." W. B. R.

Britain appears to be, that it was a favoured and flourishing portion of the Roman Empire. A very considerable number of large cities, and a greater number of towns, are known by name as having flourished in various parts of the country. The Romans brought with them their luxuries, arts, and sciences; and, accordingly, temples and theatres and towns, baths and porticos, gates, triumphal arches, and market-places arose, remarkable for their architecture and decorated with sculpture and statuary. Such was the reputation of the Romanized British architects, that they were sent by Constantius into Gaul to rebuild a ruined city. It has been said, with no less vividness than accuracy, that what Calcutta is now to London, London or York was to Rome. For four hundred years was the Roman influence at work in a large part of Britain; and that influence produced its results, not only in the arts as displayed in public and private edifices, but also in the more permanent political effects resulting from the establishment of the municipal rights and privileges of the towns.

Visible proofs of the condition of Britain during the Roman period are not unfrequently found at the present day, when some excavation discloses a tesselated pavement, or a buried arch, or military road, or when Roman coins are dug up, or sacrificial vessels, or ancient implements of war or peace. There are standing the more manifest ruins of the frontier walls—the extended lines of fortifications by which Britain was defended against the Caledonian—chiefly the wall of Severus, the height of which, in one part of its ruins, was curiously ascertained by that fervid antiquarian, Ritson. On a visit to Sir Walter Scott, Ritson, who was by nature very prone to controversy, and, with all his learning, perhaps a little insane, disputed the existence of any ruins of the wall, trusting to some information that had been given him. Scott assured him where the ruin was to be seen, and added that it was high enough to break the neck of Mr. Ritson's inaccurate informer were he to fall from it. This strong and natural expression, irritating Ritson's fiery zeal for accuracy, was carefully noted by him; and Scott was soon after astonished at finding how literally his uncalculating phrase had been taken; for a letter from Ritson stated that he had indeed found the ruin, which he had visited for the very purpose of jumping down from the wall to test the fidelity of Sir Walter's description, which his escape with an unbroken neck proved to be hyperbolical. He adds, however, that the height of the wall was such as to make the experiment dangerous; and I repeat the anecdote to give you an impression as to the state of those famous Roman ruins. So little is preserved of the national relics of the Roman-British times, and so little can be distinctly traced in the permanent influence of social or political institutions of that period, that there arises, what appears to me, another erroneous historical view of those distant eras. Knowing scarce any thing of the primitive British period, we are apt to conclude that the Britons became extinct or were pushed from their land, as the Indians in our own country are thrust away by the white population; and that, therefore, they transmitted to succeeding generations no influence or national character. In like manner, though in less degree, we are apt to fancy, because our information is imperfect, that the Roman era of British history left but few traces behind it; and hence we hastily conclude, that modern English and American character is derived only from the later elements of the Anglo-Saxon and Norman eras. Such a view is hardly rational, when we reflect that the Britons occupied the island from an unknown antiquity—that they never were driven from it, but were amalgamated with their Roman conquerors—and that Roman civilization abode there for four hundred years. The periods were of such duration, and the circumstances were such, that the influence could not have stopped abruptly as the periods respectively closed. It appears to me more reasonable and truthful, and certainly it raises the dignity of our race, to take such a view as preserves the continuity of the history, and to regard the successive periods as revolutions not destructive or overwhelming, but modifying ancient things by the introduction of new elements. The Britons underwent a Roman change, and then came, as we shall presently see, a Saxon change, and then a Norman change; and, from the successive influences of them all, there came forth a great—the greatest modern nation. The revolutions were not sudden, devastating, volcanic eruptions, leaving nothing but barren ashes and indurated lava, but rather may they be compared to a series of geological formations strewn in due and solid succession.

Before passing from the Roman period, I can do no more than advert to the early introduction of Christianity into Britain; and whether or no the gospel was first preached there by St. Paul or St. Peter, and whether or no the first Christian church was humbly and rudely built by Joseph of Arimathea, Druidical paganism passed quickly away. The remote and insular situation of the British Christians did not shelter them from the perils which were the trials of faith in its early era. It was in the tenth and last of the great persecutions, when, according to a vivid poetic phrase,

> "Diocletian's fiery sword
> Worked busy as the lightning,"*

that Alban, the first of Britain's martyrs, gave up his earthly life. English chivalry has also exulted, that the first Christian king and the first Christian emperor were natives of Britain.

The great providential agency of Rome in the history of the world was now drawing to an end—the empire was near its death—the last of the legions was withdrawn from Britain, and the emperor bade the Britons provide for their own defence. They were left with Roman arts and arms and civilization; but the heart of the people was faint, and they were helpless in the simple necessity of self-defence. From their island home they piteously entreated once more for the protection of Roman supremacy, exclaiming—"The barbarians drive us to the sea, and the sea drives us back to the barbarians."† Help could not come from Rome, whose expiring strength was sinking before the hosts of the Goth, the Vandal, and the Hun. I need not stop to say how the Britons were saved from the Pictish and Scottish invasions only by the fierce alliance of the Saxons. The country was given over again to victorious invasion and the settlement of a race of Northern heathens. Nor need I dwell on the introduction of a new national element, which, though it

* "Diocletian's fiery sword," &c. Wordsworth's Sonnet on Persecution, p. 349.

† Milton's History of Britain, p. 125.

brought misery with it, contained the germs of so much that was precious in the after-history of the land. The Saxon dominion was planted in a soil wet with blood; and it is in this ineffectual war, that early romance has placed the fabled exploits of Arthur and his peers, and the conjurations and sorcery of Merlin. The ruins of that gigantic and mysterious structure, Stonehenge, which, at this day, stands in awful silence upon Salisbury Plain, is supposed to be the monument of the treacherous massacre of three hundred British nobles by their Saxon foes.* Christian Britain was paganized again, and the faith again endured the fiery ordeal of heathen persecution. When Ethelred, the Saxon king of Northumberland, invaded Wales, and was about to give battle to the Britons, he perceived close by the enemy a host of unarmed men. He asked who they were and what they were doing, and was told they were the monks of Bangor, praying for the success of their countrymen. "Then," said Ethelred, and he said rightly, "they are fighting against us." The word went forth to attack them first; and twelve hundred of those

---

* I am not as much in the habit of quoting Wordsworth as my brother was, not being so familiar with his poems, and, perhaps, (this I say with diffidence,) relatively, not so appreciative of their merits; but his lines on Stonehenge (Excursion, b. iii.) are very grand. The parenthetical idea is magnificent:

"Not less than that huge Pile (from some abyss
Of mortal power unquestionably sprung,)
Whose hoary Diadem of pendant rocks
Confines the shrill-voiced whirlwind, round and round
Eddying within its vast circumference,
On Sarum's naked plain." W. B. R

unarmed Christian men perished by a bloody death. But fierce as was this persecution, when the Heptarchy was established, the wild superstition of the Saxons was brought under the sway of Christianity, chiefly by the mission of St. Augustine. When Paulinus visited the court of King Edwin, the king convened a council to determine whether their heathen creed should bow to the tidings which Paulinus brought; and it was there a pagan counsellor gave utterance to that beautiful imaginative argument, which, told by the old Saxon historian, has been thus rendered in modern verse:

"Man's life is like a Sparrow, mighty King!
That, stealing in, while by the fire you sit
Housed with rejoicing Friends, is seen to flit
Safe from the storm, in comfort tarrying.
Here did it enter—there on hasty wing
Flies out, and passes on from cold to cold;
But whence it came we know not, nor behold
Whither it goes. Even such that transient Thing
The human Soul; not utterly unknown
While in the Body lodged, her warm abode;
But from what world She came, what woe or weal
On her departure waits, no tongue hath shewn;
This mystery if the Stranger can reveal,
His be a welcome cordially bestowed!"*

The growth of the English Christian Commonwealth advanced with due progress in those Saxon centuries, and at length we read, in the ninth century, of the saintly and heroic reign of Alfred—the soldier and the lawgiver—who has left a name which, like one, and perhaps only one, other, stands on the page of history

* Wordsworth's Ecclesiastical Sonnets.

purely irreproachable, honoured, and faultless. I should, perhaps, run into mere common-places were I to attempt to say more respecting this famous Saxon sovereign; and I prefer, therefore, borrowing the words of Coleridge in his lecture on the character of the Gothic mind in the Middle Ages:

"I must now turn to our great monarch, Alfred—one of the most august characters that any age has ever produced; and when I picture him, after the toils of government and dangers of battle, seated by a solitary lamp, translating the Holy Scriptures into the Saxon tongue—when I reflect on his moderation in success, on his fortitude and perseverance in difficulty and defeat, and on the wisdom and extensive nature of his legislation, I am really at a loss which part of this great man's character most to admire. Yet, above all, I see the grandeur, the freedom, the mildness, the domestic unity, the universal character of the Middle Ages condensed into Alfred's glorious institution of the trial by jury. I gaze upon it as the immortal symbol of that age,—an age called, indeed, dark,—but how could that age be considered dark which solved the difficult problem of universal liberty, freed man from the shackles of tyranny, and subjected his actions to the decision of twelve of his fellow-countrymen?"*

In his fragment on English history, Burke has said that Alfred's piety—which, with all its zeal and fervour, was of an enlarged and noble kind—was the principle that supported him in so many fatigues, and fed like an abundant source his civil and military virtues. It has

* Coleridge's Literary Remains, vol. i. p. 74. Ed. 1836, Pickering.

been shown, as conclusive proof of the unfairness and the infidel tendency of Hume's history, that in it every fact is studiously concealed that would have displayed the governing principle of Alfred's life to have been an active belief in Christianity.*

From the obscurity which hangs over the Anglo-Saxon period, there shine forth, though with somewhat of mysterious dimness, four great names, which, in their several ways, characterize and illustrate the times. The earliest and most glorious of these is that which I have just noticed, King Alfred; the others are Dunstan, Canute, and Edward the Confessor. In proceeding to a brief notice of the second of these characters, I find myself approaching the neighbourhood of those questions which have been discussed with more of ecclesiastical animosity than historical candour; and it is difficult to speak of even so remote a personage as St. Dunstan, without, perhaps, touching the morbidly sensitive nerve of some prejudice or prepossession belonging to later periods. I have no desire to seek topics of this description; and, on the other hand, entertaining no opinions which I need hold in reserve, and being, unless I greatly deceive myself, incapable of saying any thing that would wound the reasonable feelings of anybody, it would be unjust, both to you and myself, were I timidly to avoid such questions when they come directly in my way. They must lie in the path of any one who proposes to examine, however superficially, the period of history which forms our subject. During the Middle Ages, and

* Quarterly Review,—"Hume and his Influence on History,"—No. 146, March, 1844, pp. 577–579. W. B. R.

even in modern times, for at least a century or more after the Reformation, you cannot, unless by a violent and irrational disruption, separate political and ecclesiastical history. The student of history desires to be instructed in forming a just estimate of the character of Dunstan, and he naturally supposes that such a subject can be candidly and satisfactorily examined; for he never dreams of writers getting angry about a man who lived nine hundred years ago. But to this day it is a vexed question with all the extreme contrarieties of eulogy and vituperation, and it is far easier to go to either extreme than to find the truth. Party animosity is a grievous evil anywhere, but nowhere more so than in historical investigation; and when I see how the candid inquiry after truth is perplexed and thwarted by it, I am reminded of that incident in the boyhood of Sir Roger de Coverley, which is told in one of those inimitable papers of the Spectator, of which he is the hero, and which abounds in such genuine English humour. "It happened to him," says the Spectator, "when he was a school-boy, which was at the time the feuds ran high between the Cavaliers and the Roundheads. Sir Roger, being then a stripling, had occasion to inquire which was the way to St. Anne's Lane; upon which the person whom he spoke to, instead of answering him, called him a young popish cur, and asked him, who had made Anne a saint. The boy, being in some confusion, inquired of the next he met, which was the way to Anne's Lane, but was called a prick-eared cur for his pains; and, instead of being shown the way, was told that she had been a saint before he was born, and would be one after he was hanged. Upon this, says the knight, I did not think fit to repeat the former question; but, going into every lane of the neighbourhood, asked what they called the name of that lane,—by which ingenious artifice he found out the place he inquired after without giving offence to any party."*

There is, I fear, no such ingenious artifice to help one in threading the avenues of history. I am tempted to add another illustration of the difficulty of discerning historic truth through the medium of party passion, which is given by Sir Francis Palgrave, the incident having occurred a few years ago in Dublin:

"A pleasure-boat, belonging to a party of Brunswickers, having been moored on the river Liffey, some of the bystanders on an adjoining quay were extremely incensed at the standard of defiance which the vessel displayed. The vane at the mast-head displayed an effigy—an Orangeman trampling on a green shamrock. This affront, aimed at the feelings of the multitude, was not to be borne. The Milesians attacked the hostile Saxon bark by hurling a furious volley of paving stones, and the unlucky crew, urged by danger or apprehension, discharged their firearms, and wounded some of the surrounding assemblage. A great commotion was excited, and the leaders of the belligerent parties were conducted to the police-office. Among the witnesses who were called was the tinman who had made the vane; and this worthy tradesman gave the most candid and unequivocal testimony in full proof of the pacific intention of the pleasure-boat, though certainly somewhat to his own discredit as an artist. The unlucky cause of so much dissension and bloodshed,—the supposed Orangeman

* Spectator, No. 125.

trampling on the green shamrock,—was, in truth, a flesh-coloured Mercury springing from a blue cloud."*

So it is in history; what is blue to one man's eye is green to another; and often, what is seen by one as the spotless purity of white, looks black and begrimed to another. For the lecturer who, in his limited time, must glance rapidly over his subjects without stopping cautiously to qualify his expressions,—for him I fear there is a special danger of his flying Mercuries being mistaken for something or other quite different.

But to return to St. Dunstan. I give him his title, notwithstanding the admonition of Sir Roger de Coverley's experience; for he stands, not only on the Romish Calendar, but his name is retained on the Calendar of the Anglo-Catholic Church.† Noble by birth, the young

* Palgrave's History of England. Preface, vol. i. p. xxxii.

† At a time when the merest justice to the Roman Catholic Church is hazardous, I will presume to deprecate the use of this word "Romish," which, kindred to the other nicknames, "Romanist" and "Papist," ought to be banished from the language of Christian scholars and gentlemen. They are words of offence and disrespect, and therefore unfit for use except as part of the Billingsgate of controversy. They are undescriptive and unsanctioned by authority. In speaking *to* a Roman Catholic, common courtesy forbids the use of such words. In speaking *of* him, surely, among scholars, the same rule of courtesy should prevail. My brother—a most resolute Protestant—was singularly free from sectarian animosities, and this slip of language was, I am satisfied, purely accidental. On the next page but one he avoids the epithet. The following words, written in confidence years before these lectures, describe his feelings and opinions to the last hour of his life,—and yet it suited vulgar and ignorant men for their own poor purposes to describe Henry Reed as an ultraist in church matters. I wish I could be sure that their eyes—those, I mean, who did him, on more than one occasion, practical injustice—would read his truthful, almost eloquent, words:

Saxon Thane exchanged his rank for the austerities of monastic life. A commanding intellect and an indomitable spirit, rare accomplishments, and a skill in the arts which excited the wonder and the awe of the people, form the character and attainments of this remarkable personage as described by all historians. But, beyond this, all is conflict and confusion of opinion, from which it is almost hopeless to attempt to draw a sure judgment. You find every variety of opinion, with no little uncertainty as to some of the facts whereon it is formed. Hume tells us that Dunstan's whole career was fraud and hypocrisy,—of course he tells you so, for that is his "universal solvent" of all ecclesiastical questions.*

"I cannot find in my heart," he writes, "any sympathy with that kind of church feeling which, when it finds the door in good condition,—hung on strong hinges and with a stout latch,—does not look with a thankful and affectionate spirit to the family within, as much as with somewhat of insolence and superciliousness to those who are without. It is, I apprehend, something of this kind which too often characterizes the self-styled—boastfully self-styled—High-Churchmanship: there is a certain temper about it which is odious to me, and at variance with what I trust and believe is the genuine heart of the church. It carries with it that unchurchlike self-obtrusion which, extremes meeting, assimilates it to that which it professes its chief aversion to. The epithet "High," in this connection, is any thing but agreeable to my ears; and I am half-inclined to think that if it is important to 'unprotestantize the Reformation,' it may not be amiss to '*unhighchurchmanize*' the church. There is danger of what Julius Hare calls 'ecclesiolatry.'" MS. Letter, March 31, 1843.

W. B. R.

* This phrase, if I mistake not, will be found in a letter from Sir Walter Scott in Lockhart, in which he says that something "might be explained by the doctrine of the 'association of ideas,' or whatever other doctrine had taken the place of that which, in my day, had been the *universal solvent* of all metaphysical difficulties." W. B. R.

Roman Catholic historical writers—Lingard and Charles Butler—uphold the probity and piety of St. Dunstan, and exhibit him as an ornament to his faith and his country. Southey denounces him as an arch miracle-monger, and as a complete exemplar of the monkish character in its worst form: he treats one of the alleged miracles as a piece of ventriloquism, and the other as a treacherous and most atrocious piece of wholesale murder. Milton, who had a hearty detestation of monastic character in every shape, must have been struck with admiration of the fearlessness with which Dunstan rebuked the vices of his king; for he speaks of him as "a strenuous bishop, zealous without dread of persons, and, for aught that appears, the best of many ages."* Palgrave explains part of Dunstan's career by a theory of partial insanity, and another writer cautiously intimates he was neither so good nor so bad as he is made out. Sir James Mackintosh characterizes Dunstan as a zealous and, perhaps, useful reformer of religious instruction, of commanding abilities, of a haughty, stern, and turbulent nature, without more personal ambition, perhaps, than is usually blended with public principle; and who, if he were proved guilty of some pious frauds, might not unreasonably pray that a part of the burden of such guilt might be transferred from him to his age.

Now, these are sorry materials to form an opinion out of, and I cannot but think how much better it would be if a Poet's charitable and catholic imagination had looked upon St. Dunstan's character, and left us a record of the vision. We should then, I believe, have been far better

* Milton's History of Britain, p. 285.

able to form a just conception of St. Dunstan's character and the powers of the mind which made him the leading and master-spirit of the Anglo-Saxon empire throughout many reigns—the Wolsey of his age.* We should have seen fanaticism or ambition, or perhaps sterner and fiercer elements, making the dark side of his character; and with this we should behold him a fearless reformer in the church, and a triumphant statesman in the kingdom. He arrayed himself against what he proclaimed to be the vices of the secular clergy, and all the energy of his indomitable spirit was exerted to establish the rule of the Benedictine order in the Saxon monasteries. Certain is it that he wielded a mighty power, for people and priests and kings trembled before him. As Primate of England and chief counsellor of the king, he is identified with the fame of that reign in which the Anglo-Saxon dominion had greater extent and majesty than it had known before—when "Edgar the Peaceful" summoned the neighbouring sovereigns to bow before his supremacy, as Napoleon, at the height of his power, received at Dresden the homage of subject monarchs. It was the result of Dunstan's administration that Edgar received the homage of eight British kings; and, on one occasion, when he sat at the helm of his barge, each one of these royal vassals was plying an oar. Dunstan was in the councils of a reign when the Saxons breathed secure from the fierce inroads of the Danes. He was honoured and powerful by the side of a king who was thus lamented in what I may give you as a brief specimen of Saxon poetry:

* Neither Henry Taylor, for Edwin the Fair had then appeared, nor Wordsworth himself appear to have fulfilled my brother's wish as to the poetic illustration of Dunstan's character. W. B. R.

"Here ended his earthly joys, Edgar, England's king, and chose the light of another world, beauteous and happy. Here Edgar departed—the ruler of the Angles, the joy of the West Saxons, the defender of the Mercians—that was known afar among many nations. Kings beyond the baths of the sea-fowl worshipped him far and wide. They bowed to the king as one of their own kin. There was no fleet so proud, there was no host so strong, as to seek food in England while this noble king ruled the kingdom. He reared up God's honour—he loved God's law—he preserved the people's peace, the best of all the kings that were before in the memory of man. And God was his helper, and kings and earls bowed to him and they obeyed his will; and, without battle, he ruled as he willed."*

This happy reign ended, and the raven—the dark and dreaded emblem on the flag of the Danes—was again seen along the shores of England. For two hundred years were these fierce barbarians of the North the terror and the scourge of the Saxon; and ever when the Danish raven was seen above the waves that beat towards England, it was the sure omen of burning dwelling-houses, of pillaged monasteries, and of a fugitive or slaughtered people. And so the warfare was waged until at length, in the eleventh century, Saxon independence was given up to Canute—that mighty Scandinavian monarch who was at once King of Denmark and Sweden and Norway and England; and, with some claim to Scotland and Cambria, it was his boast that he ruled over six nations.

* Translated from the Saxon Chronicle, pp. 116, 122,—in a note to Lingard, vol. i. p. 271.

His reign appears to have been a splendid and a prosperous one: he was called "Canute the Great," and "Canute the Rich;" and, though he lived only a little beyond the age of forty, he was called "Canute the Old;" for, in those turbulent times, the two-score years seem to have been regarded as an extraordinary duration for a king's life. It has been well said of him, that prosperity softened but did not corrupt him; and that he is one of the few conquerors whose greater and better qualities were developed in peace. A beautiful poetic light rests on the peaceful periods of his life: he was not only a conqueror and a lawgiver, but a royal minstrel; and there is still preserved from a ballad, which is said to have been long a favourite with the people of England, one stanza, which broke from him when, in his royal barge, he heard, over the waters of the river, the distant and solemn sound of the hymn that was chaunted in the minster of Ely.* There is that other beautiful and poetic story that is told of him,—so familiar that I need only allude to it,—that admirable piece of symbolical teaching so appropriate to his times, by which, on the sea-side, he won from the waves of the ocean a voice of rebuke to the flattery of his courtiers. The fitting sequel of that story is less familiar. It tells how—

"Canute, (truth more worthy to be known,)
From that time forth, did for his brows disown
The ostentatious symbol of a crown,—
Esteeming earthly royalty
Contemptible and vain."†

* This stanza will be found in a note to Campbell's Essay on English Poetry, p. 22.

† Wordsworth's Canute and Alfred on the Sea shore, p. 413.

When the Saxon dynasty was restored in the person of Edward, surnamed the Confessor, the meek and gentle piety of that saintly monarch was like a placid evening to close the Saxon day. But, looking away from the sovereign's character, the political horizon of England was darkened by lowering clouds and a stormy sunset. The weapons with which Edward strove with his turbulent and tempestuous times were juridical wisdom and saintly piety. Feeble as he was in perpetuating Saxon independence, he was endeared to after times; and a high tribute was paid to his memory when, again and again, the nation demanded that there should be given back to them "the laws and customs of the good king Edward."

It is only upon one historical point in English history that Shakspeare has touched in his tragedy of Macbeth, who was the Scottish contemporary of Edward the Confessor. There is a genuine poetic art in deepening the sense of the atrocities of Macbeth and the sufferings of Scotland under his usurpation and tyranny, by presenting the contrast of the Confessor's piety and virtues; and, most of all, the wondrous charity exerted by him on some of his subjects stricken by grievous malady. It was with Edward the Confessor that that remarkable practice began, of touching to cure the disease called the "king's evil,"—a practice which continued for nearly seven hundred years in England, for it did not cease until the accession of George the First. In France, it continued even later,—until 1770. The long duration and the universal faith in the virtues of the royal touch appear to us of the present day a most unaccountable delusion. It seems to have been attributed to some mysterious sanctity in the character or functions of an anointed king;

and when we read of it in connection with a saintly sovereign like Edward the Confessor, and in a remote age, the distance of time and the character of the monarch seem to hallow it, and one hesitates to treat it contemptuously as an absurd medical superstition. But when we come down to times less than two hundred years ago, to the reign of an English king who certainly had nothing very sacred or sacerdotal in his character,—I mean Charles the Second,—it is amazing to read of a registry which shows that, in the space of twenty years, that merry monarch touched no less than ninety-two thousand one hundred and seven persons for the "king's evil,"—the malady having, I suppose, accumulated during the Commonwealth and the Protectorate, although Cromwell appears to have played the king by trying his hand at the cure. When Francis the First, of France, was a prisoner at Madrid, after the battle of Pavia, he touched a great number of the sick; and on one day, Easter Sunday, in 1686, Louis the Fourteenth touched no fewer than sixteen hundred persons. I mention these things to show how extensively this extraordinary usage prevailed. It is not, however, my business to attempt any solution of it—to choose between the miracle of the royal touch and the marvel of a credulity which endured for seven or eight centuries, and in the minds not only of many thousands, but, as far as evidence goes, in the minds of all. But in France and in England it was accompanied with stated and solemn service of prayer, and the cure was attributed to the mercy of God rather than to the hand of man; and, therefore, I will not speak of it with mockery or contempt. I think there is truer wisdom and better feeling in simply contemplating it as the sage imagination of Shakspeare has taught us to look on it through the vision of the characters in Macbeth.

When Malcolm and Macduff have fled to England, it is in the palace of Edward the Confessor that Malcolm inquires of an English doctor—

> "Comes the king forth, I pray you?"

and the answer is—

> "Ay, sir: there are a crew of wretched souls
> That stay his cure: their malady convinces
> The great assay of art; but, at his touch,
> Such sanctity hath heaven given his hand,
> They presently amend."

When Macduff asks—

> "What's the disease he means?"

Malcolm answers—

> "'Tis called the evil:
> A most miraculous work in this good king;
> Which often, since my here-remain in England,
> I have seen him do. How he solicits heaven,
> Himself best knows: but strangely-visited people,
> All swoln and ulcerous, pitiful to the eye,
> The mere despair of surgery, he cures;
> Hanging a golden stamp about their necks,
> Put on with holy prayers: and 'tis spoken,
> To the succeeding royalty he leaves
> The healing benediction. With this strange virtue
> He hath a heavenly gift of prophecy;
> And sundry blessings hang about his throne,
> That speak him full of grace."*

* Though entirely aside from the context, I am tempted to note, that in this same scene will be found lurking one of the most beautiful

It was with this good man that the ancient and lawful lineage of the Saxon sovereigns ended, about the middle of the eleventh century. An English historian closes this era of his country's annals in these words:

"Our kings, in the castle of Windsor, live on the brink of the grave which opens to receive them. The throne

---

of Shakspeare's lines, which no "beauty-selector" or compiler of quotation-dictionaries has ever detected. It is Malcolm who says—

"Angels are bright still, though the brightest fell:
Though all things foul would wear the brows of grace,
Yet grace must still look so."

And, in this connection of quotations, I venture to quote a sprightly passage from a letter of my brother's which now lies before me:

"I was," he writes, "the other day, looking over 'Measure for Measure' to find a grand image which Froude mentions in one of his letters, but which got out of my memory after I had returned the 'Remains' to the Library. By-the-by, did you ever notice how hard it is to lay your hand sometimes upon a grand thought or image in Shakspeare, which you have lost the clue to? He puts it somewhere that you would not think of looking for it, or so incidentally that you overlook it—so differently from inferior writers, who put a flashy gilt frame round what they are proud of. I was obliged, therefore, to look over the play almost line by line, and, after all, did not find what I was looking for; but I did notice among other things a jewel of a sentence, in point of real English construction and *unparsableness*, which I thought would delight you:

'These poor informal women are no more
But instruments of some more mightier member
That sets them on.'

In the same scene, was Shakspeare thinking of a Puritan heresy—though I am not sure the error belongs to them, 'the greater the sinner the greater the saint'—when he says—

'They say, best men are moulded out of faults,
And, for the most, become much more the better
For being a little bad.'

of Edward was equally by the side of his sepulchre, for he dwelt in the palace of Westminster; and, on the festival of the Epiphany, the day after his decease, his obsequies were solemnized in the adjoining abbey, then connected with the royal abode by walls and towers, the foundations whereof are still existing. Beneath the lofty windows of the southern transept of the abbey, you may see the deep and blackened arches, fragments of the edifice raised by Edward, supporting the chaste and florid tracery of a more recent age. Within, stands the shrine—once rich in gems and gold—raised to the memory of the Confessor by the fond devotion of his successors, despoiled, indeed, of all its ornaments, neglected and crumbling to ruin, but still surmounted by the massy, iron-bound oaken coffin which contains the ashes of the last legitimate Anglo-Saxon king."

Baffled in finding the passage I was hunting, I was driven to get the 'Remains' again, for the vexation of memory haunted me. Mr. Froude was struck with what he calls 'a certain wild sublimity about it.' Speaking of respect for high places, the duke says—

> 'Respect to your great place! and let the Devil
> Be sometimes honoured for his burning throne.'"

MS. Letter, 22d October, 1843. W. B. R.

LECTURE IV.*

The Reign of King John.

Interval between the last Saxon kings and King John—Degeneracy of the Saxon race—Contagion of Danish vice—The Bristol slave-trade—The Northmen—The Normans—Their conquests—Death of Harold—Effect of the conquest on the conquerors—Their despotism—The Royal Forest lands—The Curfew—Death of William the Norman—Tyranny of his successors—Marriage of Henry the First to a Saxon princess—The Plantagenets—Richard Cœur-de-Lion—Romance of Ivanhoe—Anselm, Archbishop of Canterbury—King John, the first of the "Chronicle-Plays"—Imaginative power developed—John, a usurper—Shakspeare's view of his character—"England" the great idea of the play—Falconbridge its exponent—His character—Shakspeare's power "in minimis"—James Gurney's four words—France and Austria—Constance and Arthur—His death—Pandulph—Struggle with the Papacy—Innocent the Third—Stephen Langton—The interdict—Struggle with the barons—The Great Charter—Shakspeare's English loyalty.

THE main subject of this lecture will be the reign and times of King John. In proceeding to it, I desire to connect that period of English history with the epoch with which I closed my last lecture; and thus, by rapidly noticing the intervening times, to preserve the continuity of our historical view of England.

The last event which I spoke of was the death of that meek and saintly sovereign, Edward the Confessor, and,

* January 18th, 1847.

in his death, the ending of the legitimate dynasty of the Anglo-Saxon kings,—the race of Cerdic, the King of Wessex, which had ruled the land for more than five hundred years. This, it will be remembered, was about the middle of the eleventh century; and at the close of the succeeding century began the reign of King John. The interval of about one hundred and forty years was an eventful period, which I cannot attempt to do more than glance swiftly over.

The Saxon race had become degenerate—the race which could boast of Alfred and Athelstan—which had produced heroic kings and sent forth saintly men to bear the Christian faith unto other lands. The best part of the old Saxon character was wasted away in widespread licentiousness and debauchery. The people had grown to be sensual and self-indulgent and riotous; revelry was their habit, with no better excuse than that the Danes had taught them to drink deep.

Danish vice became also Saxon vice; and, worse an hundred-fold, a horrid slave-trade shows into what deep and cruel profligacy England, at that time, was sunk. The town of Bristol was an established slave-market; and this detested traffic was carried on by Saxons of high rank, who sold their own countrymen; and into Saxon hands the price was paid for Saxon peasants, menials, and servile vassals of every description, who were carried away from their native land to dwell in Denmark and Ireland, homeless, because in slavery.* There was such

* "Slave ships regularly sailed from Bristol to Ireland, where they were secure of a ready and profitable market." Lingard, vol. i. p. 376, ch. vii. W. B. R.

depravity in England, that, though the sensual, deaf in their debauchery and wickedness, heard it not, the cry went up to Heaven for vengeance. The national corruption seemed to provoke national retribution; and when it came, it was in fierce and bloody chastisement. "The Saxons," as has been eloquently said, "had not been left without warning. Judgment had followed judgment. The Dane had fulfilled his mission, yet there was no improvement. They had seen, too, among them, with all the stern holiness and fiery zeal of an ancient prophet, startling and terrible as the Danes themselves, Dunstan the Archbishop, who had dragged a king from his chamber of shame. Yet they would not rouse themselves: the wine-cup was too sweet, the couch too soft: 'the joys of the hall,' the story, the song, the 'glee-beams' of the harp,—these gladdened their days; and to these, in spite of the Danes and St. Dunstan, they clung faster and faster. The dream went on; the lethargy became heavier. * * * *

"At last the stroke came; more terrible in its reality than the most anxious had imagined. It was not merely a change of kings or families; not even an invasion or ordinary conquest; it was a rooting and tearing up, a wild overthrow of all that was established and familiar in England.

"There were seeds of good, of high and rare excellence in the Saxons; so they were to be chastised, not destroyed. Those who saw the Norman triumph, and the steady, crushing strength of its progress, who saw English feelings, English customs, English rights, trampled on, mocked at, swept away, little thought that the Norman, the "Francigena," was to have no abiding name in the land of his conquest; that his language was to be swallowed up and lost in that of the Saxon; that it was for the glory and final exaltation of the English race that he was commissioned to school them thus sternly. So, indeed, it was. But on that generation the judgment fell, as bitter as it was unexpected; it was, in their eyes, vengeance unrelenting and final; it seemed as if God had finally cast them off, and given them over, without hope of respite or release, to their tormentors."*

In closing the last lecture, the latest event in English history to which I alluded was the death of Edward the Confessor, the last legitimate Anglo-Saxon king. There still remained a few stormy months of the Saxon times—a disputed succession, brief and tumultuous—an unsteady tenure of the throne, and a bloody death. The eyes of the gentle and pious Edward had been spared the vision of the sufferings that were so soon to befall the nation. The wild reign of Harold, in which the Saxon dynasty passed away, occupied less than a year in that period when, after the world had completed a thousand years in the Christian era, there was strange and wide-spread dismay in the hearts of men, and dim apprehensions that the day of judgment was nigh at hand. The great comet of the year 1060 appeared; and, as it waved over England, the Saxon looked up to the sky with terror, when he beheld what seemed to him a portent of the sword of the invader or the destroyer. The Saxon vainly strove to drown his fears in revelry and riot, or else awaited in

* This striking quotation I am unable to trace to its source.
W. B. R.

dread suspense the moment when the comet should, as Milton describes it,—

> "Shake from its horrid Lair
> Pestilence and war."

In tumult and slaughter had the Saxon rule been established in Britain; and, after six hundred years duration, it ended, in like manner, in confusion and bloodshed. Brother was warring against brother for the throne, and the Norwegian king, with his pirates of the North, was summoned to unnatural alliance in the fraternal strife. Harold's short reign had its one victory, but it was a victory that left dead on the field not only the King of Norway, but his own brother. In his season of victory,—his hand wet with a brother's blood,—he was told that the ships of the Normans had set sail from the ports of France, and were approaching the shores of England.

What race of men was this that Normandy was sending forth on this voyage of conquest? The Normans, as described by an old historian, were the flower of the Swedes, the Danes, and the Norwegians. They had dwelt, indeed, long enough in France to learn a stranger's speech, but, originally, they were kindred with the Saxons; and it is curious to observe, in the progress of English history, how the various tribes of the great Teutonic race were brought into fierce collision, and how their union was again cemented by blood. The Northmen were for a long while the most adventurous and roving race of European men: they penetrated into the Mediterranean; they swept the coasts of the Northern Sea, and sailed into the navigable rivers of central Europe, striking such terror that the ancient litanies contained prayers for deliverance from the fury of the Northmen. They won from a king of France that fair province to which they gave their name of Normandy; and, in that same century, another portion of the Northmen, undismayed by the dread of an Arctic and unknown sea, are believed to have sailed westward, and, making Iceland their stepping-stone, as it were, in the ocean, to have passed onward and reached America five hundred years before Columbus.

The Northmen who settled in France became Christianized and civilized; and, in the next century, retaining all their spirit of adventure, they went forth, not as heathen pirates, but as Christian soldiers. One band of them crossed the Alps to make a Norman settlement in Southern Italy, and still farther on, to raise the Christian banner over the crescent of the Saracens in the island of Sicily. But a mightier conquest was that which a few years later was achieved over the Saxons, and by which a duke of Normandy became King of England. I need not stop to tell you how bravely the unhappy Harold met the invaders on the field of Hastings, and how he fell in that battle which sealed the destiny of Saxon independence. In less than one year after the good King Edward, the sainted Confessor, had breathed his last, the crown of England was on the brow of William the Norman.

The Norman conquest was the last of those great revolutionary changes, which successively occurred in the formation of that great community of mankind, which is now peopling the vast and scattered territory of the colonial British Empire, and the western regions of America. It was the addition of the last element in the constitution of a great modern people. We have thus seen how ancient British nationality received into itself a Roman nationality, and then the Saxon and the Dane, and, last of all, the Norman.

"The Norman conquest," says Southey, "is the most momentous event in English history,—perhaps the most momentous in the Middle Ages. So severe a chastisement was never, except in the case of the Visigoths, inflicted on any nation which was not destroyed by it."* It is an important subject of historical inquiry to ascertain the nature and extent of the changes—both social and political—which were consequent on this revolution. It is far too large a subject, even if I had the ability, for me to attempt to do more than merely touch on. The prominent events of this period are of such a character as to fill the mind to the exclusion of other less striking realities. This page of history tells of a kingdom conquered in one battle—the Saxon sovereign dead on that battle-field, and his army slaughtered or routed; it tells of Saxon fugitives in other and distant lands, and of Saxon prelates thrust out to make room for Norman ecclesiastics—of Saxon thane and Saxon peasants outcast from house and home—of the introduction of a sterner form of feudal law, and even the people's language revolutionized. It tells of that peculiar stretch of despotic power, by which, at the dismal sound of the curfew-bell, lamps and fires were extinguished at an early hour,—"the lights that cherish household cares and festive gladness" quenched by that stern bidding. When one thinks of the long, English winter-nights, this curfew-darkness

* Southey's Naval History, vol. i. p. 123.

seems almost as gloomy as that savage age, which Charles Lamb speaks of, in the essay in which he eulogizes candle-light as a kindlier luminary than sun or moon. "Wanting it," says he, "what savage, unsocial nights must our ancestors have spent, wintering in caves and unillumined fastnesses! They must have lain about and grumbled at one another in the dark. What repartees could have passed when you must have felt about for a smile, and handled a neighbour's cheek to be sure that he understood it?"* We read, too, how, when exasperated by Saxon resistance, the Conqueror swore a dreadful oath, that not one Northumbrian should escape his vengeance; and then hastened to fulfil it by his exterminating campaign in the North, in which one hundred thousand persons are said to have perished, and not a single inhabited village was left between Durham and York. It was a scene of devastation and depopulation like Hyder Ali's invasion of the Carnatic, made famous by the eloquence of Burke.

Such was the fearful penalty of the Conqueror's revenge, and scarcely less fearful was the penalty of his pleasure: the Norman monarchs must have their hunting-grounds, and the Saxon must needs give up his cultivated lands, not only to the new Norman proprietor, but even to the wild beasts. William, it has been said, "had a summary way of increasing the forest lands: no need of planting trees or waiting for the slow growth of oaks and beeches. There were then many woods in merry England, and he simply swept away the homes of the villagers who dwelt among and near them, so that the lands returned to their natural state of wilderness, and

* Popular Fallacies, xv.

the stag crouched, undisturbed, on the hearth of the peasant, or in the long fern where once was the altar of the village church."*

It is under such circumstances that, in a very brief space of time, there was established a foreign king, a foreign prelacy, and a foreign nobility; and it would seem, at least to our first impressions, that the Saxon race was not only bowed down, but crushed, beneath the Norman yoke; and that the Saxon era, with all its influences, was abruptly divided from later times by a broad line of blood, and a black line of fire and devastation. But great as were the changes, and terrible as were the sufferings, which the Norman conquest brought into England, it was not such a revolution as destroyed the continuity of the nation's life. It is said by the historian who has written with most learning on this period, that "we attribute overmuch to the Norman conquest."† This opinion seems just when we turn our thoughts away from the violence I have been speaking of, and consider that the laws of Edward the Confessor were not abolished by the victorious invader; that Saxon earls sat in the council of the realm by the side of the Norman counts; that not a few of the lesser thanes retained possession of their lands, and that the Anglo-Saxon population continued unbroken.

As the body of William the First was about to be committed to its grave, (it was in a churchyard in Normandy,) when the mass had been performed, and an eulogy pronounced on his character, a voice, from the crowd of

* Lives of the English Saints, No. vii. Introduction to the Life of St. Gilbert, p. 2.

† Palgrave's English Commonwealth, Part i. 653.

priests and people, exclaimed: "He whom you have praised was a robber. The very land on which you stand is mine. By violence he took it from my father; and, in the name of God, I forbid you to bury him in it."* It was an awful rebuke to the pride and injustice of military conquest, when a price had to be paid over the Conqueror's lifeless body to obtain a few feet of earth for the grave of him who, in his life, had added a kingdom to his ancient duchy.

The miseries of England continued during the reigns of the Conqueror's sons; and it was when all Christendom was moved by the splendid enthusiasm of the First Crusade, that the land was scourged with the ferocious tyranny of William Rufus,—the progressive wickedness of whose nature was strongly described when it was said that "never a night came but he lay down a worse man than he rose, and never a morning but he rose worse than he lay down."† He died the death of a wild beast; for all that is surely known is, that he was found in the New Forest, transfixed with an arrow and dead. Whether that arrow was sped to the tyrant's breast by the purposed aim of Walter Tyrrel, or by some one else who drew the bow in the wild spirit of revenge, or whether it was so guided by what we call chance, the people of the time beheld in his death retribution, not only on the cruelty and impiety of Rufus, but on the sins of his father, who had laid waste the homes of the Saxons to make the hunting-ground where, in the loneliness of the forest, his son miserably bled to death.

---

* Lingard, vol. ii. p. 54.

† British Critic, June, 1843, vol. xxxiii. p. 46. Article on St. Anselm.

The gradual change in the relations of the Saxon and Norman races is shown by the marriage of Henry the First to a Saxon princess, which led, soon afterwards, to the restoration of the Saxon line in the person of Henry the Second. I must pass over the tumultuous usurpation of Stephen, and the imperial reign of the first of the Plantagenets, distinguished by that great controversy worthy of all candid and careful study,—"the struggle," as Coleridge describes it, "between the men of arms and of letters in the persons of Henry the Second and Thomas à-Becket." To reach the special subject from which I have been longer detained than I anticipated, and for which I am therefore leaving myself less room, I must pass, too, over the reign of the heroic Crusader, the lion-hearted Richard, merely remarking that there may be found in the romance of Ivanhoe, not only one of the most vivid representations which Sir Walter Scott has given of the life of a distant age, but also a life-like exhibition of the relations which subsisted between the two races, when they were not yet completely amalgamated into one people. He has represented the partially extinct hostility which imbittered the feelings of the haughty Normans on the one side, and, on the other, not only the Saxon serf, but the high-born thane, whose lineage was from the kings or nobles of England before the Conquest.

It is comparatively easy to understand the hostile attitude in which, during these times, the Saxons and the Normans stood towards each other; for the angry passions of men, and the deeds which are prompted by such feelings, are always more manifest than the influences by which old animosities are appeased. It is easier to comprehend how men are brought to hate one another, than how that mutual hatred is converted to harmony and peace. Years, and countless and incalculable influences, may be needed to soothe the resentments engendered by one battle; especially when, like the battle of Hastings, it is a victory of invasion. It would be a subject of deep interest to trace the various and manifold agencies working upon the hearts and habits of the Saxons and the Normans, as they dwelt in the same region, at length producing national unity. I cannot pass by one important influence in this harmonizing process—an influence of the church, which has been thus described by a living English author:

"When Anselm (it was in the reign of the second William) came over from his Norman convent to be Archbishop of Canterbury, and his victorious countrymen thought that he, of course, would look upon the old Saxons of the soil as they did, he told them plainly, that a churchman acknowledged no distinction of race, and that his vocation was to be the friend of the poor and distressed wherever he met with them. And these principles, of course with great exceptions and deviations, were acted upon by a large portion of the Norman bishops and clergy. What was the effect? We grew up to be an English nation. The Saxon serf felt that he had a portion and a right in the soil; he recollected the sounds of his native language; he began to speak it: in due time the conquerors and the conquered became one."

The Crusades, too, had probably, by means of the predominant feeling which they inspired, helped to fuse together the Saxon and Norman elements of English nationality; and, when we reach the times of King

John, and enter the thirteenth century, we find the distinction of the two races wholly passed away.

Shakspeare's play of King John is the first, in order of time, of those "Chronicle-Plays," which he gave to his country and the world with the title, originally, of "Histories." It gives a dramatic and imaginative view of an important reign in the annals of England; and the personages, events, and dates, are subjected to the transmuting processes of a great poet's imagination, so as not only not to darken or distort historic truth, but to array it in a living light. We gain a deeper and more abiding sense of the truth, by the help of that fine function of poetic genius, by which the imagination gives unity and moral connection to events that stand apart and unrelated. As to a distant period, time works in harmony with the poet. "The history of our ancient kings," says Coleridge,—"the events of their reigns, I mean,—are like stars in the sky: whatever the real interspaces may be, and however great, they seem close to each other. The stars—the events—strike us and remain in our eye, little modified by the difference of dates. An historic drama is, therefore, a collection of events borrowed from history, but connected together, in respect of cause and time, poetically, and by dramatic fiction."*

The historic poet must carry his subject into the world of imagination; and, in dealing with the multitude of historic men and their deeds, he must do what every true artist, be he poet, painter, or architect, has to do—he must impress the mind with an harmonious sense of plurality and unity. Each character, each action, must

* Literary Remains, vol. ii. p. 161.

have its own individuality, but this must be controlled by some pervading and predominant idea which blends all the parts into unity; the very contrasts, in themselves so needful, must be subordinated to a certain concord, just as in a picture there must be a rich variety, but it must have its central point, and every thing must illustrate the main idea of it: a landscape, with all its varied imagery of nature, must have, withal, some one prevailing spirit, be it tranquil or tempestuous. You cannot have on the same canvas the waves in angry agitation and the trees in motionless repose, or else making no more than what the poet calls—

"A soft eye-music of slow-waving boughs."*

In approaching these admirable dramatic histories, I have stopped thus briefly to notice how the imagination in every sphere of art of a high order treats the multiplicity of its materials. This is so essential to the just comprehension of the historic drama, that I am tempted to borrow from a contemporary writer a fine passage on the philosophy of art and poetry:—"Every theory of beauty embraces two elements at once. One colour will not constitute a picture; and yet, over a variety of colours, there must be thrown one tint and colour. One line will not form a statue; and yet, from a multiplicity of lines, the sculptor must place before the eye some one consistent image. A building is a crystallization of forms; yet towers, pinnacles, arches and vaults, aisles and niches, fretted roofs and sculptured corbels, windows flaming with all the colours of the rainbow, and carvings wrought

* Wordsworth. Lines on Airey Force Valley, p. 192.

into a labyrinth of network,—all these, when brought together by the hand of a master, are framed and dovetailed into one grand plan, realizing one idea, permeated with one spirit. The poet brings upon the stage not one, but a multitude of characters; he represents life in all its forms, the human mind in all its phases; his very excellence consists in the comprehensiveness and versatility of his conceptions. But if he understand his art, he will link together not only his acts and events by their relation to some one end, but even the most sudden changes and incongruities by some main key-note. When Shakspeare passes at once from the awfulness of Macbeth's thoughts after the murder of Duncan to the vulgar ribaldry of the porter at the gate, he makes that ribaldry turn upon the thought of hell. So it is in music—so it is in oratory—so it is in every production of human fancy: simplicity and variety; intricacy and regularity; order amid seeming confusion, and multiplicity in apparent identity; discords harmonized; contrasts reconciled: deficiencies supplied; irregularities corrected;—these are the triumphs of art. But the triumph is achieved only when both elements are preserved together—distinct but not separate—combined but not confused."*

The first scene of the tragedy of King John has that significancy which distinguishes the openings of Shakspeare's plays—an intimation of the whole plot, the full meaning of which is regularly developed in the progress of the drama. In almost the first words, King John's royalty is spoken of as "borrowed majesty," and he is summoned by the embassy of his great contemporary, Philip Au-

* Sewell's Christian Politics, p. 18.

gustus of France, to yield his kingdom up to the rightful heir, Arthur Plantagenet, the son of his dead brother, Geoffrey. The succession of John was usurpation, beginning in fraud and violence, and continued in crime; but of the previous Norman reigns, four out of six of the kings had possessed themselves of the sceptre by the law of the strong hand. The rule of succession could, therefore, as yet be scarcely considered as established; but, instead of it, there seems to have been, in that unsettled political condition, little more than what Rob Roy calls—

"The good old rule, the simple plan,
That they should take who have the power,
And they should keep who can."*

When this is considered, and when we remember, too, that the absence of Richard on the Crusade gave peculiar opportunities to his brother John to pave the way to the succession, it is not surprising that John became the king, especially as the righful heir was in his youth, and the government had not yet attained that period when, under constitutional forms, a minority reign becomes practicable. Accordingly, at the opening of the drama, Shakspeare does not at once awaken indignation at the injustice of the usurpation, and, indeed, rather leads us to admire the calm royal bearing with which the king answers the threat of war; as if, unconscious of wrong to his nephew, he relies upon his "strong possession and his right," and confidently hurls back defiance to the King of France. We see, therefore, from the very beginning,

* Wordsworth's Rob Roy's Grave, p. 243.

how differently, and in how much finer a spirit, Shakspeare treats the character of King John, than that coarse and common mode, by which it has been represented in such black and unrelieved colours that no humanity can be found in him, and he is looked on with unmitigated horror and contempt. It has been said with reference to the "vivid speaking characters" in which Shakspeare has placed so many of the English kings in imperishable individuality before us,—"Only look at his King John, look at any historian's. Which gives you the liveliest, faithfullest representation of that prince and of his age, the poet's or the historian's? Which most powerfully exposes his vices and awakens the greatest horror at them? Yet in Shakspeare he is still a man, and, as such, comes within the range of our sympathy: we can pity, even while we shudder at him; and our horror moves us to look inward into the awful depths of the nature which we share with him, instead of curdling into dead hatred and disgust. In the historian's he is a sheer monster, the object of contemptuous loathing, a poisonous reptile whom we could crush to death with as little remorse as a viper."*

The tragedy begins with the voice of state, of diplomacy, of policy, and of the rivalry of England and France; and we shall see how, in the various characters, all the elements of mediæval life are present—the papacy and the priesthood—the monarchy and the nobility—the commonalty and the soldiery—all are there. It has, however, been ingeniously said by a German critic that—"The hero of this piece stands not in the list of person-

* Hare's Guesses at Truth, First Series, p. 355.

ages, and could not stand with them, for the idea should be clear without personification. The hero is England."* This means, as I understand it, that Shakspeare has made England the great and ever-present idea of the play; that, without any artifice of national vanity, he has so written the history of the reign of King John as to inspire a deep and fervid spirit of nationality. It is comparatively an easy thing to animate the hearts of a people with such a spirit by presenting the *glorious* parts of their country's annals; the mere touch of the memory of victories won by their ancestors will kindle enthusiasm and pride in the breasts of posterity. We can understand how the recollection, for example, of the splendid career of Edward the Third should prompt the boast of the Britons of later times:

"We are the sons of the men
 Who conquered on Cressy's plain;
And what our fathers did,
 Their sons can do again."

But it was Shakspeare's arduous achievement to fire the sentiment of patriotism with the story of a reign that was tyrannical, oppressive, cowardly,—a period of usurpation and national degradation. He has accomplished this chiefly by means of one character, which is almost altogether a creation of his mind from very slight historical materials. The fertile imagination of the poet, and his genial exuberance of happy and gentle feelings, seem to have craved something more than the poverty of the history supplies; he wanted somebody better than a king,

* Franz Horn, vol. ii. p. 196.

better than a worldly ecclesiastic, and better than the bold but fickle barons. It is in the highest order of dramatic art, and especially in the historic drama, that Shakspeare, on no other historical basis than the mere existence of a natural son of Richard, has created the splendid and most attractive character of Philip Falconbridge. Besides playing an important part himself, he fulfils something like the function of the chorus of the ancient drama; for he seems to illustrate the purposes of the history, and to make the real personages more intelligible. He is the imbodiment, too, of the most genuine national feeling, and is truer to his country than king or noble. With an abounding and overflowing humour, a dauntless courage, and a gentleness of spirit that characterizes true heroism, Falconbridge carries a generous strength and a rude morality of his own, amid the craft and the cruelties and the feebleness of those who surround him. The character, imaginary as it is, has an historical value also in this, that it represents the bright side of feudal loyalty. Honoured by the king, Falconbridge never deserts him in his hour of need and peril, when the nobles are flying off from their allegiance and a foreign enemy is at hand. It is no servile fidelity, but such genuine and generous loyalty that we look upon it as faithfulness to his country rather than adherence to the fortunes of the king. He is, as it were, the man of the people in the play, and we hear him prompting brave actions and a generous policy—encouraging the feeble king to a truer kingly career; we see him withstanding the haughty barons, and still more indignant at papal aggression. He dwells in an atmosphere of heartlessness and villainy, but it pollutes him not; rather does his presence partially purify it. It is remarkable that we do not and cannot, I think, associate him injuriously with the character of King John, with whose fortunes he is identified, but from whose vices he is wholly aloof; and I am almost tempted to apply to him what has been said of a very different character:

"His soul was like a star and dwelt apart."*

The character and position of Falconbridge in the play, seem to me finely to illustrate the workings of the principle of chivalry during this early feudal period of history,—that principle of which Mr. Burke wisely said that—"Without confounding rank, it produced a noble equality, and handed it down through all the gradations of social life. It was this opinion," said that philosophic statesman, "which mitigated kings into companions, and raised private men to be fellows with kings."† The effects of the principle of chivalry, as manifested in the intercourse of King John and Falconbridge, cannot escape observation; but the reader of the drama may probably overlook a very short passage which seems to me to illustrate the workings of it as it passes down, to use Mr. Burke's phrase, through all the gradations of life and touches the humbler range of society. It is a passage which struck the fancy of Coleridge, who was in the habit of quoting it as an instance of Shakspeare's power *in minimis;* and it certainly does show how comprehensively careful a poet's genius is of minute as well as of great things. In the list of the persons of

* Wordsworth's Sonnet written in London in 1802, p. 255.

† Reflections on the French Revolution, vol. iii. p. 98.

the play, you may notice the name of "James Gurney, servant to Lady Falconbridge." He makes his appearance once,—but once,—then only for a very little while; he does not speak till spoken to, says four words,—scarce more than four monosyllables,—then "*Exit James Gurney*," and that is all. Yet Coleridge speaks of the *character* of this person, and finds it in these very few words —that single touch of Shakspeare's pen portraying the affectionate respectfulness of an aged domestic.* When Falconbridge is about to extort from his mother the secret of his parentage, a sense of delicacy leads him to desire a conference with her alone, and he requests the attendant to withdraw, saying,—

> "James Gurney, wilt thou give us leave awhile?"

and the meek answer, which pleased Coleridge's fancy, is simply—

> "Good leave, good Philip."

I refer to the passage for a reason different from Coleridge's, and to notice the spirit of Falconbridge's playful reply, as he says—

> "James,
> There's toys abroad. Anon I'll tell thee more."

Now, I beg you to notice the familiar and affectionate tone of this intercourse, as they address each other by their Christian names, "Philip" and "James;" and then the fine, gentlemanly, and considerate feeling which prompts Falconbridge to promise the old servant—his

* Table Talk, p. 35. Ed. 1852.

old domestic friend—to tell him more after awhile, as a kind of indirect apology for even asking him to withdraw. Minute as the instance is, it is an historical illustration of the gentleness with which the genuine principles of chivalry looked down to the humble, as well as upward to the high born.

The alliances of France and Austria, which are, at the beginning, proclaimed in support of Arthur's claim to the throne of England against King John, are soon dissolved. A new wind of policy blows over them, and the friendship of king and duke, which a little before had been proffered to the helpless and injured Arthur with so much of pomp and declamatory assurance, all passes away; his cause is abandoned. new friendships and a different policy are formed on the instant. The hollowness and heartlessness of this conduct are more deeply felt when we behold the wild anguish of Constance, in desperate disappointment, clamouring for the lost rights of her child; and, as if the huge firm earth could alone support a grief so great as hers, seating herself on the ground for kings to come and bow to her loneliness and desolation.

The contrast between the beauty, the strength, and grandeur of natural feeling, and the ugliness and the instability of the politic zeal of ambitious kings and princes, is felt, not only when we are listening to the voluble utterances of maternal passion, but when we turn to the gentle exclamations of the innocent Arthur, as he would fain escape the turmoil of an ambitious destiny

> "Good my mother, peace!
> I would that I were low laid in my grave:
> I am not worth this coil that's made for me."

The peace of the grave was speedily to be the portion of this unhappy prince,—a youth whose character history has not especially deigned to record; but we can believe that he was, in truth, the thoughtful and gentle-hearted being that Shakspeare has shown to us, not only in his own actions and speech, but as he was endeared to the agitated affections of Constance. In his brief life we behold the sacrificial beauty and purity, which seem to mark him for the victim of the selfish and wicked passions that are raging around him.

The treaty between John and Philip Augustus, built on the sandy foundation of a broken faith and foresworn promises, proved an unstable and hollow armistice, as if the wild prayer of Constance, in her hour of desolation, had a speedy answer, when, deserted by earthly alliances, she cried—

"Arm, arm, you heavens, against these perjured kings!
A widow cries; be husband to me, heavens!
Let not the hours of this ungodly day
Wear out the day in peace; but, ere sunset,
Set armed discord 'twixt these perjured kings!"

In that renewed war the destiny of Arthur was sealed: he fell into the power of his victorious uncle,—the young and rightful claimant of the English crown was in the perilous possession of the wicked usurper. Two words more—a prison—death—close the story of the career of Arthur of Brittany. Impenetrable mystery hangs over his death, and all that can be discerned in the darkness of it is, the guilt of King John. How he died is not known; but history, tradition, poetry, all have laid the guilt of that death upon the conscience of King John, whose cowardice and cruelty were someway the agents of the murder. The essential guilt lies there, and it does not matter greatly, whether Arthur pined away in prison to an early death, or whether he perished in an attempt to escape, or whether John perpetrated the deed of horror with his own hand, in mid-river loneliness and midnight silence, by plunging his dagger into the bosom of his helpless kinsman, and then casting the poor child's bleeding body into the deep waters of the river Seine.

It does not belong to my subject to comment on the matchless dramatic skill of those two great scenes,—that appalling one in which the king commits Arthur to the deadly keeping of Hubert, and that other piteous one between Hubert and Arthur. In the consummate poetic art of those scenes, there is, at the same time, a no less admirable historic charity; for, in the obscurity of the history, Shakspeare has impressed the mind with a deep sense of the guilt of the king without aggravating it with needless horrors or more than human atrocity. Arthur, in the play, perishes in his attempt at escape; but to the perilous leap that caused his death he was driven by the dread of John's power; and he had already, by John's cruel purpose, endured the terror and anguish at the presence of the executioner and the sight of the instruments of torture.

When Arthur fell by the fortune of war into the hands of King John, the possession of his young rival brought security to the usurper, but it brought also temptation to make assurance double sure by converting the custody of a prison into the inviolable custody of the grave. The moral view, and, I believe, a most just historic view, which Shakspeare gives us, is this—that, however the events are separated in time, all the after-misery of the reign of King John was the penal retribution for the murder of Arthur. In consequence of it, his continental dominions passed away from him, to make up the splendid French monarchy of the Capets, and at home he struggled through a distracted reign, amid disloyal nobles and a discontented people. The sequel of the reign, after Arthur is taken prisoner, is finely told in the play, when the deep political sagacity of Cardinal Pandulph foretells the course of things. Exciting the Dauphin to claim the English throne, he bids him mark—

"John hath seized Arthur; and it cannot be,
That, whiles warm life plays in that infant's veins,
The misplaced John should entertain an hour,
One minute, nay, one quiet breath of rest:
A sceptre, snatch'd with an unruly hand,
Must be as boisterously maintained as gained;
And he, that stands upon a slippery place,
Makes nice of no vile hold to stay him up:
That John may stand, then Arthur needs must fall:
So be it, for it cannot but be so."

When the Dauphin questions what he is to gain by Arthur's fall, and doubts his success, the wily cardinal replies—

"How green are you, and fresh in this old world!
John lays you plots; the times conspire with you:
For he, that steeps his safety in true blood,
Shall find but bloody safety, and untrue.
This act, so evilly born, shall cool the hearts
Of all his people, and freeze up their zeal;
That none so small advantage shall step forth,
To check his reign, but they will cherish it;
No natural exhalation in the sky,
No scape of nature, no distempered day,
No common wind, no customed event,

But they will pluck away his natural cause,
And call them meteors, prodigies, and signs,
Abortives, presages, and tongues of heaven,
Plainly denouncing vengeance upon John.
* * * The hearts
Of all his people shall revolt from him,
And kiss the lips of unacquainted change;
And pick strong matter of revolt and wrath
Out of the bloody fingers' ends of John."

It is just before these cold-hearted and crafty speculations respecting Arthur's death, that Constance addressed the Cardinal with that beautiful and pathetic utterance of her first grief at her son's captivity:

"Father Cardinal, I have heard you say,
That we shall see and know our friends in heaven;
If that be true, I shall see my boy again;
For, since the birth of Cain, the first male child,
To him that did but yesterday suspire,
There was not such a gracious creature born.
But now will canker-sorrow eat my bud,
And chase the native beauty from his cheek,
And he will look as hollow as a ghost;
As dim and meagre as an ague's fit;
And so he'll die; and, rising so again,
When I shall meet him in the court of heaven
I shall not know him: therefore, never, never
Must I behold my pretty Arthur more."

The words fall ineffectual on Pandulph's ear; and he who, with his sacred function, might have poured consolation into the aching void of a mother's heart, answers with a rebuke. He was busy with intrigues of state, weaving meshes to catch or entangle kings; and what audience could maternal grief find with the crafty and corrupt priest, burdened with worldly policy, like such other cardinals as Wolsey and Richelieu and Mazarin and Portocarrero, the politician-ecclesiastics of modern Europe?

When, with like coldness, King Philip—he who had selfishly advocated and selfishly abandoned the cause of Constance and her son—tells her she is

> "As fond of grief as of her child,"

she gives the last justification of her impassioned sorrow:

> "Grief fills the room up of my absent child,
> Lies in his bed, walks up and down with me,
> Puts on his pretty looks, repeats his words,
> Remembers me of all his gracious parts,
> Stuffs out his vacant garments with his form;
> Then, have I reason to be fond of grief."

The appearance of Cardinal Pandulph in this play introduces another of the great contests of this distracted reign,—the struggle between King John and the papal power during that splendid period of it, the papacy of Innocent the Third. The controversy turned on the election of the Primate of England, and John's refusal to admit Stephen Langton to the see of Canterbury. When the papal claim is asserted by Cardinal Pandulph, as the legate of the pope, it is answered by King John in a high strain of defiance, which arrays the independence of his realm and sovereignty in bold antagonism against papal aggression:

> "What earthly name to interrogatories
> Can task the free breath of a sacred king?
> Thou canst not, cardinal, devise a name
> So slight, unworthy, and ridiculous,
> To charge me to an answer, as the pope.

> Tell him this tale; and from the mouth of England,
> Add thus much more,—that no Italian priest
> Shall tithe or toll in our dominions:
> But, as we under Heaven are supreme head;
> So, under him, that great supremacy,
> Where we do reign, we will alone uphold,
> Without the assistance of a mortal hand:
> So tell the pope; all reverence set apart,
> To him and his usurped authority."

And when the King of France interposes—

> "Brother of England, you blaspheme in this,"

John retorts—

> "Though you, and all the kings of Christendom,
> Are led so grossly by this meddling priest,
> Dreading the curse that money may buy out;
> And, by the merit of vile gold, dross, dust,
> Purchase corrupted pardon of a man,
> Who, in that sale, sells pardon from himself;
> Though you, and all the rest, so grossly led,
> This juggling witchcraft with revenue cherish;
> Yet I, alone, alone do me oppose
> Against the pope, and count his friends my foes."

This resistance brought upon John the penalty of excommunication, and upon the realm, in punishment of the sovereign, that more dreadful and extraordinary infliction, the papal *interdict*. This penalty—the general effect of which was to stop all religious services—was a form of ecclesiastical punishment which, according to the authority of Roman Catholic historians, was unknown in the early ages of the church, and did not come distinctly into use before the eleventh century. It is accounted for as an expedient resorted to for the purpose of counteracting and controlling feudal tyranny. In this case the sentence of a general interdict over the whole of England was proclaimed, and the effects of it have been thus described:

"As an ecclesiastical act, the features which most struck the minds of the country people were, that the daily sacrifice ceased, the doors of the churches were shut against them; that the dead were carried outside the town-gates, and buried in ditches or roadsides, without prayer or priests' offices. The images of apostles and saints were taken down or veiled; the frequent tinkle of the convent-bell no longer told the serf at the plough how the weary day was passing, or guided the traveller through the forest to a shelter for the night. Religion, wont to mix with and hallow each hour of the day, each action of life, was totally withdrawn. The state of the country resembled a raid of the Danes, or the days of old Saxon heathendom, before Augustine had set up the cross at Canterbury or holy men had penetrated the forest and the fen."*

"Closed are the gates of every sacred place,
Straight from the sun and tainted air's embrace,
All sacred things are covered; cheerful morn
Grows sad as night: no seemly garb is worn,
Nor is a face allowed to meet a face
With natural smile of greeting. Bells are dumb;
Ditches are graves—funereal rights denied;
And in the churchyard he must take his bride
Who dares be wedded."†

* Lives of the English Saints, No. 10, p. 32. Life of Stephen Langton. Hume's description of the Interdict has been often cited with praise by his admirers. W. B. R.

† Wordsworth's Sonnet,—An Interdict.

The temper of the king was not controlled by this dismal condition of a Christian land; but, with a crime-fraught conscience, the tyrant was affrighted by superstitious terrors, and the fatal predictions of a popular soothsayer. The pope invoked the alliance of France to quell by invasion and the force of arms that resistance against which the mandates and penalties of Rome had proved unavailing. Under the dread of this danger, the mean and abject spirit of John sank to its lowest and worst estate. The crown of England, that which had decked the brow of Alfred and of the Confessor and of the Conqueror, was laid at the feet of Pandulph, the papal legate, and John surrendered his kingdom to receive it back and hold it as the vassal and tributary of the pope. The infamy of John was completed and national degradation brought upon England. "The transaction," says the Roman Catholic historian, "was certainly a disgraceful act;"* and an English poet, in a higher strain of patriotic indignation, has said—

"Lo! John self-stripped of his insignia;—crown,
Sceptre and mantle, sword and ring, laid down
At a proud Legate's feet! The spears that line
Baronial halls, the opprobrious insult feel,
And angry Ocean roars a vain appeal."†

After this came the third and last great struggle of the reign, in which the confederate barons wrested from the reluctant king the Great Charter of English rights—that sealed acknowledgment of ancient rights which is an epoch in the history of constitutional freedom. In that

* Lingard, vol. iii. p. 32.

† Wordsworth's Sonnet on Papal Abuses, p. 354.

achievement, no one rendered more important services than Stephen Langton,—he whom Innocent the Third had, in fact, made the Primate of England. In the political struggle connected with the Charter, the pope was arrayed on the side of his vassal king and against the cause of English liberties; while Langton, true to his nativity as an Englishman, and to his station as the chief bishop of England, was the fearless defender of that Charter of which it has been said that—"If every subsequent law were swept away, there would still remain the bold features which distinguish a free from a despotic monarchy."

After a reign of conflict and confusion and disgrace, John dies a miserable and a suffering death; and the last words that fall upon his dying ear are the evil tidings of continued disaster. The spirit of Arthur is avenged.*

At the close of the tragedy, Shakspeare, with some disregard of chronological accuracy, brings back the nobles to their allegiance; and then, with the voice of Falconbridge—the very embodiment of patriotism and loyalty—he raises the mind from the weakness and degradation of the reign to a sense of England's power and independence. It is in a high strain of that national self-confi-

* "In the chroniclers, we have manifold changes of fortune in the life of John, after Arthur of Brittany has fallen. In Shakspeare, Arthur is at once avenged. The heart-broken mother and her boy are not the only sufferers from double courses. The spirit of Constance is appeased by the fall of John. The Niobe of a Gothic age, who vainly thought to shield her child from so stern a destiny as that with which Apollo and Artemis pursued the daughter of Tantalus, may rest in peace." Historical Illustrations to C. Knight's Shakspeare, vol. i. p. 78. W. B. R.

dence which, though it may degenerate into national vanity or swell into intolerable national pride, is part of the power which makes a people unconquerable,—it is in such a spirit that Falconbridge tells the young prince and the nobles—

"This England never did, (nor never shall,)
Lie at the proud foot of a conqueror,
But when it first did help to wound itself.
Now these her princes are come home again,
Come the three corners of the world in arms,
And we shall shock them: nought shall make us rue,
If England to itself do rest but true."

Let me add that these lines were composed by Shakspeare not long after that year in which the formidable invasion by the Spanish Armada was driven back in ruin from the shores of England. The poet's heart beat high as he beheld the banners of the ships of Spain hung out as trophies from the battlements of the Cathedral of St. Paul's, when Queen Elizabeth, in the midst of a rejoicing people, went up to that metropolitan temple to give thanks to God for the safety of her realm.

LECTURE V.*

The Reign of Richard the Second.

Henry the Third and the Edwards passed over by Shakspeare—De Montfort's Rebellion—Growth of the Constitution—The Commons—Extent of parliamentary government—Our republican institutions—The highway of nations—The Plantagenet kings—Edward the Third and the Black Prince—Chaucer—War with France—Arnold's view—Southey—From Richard the Second the "Chronicle-Plays" continuous—The fifteenth century—King John and Henry the Eighth, prologue and epilogue—Richard the Second strictly historical—Character of the king—His previous career—Popular element in France and Flanders and England—Wat Tyler's Rebellion—Its effects—Revolt of the nobles—Opening of the tragedy—Norfolk and Bolingbroke—Exile—Character of Bolingbroke—Death of John of Gaunt—Moral degradation of the king—His misfortunes elevate him—Bolingbroke's return—Divine right of kings—Richard's deposition, imprisonment, and death.

AFTER King John, the next period of English history which has been illustrated by Shakspeare's historical plays is the reign of Richard the Second. The reign of King John belongs, it will be remembered, to the first years of the thirteenth century; that of Richard the Second closed the fourteenth; so that the intervening time was not a great deal less than two hundred years,—an interval of great importance for the

* January 25th, 1847.

events that distinguished it and for the progress of the Constitution, but less familiar, for the single reason, I believe, that the light of Shakspeare's mind has not illuminated it for us. The reigns during that interval were few in number, for two of them were protracted to an uncommon length,—half a century in one case, and more than that in another. The reigns which Shakspeare has passed over are those of Henry the Third and the first three of the Edwards.

When, on the death of King John, his son Henry, in the tenth year of his age, was crowned King of England, the Earl of Pembroke, addressing his baronial peers, said,—"We have persecuted the father for evil demeanour, and worthily: yet this young child, whom ye see before you, as he is in years tender, so he is innocent of his father's doings." The appeal was not in vain. The young Plantagenet was set on the throne, enjoying the restored allegiance of his barons; but the regal power, thus fortified by returning loyalty, was also in the bonds of the Great Charter. The child-king grew to manhood, but not to the strength of manhood. Old abuses were revived, and the high spirit of the barons awoke again to resist them—by remonstrance, by opposition, and, at length, by open war. There was De Montfort, Earl of Leicester, at the head of the insurgent nobles,—he who, with his Oxford Parliament—the "Mad Parliament," as the old historians called it—took the kingdom away from the sovereign, and gave it into the hands of Commissioners. There were the vicissitudes of civil war,—the king, at one time, a prisoner, and afterwards triumphant, and Leicester dead on the field of battle. "All the months of the year," says the witty church-historian, Thomas Fuller, "may in a manner be carved out of an April day,—hot, cold, dry, moist, fair, foul weather, being oft presented therein. Such was the character of King Henry the Third's life, certain only in uncertainty; sorrowful, successful; in plenty, in penury; in wealth, in want; conquered, conqueror."*

This period of English annals is too remote, and the prominent characters in it are too dimly represented, for us to feel that lively interest which is produced by the biographical knowledge of historic personages. The study of it is, however, important, as showing the growth of the nation, and the steady and gradual progress of the Constitution. In looking back over that progress, one cannot help being struck with the small and obscure beginnings of great political institutions, and thinking how unconscious the actors must have been of the magnitude of that futurity, which was to follow their deeds. In this reign of Henry the Third, after Simon de Montfort, at the head of the baronial confederacy, had defeated his king in open battle, acting as sovereign of the kingdom, he summoned the cities and boroughs to send members to Parliament. When he cast that seed into the soil of his country, how little did he dream of the mighty and perpetual germination that it would disclose in after times! How little could he have thought, that he was laying the foundation of the popular house of the British Parliament; and, indeed, not only of the English House of Commons, but the popular representative legislatures of the Anglo-American republics in another continent! Men cannot foresee the consequences of such deeds; and,

* Church History of Britain, vol. i. p. 369.

indeed, the most enduring and happiest political institutions are those which have not grown up in the sight of one generation of men, but during the lapse of ages have risen higher and higher, and spread their branches on every side.* In examining the history of a country, you see the national life as it develops itself, first in one change, then in another; sometimes by regular and tranquil alterations, sometimes by violence, and, it may be, bloodshed; but ever, when the growth is most healthful, it is by a due course of expansion, rather than by wilful and violent changes. Thus, the steps which De Montfort took when he summoned the representation of the towns, made a path which seemed slight; but it was destined, in the providential government of the world, to become the great highway on which there should move, not only the kingly Commonwealth of England, but the republican Commonwealth of America. Indeed, I find myself borrowing here partly the language of a very happy illustration of gradual changes of government:—"New political institutions," it has been well said, "originate just as a path is made in the field. The first person who crosses the grass, treads it down. The mass of elastic verdure immediately rises up again; nevertheless, some few of the more limber stalks and slender blades are bruised and crushed, and continue prostrate on the ground; yet so slight is the impression made upon the herbage, that the clearest eyesight can hardly discover the harm. After the first passenger, other people follow; and, within a little while, marks of their footsteps begin to be perceivable. Nobody noticed the first footsteps. At what period they

* De Maistre, Essai sur le principe générateur des Constitutions Politiques.

became visible, nobody can recollect. But now, there the footsteps are, the grass has changed its colour, the depressions are distinct, and they direct other wayfarers to follow the same line.

"Not long afterwards, bits and patches of the soil, where, very recently, the grass was only flattened and trodden down, are now worn quite bare. You see the naked earth; the roots of the grass are dried, the grass is killed—it springs up no more; and then the bare places gradually and gradually extend till the brown devours the intervening green: the bareworn places join one another, all the green between them is destroyed, the continuous path is formed.

"But the path does not continue single. One passenger treads upon the bounding grass to suit his convenience; another wantonly; a third for want of thought; more footsteps, more bare places. Tracks enlarge the path on either side; and these means of transit invite so many passengers, that they break down the hedges for their further accommodation without waiting to ask the owner's leave. The trespass has received the sanction of usage; and the law, however unwillingly, is compelled to pronounce the judgment, that a public right of way has been acquired, which can never more be denied or closed."*

The right of way in the government was opened for the people during the inglorious reign of Henry the Third,—opened never to be closed; and when, in the next reign, Edward the First entered on his brilliant career of conquest, while he was consolidating his

* Palgrave's Merchant and Friar, p. 89.

kingdom by the reduction of Wales, the cause of constitutional freedom was moving onward. The movement did not stop during the degenerate rule of the second Edward,—a reign which was signalized by two battles, a victory and a defeat; of which it has been strangely but truly said, that the victory should be lamented by England as a national judgment, and the defeat celebrated as a national festival. The victory was over the Irish, and the government of Ireland is to this day England's plague; and the defeat by the Scots at Bannockburn left Scotland independent, to be united to England in due course of time by peaceful treaty. After an opprobrious reign, domestic treachery precipitated the ruin of Edward the Second,—the first of the kings of England who died discrowned. In that fine ode which the poet Gray composed, as if spoken by a Welsh bard addressing Edward the First, at the time of his invasion of Wales, and denouncing, in prophetic voice, the sorrows of his posterity, there is, perhaps, no more startling or impressive passage than that in which, foretelling the murder of his son, he bids him—

"Mark the year and mark the night,
When Severn shall re-echo, with affright,
The shrieks of death through Berkeley's roof that ring,
Shrieks of an agonizing king."*

The splendid fifty years' reign of Edward the Third raised the national spirit of England to a higher point than it had yet attained. It was an era in English history of expanding and aspiring nationality. The sovereign's high ambition of adding the crown of France to

* Gray's Bard. Poetical Works, p. 170, Reed's Edition.

that of England, carried along with it the hearts of his nobles and his people. The spirit of the nation was filled with enthusiasm by two of the most famous of England's victories, achieved by her two champions, the king himself and his warlike son, Edward, the Black Prince. The peaceful splendour of the reign equalled its martial glory. There was the pride and magnificence of chivalry, when chivalry had not yet declined to mere formal pomp and pageantry. The generous spirit and the intellectual activity of the times were displayed in the patronage of painting and the other fine arts, and architectural piles arose to perpetuate, with church and castle, the memory of an illustrious era. The character of the times was finely shown, too, in the glorious outburst of English poetry, when the first of the great English poets, Geoffrey Chaucer, displayed the power of English imagination and of the English language in a series of poems, which, in variety of feeling and scope of subject, are surpassed only by the productions of Shakspeare.

Such was the bright side of the reign of the third Edward. But, looking even at the darker side, there was good evolving out of its difficulties. War is not a game to be played at with ivory counters, and the war with France was a costly one, "whereby," says an old historian, "our nation became exceedingly proud, and exceedingly poor." The king needed money for his wars, but that very necessity proved a cause of the steady progress of the constitutional rights and liberties of the nation. It is to this period of English history that Arnold, in his history of Rome, alludes, in a passage of admirable wisdom on the growth of constitutional freedom. Speaking of the slow process by which the Roman plebeians rose to the political level of their patrician fellow-citizens, he says:—"So it is, that all things come best in their season; that political power is most happily exercised by a people, when it has not been given to them prematurely; that is, before, in the natural progress of things, they feel they want it. Security for person and property enables a nation to grow without interruption: in contending for this, a people's sense of law and right is wholesomely exercised. Meantime, national prosperity increases, and brings with it an increase of intelligence, till other and more necessary wants being satisfied, men awaken to the highest earthly desire of the ripened mind—the desire of taking an active share in the great work of government. The Roman Commons abandoned the highest magistracies to the Patricians for a period of many years; but they continued to increase in prosperity and influence; and what their fathers had wisely yielded, their sons in the fulness of time acquired. So the English House of Commons, in the reign of Edward the Third, declined to interfere in questions of peace and war as being too high for them to compass; but they would not allow the crown to take their money without their own consent; and so the nation grew, and the influence of the House of Commons grew along with it, till that House has become the great and predominant power in the British Constitution."*

The closing days of Edward's long and brilliant reign were clouded over. "Never," writes Southey, "was there a king in whose history the will of Providence may seem to have been more clearly manifested: so greatly

* History of Rome, vol. i. p. 343.

had his victories exceeded all bounds of reasonable hope, so much had his reverses surpassed all reasonable apprehension! Well might Edward have exclaimed with the preacher 'that all is vanity,' when he had survived the wife of his bosom, the son of his youth and of his proudest and dearest hopes, his prosperity, his popularity, the respect of his chiefs, and the love of his people; for, after the loss of his son, his moral and intellectual strength gave way, and he fell under subjection to an artful and rapacious woman. In this, however, posterity has been just, that it has judged of him, not by the failure of his fortunes and the weakness of his latter days, but by the general tenor and the great and abiding consequences of his long and glorious reign."

The succeeding reign of Richard the Second brings us to another of those periods of English history, which are illustrated by Shakspeare's historical plays; and, henceforward, the dramatic illustration will be found to continue uninterrupted during well-nigh a century, and during seven consecutive reigns. Of the ten "Chronicle-Plays" which Shakspeare composed from the annals of his country, eight are devoted to one grand period, and that period is thus illustrated with extraordinary completeness. It is the time between the reign of Richard the Second and Richard the Third, comprehending the intermediate reigns of the fourth, fifth, and sixth Henries, and the fourth and fifth Edwards. The subject of this era is the great civil conflict between the two branches of the Plantagenet family, the houses of Lancaster and York; and Shakspeare has represented this struggle from its earliest beginning down to the final catastrophe upon Bosworth Field. He has traced the contest back to its primal cause—to the very elements of its moral origin; and has then followed it onward through all its vicissitudes—through the multiform retribution with which, by turns, the sins of each party were visited; and, marking the ebb and flow of the bloody tide of civil war, he has traced its course to the day when the sceptre of England passed forever from the race of the Plantagenets.

Shakspeare has treated this large historical theme—England's great business in the fifteenth century—in a series of eight plays so closely connected, so interwoven with each other, following one another in so close and express succession, that they may be regarded as the eight acts of *one* grand tragedy—the drama of the historic life of very near a century. You will observe, therefore, that Shakspeare has taken one great era of English history, and that, too, in its most ample form, in its fullest extent, and he has completed the dramatic picture of it; the work is entire—it is finished. Looking, as we are apt to do, at these "Chronicle-Plays" separately, we do not appreciate the magnitude of the poet's achievement in the department of history; and it is only by taking a comprehensive view, and contemplating the unity of this series of plays, that we learn the grandeur of the theme and the sublimity of the genius which accomplished it. The tragedy of Richard the Second, the two parts of Henry the Fourth, Henry the Fifth, the three parts of Henry the Sixth, and the tragedy of Richard the Third constitute, in truth, *one* splendid drama, unparalleled, nay, unapproached, in all imaginative literature. The subject of it may be described as the decline and fall of the Plantagenet dynasty—the downfall of the dominion which had endured during an eventful period of three hundred and fifty years. The two historical plays which stand detached from this series—"King John" and "Henry the Eighth"—may be brought into relation with it by considering King John, as Schlegel proposes, a kind of prologue to the series, inasmuch as it represents an earlier period with all the varied elements of the early mediæval times; and, on the other hand, by regarding Henry the Eighth as an epilogue, representing the beginning of the new political and social condition of England in modern times. We have thus all these "Chronicle-Plays," constituting one great historical poem, in which the poet's imagination, taking the subject from the annals of his country, has created this life-like spectacle of the fortunes of kings and princes—their glories and their woes—their high estate and the deep precipitation from it—the splendour and the pride of their lives, and the tragic misery of their deaths; and, with all this, the weal and welfare of the nation, and its disasters and chastisement; and, surely, never was there such wonderful fulfilment of the wished-for vision of Milton when, in the "Penseroso," he exclaims—

"Let gorgeous Tragedy,
With sceptered pall, come sweeping by,
Presenting Thebes, or Pelops' line,
Or the tale of Troy divine,
Or what, (though rare,) of later age
Ennobled hath the buskin'd stage."

I have spoken of these historical plays as forming a connected series, and giving a continuous dramatic representation of an era of English history; it is, however, also to be borne in mind that each one of them is complete in itself, and has its own dramatic unity. I shall have occasion to use them in regular succession, and to show with what consummate skill, Shakspeare has linked these plays together—one the sequel to the other. It is when we contemplate them as the parts of one great drama, that we are most deeply impressed with their historical value and with the poet-historian's power; for it is then that we are enabled to behold the whole revolution of the wheel of kingly fortune, as it makes its large circuit through the space of near a century; it is then that we can see, in what else seems so chanceful, the hand that turns the wheel of fortune, and learn the workings of that even-handed justice, which sends its retribution, if not promptly to the guilty, slowly, but certainly, to the second and third generations of the guilty. Taking these plays as one ample poem, I know not where else to look for such varied and splendid teaching of the lessons of retributive justice. We shall see how the firmly-seated dynasty of the Plantagenets—fortified by long possession and its lineage from the Norman Conqueror—is forced by the frailties of the second Richard from the due course of hereditary succession; we shall see the Lancastrian usurpation first established with the forms, at least, of law, then raised to the highest glory of the monarchy by Henry the Fifth's splendid career of foreign conquest, and then, by the bloody strife of the Roses, utterly cast down. We shall afterwards follow the victorious progress of the house of York onward to the darkening of their fortunes, to the secret slaughter of the child-king, Edward the Fifth, and the more open death, in the face of the offended heavens the soldier's death—of the last of the Plantagenets on Bosworth Field.

In proceeding to that period of English history which is illustrated by the tragedy of Richard the Second, let me advert to the fact that, in this play, Shakspeare has treated history in a manner widely different from that in King John. In forming a drama out of the historical events of the reign of King John, the poet had no choice but to use a large liberty with the actual succession of these events, separated as they were in point of time, and to create a dramatic unity, by which the beginning and the close of the reign should be morally connected: it was necessary, too, to mould the history in such a way as to invent the dramatic action for the personages of the play. Now in Richard the Second the historical materials were very different: the history grows out of Richard's character; indeed, his character is the history, so that the poet is the historian; because, in presenting character, which is essential in dramatic poetry, he is, at the same time, telling the history. In this case, therefore, the poet follows the footsteps of the chronicler,—the play and the chronicle are in the same path. In King John, one of the most important, and certainly the noblest person of the play, Philip Falconbridge, is an imaginary character, most happily created and wisely used for the purposes of history as well as of the drama. But in Richard the Second there is no imaginary character; all the personages are strictly and actually historical. The tragedy of King John comprehended the whole of the reign—the events of sixteen years; in Richard the Second, Shakspeare has confined the drama to the close of the reign, —only a little more than one year out of the twenty-two during which Richard occupied the throne. The whole of this previous portion of the reign is omitted, and we know it in the play only by its results, and the retrospect that is occasionally given.

The opening of the tragedy of Richard the Second displays the various elements which are to be wrought to the great historical issues of the time; and it shows the condition of the realm after the lapse of about twenty years of Richard's sway. We see at once the state distracted by a turbulent and proud nobility, and division and discord in the royal family. Somewhat more gradually, the poet brings into view the character of the monarch, beneath the lofty majesty of whose demeanour, which first strikes the mind, we soon discover the fickle, arbitrary temper and the unreal strength of that pride which is to work out its own ruin in a career of folly and dissimulation and tyranny. In the play, Richard comes on the scene such a man as the previous portion of his life had made him; and to that previous period we must therefore look back in order to understand his character and his history. We must look there to discover what it was, or what causes combined to fill him with such pride; to learn what outward influences had worked upon his natural disposition so as to make him at once so haughty and so helpless. Before we proceed to the study of the tragic chastisement of his vices and his frailties, we must needs look at the origin and growth of that tyrannic pride, which rendered him so fit a subject to illustrate the retributive and chastening influences, which are the high theme of tragedy.

Richard the Second, when he succeeded to his grandfather, Edward the Third, was a boy of about eleven years of age,—that critical time of life when the innocence and purity of childhood are gone. He succeeded to a reign which, during the long term of fifty years, had been triumphant abroad and unresisted at home; and the strength and glory of that reign were well fitted to fill the mind of the boy-king with the belief that the throne was impregnable, and the sceptre had super-human might. This pride may well have been heightened, too, by the ancestral feeling inspired by the heroic character and the martial prowess of his father, Edward, the Black Prince, who, unhappily for his son, had died before the succession reached him. There was every thing in Richard's thoughts of the past to fire his pride; and, when he mounted the throne, he felt that it was upheld, not only by the moral influences of a nation's love for the memory of his forefathers, but also by the counsel and the power of the surviving sons of Edward the Third, Lancaster and Gloucester and York; and the boy little dreamed that the multitude of his uncles was to prove one of the miseries of his reign, and that, at last, a kinsman's hand was to thrust him from the throne, and to a prison, and to his grave. He could not see how much of dangerous ambition lurked in the hearts of his uncles; nor could he understand that, while the last king had bequeathed to him and to his people the glory of his foreign conquests, there was the legacy, too, of the cost of conquest and military renown; and that, in his day, the poetry of war was to be followed by that which is its inevitable sequel, the prose of debt and taxes and extortion.

It was Richard's fate to live in times when his pomp and pride became doubly dangerous. In the latter part of the fourteenth century a change was coming over the spirit of the people of Europe: there were indications, not to be mistaken, that government was no longer to be an affair of kings and nobles only, but the popular element was beginning to manifest itself, and not in England alone, but in other lands. It is a fact in European history worthy of careful study, that, at the time I am referring to, there was a contemporaneous movement of the lower classes—of the body of the people—in various countries. France felt it, and Flanders and England. The stern slavery under the feudal system was relaxing; the voice of the serf, who so long in silence had endured his bondage, was at length heard; the spirit of freedom, which heretofore had animated only the noble and the high-born, was now inflaming the hearts of those who, under the bonds of villain-service, had been part of the ownership of the soil, like a "rooted tree or stone earth-bound." There was an almost simultaneous rising of the lower orders of the people; and not being confined to any one country, it is to be explained only by general and, doubtless, various causes affecting European society and government at large. It would carry me beyond my subject were I to attempt to make any inquiry into these causes. It so happened that when the great body of the people was gradually rising in the scale of civilization, the pressure on them was increased; they rose up under it to assert their natural rights, or what may better be called, their simplest civic rights. The popular insurrections in the Flemish towns, in Paris, and in some of the French provinces, and in England, were attended with tumult and bloodshed. Long-continued and heartless neglect and oppression had engendered fierce hatred of the former masters, and political enfranchisement was sought in the wild spirit of revenge; so true is it, that "the great and hardest problem of political wisdom is, to prevent any part of society from becoming so socially degraded by poverty, that their political enfranchisement becomes dangerous or even mischievous."

This danger was encountered by the young King Richard in the early part of his reign; and I have referred to it, because the success with which it was quelled was well fitted to aggravate that pride, the formation of which in his character I proposed to trace. Richard was but sixteen years of age, when the tranquillity of his kingdom was broken by that extensive and formidable insurrection, which, from the name of its leader, is called "Wat Tyler's Rebellion." The oppression of the serfs, and the exactions under which the common people were suffering, had produced a high state of popular exasperation. Little was needed to cause an outbreak against the government. This natural sense of injury in the minds of the people was further excited and misguided by a seditious and fanatic priest—John Ball—who went about the country teaching revolutionary lessons in their most destructive forms—in sermons, with the proverb, in doggerel verse, for his text—

> "When Adam delved and Evè span,
> Who was then the gentleman?"

The insurgents assembled in the neighbouring counties, and came up to London sixty thousand strong; they seized the Tower, they threw open the prison-doors, destroyed the palace of the Duke of Lancaster, put to death many of the citizens who attempted to withstand them, and led the Primate of England to execution. It was a vast and triumphant riot; but, in the midst of it, with an intrepidity worthy of the son of an heroic father, the young king—the manly boy—rode into the metropolis, attended by only sixty horsemen, to meet and conciliate the multitude of his malecontent subjects assembled by thousands and flushed with the sudden success of their revolt. As soon as the insurgents beheld their leader struck down, they were won back again to their allegiance, it would seem, by the mere presence of their youthful sovereign;—and what could have occurred more fitted to feed the pride of such a heart as his, than the thought that he possessed such power over the hearts of thousands of his incensed and turbulent people? It made him proud of himself, and still more proud of the might of royalty.

The suppression of Wat Tyler's rebellion was succeeded by a confused and uncertain period of intrigue and conspiracy and crime. The king surrounded himself with unworthy favourites, who flattered him to his ruin. He gave himself to a career of lavish expenditure, of wanton misrule, and despotic pride. His kinsmen and his uncles became odious to him, and he to them. In Parliament, dethronement and exile were openly spoken of, and the fate of his great grandsire, Edward the Second, darkly hinted at. The discontented nobility began to confer and confederate against the king; and his own uncle, the Duke of Gloucester, placed himself at the head of one of the hostile factions. The king was beset with perils, but, what was worse, he was beset with evil counsellors, and his own evil passions. Flattery and self-indulgence had been working their mischief on his nature, and he was on the downward path of degeneracy. He could not now meet his foes as, when a boy, he went forth to meet sixty thousand infuriated rebels, and, with open intrepidity, overawe and subdue them. The boy was brave because he was innocent; but now, dark counsels of revenge and treachery seemed good to him, and poison and assassination were thought surer and easier means, by which a king could sweep his enemies from off the earth. The Duke of Gloucester was hurried away to a distant prison, where, mysteriously, he died a death of violence; and henceforth the guilt, which the king has added to his frailties and his follies, is to haunt his life to its close. Retribution, it is said, walks with a foot of velvet, and strikes with a hand of steel; and now its noiseless steps are towards this king, and its hand uplifted.

It is at this point of his reign and of his character that Shakspeare brings Richard the Second before us. The quarrel between the son of the Duke of Lancaster, Henry Hereford, called Bolingbroke, and Thomas Mowbray, Earl of Norfolk, with which the play opens, is to be decided, as the king determines, by the wager of battle, the single combat of the two noblemen—that ancient feudal form of trial, in which it was supposed Heaven would mark the righteous party by giving him the victory. The lists at Coventry are made ready for the combat; the combatants appear with their heralds and in all the pomp of chivalry, and in the presence of the king and many of the nobles. The merits of this controversy between Bolingbroke and Mowbray are involved in the obscurity which covers the intrigues and half-treasonable plots of this reign. It was one of those doubtful cases in which neither the accusation nor the defence admitted of notorious proof; and, therefore, according to the feudal jurisprudence, the trial of combat was awarded, and the Almighty was to be the judge, His will being, as it was believed, manifested by the result. To that judgment, Richard, though he awarded the trial, is not willing to commit it; and he interposes the decree of his mortal majesty at the last moment, when the trumpets have sounded, and the combatants are arrayed in complete armour, and, upon their armed steeds, are setting forward to encounter each other in deadly conflict. At that instant, the king throws down his warder—the truncheon of command—as a signal to prevent the combat. Whether this was caprice or a deeper stroke of policy and dissimulation, the reasons of the king seem hollow and insincere; and, as he professes his desire to spare the shedding of such blood as flowed in the veins of the high-born combatants, and to save the kingdom from the feuds of civil warfare that might ensue, we cannot help looking forward in the history, and thinking that the throwing down of the king's warder in the lists at Coventry may be considered the prelude to that fierce struggle between the houses of York and Lancaster, which distracted England during the greater part of half a century, and in which the best blood of the nation was poured out like water. The act of the king, on this occasion, was the beginning of a series of events, which close only with the battle of Bosworth Field; and, if his professions were insincere, and his decree tyrannical, there was fearful retribution in the future, when, in consequence of what followed this event, the nation suffered thirty years of civil war, and four kings perished by violent deaths.

The judgment which the king pronounced is arbitrary; for, instead of deciding between the parties, there is the easier tyranny of compromise by inflicting the penalty of guilt upon both of them. It is arbitrary, too, in the proportions of the penalty. Norfolk is banished for life, and Bolingbroke for the term of ten years, which is afterwards, in the same arbitrary temper, reduced to six years. It is not this inequality alone that creates a sympathy with Norfolk. We see Bolingbroke coming to the combat with a spirit that seems to exult chiefly in the consciousness of his strength,—"As confident," he boasts, "as is the falcon's flight against a bird." There is a deeper feeling in the spirit with which Mowbray meets the accusation, and confronts his adversary:

"However Heaven or fortune cast my lot,
There lives or dies, true to King Richard's throne,
A loyal, just, and upright gentleman.
Never did captive with a freer heart
Cast off his chains of bondage, and embrace
His golden, uncontrolled enfranchisement,
More than my dancing soul doth celebrate
This feast of battle with mine adversary.
Most mighty liege, and my companion peers,
Take from my mouth the wish of happy years:
As gentle and as jocund, as to jest,
Go I to fight. Truth hath a quiet breast."

This does, indeed, sound like the voice of truth; it does seem the utterance of "a loyal, just, and upright gentleman." Our pity for him, as an injured man, is deepened, when he replies so meekly, yet so feelingly, in that beautiful and pathetic lament for his perpetual exile:

"A heavy sentence, my most sovereign liege,
And all unlooked for from your highness' mouth;
A dearer merit, not so deep a maim,
As to be cast forth in the common air,
Have I deserved at your highness' hand,
The language I have learned these forty years,
My native English, now I must forego:
And now my tongue's use is to me no more
Than an unstringed viol, or a harp,

> Or like a cunning instrument cased up,
> Or, being open, put into his hands
> That knows no touch to tune the harmony.
> Within my mouth you have engaoled my tongue,
> Doubly portcullised with my teeth and lips;
> And dull, unfeeling, barren ignorance
> Is made my gaoler to attend on me.
> I am too old to fawn upon a nurse,
> Too far in years to be a pupil now;
> What is thy sentence, then, but speechless death,
> Which robs my tongue from breathing native breath?"

When the Duke of Lancaster, old John of Gaunt strives to reconcile his son to his shorter exile by telling him—

> "The sullen passage of thy weary steps
> Esteem a foil, wherein thou art to set
> The precious jewel of thy home-return,"

Bolingbroke replies in that fine and familiar strain of poetry—

> "Oh! who can hold a fire in his hand,
> By thinking on the frosty Caucasus?
> Or cloy the hungry edge of appetite
> By bare imagination of a feast?
> Or wallow naked in December snow,
> By thinking on fantastic summer's heat?
> Oh, no! the apprehension of the good
> Gives but the greater feeling to the worse."

This complaint comes to us with less of real pathos than the piteous lament of Norfolk. It is later in the drama—just at the time that Bolingbroke returns from his unfinished exile, and with the disloyal purpose of thrusting Richard from his throne and seizing the sceptre for himself—that we are told the story of what remained of the career of Norfolk:

> "Many a time hath banished Norfolk fought
> For Jesu Christ; in glorious Christian field
> Streaming the ensign of the Christian cross,
> Against black pagans, Turks, and Saracens:
> And, toiled with works of war, retired himself
> To Italy; and there, at Venice, gave
> His body to that pleasant country's earth,
> And his pure soul unto his captain Christ,
> Under whose colours he had fought so long."

No sooner is Bolingbroke banished than, as Shakspeare discloses the historical truth, we perceive that it was timid suspicion and jealousy in the breast of Richard, that prompted the sentence against his kinsman. The popular feeling, which the exile courted and won, as he went away, did not escape the notice of the king and his favourites:

> "Ourself and Bushy, Bagot here, and Green,
> Observed his courtship to the common people:—
> How he did seem to dive into their hearts,
> With humble and familiar courtesy;
> What reverence he did throw away on slaves,
> Wooing poor craftsmen with the craft of smiles,
> And patient underbearing of his fortune,
> As 'twere to banish their affects with him.
> Off goes his bonnet to an oyster-wench;
> A brace of draymen bid—God speed him well,
> And had the tribute of his supple knee,
> With—'Thanks, my countrymen, my loving friends!'
> As were our England in reversion his,
> And he our subjects' next degree in hope."

Happy would it have been for the frail and feeble Richard if, instead of letting the affections of his people be won away from him by the arts of a demagogue, he had secured them by honourable means and a dutiful sovereignty, to be at once the prop and the pride of his throne. Relieved from restraints and apprehensions of Bolingbroke's presence, the king precipitates himself still faster on his downward career of folly and crime. The wasteful pomp and pleasures of his court bring new temptations to tyrannous rapacity, and the recklessness of his character is further displayed, when, with fitful energy, he resolves to conduct the war against his rebel subjects in Ireland:

"We will ourself in person to this war.
And, for our coffers, with too great a court,
And liberal largess, are grown somewhat light,
We are enforced to farm our royal realm;
The revenue whereof shall furnish us
For our affairs in hand: if that come short,
Our substitutes at home shall have blank charters;
Whereto, when they shall know what men are rich,
They shall subscribe them for large sums of gold,
And send them after to supply our wants."

A long-continued course of self-indulgence, together with the flattery of his minions, hardens the heart of King Richard more and more; and when he is told that his uncle, old John of Gaunt, "time-honoured Lancaster," is "grievous sick," the spendthrift king exclaims, with utter and indecent heartlessness—

"Now put it, Heaven, in his physician's mind
To help him to his grave immediately!
The lining of his coffers shall make coats
To deck our soldiers for these Irish wars.
Come, gentlemen, let's all go visit him:
Pray God, we may make haste, and come too late."

The death scene of John of Gaunt is a dramatic invention, but Shakspeare has made an admirable historical use of it, by putting into the mouth of Lancaster, not only a dying man's prophecy of the ruin that is to follow Richard's riotous misrule, but also one of those magnificent poetic eulogies on England, by which the poet has fostered the national feeling of his countrymen. The misgovernment in Richard's reign grieves the spirit of the dying Lancaster; because, remembering the splendour and the strength of his father's reign, he thinks of that small island England, as—

"This royal throne of kings, this sceptred isle,
This earth of majesty, this seat of Mars,
This other Eden, demi-paradise;
This fortress, built by nature for herself,
Against infection and the hand of war;
This happy breed of men, this little world;
This precious stone, set in the silver sea,
Which serves it in the office of a wall,
Or as a moat defensive to a house,
Against the envy of less happier lands;
This blessed plot, this earth, this realm, this England."

The remonstrance and the warnings of his dying uncle are of no avail to stop the headlong course of the king; they serve but to exasperate his royal pride. Immediately on Lancaster's death, Richard, reckless of law and right, seized upon his estates—the patrimony of the banished Bolingbroke, who, by his father's death, was now Duke of Lancaster. When this last tyranny is perpetrated, the warning voice of the Duke of York, the gentlest of Richard's uncles—the last surviving son of Edward the Third—is raised, and he strives to bring the king to a better mind by the memory of his father:

"I am the last of noble Edward's sons,
Of whom thy father, prince of Wales, was first;
In war was never lion raged more fierce,
In peace was never gentle lamb more mild,
Than was that young and princely gentleman:
His face thou hast, for even so looked he,
Accomplished with the number of thy hours;
But when he frowned, it was against the French,
And not against his friends; his noble hand
Did win what he did spend, and spent not that,
Which his triumphant father's hand had won:
His hands were guilty of no kindred's blood,
But bloody with the enemies of his kin."

York warns the king, moreover, that, by the lawless seizure of Hereford's patrimony, he plucks a thousand dangers on his head, and loses a thousand well-disposed hearts. But the poison of flattery and of criminal self-indulgence, and the demoralizing irresponsibility of power, have wrought their mischief so deep into the soul of Richard, that neither rebuke nor kindly admonition, nor the fear of impending evil, can help him. He is doomed—nothing can save his sceptre or his life.

We have thus far followed, as Shakspeare and the chroniclers have traced it, the downward progress of Richard the Second, until we behold him reduced to that pitch of moral degradation, which, in this tragedy, is shown with such matchless impartiality. Morally, the king is to be sunk no lower; and let us now see how the poet-historian, with equal truth and with the large charity of a great poet's heart, raises him up again, not, indeed, to his primal power, but to our sympathy and pity. The heart, which had been hardened by flattery and the luxuries of arbitrary force, is to be softened; the sleeping humanity in his character is to be awakened; his dead conscience to be brought to life; and all this, which neither fear nor reproof nor kindness could do, is to be effected by what has been finely called "the power and divinity of suffering."* This is the very theme of tragedy; the change in Richard's character, or rather the development of those better elements in it which, in prosperity, were well-nigh utterly perishing, came from the chastisement of affliction; how it came, is shown by Shakspeare in this drama, in which he fulfils at once the high functions of poet, historian, and moralist.

The king hastens back from Ireland, because the banished Bolingbroke, regardless of his sentence, has returned to England. He has landed at Ravenspurg, his professed purpose being simply to claim his patrimony, but every step he takes is a step towards the possession of the throne. The king has returned to meet a great and growing danger—the magnitude of it making it at once awful but shadowy to his mind. He faces the danger, not with a wise or heroic self-confidence, for that he never possessed, unless it was in his youth, when he met the insurgents in London. He is now not accompanied with worthless favourites, who would delude him with flattery or tempt to criminal defences; he is surrounded by men who deal truthfully with him, and do not shrink from telling him of the sad realities that are before and around him. As soon as he touches the soil of England, he gives utterance to a strain of sensibility which, if somewhat visionary, still shows a strange blending of genuine tenderness, of royal pride, and of conscious weakness:

* Faber's Sights and Thoughts, p. 288.

"I weep for joy,
To stand upon my kingdom once again.
Dear earth, I do salute thee with my hand,
Though rebels wound thee with their horses' hoofs;
As a long-parted mother with her child
Plays fondly with her tears and smiles, in meeting;—
So, weeping, smiling, greet I thee, my earth,
And do thee favour with my royal hands."

He conjures the earth—

"Feed not thy sovereign's foe, my gentle earth!"

He invokes it to sting rebellious feet with nettles, and send forth adders to throw death upon his enemies; then, observing, perhaps, the impatient looks of his companions, he adds—

"Mock not my senseless conjuration, lords!
This earth shall have a feeling, and these stones
Prove armed soldiers, ere her native king
Shall falter under foul rebellion's arms."

When his kinsman Aumerle gently hints that his cause needs prompt and manly action, the king, looking from the earth, which he had first invoked, up to heaven, rises to a loftier state of feeling in that splendid strain of poetry—

"Discomfortable cousin! knowest thou not
That when the searching eye of heaven is hid
Behind the globe, and lights the lower world,
Then thieves and robbers range abroad unseen,
In murders, and in outrage, bloody here;
But when, from under this terrestrial ball,
He fires the proud tops of the eastern pines,
And darts his light through every guilty hole,
Then murders, treasons, and detested sins,
The cloak of night being plucked from off their backs,

Stand bare and naked, trembling at themselves?
So when this thief, this traitor, Bolingbroke,—
Who all this while hath revelled in the night,
Whilst we were wandering with the antipodes,—
Shall see us rising in our throne the east,
His treasons will sit blushing in his face,
Not able to endure the sight of day,
But self-affrighted, tremble at his sin.
Not all the water in the rough, rude sea,
Can wash the balm from an anointed king:
The breath of worldly men cannot depose
The deputy elected by the Lord.
For every man that Bolingbroke hath pressed,
To lift shrewd steel against our golden crown,
God for his Richard hath in heavenly pay
A glorious angel: then, if angels fight,
Weak men must fall; for heaven still guards the right."

The doctrine of the divine and indefeasible right of kings surely never received a more magnificent exposition; and we need not wonder that Dr. Johnson, with his high-toned toryism, referred to it exultingly, especially to prove that that political theory was of earlier origin than the era of the Stuart kings, this play having been composed during the reign of Queen Elizabeth. But it must be remembered that Shakspeare speaks dramatically; and, while he devotes this lofty strain of poetry to kingly power *jure divino*, he shows the insufficiency of the doctrine in the actual working of the government; and, what is more important, he puts it in the mouth of a king, the sacred promise of whose coronation-oath had been violated by wilful misrule, and who forgot that, if the doctrine of the divine right of royalty gave him power over his people, it imposed an awful responsibility to God, that could not be neglected without peril.

The evil tidings of growing disloyalty and rebellion came full and fast upon the unhappy Richard; and, after some fitful flashes of resolution and royal pride, he sinks into that strain of melancholy—

"For heaven's sake, let us sit upon the ground,
And tell sad stories of the death of kings;—
How some have been deposed, some slain in war;
Some haunted by the ghosts they have deposed;
Some poisoned by their wives, some sleeping killed;
All murthered:—for, within the hollow crown
That rounds the mortal temples of a king,
Keeps death his court: and there the antick sits,
Scoffing his state, and grinning at his pomp,
Allowing him a breath, a little scene
To monarchize, be feared, and kill with looks;
Infusing him with self and vain conceit,—
As if this flesh, which walls about our life,
Were brass impregnable; and humoured thus,
Comes at the last, and with a little pin
Bores through his castle wall and—farewell, king!"

King Richard is beginning to feel that he is a man; and, as chastisement brings this change across his spirit, our feelings yearn towards him. When he encounters Bolingbroke, he recovers, in some degree, the decorum of a kingly demeanour, but the sense of his degradation, the fall of his pride, breaks out again:

"O God! O God! that e'er this tongue of mine,
That laid the sentence of dread banishment
On yon proud man, should take it off again
With words of sooth! Oh! that I were as great
As is my grief, or lesser than my name!
Or that I could forget what I have been!
Or not remember what I must be now!"

He is brought to London, still a king, but, in truth, a captive; and a deeper compassion is inspired by that beautiful description of the entry into the city, which is spoken by the Duke of York. While Bolingbroke's return was hailed with the joyful greetings of all voices of the people—

> "Men's eyes
> Did scowl on Richard; no man cried, God save him;
> No joyful tongue gave him his welcome home;
> But dust was thrown upon his sacred head;
> Which with such gentle sorrow he shook off,—
> His face still combating with tears and smiles,
> The badges of his grief and patience,—
> That had not God, for some strong purpose, steel'd
> The hearts of men, they must perforce have melted,
> And barbarism itself have pitied him."

Richard resigns his throne, and is also deposed by the Parliament; or rather, it is through such formalities, that Bolingbroke dethrones him, and seizes the succession. The deposition scene in Westminster Hall, as Shakspeare has represented it, shows the last struggle of Richard's fading majesty—his unsteady mind running off perpetually in wayward motions of fancy and feeling—shrinking from the final and irrevocable expression of consent to relinquish the crown—spending what strength was left in words. Meditating on the annihilation of his royalty, and yet dreading the necessity of the slightest effort in word or deed, there comes from the very bottom of his heart that wild and piteous wish:

> "Oh! that I were a mockery king of snow,
> Standing before the sun of Bolingbroke,
> To melt myself away in water drops!"

The crown is no longer on the brow of Richard; the sceptre is no longer in his hand; and the dark shadow of his tragic death is, to my imagination, thrown distinctly forward in the few stern words in which Bolingbroke pronounces the ominous command—

> "Go, some of you, convey him to the Tower."

Richard is soon removed to the dungeon of Pomfret Castle. The prison-scene of a dethroned king seldom fails to be the death-scene. In what way he was deprived of life is doubtful; whether by the slow misery of famine, as the poet Gray has represented,—

> "Close by the regal chair
> Fell Thirst and Famine scowl
> A baleful smile upon their baffled guest,"*

or by the violence of assault, as in the tragedy. The gentle and lofty morality of Shakspeare was never more finely shown than in this,—that before Richard's soul is summoned from earth, there is added to the utterance of his anguish the contrite confession of a misspent life. You may remember how, in the tragedy of King Lear, the crazed mind of the "child-changed father" was soothed and healed, not only by Cordelia's voice, but by the remediate virtue of soft music. In the dungeon scene in Richard the Second, the poet has likewise appealed to the power of music for the different purpose of moving to a healthy wakefulness a distracted, I may say, a delirious, conscience. A sound of rude music reaches the imprisoned king; he listens in that mood in which the fancy in solitude and sorrow is so quickly apprehensive of all, even chance, impressions, and then exclaims—

* Gray's Poetical Works, p. 172.

"How sour sweet music is,
When time is broke, and no proportion kept!
So is it in the music of men s lives.
And here have I the daintiness of ear,
To check time broke in a disordered string;
But, for the concord of my state and time,
Had not an ear to hear my true time broke.
I wasted time and now doth time waste me."

When his thoughts run on into the conscious misery of his downfall, still the music calls forth a kindly feeling and a blessing; for he thinks of it as the last tribute of some humble and still loyal subject, who is lingering with affection about his prison walls:

"This music mads me, let it sound no more;
For though it have holp madmen to their wits,
In me, it seems it will make wise men mad.
Yet blessing on his heart that gives it me!
For 'tis a sign of love; and love to Richard
Is a strange brooch in this all-hating world."

Richard meets the murderous assault of Exton and the armed servants with prompt and manly valour; and his last words are expressive of the remanent feeling of royalty, and of his chastened and restored humanity.

"That hand shall burn in never-quenching fire,
That staggers thus my person. Exton, thy fierce hand
Hath with the king's blood stained the kings's own land.
Mount, mount, my soul! thy seat is up on high,
While my gross flesh sinks downward here to die."

Thus it is that Shakspeare—a great historian—teaches how tragedy—"the power and divinity of suffering"—can bring the weak, the wilful, and wicked to a better mind, and can win for them a just sympathy; so that one would fain close the story of this reign in the same compassionate spirit with which Froissart, who was an eye-witness of it, ends his chronicle of that period of English history by saying:—"King Richard was buried at Langley. God pardon his sins and have mercy on his soul!"*

* Froissart. Johnes's Translation, vol. xii. p. 193.

LECTURE VI.*

The Reign of Henry the Fourth.

Henry the Fourth's accession to the throne an usurpation—Character of the king—Error of historical reasoning—Carlyle on Cromwell—Henry's education and exile—Analogy to Macbeth—His popularity—Counsel to his son—His visit to foreign lands—Palestine—Castile—His return—Severe policy after his coronation—The Bishop of Carlisle—Shakspeare's "Chronicle-Plays" tragic—Comic element here—Falstaff and Prince Hal—Henry the Fourth's reign without national interest—Unquiet times—Plan of his crusade—Its origin and his visit to the Holy Land—Intercession of the Greek emperor for English aid—Visit of Palæologus to London—St. Bernard—Plan of crusade frustrated—Insurrection in Scotland—Percy and Douglas—Battle of Otterbourne—Mortimer—Glendower—Chevy Chase—Hotspur and Falstaff—The Battle of Shrewsbury—Death of Henry the Fourth.

When Henry of Lancaster ascended the throne of England, the regular line of hereditary succession was broken for the first time for two hundred years. The due course of the law of inheritance had been followed during that period of time, and was thus strongly fortified by prescription and consent. The rights of no lawful heir to the throne had been violated since the innocent Arthur of Brittany fell a victim to the ruthless ambition of King John. After that time the crown regularly passed from

* Monday, February 1st, 1847.

father to son, from first-born to first-born, during two centuries, until the aspiring Bolingbroke placed it upon his own brow. Not only was the rightful monarch, the frail and offending Richard, discrowned and dispossessed, imprisoned and soon slaughtered, but the legitimate heir was kept out of his inheritance by that strong Lancastrian usurpation, which was not shaken until the violated claim was revived, causing a civil war which lasted for thirty years, and in which Englishmen died by the hands of Englishmen in no fewer than twelve pitched battles.

I have endeavoured to show how the follies and vices of Richard the Second paved the way for Bolingbroke to the throne; but I purposely confined the view as much as possible to the downfall of Richard, reserving for consideration the career of his adversary, as he sought to turn the weakness and tyranny of the king to his own great gain, and to rise at last upon the ruins. This career of Bolingbroke's was probably a long and studied course of politic ambition. It proved successful, in so far as the grand object of his hopes and aspirations was attained,—he gained the throne; and we shall see whether the possession, so dearly coveted and so strenuously won, brought along with it happy days and a tranquil death.

I have spoken of the occupation of the English throne by Henry of Lancaster, as the crowning result of long-continued effort and long-cherished purposes of ambitious premeditation; yet, I am aware that, in the study of history, there is an error, which frequently deludes the student, in this way—that, looking at any remarkable achievement of political ambition, we are very apt, and naturally so, to persuade ourselves, that the ambition which has been thus successful must have been more far-seeing and more far-reaching than it really was. We can hardly believe that so great a growth has come from a small seed, and that most of its strength is to be traced to such influences as the mere course of events has given—the sun-light and the showers that have touched it, and the winds that have breathed upon it. It is with reference to a later and far more mighty usurper, that Carlyle has referred to this source of error as affecting our judgment of character; and I quote his opinion, before proceeding further with the consideration of the course of life and action, which placed the Duke of Lancaster on the throne of England. "There is an error," writes Mr. Carlyle, "widely prevalent, which perverts to the very basis our judgments formed about such men as Cromwell,—about their ambition, falsity, and such like. It is what I might call substituting the goal of their career for the course and starting-point of it. The vulgar historian of a Cromwell fancies that he had determined on being Protector of England at the time he was ploughing the marsh lands of Cambridgeshire. His career lay all mapped out, a program of the whole drama; which he then, step by step, dramatically unfolded, with all manner of cunning deceptive dramaturgy, as he went on—the hollow scheming, ὑποκριτής or play-actor that he was? This is a radical perversion, all but universal in such cases. And think, for an instant, how different the fact is! How much does one of *us* foresee of his own life? Short way a-head of us it is all dim,—an *un*wound skein of possibilities, of apprehensions, attemptabilities, vague-looming hopes. This Cromwell had *not* his life lying all in that fashion of program, which he needed then, with that unfathomable cunning of his, only to enact dramatically, scene after scene! Not so. *We* see it so; but to him it was in no measure so. What absurdities would fall away of themselves, were this one undeniable fact kept honestly in view by history! Historians indeed will tell you that they do keep it in view; but look whether such is practically the fact! Vulgar history, as in this, Cromwell's case, omits it altogether; even the best kinds of history only remember it now and then. To remember it duly, with vigorous perfection, as in the fact it *stood*, requires indeed a rare faculty,—rare, nay, impossible. A very Shakspeare for faculty, or more than Shakspeare, who could *enact* a brother man's biography, see with the brother man's eyes, at all points of his course, what things he saw; in short, know his course and him, as few 'historians' are like to do. Half or more of all the thick-plied perversions, which distort our image of Cromwell, will disappear if we honestly so much as try to represent them so in sequence, as they *were;* not in the lump as they 'are thrown down before us.'"*

Bearing in mind the necessity of guarding against this error, let us, before returning to the reign of Henry the Fourth, look back to the previous history, to see what there was which at once favoured and fomented the ambition that led him to the throne. He was the son of a younger son of Edward the Third, and his birth therefore gave him the chances of succession, which belong to a younger branch of the royal family. When he reached the years of manhood, animated by the chivalrous spirit of the times, he sought for military adventures in the distant region of Prussia, and travelled afterwards in the

* Heroes and Hero Worship, p. 198.

Holy Land. This career of foreign travel and adventure not only strengthened his character, but it kept him, for a while at least, aloof from the voluptuous misrule of Richard's court, so that when he came home, the people were ready to look upon him more hopefully and more confidently than if he had been associated, either with the pleasures of the king, or with the intrigues and conspiracies of the nobles. There seems to have been high ambition in this Lancastrian blood, for his father, John of Gaunt, having married a daughter of Pedro the Cruel, assumed, on the death of that king, the titles and arms of the kingdom of Castile. When, at a later period of his life, he led an expedition to the Spanish peninsula, he intrusted the management of his affairs in England to his son. "Before his embarkation," writes Froissart, "and in the presence of his brothers, the Duke of Lancaster appointed his son Henry, Earl of Derby, his lieutenant for whatever concerned him during his absence, and chose for him a set of able advisers. This Henry was a young and handsome knight, son of the Lady Blanche, first Duchess of Lancaster. I never saw two such noble dames, so good, liberal, and courteous, as this lady and the late Queen of England, and never shall, were I to live a thousand years, which (adds the simple chronicler) is impossible."*

The intellect and temper of Bolingbroke seem to have been those of a sagacious, wary, and prudent politician; and dim as all vision into futurity must be, he still could see enough there to tell him that Richard's tenure of the throne would be daily and daily in greater jeopardy, and

* Froissart, vol. viii. p. 4.

that if the reign should end, as such reigns are apt to end, in turmoil and confusion, power, in the season of revolution, would tend towards the strong hand and the firm mind. Richard was childless, too, and on his death the title would pass to the house of Clarence, to find there, not the vigorous grasp of a man's hand, but the more uncertain hold of a child's succession, and of a female lineage. There was, therefore, between the weakness of Richard and the strength of Bolingbroke nothing interposed but weakness. After making every allowance against that historical error of which Carlyle has warned us, we cannot but believe that the crown of England must have been a perpetual prize before the eyes of Bolingbroke, not dazzling his keen vision, but kindling the spirit of his ambition. If ever man was strongly tempted to play the demagogue, and even almost to make the character of the demagogue a virtuous one, it was Bolingbroke. The hearts of the people were with good cause falling away from the king. His crafty kinsman witnessed this, and at the same time, was conscious of his own power to win them to himself. The strong men, who belonged to an elder generation—the uncles of the king, the sons of Edward the Third—who might have stood in Bolingbroke's way, had the catastrophe of Richard's reign come sooner, were passing from the busy scene: Gloucester had been basely murdered; Lancaster was growing old, and York was content in easy and amiable loyalty. Bolingbroke must have seen how every thing seemed to conspire to make the sovereignty his destiny, and in this he felt the strong impulse to work out his destiny. There is in this respect, to my mind, something in the career of Bolingbroke parallel to that of Macbeth, although certainly with a far inferior degree of guilt. The weird sisters foretell to Macbeth that he is to be King of Scotland. The wicked prophecy sinks deep into his heart, and he never doubts the fulfilment of it; but how does this confidence affect him? He does not passively await that fulfilment; indeed, it is only once that the thought of passive expectation crosses his mind:

> "If chance will have me king, why chance may crown me,
> Without my stir."

The prophecy proves an incitement to action for its fulfilment; and, goaded, too, by the concentrated ambition of his wife, he perpetrates both treachery and murder to make himself king, because the weird sisters have promised him that he shall be king. It seems to me that there was enough in the concurring events of the times of Richard the Second to speak to the ambitious and apprehensive spirit of Bolingbroke as audibly, almost, as the mysterious voices of the witches, when they addressed themselves to Macbeth upon the blasted heath. The wicked temptations which, in the case of Macbeth, are made visible in the hideous forms of witches, are not less real because unseen in the evil passions in the heart of Bolingbroke. He had a great game to play, and it was played with surpassing skill and boldness. No part of it was neglected or mismanaged; and it is curious to observe, that he appears to have begun to lay the foundation of his kingly fortunes by courting, not his peers, not the noble and the high born, but the common people. Perhaps the power of popularity was more recognised since that recent popular movement when, in Wat Tyler's rebellion, sixty thousand men, aggrieved or misguided, rose up from the lowest level of society against the government and the laws. On that occasion, they sacked and burnt the palace of the Duke of Lancaster; a few years pass by, and Lancaster's politic son is the favourite and idol of the people; he has found it worth his while to make them his friends rather than to have them his foes. He not only won golden opinions from all sorts of men, but, with consummate art, he so demeaned himself, that ever when the people turned away with indignation, or—what is tenfold worse—with contempt from King Richard, thinking how unkingly were his courses of life, they were attracted by the very contrast to the royal reserve and stately dignity of Bolingbroke. The history in this respect is told by Shakspeare with fine poetic art in the remonstrance addressed by Henry the Fourth to his son, warning him by the contrast of his own and Richard's career. It is at once a poetic confession of a most refined and accomplished demagogue, and a description of a most unroyal king—the one controlling the people to his own uses by wielding their imagination—"the mightiest lever known to the moral world"—the other making himself cheap to their sight:

"Had I so lavish of my presence been,
So common-hackney'd in the eyes of men,
So stale and cheap to vulgar company;
Opinion, that did help me to the crown,
Had still kept loyal to possession;
And left me in reputeless banishment,
A fellow of no mark, nor likelihood.
By being seldom seen, I could not stir,
But, like a comet, I was wondered at;
That men would tell their children—This is he
Others would say—Where? Which is Bolingbroke?
And then I stole all courtesy from heaven,
And dress'd myself in such humility,

That I did pluck allegiance from men's hearts,
Loud shouts and salutations from their mouths,
Even in the presence of the crowned king.
Thus did I keep my person fresh and new;
My presence, like a robe pontifical,
Ne'er seen, but wonder'd at; and so my state,
Seldom, but sumptuous, showed like a feast;
And won, by rareness, such solemnity.
The skipping king, he ambled up and down
With shallow jesters, and rash bavin wits,
Soon kindled and soon burned; 'carded his state;
Mingled his royalty with capering fools;
Had his great name profaned with their scorns;
And gave his countenance, against his name,
To laugh at gibing boys, and stand the push
Of every beardless vain comparative;
Grew a companion to the common streets,
Enfeoffed himself to popularity;
That being daily swallowed by men's eyes,
They surfeited with honey; and began
To loathe the taste of sweetness, whereof a little
More than a little is by much too much.
So, when he had occasion to be seen,
He was but as the cuckoo is in June,
Heard, not regarded; seen but with such eyes,
As, sick and blunted with community,
Afford no extraordinary gaze,
Such as is bent on sun-like majesty
When it shines seldom in admiring eyes:
But rather drowz'd and hung their eyelids down,
Slept in his face, and rendered such aspect
As cloudy men use to their adversaries;
Being with his presence glutted, gorged, and full."

When Bolingbroke is first introduced in the drama, it is after he has been playing this politic game so long that he manifestly feels a confidence in his coming royalty It is in the very presence of the king that he proclaims himself the avenger of the murdered Gloucester; yet

Gloucester was the king's uncle as well as his. In a very few words, Shakspeare has shown how high the aspiring spirit of Bolingbroke had already risen, when he represents him saying, with reference to the assassination of the Duke of Gloucester, his

"Blood, like sacrificing Abel's, cries
Even from the tongueless caverns of the earth
To me for justice and rough chastisement."

Who would think that the king himself, as near a kinsman of the murdered man, was hearing such words from a subject's lips? And yet, in this, Shakspeare accurately portrays the relative condition of Bolingbroke and Richard.

The banishment of Bolingbroke might arrest the progress of his ambition; but every thing, in a short space of time, turns to his advantage. Froissart gives an animated account of the conversation of the nobles, who assented to the sentence of exile, but sought to sweeten it by schemes of foreign travel, and hospitality for the banished Bolingbroke. "'He may readily go,' said they to one another, 'two or three years and amuse himself in foreign parts, for he is young enough; and although he has already travelled to Prussia, to the Holy Sepulchre, Cairo, and Saint Catherine's, he will find other places to visit. He has two sisters, Queens of Castile and Portugal, and may cheerfully pass his time with them. The lords, knights, and squires of these countries will make him welcome; for, at this moment, all warfare is at end. On his arrival in Castile, as he is very active, he may put them in motion and lead them against the infidels of Granada, which will employ his time better than remaining idle in England.'"* Bolingbroke was, indeed, very active; but he had other thoughts of action than that which his considerate fellow-nobles were devising for him. He had other work than to lead the Spanish knights on a crusade against the Moors of Spain; and it was to the palace of Windsor, and not the Alhambra, that his hopes were travelling.

The arbitrary sentence pronounced upon him by Richard endeared him still more to the people; and his presence was craved the more for the very prospect of his absence. The demonstration of popular feeling on the occasion is described by Froissart with all the vivid and simple narrative of the chronicler:—"The day," he says, "the Earl of Derby mounted his horse to leave London, upwards of forty thousand men were in the streets lamenting his departure. 'Gentle earl! will you then quit us? This country will never be happy until you return, and the days until then will be insufferably long. Through envy, treachery, and fear, you are driven out of a kingdom where you are more worthy to reside than those which cause it. You are of such high birth and gallantry, that none other can be compared to you. Why, then, will you leave us, gentle earl! You have never done wrong by thought or deed, and are incapable of so doing.' Thus did men and women so piteously complain, that it was grievous to hear them. The Earl of Derby," he adds, "was not accompanied by trumpets, nor the music of the town, but with tears and lamentations." If the tears of his countrymen were calculated to soothe the sorrows of his exile, they also watered his growing pride and ambi-

* Froissart, vol. xii. p. 56.

tion. After bidding farewell to a mourning multitude, he went to receive in France the welcome of princely and royal hospitality. The Dukes of Orleans and Berry, of Burgundy and Bourbon, went forth to meet him; the meeting was joyous; and they all together, the French princes and the English exile, entered Paris in brilliant array, to receive the welcome of the King of France.

It was brief banishment; and in bold defiance of his sentence did Bolingbroke come home to rescue his patrimony out of the rapacious grasp of the king's own hand. Having formerly played, and so successfully, the demagogue to the common people, he now begins to practice the same arts upon the nobles who join his cause. He gives them thanks; and, to win them to his service, he adds the large and kinglike promises of future bounty. He proclaims himself, too, a sworn reformer, and the unrelenting adversary of the King's vicious favourites,—

> "The caterpillars of the commonwealth,
> Which I have sworn to weed and cut away."

He begins his administration of the realm by commanding them to be delivered over to execution; as if he felt in himself the irresponsible power of a conqueror, or that his foot was already on the throne, which is the seat of justice. The multitude in the city of London, which wept when the banished Bolingbroke departed, welcomed him back, as the triumphant Lancaster, with joyful acclamations. The chronicler describes how men, women, and children, dressed in their best clothes, went out to meet and to greet him, and the poet-historian has finely told of it, through the voice of the Duke of York. It is a familiar passage of rare beauty:

"The duke, great Bolingbroke,
Mounted upon a hot and fiery steed,
Which his aspiring rider seem'd to know,
With slow, but stately pace, kept on his course,
While all tongues cried—God save thee, Bolingbroke!
You would have thought the very windows spake,
So many greedy looks of young and old,
Through casements darted their desiring eyes
Upon his visage; and that all the walls,
With painted imagery, had said at once,—
Jesu preserve thee! Welcome, Bolingbroke!
Whilst he, from one side to the other turning,
Bare-headed, lower than his proud steed's neck,
Bespake them thus,—*I thank you, countrymen;*
And thus still doing, thus he passed along."*

Never did the course of usurpation run more smoothly: it seemed to flow with a natural and even tide, as if simply because Richard was weak and Lancaster was strong. Looking at the personal conduct of Bolingbroke in the course of events before he became king, and considering the strict rule of hereditary succession as the settled law of the English monarchy, the Lancastrian establishment cannot but be regarded as an usurpation; but, on the other hand, remembering the sanction given to it by the Parliament, it may be viewed as one of those revolutionary changes by which, at successive periods, the British Constitution has been modified.

* I have had some hesitation as to repeating these familiar passages; but if quotations from Shakspeare are to be omitted because they are familiar, there could be no such thing as illustrations of a lecturer's meaning. Besides, who has not observed how often in a common Shakspearian passage, a rare beauty, a new suggestion reveals itself, when presented in a new relation. I have thought it best, therefore, with but few exceptions, to allow the quotations in these lectures to remain. W. B. R.

Such opposition as was made to Bolingbroke's accession, was met with prompt and stern punishment; for it was politic to strike quickly, and, if need be, bloodily. The Bishop of Carlisle, who alone among the English clergy had kept his allegiance to Richard in his day of adversity, drew down upon himself the weary punishment of lifelong imprisonment by the fearless protest which he made against the deposition of his sovereign. The nobles, who made an ineffectual resistance to the new succession, paid the bloody forfeit of their lives. It is for the ghastly tribute of their bleeding heads that Shakspeare represents the new king uttering his first royal acknowledgments.

Having now seen by what course of events, and by what course of policy and conduct, Henry of Lancaster became King Henry the Fourth of England, we have next to consider how royalty was worn by him, and whether the crown, which had been the object of his far-seeing and far-reaching ambition, proved its own sufficient reward—whether that, which, in Lady Macbeth's words—

> "To all his nights and days to come,
> Gave solely sovereign sway and masterdom,"

gave also sleep to those nights, and tranquillity to his days.

Let me, however, first remark that, in passing from the historical illustrations which the tragedy of Richard the Second supplied us with, in the last lecture, to the illustration we may find in the two parts of Henry the Fourth, one cannot help being struck with the boundless variety of Shakspeare's historic drama, and the versatility of his genius in dealing with these successive periods. While the "Chronicle-Plays" vary in structure and character, (no two of them closely corresponding,) they are all, for the most part, *tragedies*, for the simple reason that the history of human life is chiefly tragic, especially in the great historic descriptions of men, their deeds, and their fortunes. But the two parts of Henry the Fourth contain a large proportion of the *comic* element of life. Tragedy and comedy are here combined to produce the mixed drama. As the scenes change, we behold, as we read, the interior of the palace, with all the business and the stately anxieties and perplexities of the realm, or the castles of the nobles, where the dark game of conspiracy, or the bolder work of rebellion, is preparing; and then we turn to see the frolic and revelry of a London tavern, with the matchless wit of one of Shakspeare's most remarkable creations sparkling through the sensuality and profligacy of the place. We are now at Windsor with the king, or at Bangor with the insurgent nobles; and then we are at the Boar's Head Tavern, with Falstaff and his gay companions. We see Henry the Fourth, in his palace, growing wan and careworn with the troubles of his government, becoming an old man in midlife; and then we see Falstaff fat, and, doubtless, growing fatter as he takes his ease at his inn,—an old man of more than threescore years, but with a boyish flow of frolic and spirits,—indulging his inexhaustible wit by making merriment for himself and the heir-apparent. We see in this mixed drama the tragic side of war—civil war—with the perplexity of the councils of the realm and the fierce deeds of battle; and we see the comic side—Falstaff misusing the king's press—the conscription code of the times,—not gathering *volunteers* for the war, but picking out of the community comfortable, well conditioned, non-combatant folk, who, as he calculates, will be sure to buy a release, so that he boasts to himself of having got in exchange for one hundred and fifty soldiers three hundred and odd pounds, to pay his tavern-bill, or rather to leave his tavern-bill unpaid. "I press me," says he "none but good householders, yeomen's sons, inquire me out contracted bachelors, such as had been asked twice upon the bans, such a commodity of warm slaves as had as lief hear the devil as a drum, such as fear the report of a caliver worse than a struck fowl or a hurt wild-duck. I pressed me none but such toasts and butter, with hearts in their bellies no bigger than pin's heads, and they have bought their services."

The ludicrous aspect of war and the suffering consequent upon it are further shown in Falstaff's well-known description of his soldiers—"the canker of a calm world and a long peace,"—the vagabonds he was ashamed to march through Coventry with. The link of association between the serious and the comic parts of these plays is to be found in the character of him who is the Prince Henry of the palace and the Prince Hal of his boon-companions in the tavern—for we meet with him in both places, more at home, however, in the places of his amusement than in the place of his rank. It is such mixed dramas as the two parts of Henry the Fourth, that especially illustrate the remark of Mr. Hallam, that Shakspeare's historical plays "borrow surprising liveliness and probability from the national character and form of government. A prince, a courtier, and a slave are the stuff on which the historic dramatist would have to work in some countries: but every class of freemen, in the just subordination without which neither human society nor the stage, which should be its mirror, can be more than a chaos of huddled units, lay open to the inspection of Shakspeare. What he invented is as truly English, as truly historical in the large sense of moral history, as what he read."* In the tragedy of King John we had, you will remember, as the representative of humble life and character, only James Gurney, with his conversation of four words; but in Henry the Fourth, we have, I will not say *humble* life, but English *low* life, in a company of such persons as may well be supposed to have frequented a London tavern in those days.

I am inclined to think that Shakspeare felt, that in treating dramatically the reign of Henry the Fourth he must needs expand the sphere of the drama, so as to comprehend these varied elements, in order to supply the meagre historical interest of the subject. The exuberance of his genius and of his feelings required something more than the cold, uneventful misery of the palace of the politic Henry; and accordingly going down to the lower stratum of society, he must have delighted in creating Falstaff and his associates, to make amends for the dull company of the king, and the courtiers and nobles.

The reign of Henry the Fourth is an uninteresting period of English history; especially does it want *national* interest. After all his long-sustained and successful ambition, he came to his years of royalty, and they proved years of unceasing solicitude and uncertainty. The old chronicler utters simple truth, when he speaks of "the unquiet times of King Henry's reign;" and one of the

* Literature of Europe, vol. ii. p. 395.

elder English historians accurately describes it, when he says "King Henry's reign was like a craggy mountain, from which there was no descent, but by a thousand crooked ways full of rocky stones and jetting cliffs—the first difficulties escaped, others are met with of more danger and anxiety. In such paths he walked all the time of his reign, that one danger was a step to another, and the event always doubtful; for his subjects' former desire being almost extinguished, his friends failing, and his enemies increasing, he had no other support in so painful a descent but his own vigilance and conduct,—helps, which, though they might cause him to keep on his way, yet they were not sufficient to preserve him from great weariness." And Shakspeare, with that remarkable significancy which he gives to the openings of his plays, indicates in the very first line, the character of the reign, when the king is introduced, saying—

> "So shaken as we are, so wan with care,
> Find we a time for frighted peace to pant."

It is historically true, also, when he is represented, at the beginning of the play and of his reign, meditating a crusade, planning an expedition from England,

> "To chase these pagans in those holy fields,
> Over whose acres walked those blessed feet,
> Which fourteen hundred years ago were nailed,
> For our advantage, on the bitter cross."

Whether this purpose was prompted by the desire to make atonement for such criminality as attended his accession to the throne, by the ecclesiastical service of a crusade, or with the more politic design of diverting the thoughts of the nation from the question of his title, or whether, as is most probable, it was a mingled motive of policy and of the devotional spirit of the times, it can hardly be doubted that the thought was seriously entertained by the king. When we read of such an intention at the period in which he flourished, we are apt, I think, to err from one or two causes, which lead us to think of it as altogether unreal—as a piece of mere dramatic effect. We do so, because we refer the spirit of the Crusades to an earlier era of European history, and also because modern historians are much disposed to treat such purposes as not only superstitious and visionary but hypocritical; so that when we read of this intention of Henry the Fourth's, carrying our modern notions back, we are, I believe, almost as incredulous as if we had been informed that George the Fourth had meditated a crusade. But in the case of Henry the Fourth, let it be remembered that, in early life, he had travelled to the Holy Land, and must have witnessed the gradual encroachment of the Turkish power, and the decline of the Christian empire in the East; he was too sagacious an observer not to discover that unless Western Christendom came to the rescue, the Turk could not be withstood. Moreover, it was at the beginning of Henry's reign that a Greek emperor, came from Constantinople to London to solicit from his fellow-Christians assistance for the defence of his capital and his empire against the aggressions of the Turks.* The help was not given; and in

* "When Manuel had satiated the curiosity, and perhaps fatigued the patience of the French, he resolved on a visit to the adjacent island. In his progress from Dover, he was entertained at Canterbury with due reverence by the prior and monks of St. Austin; and, on Blackheath, King Henry the Fourth, with the English court, saluted the Greek hero, who, during many days, was lodged and treated in

half a century, within the lifetime of many who were living when Henry the Fourth meditated his crusade, Mohammed with his Turks did advance, in overwhelming force, upon the capital of the Byzantine Cæsars; the Greek empire, after its life of more than a thousand years, fell; and from that day to this the Crescent, and not the Cross, has glittered in the sunbeams which shine upon the city of Constantine. It can now be no more than a mere historical speculation to think how differently the world's history might have been affected—how the cause of Christianity might have been influenced, if that ancient Christian empire in the East had been upheld,—if some holy St. Bernard had kindled the heart of European Christendom for the enterprise of a later crusade; and what a glorious destiny it would have been for Britain, if the work had been achieved by British power,—if Henry the Fourth, strong man and sagacious statesman as he was, could have devoted to such a cause the courage and wisdom by which he both gained and kept the throne of England!

The intended crusade was frustrated by impending

London as emperor of the East. But the state of England was still more adverse to the design of the holy war. In the same year, the hereditary sovereign had been deposed and murdered; the reigning prince was a successful usurper, whose ambition was punished by jealousy and remorse; nor could Henry of Lancaster withdraw his person or forces from the defence of a throne incessantly shaken by conspiracy and rebellion. He pitied, he praised, he feasted, the emperor of Constantinople; but if the English monarch assumed the cross, it was only to appease his people, and perhaps his conscience, by the merit or semblance of this pious intention." Gibbon's Decline and Fall of the Roman Empire, chap. lxvi., Milman's edition, vol. vi. p. 221. W. B. R.

danger at home. Scarcely was Henry the Fourth seated on his throne, when the flame of war was kindled upon both the western and northern frontiers of England. The people of Wales were in arms against him; and the Scots, who were, I may say, the perpetual foes of the English, came down upon the Lowlands with a strong tide of invasion. The Douglas, who led that Scottish inroad, was defeated at the battle of Holmedon Hill, and the Scots repulsed; but, while the kingdom was successfully defended, the victory proved the remote cause of new difficulties and dangers to the king. The victory was gained by the son of the Earl of Northumberland, Henry Percy, better known, as Shakspeare has made it so familiar, by the name of Hotspur. It was by the help of these same Percies, father and son, that Bolingbroke had dethroned Richard the Second and made himself king. The victory over the Scots gave to the Percies another and a new claim upon their sovereign. There are minds so constituted that nothing distresses or oppresses them more than a sense of obligation; especially will this weakness of our poor human nature betray itself in minds in which pride is a large element—pride in their own powers and resources. The gratitude is doubtless doubly burdensome when a king feels that it is to his nobles, of whom lately he was one, that he owes his crown. There is danger of their becoming arrogant, and his becoming suspicious; and the power that is built on usurpation is most apt, too, to grow jealous and tyrannical.

It is not surprising, then, to find Hotspur's victory quickly followed by his quarrel with the king, in consequence of the demand for the delivery of the prisoners taken in the battle of Holmedon. The quarrel is still further fomented by the demand, which, on the other hand, Hotspur makes on the king to ransom his brother-in-law, Mortimer, who, while leading an expedition against the Welsh, had been taken prisoner by Glendower. But Mortimer was one of that branch of the royal family, whose better title Henry the Fourth had trespassed on; and now, instead of ransoming, he accuses him of the wilful betraying his command; and replies to Hotspur's request—

> "Shall our coffers, then,
> Be emptied, to redeem a traitor home?
> * * * *
> No, on the barren mountains let him starve;
> For I shall never hold that man my friend,
> Whose tongue shall ask me for one penny cost,
> To ransom home revolted Mortimer."

The unwonted passion of the king's language betrays his sense of the unsoundness of his own title, and the jealousy of the better right of the Mortimers; and Hotspur's reply is in the finest vein of indignant vindication:

> "Revolted Mortimer!
> He never did fall off, my sovereign liege,
> But by the chance of war;—to prove that true,
> Needs no more but one tongue for all those wounds,
> Those mouthed wounds, which valiantly he took,
> When on the gentle Severn's sedgy bank,
> In single opposition, hand to hand,
> He did confound the best part of an hour,
> In changing hardiment with great Glendower:
> Three times they breath'd, and three times did they drink,
> Upon agreement, of swift Severn's flood;
> Who, then, affrighted with their bloody looks,
> Ran fearfully among the trembling reeds,
> And hid his crisp head in the hollow bank,

Bloodstained with these valiant combatants.
Never did bare and rotten policy
Colour her working with such deadly wounds;
Nor never could the noble Mortimer
Receive so many, and all willingly.
Then let him not be slandered with revolt."

The defence is in vain—the king implacable—and the conspiracy of the Percies is afoot. Hotspur theatens—

"I will lift the downtrod Mortimer
As high i' the air as this unthankful king,
As this ingrate and cankered Bolingbroke."

He speaks of his sovereign as no more than Bolingbroke; and when he learns from the elder Percies, that in the reign of Richard the Second, a Mortimer had been proclaimed the rightful heir, he adds—

"Nay, then I cannot blame his cousin king,
That wished him on the barren mountains starved.
But shall it be that you, that set the crown
Upon the head of this forgetful man,
And, for his sake, wear the detested blot
Of murd'rous subornation, shall it be,
That you a world of curses undergo,
Being the agents, or base second means,
The cords, the ladder, or the hangman rather?—
O, pardon me, that I descend so low,
To show the line and the predicament
Wherein you range under this subtle king.
Shall it, for shame, be spoken in these days,
Or fill up chronicles in time to come,
That men of your nobility and power
Did gage them both in an unjust behalf
As both of you, God pardon it! have done
To put down Richard, that sweet lovely rose,
And plant this thorn, this canker, Bolingbroke?"

The character of Hotspur, which gives so much spirit and splendour to the revolt of the Percies, furnishes various historical illustration of the character of the age. When Shakspeare introduced him into the drama, the character was already familiar to the popular mind by those fine old ballads, '*The Battle of Chevy Chase*,' and '*The Battle of Otterbourne*,' those rude strains, which had kindled the noble and heroic spirit of Sir Philip Sydney, and of which, in a well-known passage of his '*Defence of Poesy*,' he said, "I never heard the old song of Percy and Douglas, that I found not my heart moved more than with a trumpet."*

These antiquated poems supply illustration of the story and character of Hotspur, by showing that the bravery which Shakspeare has made his chief endowment had been developed in his previous life, in that border-warfare which kept the frontier of England and Scotland in perpetual turmoil. It was a state of watchful and revengeful hostilities; and, as the rugged stanza of the old ballad of Chevy Chase describes it—

"There was never a time on the march parts,
Sin the Douglas and the Percy met,
But it was marvel an the red blood ran not
As the rain does in the street."

It was in this warfare that Hotspur had acquired that indomitable confidence in his personal prowess, that physical bravery which courts danger for danger's sake, and which lives on the very excitement of encountering and

* Page 45, vol. ii. of the American edition of the Library of Old English Prose Writers, edited by Dr. Young.

overcoming the perils of war. This is one form of the soldier's character which Shakspeare has so brilliantly depicted in his history of that time.

While considering the character of Hotspur, historical as it is, I would point your attention to what is, I think, an historical use which the poet-historian makes of the character of Falstaff—an historical use at the same time that there is high poetic art in it. Hotspur and Falstaff (it seems strange to mention them together) are both, let it be remembered, soldiers. They both represent the military life and character of that period of English history; and Shakspeare has so fashioned them as to produce one of the finest and most expressive contrasts in the whole range of his dramas. The characters are thus, if you will closely examine them, made to expound each other by their very contrariety. In this there would be high poetic art; but the historical question here is this, —if, as I have sought to show, the border warfare acting upon such a natural disposition as the young Percy's, made him the impetuous, martial, danger-coveting Hotspur, what was there in the events or the social condition of that age to produce so different a form of the military character as that of Falstaff? The character of Hotspur becomes expressive of the historical causes which made him the soldier he was; and, in like manner, I think, we may discover historical causes of which Falstaff's character may become expressive. He was old enough to have seen service in the wars of Edward the Third; he had been page to the Earl of Norfolk, a valiant nobleman;* he lived on into the unwarlike and voluptu-

* "Then," says Justice Shallow, "was Jack Falstaff, now Sir John, a boy; and page to Thomas Mowbray, Duke of Norfolk."

ous reign of Richard the Second; and an old soldier, with such a sensual and self-indulgent nature as Shakspeare has given to Falstaff, would be very likely to settle down in London, to grow fat and lazy and luxurious. There are, therefore, it seems to me, historical causes of a very different kind; which, working upon two very different natures, are adequate to explain the monstrous difference between these contemporary soldiers, Hotspur and Falstaff. Each character has, therefore, its historical significancy, and the contrast between them becomes highly expressive. You find Hotspur seeking danger for danger's sake, joyous and enthusiastic at the mere prospect of it. When Worcester intimates to him a plan—

"As full of peril and adventurous spirit,
As to o'erwalk a current, roaring loud,
On the unsteadfast footing of a spear."

The quick answer is—

"If he fall in, good night!—or sink or swim;—
Send danger from the east unto the west,
So honour cross it from the north to south,
And let them grapple;—O! the blood more stirs,
To rouse a lion than to start a hare."

Falstaff has a well-settled conclusion in his mind that—

"The better part of valour is discretion."

He is by no means a constitutional coward; but, certainly, danger has in itself no charms in his eyes. Again, he is absolutely indifferent to honour, he has no sense of it or the value of it; with his intellectual activity, he convinces himself logically of the worthlessness of it:—"Can honour set a leg? No. Or an arm? No. Or take away the grief of a wound? No. Honour hath no skill in surgery then? No." Therefore he wants none of it. Then compare Hotspur's rhapsody:

"Methinks it were an easy leap
To pluck bright honour from the pale-faced moon;
Or dive into the bottom of the deep,
Where fathom-line could never touch the ground,
And pluck up drowned honour by the locks;
So he, that doth redeem her thence, might wear,
Without corrival, all her dignities."

Before the battle of Shrewsbury, Falstaff's thought is—

"Would it were bed-time, Hal, and all well."

When Hotspur, immediately after his disappointment as to the reinforcement from Northumberland, hears of the advance of the superior force of the royal army, his only wish is—

"Let them come;
They come like sacrifices in their trim.
And to the fire-eyed maid of smoky war,
All hot and bleeding, will we offer them:
The mailed Mars shall on his altar sit,
Up to the ears in blood. I am on fire,
To hear this rich reprisal is so nigh,
And yet not ours."

In this the spirit of the border warfare flashes out. The rebellion of the Percies was strengthened by confederacy with that remarkable personage, the Welsh chieftain, Owen Glendower. Of his character and career little is distinctly known, and that little through the narratives of his foes. There rests over his history the vail of a splendid mystery; and Shakspeare has represented him chiefly as seen through the obscurity of popular tradition, according to which the Welsh hero was looked on as a wizard and magician, who could not only sway the hearts of his countrymen, but could command and control the elements. Glendower had given allegiance to Richard; but, disclaiming the sovereignty of Bolingbroke, he raised the standard of revolt in Wales, and his scattered countrymen—among the rest the Welsh students at Oxford and Cambridge—hastened home to rally round his banner. He assumed the title of Prince of Wales, and made the last effort for the restoration of the independence of his country. It has been well said—

"Owyn Glendower failed, and he was denounced as a rebel and a traitor: but had the issue of the 'sorry fight' at Shrewsbury been otherwise than it was; had Hotspur so devised and digested and matured his plan of operations as to have enabled Owyn with his forces to join heart and hand in that hard-fought field; had Bolingbroke and his son fallen on that fatal day; instead of lingering among his native mountains as a fugitive and a branded felon, bereft of his lands, his friends, his children, and his wife, waiting only the blow of death to terminate his earthly sufferings; and, when that blow fell, leaving no memorial behind him to mark either the time or the place of his release, Owyn Glendower might have been recognised, even by England, as he was by France, in the character of an independent sovereign, and his people might have celebrated his name as the avenger of his country's wrongs, the scourge of his oppressors, and the restorer of her independence." While Shakspeare has done ample justice to the character of the noblest of the Percies, he leaves on our minds, with admirable impartiality, a strong sense of the selfish origin of the revolt, and the danger of such an overgrown and arrogant aristocracy. It was one of the evils of the feudal times that men did not shrink from the horrors of domestic war; because, isolated as they were,—chieftain from chieftain, and one set of vassals from another,—the relations of countrymen and fellow-citizens were not known, or at least were not felt. Hotspur, habituated, too, to his independent border warfare, was apt, on provocation, to turn his hostilities against his king, as he might do against the Douglas or any other Scottish noble. Whatever may be thought of the defect of Henry's title to the throne, there could hardly be a greater political evil than the existence of an aristocracy strong enough and proud enough to build up or to pull down the monarchy at their will. This was the pride of the Percies, as Hotspur boasted—

"My father, and my uncle, and myself,
Did give him that same royalty he wears:
And,—when he was not six-and-twenty strong,
Sick in the world's regard, wretched and low,
A poor unminded outlaw sneaking home,—
My father gave him welcome to the shore:
And,—when he heard him swear and vow to God,
He came but to be Duke of Lancaster,
To sue his livery, and beg his peace;
With tears of innocency, and terms of zeal,—
My father, in kind heart and pity moved,
Swore him assistance, and performed it too.
Now, when the lords and barons of the realm
Perceived Northumberland did lean to him,
The more and less came in with cap and knee;
Met him in boroughs, cities, villages;
Attended him on bridges, stood in lanes,

> Laid gifts before him, proffered him their oaths,
> Gave him their heirs; as pages follow'd him,
> Even at the heels, in golden multitudes.
> He presently—as greatness knows itself—
> Steps me a little higher than his vow
> Made to my father, while his blood was poor,
> Upon the naked shore at Ravenspurg."

But the pride of the Percies had its fall; and, when they were defeated at Shrewsbury, and Hotspur left dead on that field of battle, the throne of Henry the Fourth was more firmly fixed than before that proud race of nobles had levied war against him.

The unquiet times, however, were not tranquillized; and Henry's reign was, in truth, no more than a succession of conspiracies. The battle of Shrewsbury secured but a brief space of repose, which was soon disturbed by the conspiracy of the Earl of Northumberland, and Mowbray, and the Archbishop of York. This revolt was quelled, not by another battle, but by policy; and the strong king again proved too strong for his adversaries. But, while his possession of the throne was triumphantly maintained, the crown was glittering on the brow of a melancholy man. The genius of a great poet gives us the vision of the royal sadness; and it is poetry and history combined, that present the affecting spectacle of a careworn king in the scene where Henry, in the noiseless hour of the night, in the lonely splendour of his palace, with slumber estranged from his eyelids, beholding from the palace-window the silent dwellings in a sleeping city, gives utterance to that beautiful apostrophe to sleep:

> "How many thousand of my poorest subjects
> Are at this hour asleep!—Sleep, gentle sleep,

Nature's soft nurse, how have I frighted thee,
That thou no more wilt weigh my eyelids down,
And steep my senses in forgetfulness?
Why, rather, Sleep, liest thou in smoky cribs,
Upon uneasy pallets stretching thee,
And hush'd with buzzing night-flies to thy slumber;
Than in the perfumed chambers of the great,
Under the canopies of costly state,
And lull'd with sounds of sweetest melody?
O! thou dull god, why liest thou with the vile
In loathsome beds; and leavest the kingly couch
A watch-case, or a common 'larum bell?
Wilt thou upon the high and giddy mast
Seal up the ship-boy's eyes, and rock his brains
In cradle of the rude imperious surge,
And in the visitation of the winds,
Who take the ruffian billows by the top,
Curling their monstrous heads, and hanging them
With deafening clamours in the slippery clouds,
That, with the hurly, death itself awakes?
Canst thou, O partial Sleep, give thy repose
To the wet seaboy in an hour so rude;
And, in the calmest and most stillest night,
With all appliances and means to boot,
Deny it to a king? Then, happy low, lie down!
Uneasy lies the head that wears a crown."

That aching brow was soon to find repose; those sleepless eyelids were at length to be closed,—but only in the grave. "Henry Bolingbroke," it has been said, "had reigned thirteen years 'in great perplexity and little pleasure.' He had reaped as he had sown—care, insecurity, suspicion, enmity, and treason; and 'curses not loud but deep.' Having quelled the rebellious nobles, he revived the project of a voyage to the Holy Land, to recover Jerusalem from the infidels. Preparations were made for the expedition, and the king went to the shrine of St. Edward the Confessor, at Westminster, there to take his leave and to speed him on his voyage."* The hand of death fell on his careworn body there, and he was carried, to breathe his last, in the adjoining house of the abbot, and not in the palace of the Plantagenets.

* Southey's Naval History, vol. ii. p. 50.

LECTURE VII.*

The Character and Reign of Henry the Fifth.

Sorrowful but vigorous reign of the fourth Henry—His successor Shakspeare's favourite—His reign of conquest—His career as Prince of Wales—Not profligate but popular—A prince and a gentleman—His honour to Richard's memory—Veneration for his father—Relations of heirs-apparent—Statute against heresy—The Proto martyr—Contrast of the prince and his brother, Prince John—Macbeth's want of children—Henry the Fifth a genial character—His associates of early life—The character of Falstaff considered—Morgann's essay—Friendship—Hamlet and Horatio—Henry and Falstaff—Falstaff's cowardice—Mr. Senior's criticism—Henry's accession to the throne—The war with France—Battle of Agincourt—Henry's relations to his soldiers—Sir Thomas Erpingham—Death of York and Suffolk—The tragedy a triumphal song.

I HAVE endeavoured, with the help of Shakspeare's matchless historical illustrations, to recall to your minds the character of the first of the Lancastrian reigns, and to show how Henry Bolingbroke, after having climbed up the proud and royal eminence of his ambition, held the throne by strong statesmanship against the aggression of the nobles. The moral aspect of the reign, which we learn better from the page of poetry than of history, was simply this,—that Henry the Fourth wore the crown of England an anxious and melancholy man; and, while in

* February 8th, 1847.

his accession, there was more of craft and less of atrocity than in the Scottish usurper, there were, doubtless, times when, in the still hours of his sleepless nights, and in the silent chambers of his palace, and in the more secret and silent chambers of his conscience, he felt the guilty sinking of the heart—

"Better be with the dead
Whom we to gain our place have sent to peace,
Than on the torture of the mind to lie
In restless ecstasy."

The cares which saddened the royal years of the life of Henry the Fourth, did not, however, engender that sorrow which saps the strength. The strong, though sad-hearted, man held the throne until his dying day; and held it so firmly, that it passed, in due course of law, to his son, Henry of Monmouth; to whose reign, as Henry the Fifth, the regular progression of our subject has now brought us.

Of the many English sovereigns whom Shakspeare has placed in imperishable individuality before us, Henry the Fifth was manifestly the favourite of the poet's heart; and, in the multitude of the characters of all kinds whom he has portrayed or created, probably no subject was more congenial to him than the whole career of Henry the Fifth from his first introduction as Prince of Wales. Indeed, it could hardly be otherwise; for, of the nine kings who appear in Shakspeare's historical plays, there is but one—and that one, Henry the Fifth—whose character is fairly entitled to the praise of greatness, in the large sense of that term, which comprehends genuine glory and virtue. He was the only one of those crowned heads in whom royalty was united to a fine and lofty humanity. Therefore it is that, without forsaking the path of that admirable historical impartiality, in which the genius of the poet-historian forever moved, he found in the character of Henry the Fifth, and in him alone, scope for the richest panegyric which the soul of a great poet could, out of its abundant affluence, shower upon the memory of a fellow-man. I have already adverted to the variety displayed in the composition of these "Chronicle-Plays;" and, as the reign of Henry the Fifth was greatly distinguished from the other reigns, so is the drama, which is devoted to it, altogether peculiar. The reign was a short and splendid career of foreign conquest, achieved by one who was at once king, hero, and conqueror; and the play is a kind of lyrical commemoration of the victory and the victor.

Henry the Fifth had a brief reign of nine years; but this was preceded by a period of his life, the memory of which is closely connected with the estimate of his character,—the thirteen years of his father's reign, during which he was Prince of Wales. There came down to Shakspeare not only a very distinct tradition, but also complete historical consent, that Henry's career as Prince of Wales was one of unwonted levity and unworthy companionship; and, upon such tradition and such historical account, the poet has so worked as to give a most vivid impression of the life of the heir-apparent during his father's reign. The dramatic skill with which this has been done, is unquestioned; but it may also, I believe, be shown that there is equal historical fidelity; and, passing into a still higher region of thought, I think it may be shown that the poet has herein displayed that moral wisdom which is one great element of all his dramas; and, indeed, without which, poetry of the highest order cannot exist.

Respecting the career of the Prince of Wales, there appear to be two opposite and conflicting opinions. On the one hand he is represented as a low profligate, reckless, heartless, and dissolute, the perpetual inmate of taverns, and a licentious brawler. On the other side, the effort is made, and with considerable historical research, to prove that the traditional accounts of the prince's early life are altogether unfounded; that Shakspeare's representation of him, as an historical portrait, is misleading and unjust, and that the prince's life was blameless and irreproachable. Indeed, it might well be said, that a career of excessive profligacy, continued through the years of youth and into the years of manhood, could not in nature be the prelude to a kingly course so sagacious and so heroic. I do not believe that Henry of Monmouth, when Prince of Wales, lived such a life of dissoluteness and profligacy; and more confident am I that Shakspeare has not so represented it. At the same time the tradition respecting the prince was too general and too well fortified to be wholly discredited. It cannot reasonably be cast aside as a fiction by which men for a long while—and nobody can tell why—deluded themselves and others. Shakspeare is faithful to the tradition, which he has so informed with the life-giving power of the imagination as to corroborate the truth of it; and at the same time he has so portrayed Henry's princely days, as to reconcile them with his royal days, and thus to represent them in moral harmony. He does not resort to the marvel of a sudden conversion and an instantaneous growth of virtue—a monstrous and unnatural change—which would effectually hinder us from feeling the identity of the Prince Henry of one drama with the King Henry of another. With Shakspeare's guidance, therefore, we can, I am inclined to think, learn what the one, but varied, life of Henry really was; for the poet drew the history of that life from tradition, and also from the deep philosophy of human nature in his own soul.

When Prince Henry is first introduced into the drama, it is in the palace, but in the company of two of his gay companions, who visit him there. Whatever contaminating influences there were in such companionship, it was, at least, free from the vice of destroying his moral health by the poison of flattery. So far from any thing like this adulation, the conventional restraints of rank are cast aside—even the decorous formalities of society are relaxed—and there is an equality of intercourse and almost unbounded freedom in it. But all this is on the surface, and does not reach down to the real nature of the prince; for, the moment he is left alone, the first words he utters, disclose his knowledge of himself and of his companions, and his consciousness of what is due from himself to himself. We see that he has a moral self-possession—whether it will be impaired by such companionship and self-indulgence remains to be considered; but the first soliloquy shows us that, at least, he was not reckless, but that he was thoughtful; and that, whatever might be the outward show, silently and secretly he was cherishing lofty and pure aspirations:

"I know you all, and will awhile uphold
The unyoked humour of your idleness;
Yet herein will I imitate the sun,

Who doth permit the base contagious clouds
To smother up his beauty from the world,
That when he please again to be himself,
Being wanted, he may be more wondered at,
By breaking through the foul and ugly mists
Of vapours that did seem to strangle him.
If all the year were playing holidays,
To sport would be as tedious as to work;
But when they seldom come, they wished-for come,
And nothing pleaseth but rare accidents.
So when this loose behaviour I throw off,
And pay the debt I never promised,
By how much better than my word I am,
By so much shall I falsify men's hopes;
And like bright metal on a sullen ground,
My reformation, glittering o'er my fault,
Shall show more goodly and attract more eyes
Than that which hath no foil to set it off.
I'll so offend to make offence a skill;
Redeeming time when men think least I will."

This soliloquy, at his first introduction, sets before us the thoughtful element in the prince's character; and we are thus forewarned of the reserved power by which he will be able to raise himself above the loose behaviour and companionship he for a while indulges in. It is, doubtless, a perilous calculation,—present self-indulgence and prospective reformation,—and we shall see, in a subsequent passage of his life, as represented by Shakspeare, that the transition is not accomplished without a struggle. But, during this whole course of free life, the prince is never so represented as to make us forget that he is a prince and a gentleman—never so lowered as to make him forfeit all respect, or falsify the promise given by the hidden thoughtfulness of his nature. Still, the question occurs—both historically and dramatically—was this a career of wanton self-indulgence, or were there causes and impulses which gave such strange direction to his early manhood? I believe his alienation, such as it was, from the palace and the court, was in accordance both with historical truth, and the requisites of poetic art; but to show this, we must look back on his earlier days.

During the first thirteen years of his life, high as was the rank of the family, Henry of Monmouth was the son, not of a king, but of a nobleman; the years of his boyhood were spent, therefore, without the restraints and formalities of a royal household. He lived as one of the people, and learned to feel as such. This feeling of freedom was, doubtless, increased by the high-spirited boy being early initiated into military life. It is worthy of notice that, when a mere youth, he received the honour of knighthood; and, what is still more noticeable, he received it at the hands of his sovereign, the frail and unfortunate Richard the Second. To the memory of that monarch, dethroned as he was by his father, Henry of Monmouth appears to have cherished a feeling of respectful gratitude. That sentiment could exist in his mind only in conflict with the sentiment and the duty of filial piety; and it is precisely such a conflict of obligation and feeling, working upon sensitive and thoughtful dispositions, that wrests them from their even and natural course. Remember, by way of example, how the gentle and meditative spirit of Hamlet was affected, even unto the unsettling of his intellect, by the conflict between duty to his living mother, and the profound love and veneration to his dead father—it forced him to moody musing and fitful melancholy. We can conceive how, in like manner, though in a very different degree, a thoughtful character like the Prince of Wales may have had his youthful hours of painful reflection, when he was old enough to observe the establishment of his father's power upon the ruins of the fallen royalty of Richard. Having seen his first military adventures under the banner of Richard, having, too, received honours from him which would naturally sink deep into a generous heart, then in the full flush of uncalculating youth, Henry may well have looked with commiseration, at least, upon the decline and downfall of his first king, although the revolution placed the crown upon his father's brow, and showed the succession in prospect for himself. Now, I do not mean to assert that this was so; but considering what we do know of his later character and conduct, it is not an unreasonable speculation which leads us to think there were times when the breast of this young prince was agitated by the various and contending emotions of pride at the elevation of his family, duty to his father, and the lingering loyalty to the poor dethroned Richard, or pity for the memory and the misfortunes of his first chieftain. One of the first acts of Henry's reign was to cause the body of Richard the Second to be removed from its secluded grave at Langley, and with the solemn funeral pomp of kings to be interred at Westminster by the side of his queen,—"the good Queen Anne,"—in the tomb which Richard had caused to be prepared for her and for himself. It is to this act of pious loyalty that Shakspeare refers when he represents Henry, on the eve of his great battle, as praying—

> "Not to day, O Lord!
> Oh, not to day! think not upon the fault
> My father made in compassing the crown!

> I Richard's body have interred anew;
> And on it have bestowed more contrite tears
> Than from it issued forced drops of blood.
> Five hundred poor I have in yearly pay,
> Who twice a day their withered hands hold up
> Toward heaven, to pardon blood; and I have built
> Two chantries, where the sad and solemn priests
> Sing still for Richard's soul."

It will be observed, therefore, that the speculation respecting Henry's feeling towards his former sovereign—the king of his boyhood—has an actual historical basis. I will not venture to push this speculation so far as to say that the sentiment which I have just spoken of alienated his affection from his father; that he cherished such loyalty to the dead Richard's memory as to induce a slack allegiance to his living king—an unnatural estrangement from his own parent. But I do believe that there may most naturally have existed in the mind of the Prince of Wales such a state of conflicting emotion as to make the palace of his father uncongenial to him. His is not the constitution of Hamlet, and he does not, like the heart-stricken Prince of Denmark, wander through the royal chambers disconsolate, moody, and meditative; but he goes forth into the world—into the common throng of the world—into the crowded thoroughfares of life. All that is certainly known of this part of his career, leaves upon the mind an impression which associates him not at all with his father's accession to the throne, and only occasionally with his father's administration of the kingdom; and Shakspeare's representation is, therefore, in complete harmony with the imperfect historical information. The highest dramatic art and general fidelity to history are here combined to work out the poet's purpose of portraying the character of a king who should be entitled to be respected and honoured and loved; and this was to be accomplished by no fulsome adulation, by no monstrous eulogy, but by plain dealing with the imperfections of human nature.

On the one hand, it was necessary so far to preserve the relations between Prince Henry and Henry the Fourth as to avoid all imputation of a deliberate unfilial conduct, of purposed undutifulness from the son to the father. This would have cast a cloud that would have darkened all his after story. It would have been too like what has occurred at a more modern period of British history, when, in the family of the Hanoverian kings, the relation of father and son seemed to be governed by a law of reciprocal dislike and repugnance; as when, in the reign of George the First, his son, the Prince of Wales, resented, by a premeditated insult, what he spoke of as his father's "insolence" to him; and the king resented the undutiful conduct by turning the heir-apparent out of the palace: or when, some twenty years later, that Prince of Wales, after he had become George the Second, under very much the same circumstances, went through the same ceremony which had been practised on himself, by turning his son, the Prince of Wales, out of doors; so that this kind of disreputable family feud seemed to be a part of the law of inheritance,—which was again shown, too, in the case of George the Third and his Prince of Wales.* Now, inasmuch as these half-German princes

* In reference to the early Hanover kings and princes, it has often occurred to me that the later Stuarts must have been bad indeed when a moral nation, such as the English, could prefer and endure repulsive

of later days were greatly inferior to the more ancient Prince of Wales, and as history makes mention of no such scandalous squabbling between him and Henry the Fourth, whatever cause of dissatisfaction Prince Henry may have given, it was not of such a nature as to affix a lasting stain upon his name. When his father reproaches him with his habits of life, the answer is in a strain, not of insolent resentment, but of modest and placid respectful defence:

"So please your majesty, I would I could
Quit all offences with as clear excuse,
As well as, I am doubtless, I can purge
Myself of many I am charged withal;
Yet such extenuation let me beg,
As in reproof of many tales devised,—
Which oft the ear of greatness needs must hear,—
By smiling pick-thanks and base newsmongers,
I may, for some things true, wherein my youth
Hath faulty wandered and irregular,
Find pardon on my true submission."

The continued remonstrance and admonition of the king are answered simply—

"I shall hereafter, my thrice gracious lord,
Be more myself."

---

reprobates—coarse adulterers, and violaters of every domestic tie—such as were George the First and Second, and Prince Frederic. Is there not some faint analogy in our day—the points of contrast being equally marked—between Falstaff and poor Sheridan? I have somewhere seen a very sad narrative of an accidental meeting, on the road near Brighton, of Sheridan, not long before his death, and the Prince Regent; and Sheridan, in his threadbare coat, turning down a bypath to avoid his former friend. As Hostess Quickly says of Falstaff when dying,—"The king had killed his heart." W. B. R.

Neither in the history of the chronicler nor in the history of the poet does there appear any such enmity between the king and the Prince of Wales, as would throw an impediment in the way of our admiration and enjoyment of the son's character. We feel that it is a difference easily adjusted; and the prince is entitled so to speak, when he gayly tells his companions—

"I am good friends with my father, and may do any thing."

Now, while the filial relation is duly preserved, it is, on the other hand, desirable that Prince Henry should not be too intimately identified with his father's reign. It is well that he, whose glorious career is to be the theme of a poet's richest praise, should not be associated in our thoughts with an administration of the realm which was so different from his own—a reign of terror and not of loyal love—a reign of divided and not unanimous allegiance. The dominion of Henry the Fourth was that of stern, hard, suspicious power. There were conspiracies, and craft and policy were needed to countermine them; but we are glad to believe that, as Shakspeare, following the traditions, has represented it, Prince Hal took little, if any, part in such affairs of the realm. Besides, the reign of Henry the Fourth was not only an unquiet and perplexed time, but it was a dismal era of the beginning of religious persecution. It was in that reign that the stern law was enacted, by which heresy was to be punished with the slow torture of the death by fire, and the Proto-martyr of English Reformers perished at the stake.*

* Stat. 2, Hen. 4, c. 15. *De heretico comburendo.* The preamble sets forth "that divers unauthorized preachers go about teaching new

It was part of the administration of Henry the Fourth to crush the progress of the first movement of the Reformation, which began with John Wycliff and the Lollards. With a reign thus characterized by crafty policy and ecclesiastical intolerance, the young Prince of Wales happily is not identified. In this respect, Shakspeare shows a contrast between him and his brother, Prince John of Lancaster, who appears to have shared more in the councils of the king. And what is the result as to his character? He is not only the "sober-blooded boy" that Falstaff complains of, as one he could not make laugh, but, when he is engaged in suppressing the second great conspiracy of the nobles, he does so, not in open battle, like Prince Henry at Shrewsbury, but by a piece of hard and treacherous surprise. This is incomparably worse than revelry with Falstaff, and wisely and happily is

---

doctrines and heretical opinions, making conventicles and confederacies, holding schools, writing books, misinforming the people, and daily committing enormities too horrible to be heard; and that the bishops are unable to repress these offences because the offenders despise ecclesiastical censures, and when they are cited before their ordinaries, depart into another diocese; the statute therefore provides as a remedy for these evils, that the bishop shall have power to arrest and confine persons defamed or vehemently suspected of such offences till they make their canonical purgation; and, if they be convicted, to punish them with imprisonment, and a fine to the king. It then enacts that if any person so convicted shall refuse to abjure such preachings, doctrines, opinions, schools, and misinformations, or, after abjuration, shall be proved to have relapsed, then the sheriff of the county, or the mayor and bailiffs of the nearest borough, shall, on requisition, be present at the pronunciation of the sentence, shall receive the person so condemnned into custody, and shall cause him to be burnt on a high place before the people, that such punishment may strike terror into the minds of others." 1 Statutes at Large, 441. W. B. R.

Shakspeare's Prince Hal kept thus apart from his father's reign. The poet, I believe, loved this historical character too well to leave him much in the palace; and, accordingly, taking authority from the traditionary stories of the prince's lighter hours, he carried him away from the court, and transported him to a more genial and, I venture to say, a better place than the palace—a London tavern frequented by Falstaff—the moral perils of such a scene and companionship being small in comparison with those of crafty and tyrannical rule.

In presenting to our minds his splendid conception of the character of his favourite king and hero, Shakspeare would not have us believe Henry the Fifth had been trained in such a school as his father's reign. In such an element as that king's councils, he does not show him to us; it was better that the mere policy of that reign should run its course without him; and from such contact Shakspeare, for the most part, keeps him away. There is illustration of this in what has struck me as a beautiful piece of poetic art, which occurs in another of his dramas. In the tragedy of Macbeth there are intimations that Macbeth had children. Lady Macbeth, in one of the most appalling passages before the murder of Duncan, speaks of herself as having been a mother; and it is one of the pangs of Macbeth's ambition that the sceptre is to be wrenched from his family with an unlineal hand,—"no son of his succeeding," as the weird sisters predicted. But no children of Macbeth's appear in the drama: no child's voice is heard in his guilty castle, nor in his wretched palace. Why is this, but that the gentle spirit of Shakspeare, so full of fondness for children, so reverential of the beauty and the holiness of childhood, could not bring innocence into any association with the accumulated guilt of that tragedy? He could not, I believe, find it in his heart to show the children of such guilty parents. The very presence of a child of theirs would have aggravated the hideousness of the crimes of this blood-stained pair beyond the true scope of genuine tragic emotion, and even the imagination of Shakspeare could not have wrought the incongruous elements into poetic harmony.

It seems to me that it is upon somewhat a similar principle, though in a very different degree, that the career of Prince Henry is kept distinct from the career of Henry the Fourth. Retributive justice was to fall, as we shall hereafter see it did fall, with fearful force upon the descendants of the usurping Bolingbroke, but not until, in one of its more distant and mighty vibrations, it should strike, not upon the first, but second generation. The reign of Henry the Fifth was to be presented as a virtuous and glorious dominion; and retribution was not to be thought of as hanging over it. This is at once the poetic and historical view of it; and therefore it was desirable to disconnect it, as far as possible, from the primal guilt which at length brought the retribution down. It is well, indeed, that Prince Hal is a stranger in his father's palace.

But then comes the consideration, why, if estranged from the court and the royal councils, as the king describes him—

> "Almost an alien to the hearts
> Of all the court and princes of my blood,"—

the prince should be found in such companionship as that

in which he is chiefly presented, and which historical tradition tells of his having sought. What was the link of association between him and Falstaff? Whatever it was, the association did not rise to the dignity and feeling of friendship; it was companionship and nothing more—such companionship as would, however, be regulated in some degree by the laws of friendship. In the large company of the characters that people Shakspeare's plays, whether tragic or comic, I believe few instances of male friendship are presented there. It was with a true knowledge of human nature, and not with any morbid, and therefore unjust, estimate of it, that Shakspeare considered, I suppose, friendship between men as a relation that is rarely of long duration, and, more rarely, of very deep feeling. The course of the world hardly admits of it, save under peculiar and happy circumstances. We are apt, I believe, often to think that the sympathy of friendship, or even companionship, is proof of similarity of character; that men become friends and companions only because they are alike; and that no friendship can be permanent unless it be founded upon strong and complete resemblance of character and disposition. That there must be some kind of congeniality is undoubtedly true; but, with certain resemblances of mind and feelings, there may be dissimilitude, which, so far from being a hindrance to the strength of a friendship, will engender a more real and abiding affection, because the two parties are not minutely and identically alike. Even in the closer and lifelong relation of man and wife, it is reasonable to believe that some, I will not say positive *differences* of character, but varieties of disposition, will strengthen the affection due to that vow, which, in

Spenser's fine phrase, "would endless matrimony make."* The reason for this congenial influence of a certain dissimilitude of character, especially in friendship, is perhaps simply this, that one party, wanting some quality of mind or feeling, and conscious of that want, has it supplied by the differently constituted character of the friend or companion. This, of course, implies that there is present at the same time such generosity of disposition, or such a relation of the parties, as will preclude all possibility of reciprocal jealousy or pride of superiority. That being the case, their various properties make up for their mutual wants; understanding, however, that there must be preserved some main elements of direct sympathy—some ground common to them both. These principles are finely illustrated by Shakspeare in such a friendship as that of Hamlet and Horatio: they resemble each other in the excellent moral purity and manliness of their character, but in many respects, as to intellectual constitution and as to habits of feeling, it is hardly possible for two men to be more unlike. Hamlet is full of philosophy, of poetry; meditative, sensitive to the highest degree,—the equipoise of his nature disturbed by what befalls him; on the other hand, Horatio has not a particle of the poetical or philosophical constitution or temperament; he is one of the most matter-of-fact persons conceivable, with strong and genuine feelings, but with those feelings imperturbably adjusted and balanced; and it is exactly in this particular that he is the appropriate friend of Hamlet, as Hamlet himself feels. He takes Horatio as his chosen friend, because he finds in his sober-minded, judicious character

* Poetical Works, vol. v. p. 140.

something that makes up for his own infirmity of over-sensitiveness.

I have dwelt somewhat upon this train of thought, because in seeking for the point of association between the prince and Falstaff, it should be understood that possibly we may find it is "by contraries that they are joined more closely still." The chief sympathy between them, I believe, is high intellectual activity. With such a constitution of mind, Prince Henry had early in life acquired a relish for the external excitement and animation of military life; but finding no fit field of adventure, and withdrawing himself, as we have noticed, from the business of the government, he needs employment, or at least excitement, for the pent-up energies of his mind. He craves some relief that shall be at the same time excitement, and to supply this, Shakspeare gives the unparalleled wit of Falstaff. The intellect of Falstaff possesses an unwearied activity, which spends itself altogether in the direction of wit. There is no exhausting it; there is no tiring it; there is no such thing as taking it unawares. Coleridge is, no doubt, right when he says that there is no *humour* in the character of Falstaff; it is all *wit*, and that is one form of intellectual energy. Humour has more to do with feeling; it is often joined with deep pathos:—it is of the heart, but wit is of the head, and in its high forms is intensely intellectual.* It is this, and only this,

* Coleridge's words are, "Pistol, Nym, and *id genus omne*, do not please me as characters, but are endured as fantastic creations—foils to the native wit of Falstaff. I say *wit* emphatically: for this character, so often extolled as the masterpiece of humour, neither contains, nor was meant to contain, any humour at all." Literary Remains, (Ed. 1836,) vol. ii. p. 271; see also vol. i. p. 134. W. B. R.

that gives to Falstaff his power over the prince, and makes the witchery of his companionship. Falstaff, of course, feels his own power, and lays himself out (it is well worth his while to do so) to cultivate it for the amusement of the heir-apparent. He does not husband his wit, in which he was too affluent to need any economizing of it for the prince's use, but he provides materials, as when, after his visit to Justice Shallow he says—"I will devise matter enough out of this Shallow to keep Prince Henry in continual laughter, the wearing-out six fashions, and he shall laugh without *intervallums.* It is much, that a lie with a slight oath, and a jest with a sad brow, will do with a fellow that never had the ache in his shoulders! O, you shall see him laugh till his face be like a wet cloak ill-laid up."

For the lack of better employment, the prince has, from Falstaff's wit, high enjoyment, while it lasts. His other gay companions are very insufficient for him; the time hangs heavy on his hands, till Falstaff joins them. It is the stimulus of a temporary intoxication. The prince is idle, not from the love of idleness, but for want of a congenial sphere of action; he is playful to keep care away, for beneath all his playfulness there is an undercurrent of thoughtfulness, which, though covert at first, is progressive, until it assumes the aspect of almost melancholy pensiveness in his royal years. He is just in that condition of mind that he needs such a contrariety of character as Falstaff presents,—a man, who is enamoured of an idle life from pure love of inactivity, who is careless habitually, if not constitutionally. His vivacity does not, like the prince's, cover any thing—there is nothing beneath: it is a vein, however, that you cannot dig through. Besides his wit, all else is sensuality, self-indulgence, shamelessness. But, reprobate as Falstaff is, his character is not contemptible. His grossness may be disgusting, his profligacies most reprehensible—so that he may be censured or condemned—but he is not to be despised. And this presents the question of his imputed cowardice. On this point there has been a very great misapprehension, which, perhaps, even now, is not altogether done away with. The persuasion that Shakspeare intended to represent Falstaff as a coward, was so universally entertained, that when, during the last century, a very ingenious and argumentative essay, much in advance of the criticism of that day—the thin and vapid criticism of Dr. Blair and Lord Kames—when this essay appeared, vindicating Falstaff from the charge of cowardice, it was looked upon as a freak of playful paradox. But it was irrefutable argument, which has been fortified by all the fine philosophical criticism that has since been bestowed upon the Shaksperean drama. I shall not, of course, depart so far from my chief subject as to enter into that argument, and must content myself with the assurance that there is not a doubt in the case left. Falstaff is no coward; there is no constitutional timidity about him. The clue to his character in this particular is given at the very opening of the drama. When Poins says, "Well, for two of them, I know them to be as true-bred cowards as ever turned back,—and for the third, (that is, Falstaff,) if he fight longer than he sees reason, I'll forswear arms." That is the character of Falstaff's courage—he will fight as long as he sees reason, and not a moment longer will sense of honour or any thing else hold him to it. This may be dishonour, but it is not cowardice; so it is throughout, if carefully examined; and Falstaff describes himself justly when he says to the prince, "Indeed, I am not John of Gaunt, your grandfather; but yet no coward, Hal."*

---

* The "ingenious and argumentative essay" to which my brother refers is "The Essay on the Dramatic Character of Sir John Falstaff, by Morgann," which I cannot help regarding yet as a fantastical attempt to reverse a popular judgment. The isolated passages relied on, prove nothing or too much; as, for example, when Mrs. Quickly means to arrest the fat knight, she says:

"*Hostess.* Where is your yeoman? Is it a lusty yeoman? will 'a stand to't?

Fang. Sirrah, where's Snare?

Hostess. O lord, ay: good master Snare.

Snare. Here, here—it may cost some of us our lives, *for he will stab.*"

Stabbing a bailiff or a dead Percy seems to be the extent of Falstaff's positive courage; and a coward, a runaway coward, will he remain during all time. It seems to me—though this may be playful paradox too—that a far better case might be made out for poor Bardolph, who was hanged for robbing a church. For instance, Bardolph was trustworthy, or in the crisis at Shrewsbury he would hardly have been made by the prince "bearer of despatches" to Prince John and Lord Westmoreland. When Falstaff is threatened by the sheriff's officers, it is on Bardolph he calls to keep them off. When Pistol and Nym quarrel, and seem to be coming to blows, Bardolph interposes, and with his drawn sword keeps the peace. At the bridge at Harfleur, Bardolph makes at least a good show of fighting, calling his followers "on, on to the breach," and obeys Captain Fluellen's orders of attack. He uttered brave words at the bridge, and Fluellen is willing to intercede with the king, when Bardolph is to be hanged for sacrilege, but is interrupted by the stern refusal, (a little harsh from Henry's lips to his old companion,) "We would have all such offenders to be cut off." It must be admitted (I am not sure Morgann is equally candid as to *his* hero) that the "Boy," as well as Poins, disparages Bardolph as "white-livered and red-faced," as one "who faces it out and fights not," and that at Gadshill he did run with the rest; but the par-

It would, indeed, have greatly increased the difficulty of extenuating the prince's companionship with Falstaff, if the fat knight had been a pitiful coward instead of the old soldier in whom the sense of voluptuous comfort has outgrown all sense of chivalry. When the rebellion of the Percies produces a war, he is ready for military service, as affording him lawless chances of providing for himself; and when the prince tells him, "I have procured thee, Jack, a charge of foot," his only answer is, "I would it had been of horse." The rebellion calls the prince into action, and his prompt zeal shows not only that his course of life has not enervated him, but how gladly he finds a more congenial scene. It is in the midst of his loose companions that he gives his several orders:

> "Go, bear this letter to Lord John of Lancaster,
> My brother John; — this to my lord of Westmoreland,—
> Go, Poins, to horse, to horse; for thou and I
> Have thirty miles to ride yet ere dinner-time.
> Jack, meet me to-morrow i' the Temple Hall;
> At two o'clock i' the afternoon;
> There shalt thou know thy charge; and there receive
> Money and order for their furniture.
> The land is burning: Percy stands on high,
> And either they or we must lower lie."

It was by the heroism of the Prince of Wales that the victory over the Percies at Shrewsbury was won: it gave safety to his father's throne, and it redeemed his own good name.

---

tisans of Falstaff should remember the reason Bardolph gives for his flight when the prince reproaches him for cowardice:

"Faith, I ran when I saw others run."

On the whole, I submit the Bardolphian heroic theory with equal, if not great, confidence. W. B. R.

After the excitement of this campaign, he is represented as returning to his old companions; and, indeed, Shakspeare was too profound and faithful a moralist to retrieve the prince so easily—to break off suddenly his former associations. The lasting transformation of his character must cost a struggle, and this is shown in a remarkable scene which I do not remember to have seen commented upon. Mr. Senior, the eminent writer on political economy, in one of those fine critical papers with which he followed the successive appearance of the Waverley Novels, in remarking upon that rare power displayed by Shakspeare and Scott—and by few else—of combining the comic with the tragic element, observes that no tragedian except Shakspeare has ventured to make a king's son remember that "poor creature, small beer."* This occurs in the scene to which I have just alluded, as disclosing the struggle between the prince's better nature and the companionship he felt to be unworthy of it. The scene is with Poins, the most gentlemanly and least unfit of his associates. The prince says, "Trust me, I am exceeding weary." It was, doubtless, weariness of the heart—self-dissatisfaction—though he does not there say so. When Poins replies, "Is it come to that? I had thought weariness durst not have attacked one of so high blood;" the prince adds, "Faith it doth me, though it discolours the complexion of my greatness to acknowledge it. Doth it not show vilely in me to

* Lockhart's Life of Scott, vol. v. p. 247. It appears that Mr. Sonior's articles on the Waverley Novels were begun in a periodical called the London Review, which soon failed. They were continued in Quarterly Review. W. B. R.

desire small beer? * * * In troth, I do now remember the poor creature, small beer. But, indeed, these humble considerations make me out of love with my greatness." And then he runs on with a good deal of extravagance to show the mean things he was familiar with, avowing low propensities at the very time that what he truly wants is to give utterance to the better and the deeper feelings his heart is full of, but from which he is restrained by the painful misgiving that it would be thought unreal and insincere, because so unlike himself as he was known to these companions. Poins says, "How ill it follows, after you have laboured so hard, you should talk so idly. Tell me how many good young princes would do so, their fathers lying so sick as yours is." He answers, "Shall I tell thee one thing, Poins? Why, I tell thee it is not meet that I should be sad, now my father is sick; albeit, I could tell to thee, (as to me it pleases me, for fault of a better, to call my friend,) I could be sad, and sad indeed, too."

Poins's remark, "Very hardly on such a subject," provokes him to express more of his feelings:

"By this hand, thou thinkest me as far in the devil's book as thou and Falstaff, for obduracy and persistency. Let the end try the man. But I tell thee, my heart bleeds inwardly that my father is so sick; and, keeping such vile company as thou art, hath in reason taken from me all ostentation of sorrow. * * What wouldst thou think of me if I should weep?"

When Poins says, "I should think thee a most princely hypocrite," the prince adds, "It would be every man's thought: and thou art a blessed fellow to think as every man thinks; never a man's thought in the world keeps the roadway better than thine;—every man would think me an hypocrite indeed."

The conflict is this:—he has become so entangled that he cannot suffer his better nature to take its course, from an apprehension of what would most offend a disposition like his. He would, therefore, expose himself to be condemned as worse than he really is, rather than to be thought not so good as he might appear to be. Accordingly, he tries to turn away from seriousness to his old habits of diversion; but the sport is now laborious to him, and grave thoughts intrude in the midst of it, for he says: "We played the fools with the time, and the spirits of the wise sit in the clouds and mock us."

And when report is made to him—

> "The king your father is at Westminster,
> And there are twenty weak and wearied posts
> Come from the North,"

he casts off in an instant the bonds of his companionship at the approach of the dangers of a second conspiracy against his father's throne:

> "By heaven, Poins, I feel me much to blame
> So idly to profane the precious time;
> When tempest of commotion, like the south
> Borne with black vapour, doth begin to melt,
> And drop upon our bare unarmed heads.
> Give me my sword, and cloak:—Falstaff, good-night."

This is Prince Hal's last good-night to his boon companion. When they next meet it is as king and subject, and when the unchangeable impudence with which Falstaff approaches Henry the Fifth, in the midst of the royal retinue, is rebuked and repulsed with stern but not cruel severity. It is a passage in the drama of historical interest, as closing forever that levity of life which, according to common tradition, Henry had indulged.

The reign of Henry the Fifth was signalized at the outset by a magnanimous policy. Besides the funeral honours to the memory of Richard the Second, he set at liberty the representative of the strict lineal succession to the crown, and thus converted a competitor into a friend. His policy—if policy it is to be called—was to plant the throne on the affections of the nation—the nobles and the people. In the only case of conspiracy which threatened the security of his reign, he is finely represented by Shakspeare as extorting from the mouths of the conspiring nobles themselves their own condemnation, so that justice is made to appear almost self-administrant.

The great business of the reign was the war with France. Reserving the consideration of that war chiefly for the next lecture, I shall now treat it only in its connection with the character of Henry the Fifth. He revives the old claim of Edward the Third to the crown of France, and renews hostilities which had not been settled by any definite pacification. In doing so, he sought the advice of his highest and wisest counsellors; and, in asking the Primate of England to pronounce opinion on the claim, he forewarns him of the awful responsibility of his advice:

> "For God doth know how many, now in health,
> Shall drop their blood in approbation
> Of what your reverence shall incite us to:
> Therefore take heed how you impawn our person,
> How you awake the sleeping sword of war:
> We charge you in the name of God take heed:
> For never two such kingdoms did contend

Without much fall of blood; whose guiltless drops
Are every one a wo, a sore complaint
'Gainst him whose wrongs give edge unto the swords
That make such waste in brief mortality."*

I need not occupy you with the course of that invasion from the landing of Henry's army near Harfleur to one of the greatest of England's victories—the battle of Agincourt. Shakspeare has indicated the unanimity of the national feeling in this war and the universal allegiance to the king, by introducing among the soldiers, not only Englishmen, but the Welsh and Irish and Scotch, so as to make it a great British movement against a continental power. He has also shown the popular character of the war and of the sovereign, by giving considerable prominence, not merely to the nobles, but to commoners; and, indeed, to the common soldiers. If the freedom of Henry's early life had a perilous tendency to licentiousness, it gave him, on the other hand, large sympathies with his fellow-men and a power of dealing with humanity

* It was, besides, in pursuance of his father's dying advice:

"Though thou stand'st more sure than I could do,
Thou art not firm enough, since griefs are green;
And all thy friends, which thou must make thy friends,
Have but their stings and teeth newly ta'en out,
By whose fell working I was first advanced,
And by whose power I well might lodge a fear
To be again displaced; which to avoid,
I cut them off; and had a purpose now
To lead out many to the Holy Land;
Lest rest and lying still might make them look
Too near unto my state. Therefore, my Harry,
Be it thy course to busy giddy minds
With foreign quarrels; that action hence borne out,
May waste the memory of the former days." W. B. R.

in a generous and liberal spirit, which secured him the hearts of his soldiers. His intercourse with them is one of the points of description in that deservedly famous picture of the eve of the battle of Agincourt in the chorus of the fourth act:

"—— The poor condemned English,
Like sacrifices, by their watchful fires,
Sit patiently, and inly ruminate
The morning's danger; and their gesture sad
Investing lank, lean cheeks, and warworn coats,
Presenteth them unto the gazing moon
So many horrid ghosts. Oh, now who will behold
The royal captain of this ruin'd band,
Walking from watch to watch, from tent to tent,
Let him cry—Praise and glory on his head!
For forth he goes, and visits all his host,
Bids them good-morrow, with a modest smile;
And calls them—brothers, friends, and countrymen.
Upon his royal face there is no note
How dread an army hath enrounded him;
Nor doth he dedicate one jot of colour
Unto the weary and all-watched night:
But freshly looks, and overbears attaint
With cheerful semblance and sweet majesty;
That every wretch, pining and pale before,
Beholding him, plucks comfort from his looks;
A largess universal, like the sun,
His liberal eye doth give to every one,
Thawing cold fear." *

---

* Campbell, the poet, in the preface to his edition of Shakspeare, says:

"The description of the night before the battle of Agincourt will be repeated by the youth of England when our children's children shall be gray with age. It was said of Æschylus that he composed his 'Seven Chiefs against Thebes' under the inspiration of Mars himself. If 'Henry the Fifth' had been written for the Greeks, the same might have been said of it." W. B. R.

The position of Henry's army was critically dangerous. Outnumbered, enfeebled by disease and fatigue, and badly supplied, they were kept in good discipline and in good heart by the half-thoughtful, half-jocund confidence of their sovereign. In the scenes before and at the battle, Shakspeare shows in action the finest conception of a great general, the happy warrior—he

"Who doom'd to go in company with Pain
And Fear and Bloodshed, miserable train!
Turns his necessity to glorious gain;
In face of these doth exercise a power
Which is our human nature's highest dower;
Controls them and subdues, transmutes, bereaves
Of their bad influence, and their good receives."*

An historical event is dramatized when the king, overhearing Westmoreland's wish—

"Oh, that we now had here
But one ten thousand of those men in England
That do no work to-day!"

asks—

"What's he that wishes so?
My cousin Westmoreland?—No, my fair cousin:
If we are mark'd to die, we are enough
To do our country loss; and if to live,
The fewer men, the greater share of honour."

Again, when, at early morn, he greets his brothers with such fine cheerfulness and courtesy—

"Gloster, 'tis true that we are in great danger;
The greater therefore should our courage be.
Good morrow, brother Bedford!"

* Wordsworth's "Character of the Happy Warrior."

And what can be more touchingly beautiful than the respectful and affectionate greeting to the white hairs of that fine old soldier, Erpingham?—

> "Good morrow, old Sir Thomas Erpingham!
> A good soft pillow for that good white head,
> Were better than a churlish turf of France."

And when the old knight takes his leave, saying—

> "The Lord in heaven bless thee, noble Harry!"—

the king's cordial response is—

> "God-a mercy, old heart! thou speakest cheerfully."

In his season of the highest peril the spirit of Prince Hal seems to animate the king, and it is in the mood of lighter-hearted days, that he answers the message of the Constable of France—

> "Why should they mock poor fellows thus?
> The man that once did sell the lion's skin
> While the beast lived, was killed with hunting him.
> And many of our bodies shall, no doubt,
> Find native graves; upon the which, I trust,
> Shall witness live in brass of this day's work.
> Tell the constable
> We are but warrior's for the working day:
> Our gayness and our gilt are all besmirch'd
> With rainy marching in the painful field;
> There's not a piece of feather in our host,
> (Good argument, I hope, we shall not fly,)
> And time hath worn us into slovenry:
> But, by the mass, our hearts are in the trim;
> And my poor soldiers tell me yet ere night
> They'll be in fresher robes."

The battle was fought; and, at no great distance from the field of Cressy, the victory of Agincourt was won. I cannot, of course, take time to dwell on the particulars of it; to speak of the immense loss of life to the nobility of France; the consequence of their impetuous but ill-directed valour. Nor can I more than mention Henry's stern order—let us hope it was unavoidable—for the slaughter of the French prisoners. One incident alone I must refer to as finely illustrative of that period of England's history; and it is described in one of the beautiful passages of poetic description with which the play abounds—the description of the deaths of York and Suffolk. After the battle, the king inquires whether his cousin, the Duke of York, survives:

> "Lives he, good uncle? Thrice, within this hour,
> I saw him down; thrice up again and fighting;
> From helmet to the spur, all blood he was."

Exeter answers—

> "In which array (brave soldier) doth he lie,
> Larding the plain; and by his bloody side
> (Yoke-fellow to his honour-owing wounds)
> The noble Earl of Suffolk also lies.
> Suffolk first died; and York, all haggled over,
> Comes to him, where in gore he lay insteep'd,
> And takes him by the beard; kisses the gashes
> That bloodily did yawn upon his face;
> And cries aloud—'Tarry, dear cousin Suffolk!
> My soul shall thine keep company to heaven:
> Tarry, sweet soul, for mine, then fly abreast;
> As, in this glorious and well-foughten field
> We kept together in our chivalry!'
> Upon these words, I came and cheer'd him up:
> He smiled me in the face, raught me his hand,
> And, with a feeble gripe, says—'Dear my lord,
> Commend my service to my sovereign.'
> So did he turn, and over Suffolk's neck

He threw his wounded arm, and kiss'd his lips;
And so, espoused to death, with blood he seal'd
A testament of noble-ending love."

This description is an image of the English nobility; not discordant, but "keeping together in their chivalry" in the hour of battle and of death, and uttering with their last breath dutiful and affectionate loyalty to that sovereign, whose sway gave glory and harmony to the nation.

Intending this drama as a kind of triumphal song, Shakspeare has carried it, not as usual on to the monarch's death, but to the happy ending of the marriage of Henry the Fifth to Katharine of France, the daughter of King Charles. The great achievement of the war was the treaty stipulation for the permanent union of the crowns of England and France. The subjugation of the French was partial and of short duration; and the next page of history that we have to turn to, will show how the independence of France found its wondrous redemption by the splendid heroism of Joan of Arc.

LECTURE VIII.*

The Reign of Henry the Sixth.

The treaty of Troyes—Its details—The last hours of Henry the Fifth—His intended crusade—Hume's comments—Henry the Sixth an infant—His reign and these "Chronicle-Plays" unpromising subjects—Genuineness of the plays—The Minority—The French wars—State of France—The Regent Bedford—The Siege of Orleans—Joan of Arc—Various criticisms on her character—Her sincerity—Imputed witchcraft—Defective education—Her influence—Relief of Orleans—Coronation of the king at Rheims—Exemption of Domremy—Capture of the Maid—Her trial and examination—Her martyrdom—Cardinal Beaufort and the Bishop of Beauvais—The cardinal's death—Statue of the Maid at Versailles—Death of the Duke of Bedford—His monument—Magnanimity of Louis the Eleventh.

In concluding the last lecture, I pointed your attention to the fact that Shakspeare, in order to preserve unbroken the triumphant tone of the drama of Henry the Fifth, did not bring it down to the monarch's death. The historical illustration which the play furnished us, ended with the close of Henry's campaign in France and his marriage with Katharine. The war waged by England against France extended over a period of about one hundred and twenty years, broken, indeed, by various truces and interruptions; and at length, some eighty years after its

* February 15th, 1847.

origin, it was settled, to all appearance permanently, by the treaty which the victory of Agincourt enabled the English monarch to exact. The treaty of Troyes, which was concluded in 1420, was such a treaty as a conqueror negotiates, or rather dictates, in the confident strength of recent victory. It did not absolutely depose the French king; but, transferring the royal power really into the hands of the conqueror, it provided that, on the death of Charles the Sixth, the crown should pass to Henry the Fifth and his heirs. The union of the crowns of the two great monarchies was a proud achievement; but it proved no more than a splendid dream of vain ambition. It seemed as if, by the subversion of its constitutional law of succession, the ancient dynasty of France had now reached the end of its thousand-year life, and that the sceptre of Clovis was to be forever broken, when it fell from the hands of the feeble Charles. It has been well said by Arnold in his Lectures on Modern History, that—"When our object is to reproduce to ourselves, so far as is possible, the very life of the period we are studying, minute particulars help us to do this; nay, the very formal enunciation of titles, and the specification of towns and districts in their legal style, help to realize the time to us, if it be only from their very particularity. Every common historian records the substance of the treaty by which the succession to the crown of France was given to Henry the Fifth; but the treaty itself, or the English version of it which Henry sent over to England to be proclaimed there, gives a far more lively impression of the triumphant state of the great conqueror, and the utter weakness of the poor French king, Charles the Sixth, in the ostentatious care taken to provide for the recognition of his formal title during his lifetime, while all real power is ceded to Henry, and provision is made for the perpetual union hereafter of the two kingdoms under his sole government."*

The English king was in the full vigour of his days, the prime of his manhood just past, and the splendour of his reign seemed to be shining forth upon some glorious future, with the united diadem of France and England glittering on his brow. But, in less than two years, he found himself to be a dying man. Having given his death-bed injunctions for the administration of the realm and for the guardianship of his infant child, he spent his last hours in devotional exercises; and, as the penitential psalms were read, when he heard the verse—"Build thou the walls of Jerusalem," he interrupted them to declare, as a dying man, that it had been his intention to visit Palestine and free the Holy City from the Saracens. It is at once very easy and very characteristic for an historian like Hume to add the comment—"So ingenious are men in deceiving themselves, that Henry forgot in these moments all the blood spilt by his ambition, and received comfort from the late feeble resolve, which, as the mode of these enterprises was now past, he certainly would never have carried into execution."† The mode of these enterprises was, indeed, past; but, at the time, it was not known to be, and the whole reflection seems to me a piece of most unreal moralizing. It is the malice of skepticism aping the modesty and the candour of piety; and it is well worth remarking that, while Mr. Hume is confident

* Arnold's Lectures on Modern History, lect. i. p. 98, (Amer. ed.)

† History of England, vol. iv. p. 73.

enough in his speculation, to pronounce, upon no better authority, that Henry never would have carried his intention into execution, later historical research has brought to light documentary proof, which establishes the sincerity of his dying words. Immediately after the treaty of Troyes, a Flemish knight, who was a councillor to Philip the Good, of Burgundy, and had been an ambassador to the English king, was sent by Henry and the Duke of Burgundy upon a secret mission to the Holy Land. The mission was actually performed, and with success; he made a military survey of the coasts and defences of Egypt and Syria; and the two copies of this survey, intended, one for the King of England, and the other for the Duke of Burgundy, are both in existence. Accordingly, if Mr. Hume, in absence of all evidence and knowledge, had argued, not from his theory of the universal hypocrisy of all pious profession of other times, but more wisely, as well as charitably, from the possible sincerity of a dying man's declaration, he would have been much nearer the truth.

So far from its being reasonable to scoff at Henry's declaration of his purposed crusade as a self-delusion and mockery, it is not only sustained by documentary evidence of the reality of his intention, but we can well believe that a spirit so ardent and active as his, after having achieved, while yet a young man, enough to satisfy a large ambition in the way of worldly conquest, should have turned his thoughts to what was esteemed a holy war. Having won the crown of France, and being confederate with the greatest of the French nobles, the Duke of Burgundy, who also in his ducal power was almost a sovereign, Henry may well have felt that it became him to fulfil the unaccomplished purpose of his father. Had this crusade been carried into effect, it might have given to Eastern Europe security from Turkish invasion a century earlier than it was obtained; and the tranquillity of Christendom might have been saved from the alarm, which was created by the successive, and well-nigh successful, sieges of Vienna by the Turks.

On the death of Henry the Fifth, the succession passing to his only child, Henry of Windsor—the son of an English father and a French mother, an infant of no more than nine months old—the youngest successor that ever had come to the English throne was to wear the crown of both France and England. One of the old chroniclers prefaces the reign of Henry the Sixth by saying that—"The pretty hands that could not feed himself, were yet made capable to wield a sceptre; and he that was beholding to nurses for milk, did, nevertheless, distribute the sustenance of law and justice to so great and warlike nations."* Two nations, and the proud and mighty nobles of two countries, did obeisance to the baby brow of Henry the Sixth; but, when the royal child grew to manhood, he lived to learn, by bitter experience, the misery of that royalty, which his forefathers had triumphantly transmitted to him. The career that was before the poor child was calamity and disgrace in foreign war, discord and bloody strife at home, disaster in almost every variety, and, at last, a violent death.

Before proceeding to the consideration of the reign of Henry the Sixth, let me say that it is a most unpromising

* Speed, as quoted in Southey's Naval History of England, vol. ii. p. 58.

subject for us in this course. It is for several reasons. His long reign, for it was of near forty years' duration, was confusion and turmoil from the beginning to the very end of it. It was a weary period of danger and distress, but not of that description of suffering which often serves to develop heroic character, and cultivate lofty and virtuous emotions. Passing from the reign of Henry of Monmouth to that of Henry of Windsor, you see every thing co-operating to convert unanimity into discord, and not only to produce distraction, but to degrade the national enthusiasm and prostrate the character of the kingdom. The splendid achievement of foreign victory is changed for defeat and ignominy, and the record of the rest of the reign is reeking with the blood of civil slaughter. Another reason for the unpromising character of the subject is, that the history of the reign of Henry the Sixth is well-nigh in as great confusion as the reign itself, so that it becomes most difficult to trace distinctly and satisfactorily the course of events, or even to form a conception of the characters and spirit of the times; and furthermore, if we seek for personal interest in the characters of those who flourished—or rather let me say of such distressful times, who lived—then, it is hard to discover, who is entitled to sympathy and respect, and who is worthy of condemnation and hatred. There is a cloud of names belonging to that period, but so far as one's feelings are concerned, they seem to be names and nothing more. It is difficult to find one personage, either male or female, among them, in whose fortunes or character one can take any deep interest. This is owing chiefly, I suppose, to the general obscurity which hangs over the reign of Henry the Sixth, and prevents our forming any thing like a distinct conception of the characters of the men of the times or of the principles of action in the events.

Again, there is another reason which affects the interest in this reign, at least for our present purposes, and that is the manifest inferiority of the dramas Shakspeare has devoted to it, when compared with his other "Chronicle-Plays." It is that very inferiority which has made the authorship of the three parts of Henry the Sixth a question; and it is difficult to believe them the productions of the same poetic genius that gave to English history and English poetry the other historical plays which bear a stamp that no one can mistake. The question whether or no Shakspeare was the author of the three parts of Henry the Sixth, is a literary question not belonging to my present course; and, while I do not enter upon it, I cannot help lamenting that there is such grievous inferiority in these three plays, in which I fear I cannot find a passage furnishing valuable historical illustration, or of such poetic excellence, that I should desire to repeat it to you. The chief value of the poet's historical illustration is, that it gives unity to the apparent inconsistencies of human character, and also to a multitude of events; it helps us to comprehend the facts, because, disconnected as they may be, and therefore unimpressive, they are put into order and harmony by the power of the imagination. Unfortunately, it is just at the period of English history when we should need this assistance, that it fails us; for really these three parts of Henry the Sixth are nearly as confused as the *literal* history of the times; and if the lamp of philosophic history is shining very feebly and unsteadily in the prose, the light of poetry is equally dim in these dramas. I am sure that I could not interest you in retailing the military vicissitudes of this reign—the alternations of victory and defeat, or the dark and obscure schemes of rival factions; and yet, what else is there in the history of the reign? So that we have before us, I apprehend, not only a difficult, but (I am inclined to believe) almost an impossible, subject.

From four of Shakspeare's plays, the Richard the Second, the two parts of Henry the Fourth, and Henry the Fifth, we have been enabled to draw historical illustration of the ascendency of the Lancastrian kings—the rise and progress of the Plantagenet family, from the time when Richard threw down his warder in the lists at Coventry, to the period of the highest glory of the race on the field of Agincourt: Four plays, attributed to Shakspeare, are given to the sequel of the decline and fall of the Lancastrians, and the rising fortunes and dominion of the house of York.

The reign of Henry the Sixth may be divided, in order to assist the mind in taking a view of it, into two periods; the first, chiefly during his minority, being occupied with the continuance and conclusion of the war in France, and the other with the civil wars of the houses of York and Lancaster. The first of these forms the subject of the First Part of Henry the Sixth, which opens with the funeral of Henry the Fifth. This opening is intended, it has been suggested, to show that the death of that king, who was the conqueror of France and the idol of England,—who, by his extraordinary talents and energy, obliterated almost the memory of the circumstances under which his father obtained the throne,—was the starting-point of a long period of error and misfortune, during which France was lost, and England torn to pieces by civil war. By way of showing the irreparable loss the nation suffered in the death of Henry the Fifth, and as a dramatic anticipation of later events, the nobles and princes of the blood, to whom were committed the management of the kingdom and guardianship of his infant son, are represented as beginning their disputes over the bier of their deceased sovereign. The success which had attended the military career of Henry the Fifth in his invasion of France, did not, immediately after his death, fail his countrymen. The Duke of Bedford, as Regent, prosecuted the war, and it proved no less to him a career of victory. Low as the power of France was reduced by the battle of Agincourt and the treaty of Troyes, it was destined to sink still lower before the unabated strength of the great generals of Henry the Fifth, Bedford, and Salisbury, and Talbot, strengthened too, as they were, by the alliance of the Duke of Burgundy. The tide of victory and conquest continued to set in the same direction. The poor half-crazed, or more than half-crazed, French king, Charles the Sixth, had quickly followed Henry the Fifth to the grave, and his son, afterwards Charles the Seventh, was scarcely recognised, even with the title of dauphin. His adherents, discomfited wherever encountered, were driven from a large portion of their country; Paris was in the occupation of the new dynasty; and the whole Burgundian people, almost a nation in themselves, had withdrawn their allegiance from the ancient race of the Capetian kings, and were the willing subjects of the English infant, whom the fortune of war had placed on the throne of France. The hope of independence was nearly extinct; the might of the island-strangers, thus far irresistible, had little more to do in fulfilling the work of subjugation; and France was sunk so low as if to give the greater splendour to that wondrous restoration which was to be achieved by a poor, unlettered peasant girl.*

The course of English conquest in France seemed to be drawing to its completion. It remained to carry the war into the country beyond the Loire, and there to extinguish the last hopes of French independence. The Regent Bedford added fresh troops to an army that was growing almost veteran on the soil of France, and being strongly reinforced by the Duke of Burgundy, sent a large force, under the command of the Earl of Salisbury, to take the city of Orleans, the possession of which was important, as commanding the passage of the Loire and the entrance into the southern provinces. If Orleans should be taken, the troops of Bedford and of Burgundy could enter without hinderance into the open country; and nothing but the mountains of Auvergne could shelter the dauphin, if he ventured, with his small court and reduced army, to remain on the soil of his native country. At the

* There is a striking passage of De Serres, quoted in a note to Southey's Joan of Arc, and requoted in Creasy's "Battles," in the chapter on the Battle of Orleans: "In sooth, the estate of France was then most miserable. There appeared nothing but a horrible face, confusion, poverty, desolation, solitarinesse and feare. The lean and bare labourers in the country did terrifie even theeves themselves, who had nothing left them to spoile but the carkasses of these poore miserable creatures, wandering up and down like ghostes drawne out of their graves. The least farmes and hamlets were fortified by these robbers, English, Bourguegnons, and French, every one striving to do his worst; all men-of-war were well agreed to spoile the countryman and merchant. Even the cattell, accustomed to the larume bell, the signe of the enemy's approach, would run home of themselves without any guide by this accustomed misery." W. B. R.

advance of the English army, the small towns surrendered after faint and ineffectual resistance; and it was manifest to both nations, that the issue of sovereignty on the one side, and of independence on the other, was to be decided at the city of Orleans. The day was near, when the long contest between the two kingdoms was to be decided forever, after having now been protracted through several generations; for, from its origin, in the reign of Edward the Third, it had lasted about ninety years. The final judgment was to be made in a great national struggle, which the victories of neither Cressy nor Poictiers nor Agincourt could determine. The city of Orleans proved no easy conquest; it was bravely defended, and Salisbury, the English commander, was killed during the siege. The siege was protracted for months, and at last converted into a blockade, to reduce the garrison by famine. With all their fortitude and endurance, and notwithstanding occasional relief, they were bound in more and more hopelessly; and nothing short of an almost miraculous interposition could save them, and with them the independence of their country.

It was exactly in such unlooked-for relief, by an almost miraculous interposition, that succour did come to that beleaguered garrison and to France. It was at that crisis of the war that Joan of Arc came from the village of Domremy, on the borders of Lorraine, to rescue her country from foreign dominion, and to win for herself the imperishable title of the Maid of Orleans.

The representation which is given of the character of Joan of Arc, in the First Part of Henry the Sixth, has been ingeniously defined and commented on by one of the latest and best editors of Shakspeare, and one of his most genial critics: he says, "We find her described in the chronicles under every form of vituperation—'a monstrous woman,' 'a monster,' 'a romp,' 'a devilish witch and satanical enchantress,' 'an organ of the devil.' She was the main instrument through which England had lost France; and thus the people hated her memory. She claimed to be invested with supernatural powers, and thus her name was not only execrated, but feared. Neither the patriotism nor the superstition of Shakspeare's age would have endured that the Pucelle should have been dismissed from the scene without vengeance taken on imagined crimes; or that confession should not be made by her, which should exculpate the authors of her death. Shakspeare has conducted her history up to the point when she is handed over to the stake. Other writers would have burned her upon the scene, and the audience would have shouted with the same delight that they felt when the Barrabas of Marlowe was thrown into the cauldron. Shakspeare, following the historian, has made her utter a contradictory confession of one of the charges against her honour; but he has taken care to show that the brutality of her English persecutors forced from her an inconsistent avowal, if it did not a false one, for the purpose of averting a cruel and instant death. In the treatment which she received from York and Warwick, the poet has not exhibited one single circumstance that might excite sympathy for *them*. They are cold, and cruel, and insolent, because a defenceless creature, whom they had dreaded, is in their power. Her parting malediction has, as it appears to us, a special reference to the calamities which await the authors of her death:—

'May never glorious sun reflex his beams
Upon the country where you make abode!

But darkness and the gloomy shade of death
Environ you.'

"But in all the previous scenes, Shakspeare has drawn the character of the Maid with an undisguised sympathy for her courage, her patriotism, her high intellect, and her enthusiasm. If she had been the defender of England, and not of France, the poet could not have invested her with higher attributes. It is in her mouth that he puts his choicest thoughts and his most musical verse It is she who says—

'Glory is like a circle in the water,
Which never ceaseth to enlarge itself,
'Till by broad spreading it disperse to nought.'

It is she who solicits the alliance of Burgundy in a strain of impassioned eloquence which belongs to one fighting in a high cause, with unconquerable trust, and winning over enemies by the firm resolves of a vigorous understanding and an unshaken will. The lines beginning—

'Look on thy country—look on fertile France,'—

might have given the tone to every thing that has been subsequently written in honor of the Maid.* It was his

* I am at a loss to conjecture why these striking lines were not quoted in full, and add them in a note:

"Look on thy country—look on fertile France,
And see the cities and the towns defaced
By wasting ruin of the cruel foe!
As looks the mother on her lowly babe,
When death doth close his tender-dying eyes,
See, see the pining malady of France;
Behold the wounds, the most unnatural wounds,

accurate knowledge of the springs of character which, in so young a man, appears almost intuitive, that made Shakspeare adopt this delineation of Joan of Arc. He knew that, with all the influence of her supernatural pretension, this extraordinary woman could not have swayed the destinies of kingdoms, and moulded princes and warriors to her will, unless she had been a person of very rare natural endowments. She was represented by the chroniclers as a mere virago, a bold and shameless trull, a monster, a witch, because they adopted the vulgar view of her character—the view, in truth, of those to whom she was opposed. They were rough soldiers, with all the virtues and all the vices of their age; the creatures of brute force; the champions, indeed, of chivalry; but with the brand upon them of all the selfish passions with which the highest deeds of chivalry were too invariably associated."*

This is all that can be said of the character of Joan of Arc as it appears in the drama; and I have quoted Mr. Knight's comment at length, because I must confess that I have not been able to raise my admiration of the dramatic treatment of her character so high. It has relative merit when compared to the treatment of the same subject

---

Which thou thyself hast given her woful breast!
Oh! turn thy edged sword another way;
Strike those that hurt, and hurt not those that help!
One drop of blood drawn from thy country's bosom
Should grieve thee more than streams of foreign gore.
Return thee, therefore, with a flood of tears,
And wash away thy country's stained spots." W. B. R.

* Charles Knight's Pictorial Shakspeare. Essay on Henry the Sixth and Richard the Third, p. 131.

by the chroniclers, but it still falls, I think, very far short of what is justly due to beauty and purity and heroism of female character. I believe that the matured genius of the poet would have rendered such tribute in spite of national prejudice and universal injustice; and one cannot help lamenting that the subject fell into his hands only in the early and immature period of his imagination, to which the composition of the play, if it really was his, is ascribed.

The dispassionate and unprejudiced estimate of the character of the Maid of Orleans belongs, however, to a later age than that of Shakspeare; and the national animosity which hindered it, has, in this case, died away, so that she is now a heroine to Englishmen, no less than to Frenchmen, and, indeed, a Christian heroine to all Christendom.* The poets of Britain and of Germany have drawn genuine inspiration from the memory of her life.† But let me notice that, while there is better spirit of justice in dealing with her history, the modern judgment differs from that which was contemporary with her in this respect, that now the supernatural element is excluded; and the question is, whether she was a sincere and self-deluded enthusiast, or a wilful impostor. For-

* "Joan of Arc a heroine to Englishmen no less than to Frenchmen." Arnold's Lectures, p. 96.

† My brother was not familiar with the German language or its literature. His allusion is here, of course, to Schiller's "Maid of Orleans," with which, accident had made him acquainted in the translation by the late William Peter, the British consul in Philadelphia—a gentle man who, during his residence in our city, gained many friends. He was a poet of no mean pretensions and a thorough scholar. My brother always spoke of him highly and affectionately. W. B. R.

merly, the supernatural character of her mission was not doubted, and the question then was, whether the mission was from above or below. By those who were hostile, her influence was not regarded as a cheat and an imposture, but it was witchcraft—it was sorcery and satanic inspiration—some strange dealing with the powers of darkness. The Duke of Gloucester issued a proclamation to reassure his soldiers against the *incantations* of the girl, and the Duke of Bedford spoke of her as a "disciple and lymb of the fiend, that used false enchauntments and sorceries." Nobody seems to have had a doubt that she possessed supernatural power; and the only question was, whether she brought with her "airs from heaven or blasts from hell." The severe rationalism of modern times has, however, wholly changed this interpretation of her character and career, which may be admired and applauded, but must not be traced to any higher cause than such as serve to explain the ordinary affairs of daily life. The modern mind recoils so violently from the admission of any thing more than mere human agency in the course of human affairs, and the whole subject of belief in miraculous interposition is so completely systematized by formal treatises upon the "Evidences," which prescribe the occasions on which a miracle may reasonably and appropriately be recognised, that the achievements of the Maid of Orleans must find an explanation in some of the more customary principles of action. And yet I do not see that there is any great difference between saying that she was supernaturally commissioned to redeem her country from foreign dominion —a proposition which most minds would probably shrink from—and saying that, in the providential government of the world, it came into her heart to save France from

English conquest—a proposition which, perhaps, none would have any difficulty in admitting.

This, at least, is clear: that what she said respecting her motives and the influences upon her mind, she did sincerely and steadfastly believe. No authority could shake, no sophistry could beguile, her deep convictions of what she held to be the truth, though the whole world should discredit it. She said she was commissioned by Heaven to raise the siege of Orleans and to crown Charles the Seventh at Rheims—two acts very remotely possible, nay, to human foresight, almost impracticable. And who was she that gave such wondrous promise? A humble shepherd girl, a mere child, (for she was but nineteen years old,) ignorant of the world—of every thing but the mighty workings of her own soul—unfriended, and, indeed, with no earthly support of any kind, with no mortal countenance to cheer and encourage; and yet what this poor girl said she was commissioned to do, that exactly she *did* do. Her mission was fulfilled; and while, perhaps, no one can confidently assert, or confidently deny, that her mission was, as she believed, divine, certainly in the world's history there is not to be found such an achievement of unassisted human enthusiasm.

The heroism of the Maid of Orleans has this surpassing merit: that it combines in beautiful proportions and harmony the elements of piety, of patriotism, and of freedom. She was what she was from the love and the fear of God from love of her native land, and from the love of liberty. In childhood she tended her father's flocks. Her education was that of a peasant girl; she could neither read nor write, but she could repeat her Pater Noster and Ave Maria. She was known as a kind-hearted girl, who would dutifully nurse the sick and help the wayfarer; and acts of devotion were more congenial to her than the sports of childhood. At her trial—that trial which ended in her death and the eternal shame of her judges—the sacristan of the village church bore witness, that she was wont to chide him when he neglected to ring the church bells at the appointed hours of service, and to win him to more fidelity in his office. To her secluded home and her apprehensive spirit there came tidings—brought, no doubt, by many a weary wayfarer—of the evil that was besetting the monarchy of France. She heard with indignant loyalty, how her sovereign was, by a series of disasters, becoming a vassal; how British invasion, with Burgundian alliance, was spoiling her native land. How it was that the thought came into her soul that *she* was to be an instrument to save her country and her king, no history can tell, no philosophy can explain; and we must fain content ourselves, I suppose, with the poor theory that it was enthusiasm—political and religious enthusiasm combined, and working on an ardent imagination and a lofty spirit. It was her own belief that the canonized dead appeared to her; that she saw the forms and "heard the voices of her guardian saints, calling on her to re-establish the throne of France and expel the English invaders." The apparitions began, she said, when she was thirteen years old, and they continued during several years. She beheld them at noonday, and in the open fields; majestic forms floated before her sight, and the sound of mysterious voices reached her ears. One awful form announced itself as an archangel; and so strong and sincere was her faith in these appearances, that, on her trial, with that placid and serene confidence which she displayed on that occasion, she said to her judges—"I saw him with my eyes as plainly as I see you now." And when further questioned, she added—"Yes, I do believe firmly, as firmly as I believe the Christian faith, and that God has redeemed us from the pains of hell, that those voices came from God and by his command." Animated by such faith, she went forth to inspire new zeal into the hearts of her fainting countrymen; and it is a familiar story, how her presence quickly proved a power of victory, and her voice kindled that hopeful courage, which gives a people their liberty and guards their independence. The enthusiasm that was caught from her by her countrymen at the same time struck terror and dismay into the hearts of their adversaries; her voice was the trumpet-signal of the restoration of her country's freedom; and it has been nobly said in those lines, which burst so finely from a youthful poet's heart—from the impassioned soul of Southey—

> "When she spake the trump was heard
> That echoed ominous o'er the streets of Rome,
> When the first Cæsar tottered o'er the grave
> By freedom delved;—the trump whose chilling blast,
> On Marathon and on Platea's plain
> Scattered the Persian."

In the almost incredibly short space of seven days after her arrival at Orleans, she raised the siege of the city; and, of those seven days, three were by her direction devoted to public prayer. The supernatural terror which had seized the English soldiers was so great, that, at the battle of Patay, they—among them no doubt were some of the veterans of Agincourt—fled in panic-struck confusion.

The remaining promise of Joan of Arc was speedily fulfilled when the dauphin entered the city of Rheims in triumph, and was crowned Charles the Seventh. During the coronation, the Maid of Orleans stood before the high altar of the cathedral, with her banner unfurled; and, afterwards, when asked on her trial—"Why was your banner thus honoured beyond all other banners?" she answered—"It had shared the danger; it had a right to share the glory."

It was a beautiful trait of female heroism that, while this extraordinary woman was not only displaying a dauntless intrepidity in the hour of battle, and not only animated the soldiers, but led them into the thickest of the fight, she refrained from staining her womanhood with the blood of even the enemies of her country.* The white banner which she bore in battle, and which was seen in her hands in the fiercest of it, she had taken, as she declared on her trial, on purpose to spare the sword and lance; that she wished not to kill any one with her own hand, and that she never had. She wore, it is true, the old sword which was mysteriously obtained for her from the church-vault of St. Catherine at Fierbois, but only as a part of her suit of armour and for defence. Among the curious particulars of her story, one of the homely incidents which give such reality to our impressions of her life, was the use of it on one occasion as a bloodless weapon of offence. When the sudden change in the fortune of war raised the spirits of the French sol-

* How untrue, therefore, is Schiller's delineation of "The Maid:" he makes her bound by a vow to kill, and never to give quarter. The crisis of her fate comes from an act of mercy. W. B. R.

diers from their depression, the excitement led to disorders which defied discipline. The Maid, encountering one of the riotous parties revelling in company with a worthless female camp-follower, beat them with the flat of her sword, so that the mysterious weapon broke in her hands. When this ill-omened accident was reported to the king, he said to her—"You ought to have taken a stout stick and laid that well on them, instead of risking the sword which came to you divinely, as you say."*

Orleans being relieved and Charles the Seventh crowned at Rheims, the Maid regarded her mission accomplished and her duty done. She sought release from her strange, unwomanly service. "I wish," she said, "this gentle king would allow me to return to my father and mother, to keep my flocks and herds as before, and do all things as I was wont to do." This, let it be observed, was at the very height of her triumph and power; amid the splendour and attraction of such proud scenes, and amid the grateful honours rendered to her by king and captains and courtiers, her thoughts travelled back to the simple life of her childhood and the secluded pastures of Lorraine. Her father and kinsfolk had come to witness her triumph, and gladly would the shepherd girl have gone back with them to her quiet home and the village church. She was, however, prevailed on by universal entreaty to forego her own wishes; but, while in her

* Is there not some skepticism—an insinuated doubt—in this "*As you say*" of the king? I wonder that my brother missed the chance of a fair criticism on Hume, who calls Charles the Seventh "*the good king.*" Why, it is, indeed, not easy to say. History scarcely produces a character less entitled to this praise, and more in contrast with the heroism that rescued him. W. B. R.

after career she displayed the same courage in battle, it was observed that she seemed no longer to feel the same persuasion that she was acting at the command and under the guidance of Heaven.

Another remarkable proof of the preservation of the simplicity and innocence of her character is to be found in the fact, that she only did not solicit, but declined, all rewards; all of royal favour that she asked was that the village of her birth should be thereafter exempt from all taxation. For three hundred years and more did this memorial of her services continue; and, until the French Revolution ruptured so many historic associations, the stated return on the registry of taxes opposite to the name of the village of Domremy was in these words: "Nothing on account of the Maiden."*

Again, at another period of the war, did Joan of Arc determine to retire; but again was she persuaded to remain with the army; and again and again in assaults and skirmishes was she distinguished by her accustomed valour. But her glorious career was drawing to its dark and tragic close; so true is it, as has been eloquently said, that—"There is seldom a line of glory written upon the earth's face, but a line of suffering runs parallel with it; and they that read the lustrous syllables of the one and stoop not to decipher the spotted and worn inscriptions of the other, get the least half of the lesson earth has to give."

The death of Joan of Arc has a connection with English history—an opprobrious connection; for upon that history it has left a reproach, which all the tide of time

* "Néant à cause de la Pucelle." W. B. R.

cannot wash away. The battle in which she was taken prisoner was not with the English, but with the Burgundians. In the course of a few months, however, she was purchased by the English of John of Luxemburg, whose prisoner she was, for ten thousand livres. When the news of the captivity of the Maid was received, Paris, still in the occupation of the English, was filled with rejoicing; the bells in the old towers of Nôtre-Dame were rung, and a solemn *Te Deum* and thanksgiving were celebrated;—all this because one woman was taken prisoner; and, O, shame! the celebration was by the order of the Regent Bedford—he who, a few years before, had stood by the side of his heroic brother, King Henry the Fifth, on the perilous field of Agincourt, with an army outnumbered, needy, and enfeebled, but not disheartened.

Joan of Arc was placed in strict confinement; she was loaded with fetters, and English archers kept guard over her. Her death was determined on; but more than her death was needed. Her enemies were crafty as well as cruel; and their purpose was to dispel the popular feeling of awe which had given strength to her countrymen and struck terror to her enemies. It was by a subtle barbarity that she was delivered over to an ecclesiastical tribunal for trial—the mockery of justice. The guilt of this proceeding rests upon both countries—England and France. With Englishmen did the trial originate, and by Frenchmen was it conducted. The Bishop of Beauvais proved a ready instrument, and was appointed first judge; another French ecclesiastic the second, and another discharged the function of accuser. Near one hundred doctors of theology were present to assist with their counsel; and all this authority and learning were arrayed against a young, unlettered, and friendless peasant girl. She appeared in her military dress, but loaded with chains; and during fifteen days was the torment of her examination continued, vexing the memory even of her innocent childhood. The mind is apt to be attracted in the history of Joan of Arc, chiefly, if not exclusively, by her amazing martial prowess; but equally wonderful was the constancy displayed upon her trial. When we think of the deep sensibility of her nature, her ardent imagination, her high-wrought enthusiasm, and memory fraught with such marvellous recollections, it is most wonderful to note the sober good sense and calm wisdom of her answers; and, still more, the placid faith and beautiful charity which shone through them.*

She was asked whether she knew herself to be in the grace of God. It was a crafty and a murderous question, for it was framed in the hope of extorting an answer that should prove the sentence of her own condemnation. The malice of the question was baffled by the simplicity of her answer:—"If I am not in the grace of God, I pray God it may be vouchsafed to me; if I am, I pray God I may be preserved in it." A profound humility proved the highest wisdom. With undiminished malevo-

* It was once my good fortune—a rare one in this country, where the book is not often met with—to read the examination of Marie Antoinette, the dethroned Queen of France, before the revolutionary tribunal—the questions and the answers as printed in the Moniteur. The original newspaper on its homely brownish paper as published, I presume, the next day, was before me. It brought the ghastly scene of her martyrdom more vividly to my mind than any elaborate eloquence—from Burke down to Lamartine. It has been recalled to my memory by this examination of "La Pucelle." W. B. R.

lence, she was asked whether the saints of her visions hated the English nation; and when she replied—"They love whatever God loves, and hate whatever he hates," the irritated inquisitor pursued her with the question—"Does God, then, hate the English?" and her answer was —"Whether God may love or hate the English, I know not; but I do know that they shall be driven forth from this realm by the King of France—all but those who shall die in the field." It seems to me that there is nothing more impressive in her story than the simple serenity, the sagacity, as well as the piety of her answers, as will appear from a few of them:

"When you took the banner, did you ask whether it would make you victorious in every battle?" "The Voices," answered she, "told me to take it without fear, and that God would help me." "Which gave the most help, you to the banner or the banner to you?" "Whether victory came from the banner or from me, it belonged to God alone." "Was the hope of victory founded on the banner or on yourself?" "It was founded on God, and naught besides."

"If another person had borne it, would the same success have followed?" "I cannot tell. I refer myself to God."

"Why were you chosen sooner than another? "It was the pleasure of God that a simple maid should put the foes of the king to flight."

"Were you not wont to say, to encourage the soldiers, that all the standards made in semblance of your own would be fortunate?" "I used to say to them—'Rush in boldly among the English!' and then I rushed in myself."

The tones of innocence and truth could find no entrance into the hearts of the ruthless judges who had foredoomed her. The cruelty of her persecutors gave no respite even to the short and bitter time between her condemnation for sorcery and heresy and the last hour when, in the market-place of Rouen, she was bound to the stake. The young and heroic brow which, during her whole life, had been bowed in frequent and faithful devotion, and which had been pressed by the helmet in her country's battles, was made to bear a mitre with the cruel and false inscriptions of—"RELAPSED HERETIC, APOSTATE, IDOLATER." While engaged in her last devotions she asked for a crucifix. There was none at hand, but an English soldier made a cross of rude form by breaking his staff. This was the only act of mercy or pity which appears to have been shown to her by her English foes. The flames lapped her body, and the Saviour's name was the last word that was heard from her lips.

Of this awful and inhuman tragedy the French Bishop of Beauvais was an official spectator, and so was the English Bishop of Winchester. It was the last prelate—the Cardinal Beaufort—who, implacable even by the death of their victim, ordered the ashes and the bones of the "heretic" to be gathered up and cast into the river Seine. And who was this Cardinal Beaufort, Bishop of Winchester? What was his life, and what the ending of it? We have seen how the career of Joan of Arc was mysteriously turned from the simplicity and lowliness of her birth, and from the path of womanhood; and now, in brief comparison, let us look at the life and death of the haughty ecclesiastic who exulted over her martyrdom.

Henry Beaufort was a natural son of John of Gaunt,

Duke of Lancaster, and brother, therefore, of Henry the Fourth, and uncle of Henry the Fifth. Preferment in the church was not wanting to him, but it gave not enough to satisfy either his avarice or his ambition; and he added political to ecclesiastical power. During the minority of Henry the Sixth, his aspiring and turbulent spirit was not the smallest element of disorder in those times. The tranquillity of the realm was broken by the quarrels and the rivalry of the Bishop of Winchester and the Duke of Gloucester; and the Regent Bedford was constrained to return to England to quell their controversy. The prelate was honoured with ecclesiastical dignities conferred by the pope; he was made a cardinal, and appointed captain-general of a crusade against the followers of John Huss, in Bohemia. We have seen how the peaceful life of Joan of Arc was turned from its natural course into the stormy channel of war; and so it is with this cardinal, the duty of whose life lay in the pacific duties of the church. But how different was the change! She sought a soldier's life to defend her king and country; and he, for aggression and religious persecution, levied his band of five thousand archers. She put away reward from herself; while he accumulated wealth that distinguished him as the "Rich Cardinal." She, even in battle, forebore staining her hand with blood; he participated in the fiery blood-shedding of her martyrdom; and on his memory rests, too, the dark suspicion of having caused the treacherous murder of his kinsman, Gloucester. Joan of Arc perished in the bloom of early womanhood, but Beaufort lived not only the threescore years and ten, but to be an aged man of eighty years. She died a death of torture at the stake; and, fixing her fading vision on the cross rudely and hastily made by a soldier's hand, gave up her spirit meekly in prayer. He died in his palace in his bed; perhaps it was "his bed of the golden cloth of Damascus," so gorgeous that he bequeathed it a legacy to the Queen of England; and now that he had reached the mortal limit of his fourscore years of princely pomp and royal opulence, his restless spirit raised new hopes of ambitious regency upon the deaths of Bedford and Gloucester; and, still more, the triple crown of the papacy was a distant vision to the eyes of the aged and aspiring cardinal. One of the chroniclers, upon the testimony of the chaplain who witnessed his last days, narrates that Beaufort on his death-bed uttered the miserable question—"Why should I die, having so much riches? If the whole realm would save my life, I am able either by policy to get it or by riches to buy it." And Shakspeare has wrought the history and tradition of Cardinal Beaufort's last hours into that awful scene of impenitent misery and terror upon a death-bed, where the meek and pious monarch, Henry the Sixth, is introduced, uttering over the dying man's struggles the words of piteous intercession:

> "O thou eternal Mover of the heavens!
> Look with a gentle eye upon this wretch!
> Oh, beat away the busy meddling fiend
> That lays strong siege unto this wretch's soul,
> And from his bosom purge this black despair!
> * * * *
> Lord cardinal, if thou thinkest on heaven's bliss,
> Hold up thy hand—make signal of thy hope—
> He dies, and makes no sign.*

* The historical student is aware that there is "another side" even in Cardinal Beaufort's case; and that Doctor Lingard, the Roman

The world that was not worthy of Joan of Arc while she lived, has striven to make some amends to her memory, against which the spirit of persecution has been revived only in the more devilish form of the ribald wit and blasphemy of Voltaire. On the spot where she was sacrificed, a monument has long stood to commemorate her character and national services. The poetic genius of Southey and of Schiller has celebrated her memory, and historians have reverently collected all the evidence of her story.* But, perhaps, the most beautiful tribute

Catholic historian, asserts that Shakspeare was all wrong, and was misled by prejudiced chroniclers, such as Hall; and that the cardinal's old age was devoted to pastoral duties and religious exercises. (Vol. iv. p. 83.) My brother, though evidently on the Shakspearian side of the question, did not bring out one of Beaufort's atrocities as strongly as he might have done. Lord Mahon, in his Quarterly Review essay, says, speaking of the Maid's execution:—"Several of the prelates and assessors had already withdrawn in horror from the sight, and others were melted into tears; but the Cardinal of Winchester, still unmoved, gave orders that the ashes and bones of the heretic should be collected and cast into the Seine." On the vexed question of Beaufort's real guilt or innocence, I am incompetent to form an opinion; but, taking his death-bed horrors as truth, there are four lines at the close of the scene which, in charity, should be quoted. Warwick says—

"So bad a death argues a monstrous life."

To which the king gently answers—

"Forbear to judge, for we are sinners all—
Close up his eyes and draw the curtain close
And let us all to meditation." W. B. R.

* I find the following most recent tribute to the memory of "The Maid" in the little volume to which I have already more than once referred in these notes:

"I will add but one remark," says Professor Creasy, "on the character of the truest heroine that the world has ever seen. If any that has ever been paid to the memory of the Maid of Orleans, has been that, in our own day, of a sister woman and sister countrywoman by that daughter of the King of the French—the princess who, in the statue of Joan of Arc, has left a memorial that she shared the genius and the inspiration of Thorwaldsen or Canova. An English writer has well said—

"Who that has ever trodden the gorgeous galleries of Versailles, has not fondly lingered before that noble work of art—before that touching impersonation of the Christian heroine—the head meekly bended, and the hands devoutly clasping the sword, in sign of the cross, but firm resolution imprinted on that mouth, and beaming from that lofty brow? Whose thoughts, as he paused to gaze and gaze again, might not sometimes wander from old times to the present, and turn to the sculptress—sprung from the same royal lineage which Joan had risen in arms to restore—so highly gifted in talent, in fortunes, in hopes of happiness, yet doomed to an end so grievous and untimely? Thus, the statue has grown to be a monument, not only to the memory of the Maid, but to her

---

person can be found in the present age who would join in the scoffs of Voltaire against the Maid of Orleans, and the heavenly voices by which she believed herself inspired, let him read the life of the wisest and best man that the heathen nations ever produced. Let him read of the heavenly voice by which Socrates believed himself to be constantly attended; which cautioned him on his way from the field of battle at Delium, and which, from his boyhood to the time of his death, visited him with unearthly warnings. Let the modest reader reflect upon this; and then, unless he is prepared to term Socrates either fool or impostor, let him not dare to deride or vilify Joan of Arc." Decisive Battles of the World, vol. ii. p. 101: "The Battle of Orleans."

W. B. R.

own: thus, future generations in France—all those, at least, who know how to prize either genius or goodness in woman—will love to blend together the two names—the female artist with the female warrior—

MARY OF WURTEMBURG and JOAN OF ARC."*

The execution of the Maid of Orleans proved ineffectual in restoring the fortune of the English arms; and, though the contest was protracted, neither the wise and strong regency of Bedford, nor the valour of Talbot, could save the conquests in France. The Duke of Burgundy broke off from the alliance with England, and returned to his allegiance to the French king. The fit and final catastrophe to a war which had lasted in all near one hundred and twenty years, was the expulsion of the English. The original claim of the King of England to the French crown had no foundation in justice; and, happily for both nations, the independence of France was re-esta-

* This is an extract from a most picturesque article in No. 138 of the Quarterly Review, now known to be by Lord Mahon—the present Earl Stanhope—and since separately published as his, in a popular form. Much of the materials, and, occasionally, passages of the lecture, are derived from this article; and I have not thought it worth while to distinguish them further than by this general acknowledgment. It occurs to me here to note, as this work is passing through the press, we have the intelligence that Earl Stanhope has recently—and it was one of his first acts on succeeding to his title—created a prize essay at Oxford on "English Historical Composition." At this time when a great deal of nonsense is talked and written on both sides of the Atlantic about "the cold shade of the aristocracy," it is pleasant to those who still think well of ancient institutions to find noblemen like Lord Stanhope and Lord Carlisle actively contributing to the cause of popular letters. W. B. R.

blished, and the continental conquests of the Plantagenets ceased forever.

During that war in France, the Duke of Bedford died—his regency unaccomplished, but distinguished for wisdom and ability; he was buried in one of the old cathedrals of France, and a stately monument erected over his body.

It was said by an old chronicler that, in the next French reign, King Louis the Eleventh—"By certain indiscreet persons was counselled to deface the tomb of the Duke of Bedford in the cathedral church of our Lady in Rouen, being told that it was a great dishonour both to the king and to the realm to see the enemy of his father and theirs have so solemn and rich memorial. He answered, saying, What honour shall it be to us or to you, to break this monument and to pull out of the ground the dead bones of him who, in his lifetime, neither my father nor your progenitors, with all their power, puissance, and friends, were not able to make flee one foot backward; but who, by his strength, wit, and policy, kept them all out of the principal dominions of the realm of France, and out of this noble and famous duchy of Normandy. Wherefore, I say, first—God have his soul, and let his body lie in rest, which, when he was alive, would have disquieted the proudest of all; and, as for the tomb, I assure you it is not so decent or convenient as his honour and acts deserved, although it were much richer and more beautiful."*

This was a piece of generosity which one would hardly

* Lingard cites for this surprising act of Louis the Eleventh, Stow, p. 475; Hall, 129.

have expected from a man so cold-hearted and unscrupulous as Louis the Eleventh; and, as the incident is told in the simple language of the chronicler, it has a poetic aspect, and recalls—once scarce knows how—those simple lines of Coleridge which Walter Scott was fond of quoting:

"The knight's bones are dust,
And his good sword rust;—
His soul is with the saints, I trust."*

It was my intention to have included in this lecture that part of the civil war which belongs to the reign of Henry the Sixth; but the truth is, I have been glad to escape into the French history connected with that reign, and I could not forbear dwelling upon the story of Joan of Arc longer than I at first contemplated.

The next lecture must, therefore, comprehend the subject of the war of the houses of York and Lancaster from its origin to the end of the reign of Richard the Third.

* Christabel. Poetical Works, p. 276, Am. ed.

LECTURE IX.*

The Wars of the Roses.

Closing scenes of the Plantagenet dynasty—Want of interest in the War of the Roses—The question of genealogy—No actuating principle in the contest—Its obscurity—A series of bloody battles—Saintly character of the king—His solitary sadness—Loss of the French conquests—The Duke of Suffolk—Popular tumult—Jack Cade—The Temple Garden—Richard of York and Somerset—The battle of St. Albans—The Earl of Warwick, the king-maker—Henry's captivity—The Parliament—Margaret of Anjou—Her character—King René—Injustice of English writers to her memory—The battle of Wakefield—Two crowned Kings of England—The slaughter at Towton—Tewksbury—The queen—Sir Walter Scott's tribute to her—Political effects of the civil war—Death struggle of the military power of the nobles—The last of the barons—Clifford—No feud among the people or vassals—The separation of the church from the conflict—Education—The foundation of Eton.

THE first part of the reign of Henry of Windsor being connected with the close of the war against France, I was tempted, in the last lecture, to digress in some measure into French history, partly because one could hardly help expatiating on the splendid and sad story of that Christian heroine, the Maid of Orleans, and partly because I would fain escape, at least for a little while, from the unpromising and unsatisfactory subject

* February 22d, 1847.

that must be encountered now—I mean the history of that hateful civil feud between the families of York and Lancaster, which has nothing attractive in it save its pretty symbolical title of the "War of the Roses." The subject which I have now to treat of is the civil war between the two branches of the Plantagenet family, from the origin of their contention down to the defeat and death of Richard the Third at the battle of Bosworth Field, when the body of that last of the Yorkists was stripped and thrown across a horse's back, like a slaughtered wild beast, besmeared with blood and dirt, and thus carried to an unhonoured burial at Leicester. So it was, that, after more than three centuries of majestic rule and after fourteen reigns, the dominion of the Plantagenet dynasty in England, the Saxon and the Norman race combined, passed away forever.

Taken in its fullest extent, down to the battle of Bosworth Field, this civil war occupied a period of thirty years, embracing what one of the old English chroniclers has entitled "the *troublous* season of King Henry the Sixth, the *prosperous* reign of King Edward the Fourth, the *pitiful* life of King Edward the Fifth, and the *tragical* doings of King Richard the Third." A struggle so protracted and so sanguinary as it was has not been without permanent political consequences, which I will endeavour to indicate in the course of this lecture; but, however important were these remote results in the national progress of England, they do not give an interest to the story of the struggle itself. If the War of the Roses be considered by itself—separated, on the one hand, from the earlier events, with which it is morally connected by retribution for ancestral guilt, and, on the other hand, from the later times, in which unlooked-for consequences are seen—there cannot, I think, be found an era of history more unsatisfactory. It is scarcely possible, it seems to me, to awaken in our minds any strong feeling on either side of this domestic warfare by the statement of the respective claims of the two parties. The particulars of the genealogical question are no sooner received into the mind than they are very apt to escape out of the memory. It is enough, however, to remember, for the purpose of understanding the issue, that both parties trace their claims back to a common ancestor, Edward the Third. There being no descendants from either the first or second son of that sovereign, the controversy lay between the posterity of the third and fourth sons. The three Lancastrian kings, being descended from the fourth son, had occupied the throne for more than half a century, to the exclusion of the lineage of the third, to whom the rights of the Duke of Clarence had descended in due course of inheritance.

Now, a judgment on the respective merits of the Yorkist and Lancastrian claims can only be formed after determining whether the law of the English monarchy is indefeasible, unalterable, hereditary right, or whether the rule of succession may undergo a change by the action of Parliament, as the great national council. Historians, accordingly, are found with York or Lancaster predilections and prejudices, as they respectively incline to the theory of the absolute, hereditary right of the monarch, or to that of the supremacy of the Parliament. But, whatever be the merits of this question, they are not of such a nature as to inspire us with an interest in the war, for the sake of any principle involved in it. And this is so, not because the modern mind, or our republican minds, prevent our entering into the spirit of this ancient commotion of the monarchy, but because the parties to the war do not appear themselves to have felt the respective principles as great actuating impulses. There is a great deal to show that the war was a contest of passion far more than of principle. The theoretical cause of the war was perhaps the least efficient, and is quite inadequate to explain such vindictive and incessant and protracted warfare. Had not other causes co-operated, blood never would have been shed so freely and fearfully; and it would, I believe, be as reasonable to say, that the two parties fought because the Yorkists wore the white rose, and the Lancastrians the red, as to ascribe the war wholly to the question of genealogical right. The Yorkists were not warring in support of the principle of indefeasible succession, nor were the Lancastrians warring for the principle of the constitutional authority of parliamentary establishment. If they had been, however we might incline to one principle or the other, we might gain an interest in a contest, in which we could contemplate and admire men laying down their lives for a principle. This war, in which Englishmen were slaughtering Englishmen, was the most destructive that England had ever been engaged in; this fraternal ferocity was the cause of the loss of more lives than all the wars with Wales, Scotland, and France; and the difficulty is to discover the real motives to such a series of cruelties and carnage. Full as history is, from ancient years down to the present day, of wars, wicked from the frivolity or the insanity of the occasion of them—ready as nations have been to plunge into hostilities—it still is incredible that the war of York and Lancaster was waged only on such a point of controversy as the real issue between the two contending parties. The only cause assigned is inadequate to give an interest to the struggle; and no other cause, that I am aware of, has been discovered, which would better attract the mind to the study of it.

Besides the absence of intrinsic interest in the subject, a most vexatious obscurity envelops the whole period of this civil war. It is very true, as has been said, that "The peculiar hardship in explaining the transactions of those days is, that we do not know what we have to explain, or whether we have any thing to explain at all. We have to solve a theorem without a proposition." We have, indeed, a considerable number of facts distinctly ascertained, but often utterly inexplicable; we know their dates, too, so that we can follow them in order of time; but, as to the sequence, the connection of one with the other, it is utter darkness. One can make his way through this region of history, only as a man travels along an unknown road in a dark and stormy night. There comes a flash of light, giving a lurid and momentary conception of what is near; and, confiding in the knowledge thus gained, you venture onward in the dark, till again you are startled by another flash, that shows how, in a little distance, all your expectations of what lay before you are illusive, and that every thing around you is totally different from what it was just now:

"The road is black before your eyes,
Glimmering faintly where it lies;

Black is the sky—and every hill,
Up to the sky, is blacker still."*

Now and then the darkness of the storm seems to be breaking, and light is caught from between the flying clouds, from the moon, or from a starlit space in the sky; and then, just as we are promising ourselves the calm vision of a tranquil hour, the tempest, that was only lulled, comes back again worse and darker than ever. So it is in the uncertain and confused history of these civil wars. We get the lurid and fitful light from the fields of twelve battles, and that is nearly all that one has to guide his steps by. Ever and anon, when there is some show of reconciliation between the factions, promising a little more clearness of historical knowledge, the strife is renewed with tenfold bitterness, and we are left in tenfold obscurity. If, in the fierceness of the warfare, we look up to heaven to discover why, in the providential government of the world, brother is thus furiously arrayed against brother for deadly carnage, we look up in vain for the meaning of it all, and seem to learn no more there than when we look to the high-reaching wickedness of the earthly passions of the moral combatants:

"Black is the sky—and every hill,
Up to the sky, is blacker still."

Such is the obscurity enveloping much of the history of the War of the Roses, that one of the latest and most laborious of the historians of England makes the candid admission, that he has omitted altogether from the text of his history the principal events of one of the years—

* Wordsworth. The Waggoner.

"Because," he says, "in our ignorance of their causes, it is difficult to connect them together." He finds himself unable to do more than merely mention them in a note.*

But, as we shall not gain any more light by merely complaining of the darkness, let us make some attempt to set our steps forward in it. We have seen how, in the reign of Henry the Fifth, that sovereign enjoyed, in a high degree, the unanimous and affectionate allegiance of his people; and let us, in the first place, consider whether there was any thing in the character of his son, Henry the Sixth, that was calculated to alienate from him the duty and the love of his subjects. It may be truly said of this king that, having begun his reign in the months of infancy, he carried forward into the years of manhood a most childlike spirit; the very innocence and simplicity of childhood seem never to have deserted him. One of the chroniclers has said of him—"King Henry was a man of meek spirit and of a simple wit, preferring peace before war, rest before business, honesty before profit, and quietness before labour: and to the intent that men might perceive that there could be none more chaste, more meek, more holy, nor a better creature, in him reigned shamefacedness, modesty, integrity, and patience to be marvelled at, taking and suffering all losses, chances, displeasures, and such worldly torments, in good part and with a patient manner, as though they had chanced by his own fault or negligent oversight. He gaped not for honour, nor thirsted for riches; but studied only for the health of his soul, the

* Lingard, vol. iv. p. 104.

saving whereof he esteemed to be the greatest wisdom, and the loss thereof the extremest folly that could be." Another describes him—"Patience was so radicate in his heart that, of all the injuries to him committed, which was no small number, he never asked vengeance nor punishment, but for that rendered to Almighty God, his Creator, hearty thanks, thinking by this trouble and adversity his sins were to him forgotten and forgiven. This good, this gentle, this meek, this sober and wise man did declare and affirm, that those mischiefs and miseries partly came to him for his own offence, and partly for the heaping of sin upon sin wretchedly by his ancestors and forefathers."

The whole life of this king sustained the truth of these descriptions of his character; and surely his offence to his turbulent countrymen was nothing more than his pure inoffensiveness—his unresenting meekness:

> "The universal stock of the world's injury
> Would be too poor to find a quarrel for him."*

Like his ancient predecessor, the sainted Saxon, King Edward the Confessor, the lot of Henry the Sixth was cast in an age of violence, and he brought nothing to it but a gentle spirit. Through all the tumults and the blood-shedding of the reign, the poor monarch wanders in a kind of solitary sadness of heart, the most inappropriate being in the world. It was said by that ill-fated artist, the late Mr. Haydon, speaking of the angelic disposition of a fellow-artist, that he always seemed to him

* "A Fair Quarrel," by Middleton and Rowley. Quoted in Henry Taylor's "Statesman;" and in "Lamb's Specimens," vol. i. p. 143.

to have been born in the wrong planet. One cannot help having something of the same feeling towards the memory of one so inappositely virtuous as this good man and feeble king, Henry of Windsor.

While the character of the king was negative in its influence upon the nation, there were several causes which, in the course of events, proved positive agencies of disaffection to the Lancastrian dynasty. During the minority, while Bedford was regent in France, the administration at home was perplexed and discordant, and the protector Gloucester had to struggle against the factious ambition of his rival, Cardinal Beaufort. The mysterious iniquity of the times begins to show itself, when the Duke of Gloucester is found dead in his bed, murdered, it was believed, but how, why, or by whom, no one to this day has discovered, so that the fact of murder has become a question. In a short space of time, the aged, rich cardinal expires; and Bedford is dead too, so that the great Lancastrian chiefs have passed away before the worst troubles of the reign begin.

The national vanity of the English, which had been so highly stimulated by the victory of Agincourt and the short-lived conquest of French territory, was now exasperated by the reverses of the war in France, and the loss of their continental dominions. The glory of the Plantagenets was waning, and the King of France was getting his own again; fortress after fortress was given up by the English; and when the nation found themselves deprived of all that lately they so proudly held of French soil, save a mere foothold on the sea-shore, they turned, in the maddened passion of disappointed pride, to take vengeance upon some one who might be made answerable for the disasters of the government. The national fury fell upon the Duke of Suffolk, as chief minister of Henry's government. He was impeached and tried; and the king, probably to save his life from the phrensy of faction, banished him from the kingdom. On his passage to France, the vessel that carried him was captured by a ship of the royal navy; he was ordered on board, received with the ominous salutation—"Welcome, traitor!" a mock trial was held, sentence of death pronounced; he was lowered into a small boat, which bore an executioner, a block, and a rusty sword; his head was hacked off, and his corpse cast ashore upon the Dover sands. This much is known, and then comes the cloud over the history, and we are all in the dark again.*

The murder of Suffolk seems to have been one of those deeds which are perpetrated by lawlessness usurping the place of law—the wild spirit of revenge claiming the power of justice. We know just enough of it to regard it as one of the ominous signs of perturbed times. It is a symptom of misgovernment and of domestic discord; and quickly there appears, in the shape of popular insurrection, another sign of approaching anarchy. You begin to hear the first sounds that give signal of the coming convulsion that is to shake the whole fabric of the realm;

* It has been cleverly said "that we are certain he was put to death, certain he was put to death violently, and we are so thankful for these two known quantities, that we consider the problem easy, and the event almost a natural one, though the facts, as they have come down to us, can only be paralleled in modern description, by imagining that Lord Brougham, while crossing to Havre, after having been supplanted in the chancellorship, had his head chopped off on the paddle-box of the Grand Turk steamer, and no inquiry made about it." H. R.

you discover the premonitions of the political pestilence that is to devastate England. Popular tumult is the first eruption of the disease, and just such an insurrection as that which was headed by Jack Cade, is the form the tumult is apt to take. It is licentiousness proclaiming freedom by the destruction of all rule and order; it is ruffian ignorance taking advantage of popular discontent by promising absurd and impracticable reformations. Wat Tyler's rebellion, some seventy years before, seems to me to have been a much more reputable insurrection than Cade's. Then the populace rose, because the power of government was oppressive upon them, and now, because they felt that the authority of law was too feeble to preserve subordination. The people were estranged from the sovereign; they had, in their discontent, a restless desire for change—they knew not what it should be; and a low demagogue started them—to flatter them with promises,—"There shall be in England seven half-penny loaves sold for a penny: the three-hooped pots shall have ten hoops; and I will make it felony to drink small beer: all the realm shall be in common, and in Cheapside shall my palfrey go to grass." Whether or no Cade's rebellion was fomented by the Duke of York, for the purpose of promoting his own aggrandizement out of the increased confusion, is one of the multitude of uncertainties of the history. York's claim to the crown is not yet made; but the troubles of the reign next take the form of the feud between York and the Lancastrian chief, the Duke of Somerset. It is a dispute between them, that Shakspeare has made the subject of the scene in the Temple garden, in which the origin of the adoption of the respective badges of the two great parties is accounted for. The scene, however, is a purely dramatic creation, without historic authority, as far as is known; and I am not aware that history gives any explanation of the adoption of the white and red roses as the emblems of the Yorkists and Lancastrians, respectively. In that scene York, being unable to obtain an oral expression of opinion respecting his hereditary rights, is represented saying—

> "Let him that is a true-born gentleman,
> And stands upon the honour of his birth,
> If he suppose that I have pleaded truth,
> From off this brier pluck a white rose with me;"

and Somerset adds—

> "Let him that is no coward, nor no flatterer,
> But dare maintain the party of the truth,
> Pluck a red rose from off this thorn with me."

The angry scene closes with Warwick's prediction:

> "This brawl to-day,
> Grown to this faction, in the Temple garden,
> Shall send, between the red rose and the white,
> A thousand souls to death and deadly night."

Before the claim of the Duke of York to the throne was openly asserted, the thoughts of the nation were, during some years, habituated to look to him as the future sovereign in due course of inheritance, he being the heir presumptive, and Henry the Sixth being then childless. The Duke of York became still more prominent in connection with royalty, by being made protector during the disability of the king. To the eyes of the nation, and to his own, the crown was visible as his future possession, until the birth of the Prince of Wales, the son of Henry the Sixth, changed the prospect, and the throne could be reached by the family of York only by a revolutionary change.

The battle of St. Albans, which is regarded as the beginning of the civil war, appears to have been an unpremeditated conflict. The Yorkists gained the battle, and the king fell into their power. The fact of the battle is quite intelligible; but immediately after it all that the triumphant Yorkists ask, is *pardon:* they renew their oaths of fealty to King Henry, and appear perfectly satisfied, simply because Somerset was killed in the battle. Soon afterwards the gentle king reconciled the contending parties, and a solemn procession to St Paul's Cathedral took place, in which the leaders of the two parties made a beautiful show of concord by walking hand in hand with each other. It was a very fine spectacle, but it was nothing more than a spectacle. The regal ambition in the soul of York was never quenched; and besides that, it was not forgotten, that in the conflict at St. Albans, Somerset, and Clifford, and Northumberland had fallen by the sword of their Yorkist foes; and now there was burning in the bosoms of their sons and retainers a lust for vengeance, which years did not extinguish. Moreover, there was the queen, the indomitable Margaret of Anjou, of whose character I shall speak presently. She was naturally suspicious of the adverse influences, which she saw gathering round her husband's throne; and the Yorkists strongly reciprocated the feeling of jealousy, as they came to know the might of that strong-willed woman.

The reconciliation endured but a little while, and then came another battle, the Yorkists again victorious: but to the great perplexity of the historical student, the victory is scarcely completed before the fortunes of the conquerors are suddenly depressed, one can hardly tell how or why: the Yorkist army disbands itself, and the leaders flee away to their strongholds. It was then that the fortunes of the faction were retrieved by perhaps the most remarkable personage in this war—Richard Nevil, Earl of Warwick, "the king-maker," as his successful prowess well entitled him to be styled. Warwick returned, rallied the disbanded army of the Yorkists, gained the battle of Northampton, drove the queen into exile, and brought his sovereign, helpless King Henry, captive to London,—the victorious nobleman all the while paying the show of respectful homage to his prisoner-king. Professions of allegiance were still studiously continued. It was a civil war, and not yet a war of succession. But now another change comes over the character of the contest, for while the parliament was in session for the purpose of harmonizing the dissentions, the Duke of York walked into Westminster Hall, and moving on to the throne, he placed his hand upon it and stood silent in that attitude. Every voice was hushed. The primate of England, after a short pause, inquired whether he would visit the king, and the answer was, "I know of no one in this realm who ought not to rather visit me." These words, and the significant gesture, proclaimed for the first time, and in the presence of the assembled parliament, that Richard Plantagenet laid claim to the throne of England. The claim was soon formally submitted to parliament, and there was presented, for the first and the last time in English history, the extraordinary spectacle of a king reigning and a king claiming confronted, as it were, and maintaining their rights in the presence of the great council of the realm. When the subject was first stated to King Henry, he said, with a simplicity and earnestness that were impressive—"My father was king; his father was also king; I have worn the crown forty years from my cradle; you have all sworn fealty to me as your sovereign, and your fathers have done the like to my fathers. How, then, can my right be disputed?"

The decision of the lords in parliament was the timid and unsatisfactory result of compromise—that process by which men, in their dread of encountering either one of two dangers, bring both upon themselves. Henry's possession of the crown was confirmed; but, on his death, to the exclusion of his son, the Duke of York and his heirs were to succeed. This wretched bargain was the occasion of another solemn procession of amity to St. Paul's.

It is at this crisis of the war that we may best turn to the character of Queen Margaret; for upon her was the cause of the Lancastrian succession now dependent. From Shakspeare and the chroniclers we receive a very harsh impression of the character of Margaret of Anjou, for they present her in repulsive, if not hideous, colours. She is portrayed unfeminine, arbitrary, revengeful, licentious, and even her energy and fortitude are distorted into unnatural ferocity and obduracy. I greatly distrust this representation, not because I am able to find historical authority for a different and better character, but because there was so much that would almost irresistibly render the English judgment on her memory prejudiced and unjust. The marriage-contract between her and Henry the Sixth stipulated for the cession of territory to her father, René of Anjou, that amiable, but, perhaps, somewhat fantastic person, who was happy in the pompous possession of three regal titles, without a rood of land in either of his kingdoms, Naples, Sicily, and Jerusalem; and who spent his days in a sort of pleasant dream of the innocent play of chivalry, and the songs of troubadours. Margaret came to England a Frenchwoman, to be the Queen of England, just at the time when English pride was exasperated by French victories; and, moreover, she was soon placed in the unnatural attitude of supplying by her character the feebleness of her husband's rule. The almost feminine gentleness of Henry's disposition gives an offensively masculine character to Margaret's life. She could not but see that the throne was environed with dangers, the perils of false friends and open enemies. She could not but see the helplessness of her royal husband; and she ought not to be judged too severely, when we consider that if her natural temper led to it, so also did the necessity of the case constrain her to do one of the worst things a woman can do, make a man of herself. And this was done, not as by her illustrious countrywoman, the Maid of Orleans, under religious influences, but for purposes of worldly policy. Still, these purposes were the defence of her king and husband, the possession of the throne, and the maintenance of the hereditary rights of her son. She may have been all that the English chroniclers and the English dramatist represent; but I do distrust it, because she was in the very position —the relation to a divided and misgoverned people—that would inevitably cause a great deal to be attributed to her, for which she may not have been rightfully responsible. Considering all the circumstances—more than I can stop to treat of—how natural, and yet how unjust, would it be for the adverse party to trace every obnoxious measure of the government, and many an atrocity in the war, to the Frenchwoman on the throne—the strong and determined wife of an irresolute and unregarded king.

I dare say that, in her way of life, there may have been much that is revolting to our sense of female character; indeed, it could not be otherwise; for a woman can hardly play a man's part in the work of the world without grievous detriment to her own nature. But one is still entitled to contemplate Queen Margaret, not as a vulgar and hideous Amazon, but as a woman under the dire necessity of mingling in scenes of war. After the parliamentary compromise, in which the succession of her son was sacrificed, we can behold her as an heroic matron warring for the rights of her child when the father's feeble hand could not defend them. She gathers an army, which the Duke of York, contemptuously encountering, pays a bloody penalty for the folly of rashly despising an enemy. He was slain at the battle of Wakefield; and, in as short a time as two months after he had walked in procession to St. Paul's, as the newly-declared heir-apparent, his gory head, insulted with a paper crown, was set upon the gates of York. After such a catastrophe, the reader of history naturally looks for the establishment of Lancastrian supremacy; but no—the rights of the Duke of York, and the feudal inheritance of vengeance for his death, pass to his son, the Earl of March, a youth of nineteen years of age; and from this time, the war becomes more ferocious than ever, and with a deeper thirst for revenge. The warlike queen pursues her success by the rescue of her husband from his captivity, but the young Duke of York enters London, and is proclaimed King Edward the Fourth.

The coronation of the new monarch was postponed until further hostilities should give him stronger possession of the throne. There were now two kings in the land, Henry the Sixth and Edward the Fourth; and the battle that soon followed between the two royal armies, shows, more impressively, perhaps, than any other in the war, to what fearful issues of carnage and bloodshed the passions of faction and civil war can drive men of the same kindred and the same homes. No foreigner shared in the strife; there were none but Englishmen present, and of them more than one hundred thousand were drawn up, in no very unequal division, in hostile array on the field of Towton. Both sovereigns were present, King Edward and King Henry, or, perhaps we had better say, Queen Margaret. Proclamation had been made that no quarter should be given; and faithfully and fiercely was the order obeyed, so that it proved probably the bloodiest battle in British history. The desperate conflict lasted more than a day; and some idea may be formed of the slaughter, when it is said the number of the Englishmen slain exceeded the sum of those who fell at Vimiero, Talavera, Albuera, Salamanca, Vittoria—five great battles of the Peninsular War—and at Waterloo combined.* This enormous shedding of English blood was by English

* I do not know the authority for this exact statement. In Southey's Colloquies, vol. i. p. 210, *Montesinos* says:—"More Englishmen fell at Towton than in any of Marlborough's battles or at Waterloo." Lingard says that Edward the Fourth, in a confidential letter to his mother, while he conceals his own loss, tells her that his heralds counted twenty-eight thousand Lancastrian dead on the field. "It was," says the historian, "a decisive victory, but it cost the nation a deluge of blood." W. B. R.

hands. The battle ended in the total rout of the Lancastrians, and the crown was firmly placed on the brow of Edward the Fourth.

So decided a victory, one would imagine, must have closed the contest; but no; for ten perilous years was the struggle continued, chiefly by the indomitable energy of Queen Margaret. Poor King Henry took refuge in the secluded regions of the North of England, but was betrayed and committed prisoner in the Tower of London, while his queen, eluding her enemies, is with difficulty followed in her rapid and unwearied movements, at one time rallying her English partisans and risking battle, again seeking alliance and help from the King of France. Perils by land and perils by sea making up the wild story of her adventures, we hear of her at one time shipwrecked, and, at another, falling into the hands of a band of roving banditti. She struggled to the last—as long as she had a husband or a child whose rights were to be contended for.

The later years of the war are no less perplexed than the beginning; and I do not know that, in the events that follow, there is to be discovered any thing especially characteristic of the age or expressive of the spirit of the times, except the conduct of that great feudal lord, the Earl of Warwick. It was chiefly by him that Edward the Fourth had been helped to the throne; and, when the king-maker found cause of quarrel with the monarch, he turned his allegiance away, and the greatest of the Yorkist chieftains was afterwards an adherent of the Lancastrians. King Edward became the prisoner of the proud nobleman, and one of the extraordinary spectacles which England exhibited in this war, was that of two rival kings, each confined in prison and at the same time. The king-maker was strong enough to lift up the prostrate Lancaster. Edward the Fourth fled from the palace and the kingdom; and his imprisoned rival was led forth from the Tower to hear the streets of London resounding once more with the name of King Henry. This surprising restoration gave, however, but a brief respite to the Lancastrian family before its final overthrow. The fugitive Edward returned to recover the crown, and, as it proved, to extinguish the opposing dynasty. He landed at Ravenspurg—the very place, as has been observed, where Bolingbroke, the Lancastrian progenitor, landed, when he came to deprive Richard the Second of the crown and to usurp it for himself; so fatal was that spot for the Plantagenets, first of the one and then of the other line. The landing of Edward at Ravenspurg has been compared to the return of Napoleon from Elba, when he came to shake the Bourbons again from the throne so lately restored to them. The comparison holds good as to the boldness and rapidity of the exploits; for, in about forty days, the counter-revolution of Edward was completed.

In regard to the first reception and the final results, the parallel fails. When Edward landed, he found that none durst speak in his favour for dread of Warwick; and he could advance into the country only, as Bolingbroke had done, under the crafty plea that he came to claim no more than his duchy. The disguise was, ere long, thrown off: he fought and gained a battle in which his chief adversary, the king-maker Warwick, was left dead on the field. He entered London in triumph, was king again, and poor King Henry, of whom we never hear any thing, except when something is done to him, was remanded to the Tower, never again to leave it alive.

The last convulsive effort of Queen Margaret was made at Tewkesbury, where the Lancastrian party met with its final defeat. The misery of the hapless queen was completed by the barbarous murder of her only child, the young Prince of Wales, who was stabbed to death, it is supposed, by King Edward's brothers, Clarence and Gloster—the horrid deed which Shakspeare has fitly made one of the phantoms that haunted the death-dream of Clarence:

> "Then came wandering by,
> A shadow like an angel, with bright hair
> Dabbled in blood;—and he shriek'd out aloud,
> 'Clarence is come—false, fleeting, perjur'd Clarence,
> That stabb'd me in the field by Tewkesbury;—
> Seize on him furies,—take him to your torments.'"

The murder of the old king, the harmless Henry, soon followed, the bloody release to his grieved spirit being given by the dagger of the Duke of Gloster—if popular belief has rightly rested on that, one of the dark deeds which belong to the history of the tower of London. The Lancastrian king and the Lancastrian heir having been destroyed, their great champion, the queen, Margaret of Anjou, is left alone; and, so far as the story of her life is connected with the annals of England, the last image which we have of her is, as she stands in the tragic sublimity of wo, discrowned, widowed, childless, captive, and desolate.*

* After five years of captivity in England, she was ransomed by the King of France and returned to her native country; where, in about

For sixteen years had the War of the Roses lasted, and eleven fierce and bloody battles had been fought by English with English alone within the narrow limits of England. Children had grown up with no other spectacle of their native land than as a battle-ground on which their countrymen were shedding one another's blood; and now that the war was at an end—at least so far as the undisturbed occupation of the throne of England was affected by it—the question naturally presents itself—What meaning had this war? Can it be possible that all

---

five years more, her eventful and unhappy life came to its end. The latter part of her life is a subject that has fallen into the hands of Shakspeare's great successor in imaginative historical literature. In the romance of "Anne of Geierstein" Sir Walter Scott has introduced the character of Queen Margaret during the last years of her life, and he has represented her with a finer justice than is awarded to her in the dramas. It is with admirable impartiality, and with the highest art, that Scott has dealt with the majestic ruin of Margaret's mighty and ambitious spirit, when, as he describes her, during the interview with the young Lancastrian in the Cathedral of Strasburg—"Though rivers of tears had furrowed the cheek—though care, disappointment, domestic grief, and humbled pride had quenched the fire of her eye and wasted the smooth dignity of her forehead—her noble and majestic features even yet showed the remains of that beauty which once was held unequalled in Europe."

Scott has traced the course of Margaret's aspiring and restless spirit on to her death, and even to the last sound of the solemn dirge over her grave. It is over the close of her story that Scott cites the lines entitled from an "Old Poem," but, doubtless, his own:

> "Toll, toll the bell—
> Greatness is o'er;
> The heart has broke,
> To ache no more.
> An unsubstantial pageant all—
> Drop o'er the scene the funeral pall."

H. R

this ferocity and havoc was significant of nothing more than the contest for the throne? Can it be that the mere question, which of two cousins should fill the throne —whether Henry Plantagenet or Edward Plantagenet should wear the crown—drove the multitudes of men to such fierce extremities of civil strife? Was all the misery and bloodshed of this war expended for no other consequence than a dubious settlement of succession? We should, indeed, study history very superficially if we thought so.

In the progress of constitutional freedom there was a great and permanent consequence of this civil war, which outweighs a thousand-fold the importance of any right of York or Lancaster. It was a result which the combatants on neither side contended for, and, indeed, they could not have dreamed of it. It was this: the devastation of the war wrought the downfall of English feudalism, and thus effected a great revolution in the aristocratic element of the Constitution. The war was the unconscious death-struggle of the martial power of the nobility. It would seem as if feudalism was to display its greatest splendour immediately before it was extinguished—as if it were to rise to its highest prowess immediately before it fell into irretrievable exhaustion. As the sun of feudal power in England went down, it blazed forth with the light of a larger and redder orb through the clouds of war that gathered around its setting.

During the whole extent of England's history, under the Saxon, Dane, or Norman, the mightiest of her barons was the king-maker Warwick. It was his power that made Edward king, and his that unmade him. It was his power that dethroned King Henry, and it was his that restored him. Each monarch in turn became the captive and prisoner of this great earl. With princely revenues and estates, Warwick's vassals were an army; and some notion may be formed of the force he could, at will, bring armed into the field, from the fact that he is said to have daily feasted, at his numerous manors and castles, upward of thirty thousand persons. The other nobles possessed, in their degree, the power of an armed feudal retinue, ready to follow their lord to battle in any cause of his choosing; and thus there was a baronial power of which modern England shows only the shadow. As the traveller now beholds the stately walls of Warwick Castle, or wanders amid the ruins of Kenilworth—

> "Where battlement and moated gate
> Are objects only for the hand
> Of hoary Time to decorate,"—*

he can scarce, with all the impulse given to his imagination, call up the vision of the armed hosts which, some three hundred years ago, could, at a moment's summons, be gathered there in battle array.

The war of York and Lancaster was a self-exhausting contest of the nobles. At the battle of Northampton the order was given through the field to strike at the lords, knights, and esquires, rather than at the common people. In the course of the war eighty princes of the blood were killed, and the ancient nobility nearly annihilated.

Every individual of two generations of the families of Somerset and Warwick fell on the field or on the scaffold.

* Wordsworth's Lines to a Lady. Works, p. 411.

Many of those who escaped the carnage were impoverished and outcast from their homes. "I myself saw," says Philip de Commines, "the Duke of Exeter, the King of England's brother-in-law, walking barefoot after the Duke of Burgundy's train, and earning his bread by begging from door to door."* The martial fierceness of a feudal nobility was tamed; and, with the decline of the force which feudalism armed them with, the way was prepared for converting them into the pacific aristocracy of more modern times. This change was wrought upon the generation of nobles during the civil war by the varied influences and lessons of adversity. Feudal pride had its fall, and feudal vengeance was softened to a gentler feeling. In this change there was a silent and momentous revolution; and it may, perhaps, be illustrated to you by the romantic story connected with the change as exemplified in the family of the Cliffords. At the first battle in the war, Lord Clifford was slain by the Duke of York; and the filial vengeance which fired the breast of the next Lord Clifford was scarce appeased, when, in the same battle in which York was slain, his son, young Rutland, was stabbed by Clifford, whose unpitying warfare earned for him the titles of "the butcher" and the "black Clifford." His death on the bloody field of Towton gave the Yorkists their retaliation, and the title of Clifford passed to his son, a young child, whose mother fled with him to find safety amid secluded lakes and mountains in the North. To elude the unrelenting pursuit and search of his enemies, the boy was trained in the simplicity and severity of a shepherd's life, with no more than dim

* Memoires de Commines, Liv. iii. ch. iv.

remembrances of his father's bloody death, and of the perils he must have witnessed in his early childhood, or seen reflected from his mother's brow. In shepherd's garb he learned to love the simple folk and the mute creation with whom his days were spent; he carried, too, into all his after life, peacefully protracted, as it was, to a good old age, a passion for the tranquil pursuits of science; for, while tending his flocks, he gazed from the lonely mountain-top upon the stars, and the beauty and peace of their placid motion sank deep into the soul of the fierce warrior's child. His fathers, through many a generation, had been surrounded by all the pomp of chivalry and by their troops of vassals; but, for this boy—

> "To his side the fallow-deer
> Came and rested without fear;
> The eagle, lord of land and sea,
> Stoop'd down to do him fealty."*

It was not until after more than twenty years—not until after the dynasty of the house of York had passed away—that the young Clifford was restored to his estates, to which he came, doubtless, a wiser and a better man than any of his stern progenitors; for, as a poet has commemorated the story of his life, which history has hardly heeded, this Clifford was one—

> "Who long compelled in humble walks to go,
> Was softened into feeling, soothed, and tamed.
>
> Love had he found in huts where poor men lie,
> His daily teachers had been woods and rills,

* Wordsworth's Song at the Feast of Brougham Castle. Works, p. 187.

The silence that is in the starry sky,
  The sleep that is among the lonely hills.

In him the savage virtue of the race,
  Revenge, and all ferocious thoughts were dead:
Nor did he change; but kept in lofty place
  The wisdom which adversity had bred.

Glad were the vales, and every cottage hearth;
  The shepherd lord was honoured more and more:
And ages after he was laid in earth,
  'The good Lord Clifford' was the name he bore."*

One of the most remarkable facts connected with this period of history is, that, when the Wars of the Roses were over, after all the aggravated and unsparing hostilities, little animosity appears to have remained among the survivors and their descendants. The solution of this fact is this, I believe:—that, having taken the field simply as retainers of nobles opposed to each other, they ceased to cherish belligerent feelings, when the relation to their superior lord ended. The vassal of Clifford, for example, and the vassal of Salisbury fought fiercely with each other; but, when they ceased to be the fighting vassals, they looked upon each other as fellow-countrymen, and so their hatred was spent.

After dwelling upon the evils of these distressful times, I wish not to overlook the good that was silently working out from them. While the two aristocratic factions of the realm were sweeping along with the tide of war a large portion of the people, composed of the multitude of their retainers, there was still a mass of the popula-

* Wordsworth's Song at the Feast of Brougham Castle. Works, p. 188.

tion that kept aloof from the strife, who neither shared in it nor suffered by it. There was happily no ecclesiastical element in the war; the church was not known in it—it was neither Yorkist nor Lancastrian; and no bishop or abbot appeared in it, except to stay, if possible, the shedding of blood, or to give sanctuary to the helpless or comfort to the suffering. While the feudal power of the nobles was sinking, the common people were rising. It has been well observed by Southey, that—"Inasmuch as both parties exerted themselves to bring into the field all the force they could muster, the villeins in great numbers were then emancipated when they were embodied in arms; and great numbers emancipated themselves, flying to London and other cities for protection from the immediate evils of war; or, taking advantage of the frequent changes of property, and the precarious tenure by which it was held, to exchange their own servile condition for a station of freedom with all its hopes and chances."

It is to be observed, too, that, ferocious and sanguinary as the civil war was, its fury spared the cities and towns. There was no burning or sacking of towns; there was no pillaging or devastation of churches or monasteries, so that a peaceful current of good was still flowing underneath the war. It is a noticeable fact that, during the perturbed reign of Henry the Sixth, as if at once to meet—what could not then have been foreseen—the wants of the people as they rose from feudal servitude, schools in London and throughout the realm were extensively endowed.*

* The spread of education was one of the innovations, it will be remembered, that excited the ire of Jack Cade when his ruffians brought Lord Say a prisoner to him, and Cade tells him—

Having spoken, somewhat contemptuously, perhaps, of the utter insignificance of Henry the Sixth, in the warlike doings of his reign, I must add, in justice, that his memory is finely redeemed, for national gratitude is due to him for that college at Cambridge, the gorgeous Gothic architecture of which has made the name of King's College famous over the world. He was also the founder of Eton College—that great school which stands by the side of the ancient palace of England's kings, and with the red-cross flag on Windsor Castle waving in sight of it. Instead of leaving your mind with a contempt for the good King Henry the Sixth—instead of dismissing the subject with the last thought of his gentle unfitness for a warlike reign, I am glad to turn to a vindication of his memory—a plea for gratitude that, not long since, was wisely and appropriately uttered in Eton College:

"If we were required to point out the most disastrous period of English history, we should, perhaps, fix upon the reign of Henry the Sixth. In his earlier years he saw the foreign possessions acquired by his father's victories, successively wrested from his hands; and, towards its close, he saw his kingdom wasted by the fury of civil war, and the blood of his subjects profusely shed in the

---

"Thou hast most traitorously corrupted the youth of the realm, in erecting a grammar school; and, whereas, before, our forefathers had no other books but the score and the tally, thou hast caused printing to be used; and, contrary to the king, his crown, and dignity, thou hast built a paper-mill. It will be proved to thy face that thou hast men about thee that usually talk of a noun, and a verb, and such abominable words as no Christian can endure to hear." H. R.

unnatural contest. He himself, meanwhile, appeared in no degree to influence the progress of events, which were to terminate in the loss of his sceptre and his life. Transferred from a throne to a prison, and again from a prison to a throne, he seemed to be the sport of fortune; a merely passive instrument in the hands of others; a spectator, rather than an actor, in the eventful drama. His thoughts and affections were fixed upon very different objects from those for which worldly ambition contends. Bent on securing for himself an imperishable crown, he felt little solicitude about the perishable crown which was to be the prize of the victor in the bloody strife. The world, therefore, while it has bestowed on him some portion of its pity, as on one who underwent much unmerited suffering, has pronounced him unfit for the station which he filled, and utterly useless in his generation. Yet it has pleased the Almighty to ordain that this despised, this suffering monarch, should exercise a more powerful and more permanent influence over future ages than many princes whose exploits are the theme of the world's applause. What traces can we now discern of the effects of his father's victories? They form a page, a brilliant page, in history, on which we dwell with exultation, and which has inspired many a bosom with the desire of military glory. But, as to any present influence on the interests of the country, they are as if they had never been; whereas, the foundation of Eton College exercises an influence which is now felt, and will continue to be felt to the remotest times. To the intellectual and moral training, to which the youthful mind is here subjected, perhaps is owing more than to any other single cause, the formation of that national character, which has, under the Divine blessing, raised England to its eminent position among the people of the earth."*

---

* This is an extract from an address delivered after a confirmation, at Eton College, in 1844, by Dr. Kaye, Bishop of Lincoln, and quoted in a little work that I found in my brother's library, entitled "The Unity of History, or Outlines of Lectures on Ancient and Modern History considered on the principles of the Church of England," by the Rev. C. J. Abraham, London, 1845. W. B. R.

LECTURE X.*

Richard the Third—Henry the Eighth.

The character of Edward the Fourth—His death—Richard's usurpation—Its character of intrigue and violence—The princes in the Tower—Attempted vindications—Their inefficacy—Sir Thomas More—Richard's deformity, mental and physical—Effect of personal deformity—Commanding intellect of the king—Power of will—No sympathy—No repentance—Contrast of Macbeth—Richard's dream—The last of the Plantagenets—The Tudor kings—Henry the Eighth—The progress of society and government—Henry's reign nearly contemporary with Shakspeare—The play of Henry the Eighth history—Wolsey's character—Catharine of Arragon—Wolsey's fall and death—The approaching Reformation—Henry's character the worst in history—His death—Conclusion.

AFTER the close of the War of the Roses, and the death of that good man, King Henry the Sixth, the throne of England was peacefully held by Edward the Fourth, who kept until his death the possession, which had cost so much peril to himself and havoc in the realm. The battle of Tewkesbury was followed in Edward's reign by twelve years of peace and of exhaustion; and, at the end of that time, during which there were scarce any events of importance or interest, the monarch died a death, which had become most unusual in the York

* March 1st, 1847.

family—he died in his bed; for it may be mentioned as one of the indications of the sanguinary character of the times, that the lives of his father and grandfather and his three brothers, ended bloodily or violently. The character of Edward the Fourth was briefly this: he was a warlike and a voluptuous prince, equally ready for the perils of war and the pleasures of peace. The military hardships of his early life seem to have been regarded by him as warrant for the uncurbed licentiousness of his undisturbed royalty. One of the elder English historians, in summing up his character, says that—"He lived too fast; and that, while no man acted with more vigour and spirit in all the distressed and dangerous situations of his affairs, yet, when the danger or difficulties were over, he relapsed constantly into a sauntering way with the fair sex." What precisely the historian meant by a sauntering way with the fair sex, I need not stop to describe further than to say that, while Edward displayed in his belligerent days an energy and dauntless intrepidity like that of as stern and indefatigable a warrior as Cromwell, in his peaceful years he sank into the easy morality of as gay a voluptuary as Charles the Second. It is one of the dark truths of human nature, that men can mingle with all the levity of loose pleasures the perpetration of deeds of appalling ferocity; for the heart becomes so indurated by continued self-indulgence, that the conscience will be troubled no more by crimes of cruelty and bloodshed than by its frolic immoralities. The close of the career of this voluptuous prince, King Edward the Fourth, was darkened by the guilt of fratricide. The share he had in the murderous killing of his brother, Clarence, is finely represented by Shakspeare as embittering his last hours. Immediately on being informed of the death of Clarence, he is solicited by Lord Stanley to pardon one of his servants, and his perturbed conscience finds voice in the answer to the suit:

"Have I a tongue to doom my brother's death,
And shall that tongue give pardon to a slave?
My brother killed no man, his fault was thought,
And yet his punishment was bitter death.
Who sued to me for him? Who in my wrath
Kneel'd at my feet, and bade me be advised?
Who spoke of brotherhood? Who spoke of love?
Who told me how the poor soul did forsake
The mighty Warwick and did fight for me?
Who told me in the field at Tewksbury
When Oxford had me down, he rescued me,
And said,—Dear brother, live, and be a king?
Who told me, when we both lay in the field,
Frozen almost to death, how he did lap me
Even in his garments, and did give himself,
All thin and naked, to the numb-cold night?
All this from my remembrance brutish wrath
Sinfully pluck'd, and not a man of you
Had so much grace to put it in my mind."

Edward's undisturbed occupation of the throne gave deceitful promise of the security of the house of York, and of the return of tranquil times. Even during the peaceful part of his reign, the elements of discord were secretly fermenting, and the evil eye of the strongest man of the Yorkist race was watching the chances for usurpation. The death hours of Edward the Fourth may well have been embittered, not only by the memory of many an act of ruthless violence, but by gloomy forebodings for his young heir, to the unformed strength of whose hands the sceptre was to pass. Edward the Fifth succeeded to his father's throne when but thirteen years old, and he reigned for less than thirteen weeks. His name stands on the list of English sovereigns, and his statue may fill a niche with the images of the rest; but there is only the name and shadow of a reign. Under the dark protectorship of his uncle, the Duke of Gloucester, the youthful sovereign went speedily from the palace to a prison, and found secret death and burial within the gloomy precincts of the Tower of London. Whatever there was of justice in the original claim of the York family to the throne, it was established with so much wrong and iniquity that it had no sure foundation to rest on; and after Edward the Fourth's triumphant career, retribution fell heavily on his sons and successors. Indeed, when we consider the mingled right and wrong in both the Lancastrian and York titles, it would seem as if the good in each was rewarded with a brief season of success, after which the meed of misery was awarded to the guilt. The ruin of the house of York was not only the retributive consequence of its crimes, but it was to be effected by the atrocities of him who was to be the last of the dynasty.

It is not necessary that I should follow with any comment the usurpation of Richard the Third. It is a familiar story of craft and cruelty directed to the accomplishment of a purpose, which, probably, had long been present to his thoughts. It is one of the miseries of civil war that it destroys all sense of security of life or of possession of any kind; and it is then, when the whole fabric of society is unstable, that the worst passions display themselves and roam abroad in all their force. Witnessing, during the early part of his career, the confusion and anarchy of the War of the Roses, Richard may well have seen that, if the chances of an unsettled time did not better his prospect of inheriting the crown, still the mind of the people had become familiar with sudden and revolutionary changes and scenes of bloodshed. The times and the bold and unscrupulous usurper were fitted for one another; and the accession of such a man as Richard, and such a reign as his, seem no more than the natural sequel to the civil war.

When we consider the process of the usurpation, and some of the means employed to accomplish it, we seem to be passing from the days of open feudal violence to the times of modern intrigue. If, in the previous period the nobles were seen armed in the field, and openly warring for one or the other claimant, we now find the Duke of Buckingham in the meaner attitude of the demagogue. He is seen, not like "the king-maker" Warwick, making a path to the throne with his sword, but giving his tongue to falsehood and deceit,—playing a deep game of hypocrisy and fraud. The speech of Buckingham to the people, when he endeavours to insinuate Richard's title to the crown into their minds, is for all the world like the craft of a modern politician, stimulating a factitious public opinion for selfish purposes:

"When my oratory grew to an end
I bade them, that did love their country's good
Cry—God save Richard, England's royal king!
Glos. And did they so?
Buck. No, so God help me! they spake not a word,
But like dumb statues or breathless stones,
Stared on each other, and look'd deadly pale:
Which when I saw, I reprehended them,
And ask'd the Mayor, what meant this wilful silence.

His answer was—the people were not used
To be spoke to but by the recorder.
Then he was urged to tell my tale again;—
'Thus saith the duke,' 'thus hath the duke inferred,'
But nothing spoke in warrant from himself.
When he had done, some followers of my own,
At lower end o' the hall, hurled up their caps,
And some ten voices cried—'God save King Richard!'
And thus I took the vantage of those few.
'Thanks, gentle citizens and friends,' quoth I,
'This general applause and cheerful shout
Argues your wisdom and your love to Richard;'
And even here brake off and came away."

Again, in this previous period, the deaths of violence, even when not in battle, were open deeds of atrocity and bloodshed, as that which caused

"The piteous moan that Rutland made,
When black-faced Clifford shook his sword at him,"

or when Prince Edward was stabbed in the field at Tewksbury; but now there is a transaction secret and mysterious—dark assassination—the dread doings in the Tower of London, such as the killing of Clarence, or the more piteous murder of the princes, when Tyrrel was intrusted with the keys of the Tower for only twenty-four hours; the murder, which he feared to look on, but is represented as describing:

"The tyrannous and bloody act is done,
The most arch-deed of piteous massacre
That ever yet this land was guilty of.
Dighton and Forrest, whom I did suborn
To do this piece of ruthless butchery,
Albeit they were flesh'd villains, bloody dogs,

Melting with tenderness and mild compassion,
Wept like two children, in their death's-sad story,
'O, thus,' quoth Dighton, 'lay the gentle babes'—
'Thus, thus,' quoth Forrest, 'girdling one another
Within their alabaster innocent arms.
Their lips were four red roses on a stalk,
Which in their summer-beauty kiss'd each other.
A book of prayers on their pillow lay,
Which once,' quoth Forrest, 'almost changed my mind;
But O, the devil'—there the villain stopped;
When Dighton thus told on—'We smothered
The most replenished sweet work of Nature,
That from the prime creation e'er she framed.'"

There is no event connected with the history of Richard the Third, which has added more to the accumulated odium that rests upon the tyrant's memory, than the mysterious death of his young kinsmen, the two princely Plantagenets, who are believed to have been cruelly assassinated in the Tower. Out of the mystery which shrouds the story, there have been spun speculations, intended to discredit the tradition, which traced the horrid guilt to the stern usurper; but the popular belief has been too widely spread to be shaken, and it is thought to stand upon the basis of truth. An impressive confirmation was given to it, when, nearly two hundred years after the time the murder was secretly perpetrated, some excavations in the Tower of London, during the reign of Charles the Second, brought to light the bones of two striplings, contained in a chest, buried where no intentional search was likely to discover it; and when its ghastly and mouldering contents were disclosed, the voice of the murdered children spake, as it were from their secret grave, to chase away the mystery that hung over the story of their death So little doubt was entertained as to the identity of the mortal remains thus discovered, that the bones were removed and received royal sepulture.*

It is not only from the reproach of having caused the murder of the princes, that attempts have been made to relieve the memory of Richard the Third. The bolder effort of a still more general vindication has, from time to time, been made; and not only the innocence of his life been asserted, but also the goodness of his disposition and the comeliness of his personal appearance. It has been contended, that the popular notion of Richard's character is a party delusion, by which his mind, his morals, and his make, have all been misrepresented,—that it is all a matter of Lancastrian prejudice, which Shakspeare has injuriously fomented, and that, as to his personal appearance, the crooked back, and the shrivelled arm, and the deformity of face, were all exaggerations and distortions of nothing more than low stature and a stern visage. The most noted of Richard's apologists and advocates was Horace Walpole, who startled the reading world by his historic doubts on this subject. The paradox was not original, for it had been the burden of an old book many years before Walpole's time; and lately an Englishwoman, whose name I do not now recall, has written a book to prove that Richard was "truly a marvellous proper man," who has been used very badly by posterity.†

Such historic doubts are entitled to consideration, for certainly it is not unfrequently found, that gross traditional errors have gained a place in history, and it is

* The disinterment of these supposed royal remains was in 1674. See Appendix to chap. vii. vol. iii. Lingard.

† This I presume to be Richard the Third as Duke of Gloucester and King of England, by Caroline A. Halstead. London, 1844. W. B. R.

never too late to vindicate and assert the truth; to rescue it, when beleagured by triumphant falsehood, is the worthy duty of a strong and intrepid intellect. In the present case, the attempt to turn the current of historical opinion has proved vain, and all the ingenuity of argument and parade of testimony have failed in redeeming the memory of Richard from the detestation with which it so long has been regarded. Under its load of obloquy the most accurate and judicious historians are still content to leave it.

In the dramatic delineation of the character of Richard, Shakspeare followed the description and the narrative given by Sir Thomas More and the chroniclers, and has produced his own conception of the character in correspondence with the popular notion. Shakspeare followed faithfully the best historical authorities of his day, in whom, as well as in the poetic portraiture, there may have been some exaggeration—a deeper shade may have been given to the blackness of guilt; but still we are safe in believing, that the truth was much nearer to that side than to the extreme opinion that lies so much farther in the opposite direction.

It would not be possible, on an occasion like this, to enter into an examination of the conflicting arguments and testimony respecting Richard's memory, but the question respecting his bodily deformity will serve to illustrate the nature of the controversy as to his character. The Richard of the drama speaks of himself

"As rudely stamped, curtailed of fair proportions,
Cheated of feature by dissembling nature:
Deformed, unfinished,—sent before my time
Into this breathing world,—scarce half made up,
And that so lamely and unfashionable,
That dogs bark at me, as I halt by them."

Now, this is dramatic exaggeration—it is intended to be so; it is not meant for description, as persons who read unimaginatively misconstrue it, but is meant for Richard's morbid exaggeration of his own personal defects, especially as felt in envious contrast with the elegance of face and form of his voluptuous brother, Edward the Fourth. This utterance of malignant and spiteful feeling ought never to be mistaken for literal description; for though men have what Madame de Sevigné, I believe, calls the privilege of ugliness, it would be a supernatural abuse of that privilege, if a man were, as Richard speaks of himself, so ugly as to set the dogs barking. So it is throughout the play: the references to Richard's personal appearance are, and are intended to be, exaggerations of dramatic passion.

But the general popular impression as to Richard's bodily unsightliness, seems to show how intense was the hatred of his character—how odious the recollection of his life. The detestation which he had inspired aggravated the conception of his personal defects: and he was, perhaps, thought tenfold more deformed than he really was, because his body was the visible exponent of the spiritual deformity of his nature. If Richard was the comely person his modern apologists maintain, then the notion of his deformity could have its origin only in the deep conviction of the inhuman wickedness of his invisible nature: men must have made him crooked and hideous because his life was so. There is an ingenious and humorous essay of Charles Lamb's, on the danger of confounding moral with personal deformity, in which he remarks, among other illustrations, "that crooked old woman, I once said, speaking of an ancient gentlewoman, whose actions did not square altogether with my notions of the rule of right. The unanimous surprise of the company, before whom I uttered these words, convinced me that I had confounded mental with bodily obliquity, and that there was nothing tortuous about the old lady but her deeds."* Now, if this mistake occurred with regard to King Richard, it proves that if the physical deformity was not there, the moral deformity, in all probability, was.

It would be both an idle and impossible inquiry to seek to ascertain the degree of Richard's bodily deformity, but the fact of some deformity appears highly probable, and, indeed, has an historical significancy in connection with the almost incredible inhumanity of his character. The consciousness of bodily deformity, even though it be slight, is found to embitter minds of a certain cast—to poison their spirits—and, by wrenching their dispositions from their natural course of feeling, to fit them for unnatural paroxysms of passion, or for envenomed ferocity against their more favoured fellow-men. In other minds, more happily constituted, the same consciousness proves altogether innocuous, and like any other inscrutable affliction, it subdues and softens the spirit without making it savage. Remember, for instance, how different was the influence of such consciousness upon the character of Sir Walter Scott and Lord Byron, afflicted as they were with much the same kind of bodily defect. It is well observed by Mr. Lockhart, in his biography of Scott, that the novel of the Black Dwarf derives "a singular interest from the delineation of the dark feelings so often connected with

* Lamb's Prose Works, vol. i. p. 246.

physical deformity—feelings which appear to have diffused their shadow over the whole genius of Byron ; and which, but for this single picture, we should hardly have conceived to have passed through Scott's happier mind. All the bitter blasphemy of spirit which, from infancy to the tomb, swelled up in Byron against the unkindness of nature, which sometimes perverted even his filial love into a sentiment of diabolical malignity, all this black and desolate train of reflection must have been encountered and deliberately subdued by the manly parent of the Black Dwarf."*

The dark record, which history has made of Richard's life and reign, becomes the more credible when we reflect upon this desolating and demoralizing influence of the consciousness of deformity. Shakspeare's profound philosophy is shown in his making this an element in Richard's character. He is represented as feeling himself marked by nature to stand apart from his fellow-men—separated from the species. He stands in utter and awful moral loneliness; and as all social feeling is extinguished, the humanity of his nature dies with it, and all that is left is an almost supernatural selfishness, proud and self-assured—

"I that have neither pity, love, nor fear;
I have no brother, I am like no brother,
And this word *love*, which gray-beards call divine,
Be resident in men like one another,
And not in me. *I am myself alone.*"

I have several times adverted to the peculiar significancy of the opening scenes of Shakspeare's plays, and it

* Life of Scott, vol. v. p. 175.

may now be observed, that of them all, Richard the Third is the only one that opens with a soliloquy, as if to indicate the moral solitariness of the character.

The career of such unusual and savage self-dependence could be sustained only by the power of commanding intellect. Accordingly, there is found in Richard such power in all its magnitude: there is intellect, and nothing but intellect. Coleridge has observed, that "pride of intellect is the characteristic of Richard, and that Shakspeare has here, as in all his great parts, developed in a tone of sublime morality the dreadful consequences of placing the moral in subordination to the mere intellectual being."* Struggling first for the aggrandizement of his family, Richard struggles afterwards for himself. To bravery in battle he adds craft and hypocrisy, because he finds them the best instruments for some purposes, and not because he is solicitous to screen his crimes from the world or himself. He feels his intellectual strength, and has an exulting pride in the exercise of it. He was one of these bold bad men, who rise up in revolutionary times, when ambitious and unprincipled nobles stoop from their high station to the vilest arts of the low-born demagogue; one of those aristocratic Jacobins, who are seen in seasons of anarchy, seeking to build up a tyranny on the ruins of their own order. Richard is arrogant with the pride of birth and the recollection of past dangers, as when he boasts—

"I was born so high
Our aiery buildeth in the cedar's-top,
And dallies with the wind and scorns the sun."

* Lectures on Shakspeare and other Dramatists, vol. i. p. 187.

The intense intellectual force of Richard's character, with the utter absence of moral elements, produces throughout an overweening self-assurance that is troubled with no misgivings, but breaks out perpetually into a species of malignant merriment. He is so sure of his game always, that he exults in anticipation of success, and vents his exuberance of spirits in that most hateful mode of expression, sarcastic irony—one of the sure signs of a bad heart. When he is planning his brother's murder, he looks after him as he is led to the Tower:

> "Go tread the path that thou shalt ne'er return.
> Simple plain Clarence, I do love thee so,
> That I will shortly send thy soul to heaven,
> If Heaven will take the present at our hands,"

His exultation rises at the prospect of the death of his other brother, Edward the Fourth:

> "If I fail not in my deep intent,
> Clarence hath not another day to live.
> Which done, God take King Edward to his mercy,
> And leave the world for me to bustle in."

The Duke of Buckingham has been the mean and wicked partner of Richard's usurpation. The strong man has whirled him along in the progress of his crimes—he has used him, not as a staff to lean on, but a tool to subserve his purposes. The moment the frail Buckingham falters at the proposed murder of the princes, Richard casts him off as a worthless thing to be trampled on without fear or compunction:

> "I will converse with iron-witted fools
> And unrespective boys; none are for me
> That look into me with considerate eyes.

High-reaching Buckingham grows circumspect;
The deep-revolving, witty Buckingham
No more shall be the neighbour to my counsels.
Hath he so long held out with me untired,
And stops he now for breath? Well, be it so."

The fate of this wicked and discarded favourite is sealed. He feels that it is not enough that he is degraded—he must die; and, after a vain struggle against his destiny, his partnership with the usurper's crimes ends with a bloody death by the tyrant's order.

Immediately after Richard has cast Buckingham from his counsels, he looks about for other men, more pliant implements; and he recovers his wonted animation when he utters that cold-blooded piece of irony in the question to Tyrrel—

"Dar'st thou resolve to kill a friend of mine?"

exactly as if murder was a perfectly amicable transaction.

Richard's short reign of three years was a weary period; and, whether we look at his character in history or in the drama, we escape from it with pleasure, for there is nothing to relieve—nothing to mitigate it. The contemplation of even his commanding intellect—the tremendous force of his will—becomes odious; for we see that it owes much of its strength to abandonment of all principle of right. It is one of the dreadful lessons of history, that men have often risen to power simply by what has been well described as—"The fearful resolve to find, in the will alone, the one absolute motive of action, under which all other motives, from within and from without, must either be subordinated or crushed;" men who, knowing no other principle but that might is right, are "the Molochs of human nature, who are indebted for the larger part of their meteoric success to their total want of principle, and who surpass the generality of their fellow-creatures in one act of courage only—that of daring to say with their whole heart—'Evil, be thou my good!'"*

It is not possible to discover either in the history or the drama of Richard a single point for even a momentary sympathy to rest on—there is no room for the least transient pity of the misery of guilt. Richard had no suffering that we can see—he is happy in his crimes, and they make him prouder of his power. He has no compunctions of conscience, no remorseful remembrances; and it is in this he is represented so differently from the Scottish usurper and tyrant. There is scope for a grand contrast between Richard and Macbeth, but let me only notice that never from Richard's lips do we hear the piteous utterance of the guilt-oppressed weariness of life that weighed down the once guiltless spirit of Macbeth.

Richard never felt that he had lived long enough; and, as to troops of friends, the lonely-hearted and proud man set no value on them. The tyrant's indurated and stony conscience seemed to sustain with ease the awful superstructure of his crimes; the prospect of what he thought a necessity of more and more guilt—"sin plucking on sin"—disturbs him with no such agony of ineffectual reluctance as that which appears in Macbeth's brief utterance to Lady Macbeth—

"Oh, full of scorpions is my mind, dear wife!"

---

* Coleridge's Statesman's Manual. Appendix B, p. 262.

When Richard's crimes are perpetrated, he seems to think of them no more—by a strong effort of the will, he dismisses them from his mind. The guilty past is no burden to him; there is no such heart-wasting, hopeless memory as appears in the solemn irony of Macbeth's words to the physician:

> "Canst thou not minister to a mind diseased?
> Pluck from the memory a rooted sorrow,
> Raze out the written troubles of the brain,
> And with some sweet oblivious antidote,
> Cleanse the stuff'd bosom of that perilous stuff
> Which weighs upon the heart?"

The long-sustained obduracy of Richard's spirit at length breaks down, like that of the strong-willed woman, Lady Macbeth, in the mysterious condition of perturbed sleep. The waking tyrant never loses his self-command, but the pride of his wicked heart is shaken by fearful visions of the night; it is only when appalled by them that conscience begins to assert its authority on the eve of his death. It is a curious fact, that what might be regarded as a mere dramatic invention—I mean the agitated dream of Richard on the eve of the battle of Bosworth Field—is supposed to have an historical foundation, and is treated by accurate historians as of actual occurrence. The story is, that Richard, rising from his fearful sleep, harrassed and haggard and disturbed, found it necessary, as battle was about to be joined, to explain to his attendants the change which had come over his spirit, and which his looks betrayed. When the mysterious shapes, which in his dream hovered around his couch, are represented by the poet as the ghosts of those who had been murdered by him, it is to be interpreted as the embodiment of the hauntings of a guilty conscience—the presence of remorse made vocal and visible. It seems monstrous, either in scenic representation or in the mere reading of the play, to find the ghosts set down among the persons of the drama—ghosts enumerated along with citizens, soldiers, and the rest; but they are not so to be thought of; if Richard's dream on the night before the battle is an historical fact, then the poet has given it a sublime moral significancy, by idealizing the horrid phantoms of sleep into the shadowy form of the dead whose blood had stained the tyrant's hands. The long and unchecked career of guilt had so closed the avenues to Richard's conscience, that nothing but a miracle or the mysterious agencies of sleep could open the way to it; and thus, in the first awakening from his vexed sleep, the terrors of conscience throng around him for the first time:

> "My conscience hath a thousand several tongues,
> And every tongue brings in a several tale,
> And every tale condemns me for a villain.
> Perjury, perjury in the high'st degree,
> Murder, stern murder, in the direst degree,
> All several sins, all used in each degree,
> Throng to the bar, crying all—Guilty! guilty!
> I shall despair. There is no creature loves me,
> And if I die, no soul will pity me.
> Nay, wherefore should they? since that I myself
> Find in myself no pity to myself.
> Methought, the souls of all that I had murdered
> Came to my tent, and every one did threat
> To-morrow's vengeance on the head of Richard."

The terror of Richard's dream did not unman him when danger came in the more familiar form of an armed enemy, and the last of the Plantagenets fell, fighting with a bravery worthy of that heroic race which had reigned in England for more than three hundred years, and which now reached a bloody catastrophe on Bosworth Field. The crown of England, which had been carried by Richard to the battle, being found after the fight was over, was placed on the brow of the Earl of Richmond, who, on the field of his victory, was hailed "King Henry the Seventh."

The first of the Tudor kings held the throne by conquest, and by his Lancastrian blood; and a matrimonial alliance with the family of York gave further security to his possession. To borrow the fine image of Mr. Hallam —"Lest the spectre of indefeasible right should stand once more in arms on the tomb of the house of York, the two houses of parliament showed an earnest desire for the king's marriage with the daughter of Edward the Fourth, who, if she should bear only the name of royalty, might transmit an undisputed inheritance of its prerogative to her posterity."* The child of that marriage, Henry the Eighth, succeeded to the throne with the first undisputed title that England had known for more than one hundred years. The beginning of the reign of Henry the Eighth is just at the transition period from mediæval to modern history, when the feudal baronial power had been exhausted by the War of the Roses, and the monarchy, gaining strength from the ruin of the nobility, had been further fortified by the sagacious dominion of Henry the Seventh. At the opening of the sixteenth century, England takes its place in history as one of the

* Hallam's Constitutional History, vol. i. p. 12.

great monarchies of Europe about the same time that the monarchal polity of France attained a similar supremacy.

In the progress of the constitutional government of England, and for the ultimate advancement of constitutional freedom, the work which appears to have been assigned to the Tudor generation of kings was, the extinguishing of the multitudinous tyranny of a feudal aristocracy; and this was accomplished by the elevation of the monarchal element in the government. At no period of English history has there been such an imperious tone and such arbitrary conduct employed by the kings as under the Tudor dynasty—a succession of tyrants from the seventh Henry to Elizabeth, who wrought the monarchy to such a pitch of prerogative, that the lofty pile fell to its foundation during the Stuart dynasty, when Charles the First laid his head on the block.

Before passing to what must be a very rapid view of the period of history that remains, let me call your attention to the fact, that the drama of Henry the Eighth was composed by Shakspeare at the distance of only a little more than half a century from the events which it illustrates. These events are, it is true, now seen by us through the haze of a longer time; but to the poet and his contemporaries, they had all the distinctness of comparatively recent occurrences; and, as such, the imagination had a difficult task in dealing with them. The poetic process, when employed on subjects of a recent and familiar nature, must needs be managed with excellent judgment and high imagination; to Shakspeare, therefore, the subject of Henry the Eighth was very much what the period of Washington's administration, or the reign of George the Third or Louis the Sixteenth, would be to a dramatic poet of the present day. The character of the play is, on this account, in many respects different from that of his other "Chronicle-Plays;" lofty as is the poetry in it, the whole tone of it eminently shows how Shakspeare's genius takes rank with history. The play of Henry the Eighth is history, and history in its highest and purest state.

Coleridge said of this play that—"It is a sort of historical masque, or show-play."* It opens with a description of the gorgeous meeting of King Henry and the French monarch, Francis the First, at the "field of the cloth of gold," and it ends with the procession at the christening of Queen Elizabeth. The deep interest of the play, however, is not in its scenes of pomp and display, but in the silence and stillness of the tragic misery that it tells of.

In previous reigns we have seen the monarchy of England swayed or sustained by the great nobles—princes of the blood or potent feudal barons—standing round the throne; but the great change that has come over the kingdom in this respect is apparent, when we see, in Henry's time, that the mightiest man in the realm, one who controls even the tyrant's policy, and guides the government, is a low-born commoner; who, rising upon church preferment, becomes the chancellor of the kingdom and the king's chief minister. The politic statesmanship of Cardinal Wolsey is a power that transcends what was displayed by the great Earl of Warwick or any of the early feudal baronage. The early part of the

* Literary Remains, vol. ii. p. 91.

drama represents the angry and resentful pride of the nobles, as they fret under the pomp and power of the great cardinal, whose splendid ambition has mounted over all the high born of the land. The impetuous Duke of Buckingham with rash passion provokes a controversy, and braves the authority of Wolsey; but the moment that power strikes him, he feels—

> "The net has fallen upon me. * * *
> * * * My life is spann'd already:
> I am the shadow of poor Buckingham,
> Whose figure even this instant cloud puts on,
> By dark'ning my clear sun."

He dies on the scaffold, and his death is a bloody proclamation of Wolsey's power.

The tragic part of the drama is made up of a succession of changes from grandeur to debasement; and the next in the series is the downfall of Queen Catharine, repudiated as a wife and degraded from the throne. Her story is a familiar one, which I need not trace and I cannot now pause to expatiate on. Let it be borne in mind that Catharine of Arragon, when she came to England, betrothed to the heir of England's throne, brought, as the daughter of Ferdinand and Isabella, not only her splendid dowry, but the pride of the proudest monarchy of Europe; she came from the palace that had lately rejoiced in those wondrous achievements by which the spaces of Christendom were enlarged; for in one and the same year did Ferdinand and Isabella remove from the soil of Spain the long-enduring dynasty of the Saracens, and send forth Columbus to search the dark waters of the West. For near twenty years was this proud Castilian woman Queen of England, the honoured wife of

Henry the Eighth. The poet-historian, I will not say narrates, but exhibits with historical fidelity the course of proceeding by which Catharine was wickedly cast aside to make room for Anne Boleyn. There cannot be any thing more impressive or affecting, than the variety and revulsions of feeling that pass over the afflicted spirit of this queenly matron, whether we behold her in stately yet suppliant remonstrance with her heartless husband, or—beleaguered by the crafty counsels of the two cardinals, Wolsey and Campeius—she turns from the king to address a more impassioned utterance to Wolsey:

"Sir,
I am about to weep; but, thinking that
We are a queen, (or long have dreamed so,) certain
The daughter of a king, my drops of tears
I'll turn to sparks of fire."

In a former part of this course, we had occasion to consider the character of Constance wildly clamouring for her son's royal claim, and afterwards that of Margaret of Anjou indomitably warring for her son's inheritance; but the noblest matron of them all is Queen Catharine, in whom are seen all the feelings of the wife, the mother, and the queen—the pride of birth and of place—the consciousness of irreproachable purity—the anguish of the bitterest wrong—the sense of loneliness in a foreign land—all sinking down with something of placid piety, into the most piteous dejection. She knows how desolate she is—

"Shipwreck'd upon a kingdom where no pity,
No friends, no hope; no kindred weep for me;
Almost no grave allowed me."

But almost in the same breath she has the fortitude to say to Wolsey—

> "My lord, I dare not make myself so guilty
> To give up willingly that noble title
> Your master wed me to: nothing but death
> Shall e'er divorce my dignities."

She had warned the great cardinal—

> "Take heed, for heaven's sake, take heed, lest at once
> The burden of my sorrows fall upon ye."

The next of these sublime reverses—the change from "mightiness to misery"—is the downfall of Wolsey. The worldly and ambitious ecclesiastic had been odious in his pride of power—in his days of magnificence; but now, with no more than the actual facts of history, the poet, as has been well said—"By his marvellous art, throws the fallen man upon our pity. He restores him to his fellowship with humanity by his temporal abasement. The trappings of his ambition are stripped off, and we see him in his natural dignity. He puts on the armour of fortitude and we reverence him."

Wolsey had dwelt in an atmosphere so radiant as to dazzle him; but now a sudden change of fortune sweeps it away, and he sees the world in the pure air and calm light of heaven. He bids farewell to all his greatness in a strain of poetry, not as piteous, certainly, but as heartfelt as that with which the soul-stricken soldier bade farewell to the plumed stood and the big wars that make ambition virtue. There is the lingering sorrow for lost power—

> "No sun shall usher forth my honours,
> Nor gild again the noble troops that waited
> Upon my smiles."

He looks sorrowfully to the destitution that is before him—

> "My high-blown pride
> At length broke under me; and now has left me
> Weary and old with service, to the mercy
> Of a rude stream that must forever hide me."

It is not until the tears and the affection of his servant Cromwell touch the hidden humanity in the proud man's heart, that Wolsey rises to the higher strain of that solemn admonition:

> "Mark but my fall and that that ruin'd me.
> Cromwell, I charge thee, fling away ambition.
> By that sin fell the angels—how can man, then,
> The image of his Maker, hope to win by it?
> Love thyself last; cherish those hearts that hate thee.
> Corruption wins not more than honesty.
> Still in thy right hand carry gentle peace
> To silence envious tongues. Be just and fear not.
> Let all the ends thou aim'st at be thy country's,
> Thy God's, and truth's: then, if thou fall'st, O Cromwell,
> Thou fall'st a blessed martyr."

The dramatic narrative of the close of Wolsey's life becomes manyfold more impressive from being told to the discrowned Queen Catherine in answer to her gentle inquiry—

> "Did'st thou not tell me
> That the great child of honour, Cardinal Wolsey,
> Was dead?
> * * * *
> Prythee, good Griffith, tell me how he died:
> If well, he stepp'd before me, happily,
> For my example."*

* It is observed by Lord Campbell, in his Lives of the Chancellors of England, that the subsequent part of Henry's reign is the best

And then, after she has listened to the narrative of his deeds of beneficence and his death of humility, her gentle comment—

> "After my death I wish no other herald,
> No other speaker of my living actions,
> To keep mine honour from corruption,
> But such an honest chronicler as Griffith.
> Whom I most hated living, thou hast made me,
> With thy religious truth and modesty,
> Now in his ashes honour: Peace be with him!"

This forgetfulness of her injuries—this placid forgiveness of her adversary—is made to be the appropriate prelude to her own death. Through the subdued emotions of charity to the memory of the dead, and of resignation to her own woes, the Castilian pride of the noble-minded and afflicted Catharine shines forth faintly in her dying injunctions to her attendants:

> "Although unqueen'd, yet like
> A queen, and daughter to a king, inter me."

---

panegyric on Wolsey; for, during twenty-nine years, he had kept free from the stain of blood or violence the sovereign, who now, following the natural bent of his character, cut off the heads of his wives and his most virtuous ministers, and proved himself the most arbitrary tyrant that ever disgraced the throne of England.

The same author, in closing the biography of Wolsey, remarks:—"I shall not attempt to draw any general character of this eminent man. His good and bad qualities may best be understood from the details of his actions, and are immortalized by the dialogue between Queen Catharine and Griffith, her secretary, which is familiar to every reader."

Nothing need be added to a dialogue which has been well described as "not merely the noblest poetic impersonation, but the most fair and impartial historic estimate, of Wolsey's character." H. R.

The tragedy of Henry the Eighth gives intimation of the vast changes that were approaching. The great ecclesiastical revolution of the sixteenth century is distantly alluded to, when Wolsey speaks of Anne Boleyn as a spleeny Lutheran, and of Cranmer's rise :

> "There is sprung up
> An heretic, an arch one, Cranmer; one
> Hath crawled into the favour of the king,
> And is his oracle."

And, looking forward into one of the last allusions in Shakspeare's historical plays, it is to America, when, in poetic anticipation of the reign of James the First, it is said—

> "Wherever the bright sun of heaven shall shine,
> His honour and the greatness of his name
> Shall be and make new nations. He shall flourish,
> And, like a mountain cedar, reach his branches
> To all the plains about him."

Of the character of Henry the Eighth it may be said, without exaggeration, that it contained all the worst qualities of the worst man that ever reigned in England. Despotic over the nation, he carried a bloody and inhuman tyranny into his own household; and all the time he was so busy handling his conscience, fondling it, and talking about it, and the distress its tenderness caused him, and his scruples and his sense of duty; so that he seems to have lived and died in the self-complacent conviction that he was one of the most virtuous, and certainly the most conscientious, creature in the world. Strange to say, too, his subjects seem to have had an abject affection for him; and, with a series of atrocities indisputably resting upon his memory, posterity has but imperfectly fulfilled its duty of hatred of him. The explanation given of this by Mr. Hallam is thus:—"The main cause of the reverence with which our forefathers cherished this king's memory was, the share he had taken in the Reformation. They saw him, not, indeed, the proselyte of their faith, but the subverter of their enemy's power —the avenging minister of heaven, by whose great arm the chain of superstition had been broken and the prison-gates burst asunder. As the poet Gray has finely glanced at this part of his history when he speaks of him as—

"The majestic lord
That broke the bonds of Rome."

A curious explanation of the inadequate condemnation of Henry's character is given by another writer, who remarks:—"It is extremely difficult to attach any moral responsibility to one who appears to have been so utterly unconscious of it himself. We cannot contemplate murder and robbery apart from the homicide and the felon. No reader ever throws down his book in disgust at the revolting character of Bluebeard; few experience any personal abhorrence at the Emperor of Morocco, though his courtyard is ornamented with pyramids of human heads, freshly furnished every day. History is unfortunately nowise deficient in examples of graduated barbarity to suit any conceivable occasion; but its moral would be lost and its occupation gone, if it could not also generally exhibit the temporal wages of sin. Even Caligula used to wander through the measureless and hollow-sounding corridors of the palace, followed by gibbering phantoms and eagerly praying for the dawn. Even Nero started at the unearthly trumpet which sounded nightly over the grave of his murdered mother.* Even Charles the Ninth saw bloody streaks in the sky, and heard strange noises on the leads of the Louvre. But no remorse ever disturbed the rest or affected the dreams of Henry. No occasional misgivings that he was not the best king, the most faithful Catholic, the truest friend, the most loving husband in Christendom, ever crossed the royal mind. Wife after wife, friend after friend, councillor after councillor, perished by the axe of his slaves; but no troublesome spectres stalked through the groves of Richmond or marred the tiltings at Greenwich. At last, his own familiar friend is condemned; but no blood-boltered Cromwell rises at the council-board or shakes his gory locks in St. George's Hall. The unconscious monarch continues his murders and his marriages, troubled by nothing but the gout, and lamenting nothing but his poverty, and dies at last committing his soul to the Blessed Virgin with as much confidence and complacency as if he had lived the life of François Xavier. When we include, in our recollections of this man, the facts that he was destined for the Archbishopic of Canterbury, that he gravely discussed theological questions, propounded and defended theses of divinity, and earnestly and vehemently disputed on serious points of religion, it is enough to confuse the gravity of our reason

* Tacitus Ann. xiv. 10. "Quia tamen non, ut hominum vultus, ita locorum facies mutantur, obversabaturque maris illius et litorum gravis adspectus (et erant, qui crederent, sonitum tubæ collibus circum editis planctusque tumulo matris audiri) Neapolim concessit." W. B. R.

and judgment, and to give to the whole of his reign and actions the air of a grotesque and barbarous pantomime."

I should have been glad, in coming to the end of the many historic personages whom we have been considering, to have closed with one whose memory could be regarded with less of detestation; but, as I have no choice, I would fain help you to as hearty hatred of Henry the Eighth as historic truth demands. I cannot add force to the language of an author who has said—"It is fearful, but not unsalutary, to cast a parting glance at Henry the Eighth after his work upon the earth was done. His broad and vicious body lay immovable and helpless, a mere corrupt and bloated mass of dying tyranny. No friend was near to comfort it, not even a courtier dared to warn it of its coming hour. The men whom it had gorged with the offal of its plunder, hung back in affright from its perishing agonies, in disgust from its ulcerous sores. It could not move a limb nor lift a hand. The palace-doors were made wider for its passage through them, and it could only then pass by means of machinery. Yet, to the last, it kept its ghastly state, descended daily from bedchamber into room of kingly audience, through a hole in the palace ceiling, and was nightly, by the same means, lifted back again to its sleepless bed. And, to the last, unhappily for the world, it had its terrible indulgences. Before stretched in that helpless state of horror, its latest victim had been a Plantagenet. Nearest to itself in blood of all its living kindred, the Countess of Salisbury was, in her eightieth year, dragged to the scaffold for no pretended crime save that of corresponding with her son; and, having refused to lay her head on the block, (it was for traitors to do so, she said, which she was not,) but, moving swiftly round, and tossing it from side to side to avoid the executioner, she was struck down by the weapons of the neighbouring men-at-arms; and, while her gray hairs streamed with blood, and her neck was forcibly held down, the axe discharged, at length, its dreadful office. The last victim of all followed in the graceful and gallant person of the young Lord Surrey. The dying tyranny, speechless and incapable of motion, had its hand lifted up to affix the formal seal to the death-warrant of the poet, the soldier, the statesman, and scholar, and on the 'day of the execution,' according to Holinshed, 'was itself lying in the agonies of death.' Its miserable comfort then was, the thought that youth was dying too; that the grave which yawned for abused health, indulged lusts, and monstrous crimes, had, in the same instant opened at the feet of manly health, of generous grace, of exquisite genius, and modest virtue. And so perished Henry the Eighth."*

And here, just across the threshold of modern, as distinguished from mediæval, history, this course of lectures comes to its conclusion. When I think of the distant period of history with which this course began, I am almost afraid to think of the extent of time and the multitude of characters I have attempted to speak of. With a very strong sense of the necessity of leaving a vast deal unsaid, and of the danger of passing over what ought not to be neglected, I have used all possible pains to make the most of the time you have kindly given me. I part with my subject at present

* Forster's Treatise on Popular Progress, p. 48.

with the hope that, hereafter, I may possibly resume it, by treating either some of the many grand historical subjects which remain in the period of the Middle Ages, *or by advancing into the ampler field of modern history*, and onward into the neglected annals of our own country.*

Let me add a word or two of explanation respecting the method of the course I am now concluding. In it, I have purposely refrained, as far as possible, from mere historic narrative, and have aimed at such comprehensive comment as might illustrate the character and spirit of those distant times, and of the men who lived in them. I ventured to hope that in this way I might revive some historical recollections—might deepen some historical impressions, and, perhaps, inspire an interest in the study of history.

With regard to the poetical illustrations which I have introduced from Shakspeare's "Chronicle-Plays," I wish to explain, that I have not thought it worth while to occupy your time with pointing out the deviations in those plays from the literal truth of history. I have used those illustrations as contributing to the general truth of history—to its moral significancy, and because I had it at heart to show that by the help of the imagination, disciplined in the service of truth, we gain that sense of the reality of past ages, and of our fellow-beings who peopled them, which makes history a living picture.

To these words of explanation let me add that I very heartily feel the kindness and attention for which

* These hopes, alas, were never fulfilled. W. B. R.

I am indebted to the class. That kindness has been a very great encouragement while I have been going on with the preparation of these lectures; it furnishes me with most agreeable recollections, and the hope of a recurrence of your friendliness, if a similar intercourse should hereafter be renewed.

FOUR LECTURES

ON

TRAGIC POETRY,

AS ILLUSTRATED IN

Shakspeare's Four Great Dramas.

TRAGIC POETRY.

LECTURE I.*

King Lear.

THE subject which I ask you to carry in your thoughts during this brief course of lectures is—"Tragic Poetry, especially as illustrated by the four great dramas of Shakspeare." I do not propose to enter upon a strictly critical examination of these tragedies. I dwell upon them as they are illustrative of the aim and the scope of tragic poetry. I wish to inquire, how a true poet deals with the human heart when he awakens its solemn sympathies, and why it is that such sympathies—the sentiments of pity, sorrow, and even anguish—are stirred within the soul by the agency of the imagination.

When I speak of the four great dramas of Shakspeare, I trust it is understood, that I am not expressing merely a private preference of my own—an individual judgment. Universal consent has recognised them as

* December 6th, 1842.

undoubtedly the highest efforts of his genius; and, what I wish you to observe is, that when the inspiration of the poet was in its loftiest region, that region was "Tragedy." The upper air of poetry is the atmosphere of sorrow. This is a truth attested by every department of art—the poetry of words—of music—of the canvas and of marble. Now, as poetry is a glorified reflection of life and nature, why is this? Simply because, when a man weeps, the passions that are stirring within him are mightier than those feelings which prompt to cheerfulness and merriment. The smile plays upon the countenance; the laugh is a momentary and noisy impulse; but the tear rises slowly and silently from the deep places of the heart. It is at once the symbol and the relief of overwhelming feeling—it is the language of those emotions which words cannot give utterance to. Words and smiles and laughter all have to do with impulses that are on the surface, and which we freely express to one another in the trivial and social intercourse of daily life; but let any one study his own heart, and he will know that there are passions, whose very might and depth give them a sanctity, which we instinctively recognise by veiling them from the gaze of others. They are the sacred things of the temple of the human soul, and the common touch would only profane them. In childhood, indeed, when its little griefs and joys are blended with that absence of self-consciousness which is both the bliss and the beauty of its innocence, tears are shed without restraint or disguise. But, when the self-consciousness of manhood has taught us that tears are the expression of those passions which are too sacred for exposure, the heart will often in silence break rather than violate this admirable instinct of our nature. Indeed, the more a man reflects on these things, the more confirmed will be the spirit of reserve in him—the more will he shrink from "wearing his heart upon his sleeve." Hence it is that the highest department of poetic art belongs to tragedy, embracing, as it does, in its range the most awful emotions that human nature is capable of—an old man's agony from the wrongs of filial impiety, as in King Lear; the heart-wasting misery of criminal temptations and a blood-stained conscience, as in Macbeth; the strife of a young and noble spirit contending with vice and an adverse destiny, as in Hamlet; and the phrensy of an abandoned faith, as in Othello.

If it has been shown that the highest department of the art belongs to tragic poetry, assuming, as it may do, either the epic or the dramatic form, it may still be asked—What are its moral uses? The inquiry is a just one; and, to the best of my ability, I will endeavour in some degree to give an answer to it—on this condition, however, that I am not expected to answer it in any mere utilitarian spirit. Indeed, one main design of these four lectures will be to show what salutary influences belong to tragic poetry—how the poet's sad imaginings are calculated to chasten, to elevate, and to purify—an agency which justified so sage and solemn a spirit as Milton's in styling the lofty, grave tragedians—

"In chorus or iambic, teachers best
Of moral prudence, with delight received,
In brief sententious precepts, while they treat
Of fate, and chance, and change in human life;
High actions and high passions best describing."*

* Paradise Regained, book iv. ver. 261.

When Milton thus spake, it was in immediate reference to the Athenian tragic drama; but the words have a more universal application as finely describing the themes of all tragedy:

> "Fate, and chance, and change in human life,
> High actions and high passions best describing;"

themes involving what is most momentous in man's moral nature. The great poet, in all ages of the world, has been a genuine moralist; and, when morality perished upon the pages of philosophy, it has been kept alive by the inspirations of poetry. Most of all has the tragic poet best told the strange story of man's nature—the conflict of its passions, the wild commingling of good and evil elements, their ceaseless agitation, and all that makes up the mystery of the human heart—the strange mystery that dwells in the breast of every human being.

The influence of any department of poetry must be sought in that sphere of action and passion which is its archetype; for all poetry, that is truly such, is the imaginative representation of life. Now, tragic poetry has its original in the sorrows and misery that float like clouds over the days of human existence. Afflictions are ever travelling across the earth upon errands, mysterious, but merciful, could we only understand them; and the poet, picturing them to us in some sad story of his own, teaches the imaginative lesson of their influence upon the heart. He shows what that heart is capable of; its often unknown power and energy and endurance; the passions that are slumbering there; the feelings which may be wrought either to a pitch of wickedness or to some lofty mood of heroic virtue. I say again, that to the poet, and chiefly to the tragic poet, belongs the function of unravelling that greatest of all earthly mysteries—the human heart. And this is done for salutary uses; for be assured that mighty poets are inspired with the power of portraying the soul in its strength and its weakness, not for the effeminate purpose of mere sentiment, but that we may the better know our own natures—the better learn what the spirit which abides within us is capable of. Whether that teaching of the poet is made practically influential upon character, or the impressions be suffered to pass away in sentimental inactivity, in violation of that law of our moral being which tells us that feelings, no matter how virtuous, will surely perish unless they are converted into active principles, is another consideration to which I may revert hereafter. But the question now is as to the moral design of tragedy, not whether its uses are neglected. The great critic of antiquity, with all the sublime solemnities of his country's dramatic literature in his thoughts, in the presence, as it were, of that spectral mystery of fate which overshadowed Athenian tragedy, has told us that—"Tragic poetry is the imitation of serious action, employing pity and terror for the purpose of chastening such passions."* A great modern poet tells us that—

"It were a wantonness, and would demand
Severe reproof, if we were men whose hearts
Could hold vain dalliance with the misery
Even of the dead: contented thence to draw
A momentary pleasure, never mark'd
By reason, barren of all future good.
But we have known that there is often found

* Aristotle's Treatise on Poetry, chap. vi.

> In mournful thoughts, and always might be found,
> A power to virtue friendly."*

Now, it is my purpose to trace this "power to virtue friendly" in tragic poetry, designed as it is to shadow forth imaginatively the mournful thoughts of our actual life, and to show that the poet gives us the best insight into our nature—teaching us, by his imaginative realities, how the heart may be hardened; how it may be melted; that thus we may the better know what should be our true dealings with the principles and passions of our fellow-beings and of ourselves. This is the profound and simple morality of that drama which is to be my illustration this evening.

But let me introduce the contemplation of that sublime production of art, the tragedy of King Lear, by first presenting a simpler example of pathetic poetry, to show "the power to virtue friendly" which abides in mournful thoughts. There is a tradition respecting one of the ancient ecclesiastical edifices in the North of England, that it was founded by the mandate of a mourning mother—the first impulse when her despairing, obdurate, and voiceless grief was turned into tranquil resignation for the fate of her only son, a gallant youth who perished pitiably in the rocky chasm of the river Wharf. The story and its moral are told in the unaffected stanzas of a ballad:

> "Young Romilly through Barden woods
> Is ranging high and low
> And holds a grayhound in a leash,
> To let slip upon buck or doe.

* Wordsworth's Excursion, b. i. Works, p. 401.

The pair have reached that fearful chasm,
How tempting to bestride!
For lordly Wharf is there pent in
With rocks on either side.

This striding place is called the Strid,
A name which it took of yore:
A thousand years hath it borne that name,
And shall a thousand more.

And hither is young Romilly come,
And what may now forbid
That he, perhaps for the hundredth time,
Shall bound across the Strid?

He sprang in glee, for what cared he
That the river was strong, and the rocks were steep?
But the greyhound in the leash hung back,
And check'd him in his leap.

The boy is in the arms of Wharf,
And strangled by a merciless force;
For never more was young Romilly seen
Till he rose a lifeless corse.

Now there is stillness in the vale,
And deep, unspeaking sorrow:
Wharf shall be to pitying hearts
A name more sad than Yarrow.

If for a lover the lady wept,
A solace she might borrow
From death, and from the passion of death;—
Old Wharf might heal her sorrow.

She weeps not for the wedding-day
Which was to be to-morrow:
Her hope was a farther-looking hope,
And her's is a mother's sorrow.

He was a tree that stood alone,
And proudly did its branches wave;

And the root of this delightful tree
  Was in her husband's grave!

Long, long in darkness did she sit,
  And her first words were, 'Let there be
In Bolton, on the Field of Wharf,
  A stately Priory!'

The stately priory was rear'd;
  And Wharf, as he moved along,
To matins join'd a mournful voice,
  Nor fail'd at even-song.

And the lady pray'd in heaviness
  That look'd not for relief!
But slowly did her succour come,
  And a patience to her grief.

Oh! there is never sorrow of heart
  That shall lack a timely end,
If but to God we turn, and ask
  Of him to be our friend!"*

I need not stop to show how, in this story, there came from mournful thoughts a power to virtue friendly. The science of ethics could not teach a more precious lesson than is conveyed by the reflection, that the darkness of a lonesome heart in which the mourner sat, caught its first ray of light by the resolve of an *act* of piety. It was thus the heavy cloud of hopeless sorrowing was scattered; it was thus that the widowed mother's spirit, while yet on earth, found a home in the calm and unclouded region of holy emotions, and her aspirations and the chaunted services of the church and the voice of the waters of the fatal river all blended together to consecrate the place.

---

* Wordsworth's Force of Prayer. Works, p. 356.

From these simple verses let us now turn to learn how the same truth is conveyed in one of the most awe-inspiring productions of Shakspeare's genius—the tragedy of King Lear. Let us seek to discover the salutary influences of that tumultuous and solemn agony with which it is filled, and thus verify the words of the great critic of antiquity, that "tragedy is meant to chasten the passions of the soul by the agency of terror and pity." These are the wise words of him whom Greece, in the abundance of all that the intellect of man can achieve, gave as worthy to be the philosopher and critic of her poets, and who brought his art of criticism from a reverential gazing upon the pages of Homer, and reverential insight into the deep places of his own heart. Let me here ask whether the truth of this principle, which I am about to take as my guide through these lectures, is not recognised in its analogy to the outer world—whether there is not a violent, and it may be, a terrific, chastening of the elements without, like the painful purification of the moral elements within us. A heavy and pestilent atmosphere may be gathering around us, the seeds of disease and death floating upon it. Then there is a lurid threatening of the tempest—a hurried movement of the clouds; and the wind, which had been ominously moaning, comes rising up from beneath the horizon like the terrific phantom that haunted the palace of Dion—a sullen spectre—

"Sweeping, vehemently sweeping,
Like Auster, whirling to and fro
His force in Caspian foam to try;
Or Boreas, when he scours the snow
That skins the plains of Thessaly;"*

* Wordsworth's Dion. Works, p. 359.

and when the tumult of the elements is over, there is a pure air to breathe; and overhead is the blue sky, into whose infinite depth the eye cannot look without a sense of better things, than when it is ever bent downwards to what is low and corrupt—the measurable meannesses that entangle our footsteps. Now, akin to this is the strife of passions, which passes away and leaves in the soul a calm and a purity it knew not before. Or, again, the rain weeps upon the earth, and, ere the drops are dried—while glistening with the rays of the returning sun—the grass will begin its silent growth in the valley; and so it is that, by the virtue of pathetic influences, gentle emotions will spring up from the soil of a saddened spirit.

The significancy of the very titles of Shakspeare's plays at once tells us that the interest of "King Lear" is meant to centre chiefly about the aged monarch—an ancient British king. The first step in the accurate study of any great dramatic poem is to consider the locality and the period, so far, at least, as they serve to cast their lights and shadows upon the characters. The idea of place is definite, strikingly so by virtue of such local description as of the Dover Cliff, impressing the imagination with the knowledge that Britain is the scene. This serves, too, to make it a home story; and such, indeed, it was, when Shakspeare, not inventing the plot, simply took it as an old legend of the land, to be made forever a living thing by the life-blood infused into it by a poet's genius. While it is thus distinct as to place it is all shadowy as to time; you must go back beyond the Norman Conquest, the Saxon, the Dane, or even the Roman; back into a region which the ray of historic light dimly penetrates, only to show in the misty confusion the strange shapes of fable and romance. All that can be learnt is, that Lear and his daughters lived a long time ago; and it only concerns us to observe that it was in some age earlier than the Christian era, when men fancied that their destinies were ruled by the stars, and put up their prayers to gods passionate like themselves. This is important; for the wild and stormy tumult of the drama is more in unison with a period of paganism than it could be with any age of true faith. Lear is a barbaric chieftain—a heathen monarch; and the wilfulness of offence at an unoffending child, and the agonized imprecations upon his wicked daughters, befit a heathen's lips. The lurid atmosphere of the tragedy could not have been harmonized with the radiance of Christendom; and, therefore, the imagination is skilfully guided into a pagan land; for it is in the very first scene that one mythological oath after another is uttered by the king, swearing by Apollo, Jupiter—

> "By the sacred radiance of the sun;
> The mysteries of Hecate and the night;
> By all the operations of the orbs
> From whom we do exist and cease to be."

Except in these two respects—distance from the distinctness of historic time and from the calmness of a Christian age—it matters not how many centuries ago we fancy the story; indeed, it is better that a great work of imagination should stand aloof from chronology. Like the relation between parent and child, on which the tragedy rests, it is not circumscribed by time; and, as long as there shall be parental feeling on the earth—as long as there shall be filial piety, there must be sympathy with the "child-changed father" in this wondrous poem.

The first impression that is given of Lear's character is that of *selfishness*, arising from the habitual exercise of power. He is fourscore years old, and his heart has been hardened by that which is well-nigh sure to harden the heart of any man—the possession of irresponsible strength. His only law is his own absolute will, now feebly guided by an intellect which time has begun to work on: the gods are only ministers to his oaths and imprecations. He stands before us the very personation of unlimited despotism, lawless and selfish. He is surrounded by courtiers, but they are not counsellors. The only council-chamber is his own mind; and there he matures, in the lonely dignity of a tyrant's will, the "dark purpose" as he calls it, of his abdication and the division of his kingdom. In the very act of putting off royalty, every word and motion of the aged man is kingly—the speech and action of one so long habituated to the use of arbitrary authority—so that when he purposes to lay it down, there is despotism in the very resignation. As if the issues of life were in his mortal hands, he decrees the course of his remaining days:

> "'Tis our fast intent
> To shake all cares and business from our age,
> Conferring them on younger strengths, while we
> Unburthen'd crawl toward death."

This passage, it seems to me, suggests one of those dim presentiments which Shakspeare frequently employs, as darkly prophetic of the future in his dramas. We feel as if this absolute planning for the future, even for the remnant days of his old age, can hardly come to good. Human power is reaching beyond its limits, and the pride of power, so confidently resolving upon freedom from all cares, seems to shadow forth its own disappointment. The anxieties of not only sovereignty but of humanity are to be laid aside; yet, at the very moment when, with kingly self-confidence, he is sending this decree forth that he will travel onward unburthened to the grave, we seem to have a mysterious forewarning—low words of admonition—that burdens a thousand-fold weightier shall be heaped upon him. Troubles to come are casting their shadows before and darkening the splendour of his pride. We may fancy Lear, like another ancient barbaric king of Britain, intoxicated with the lifelong use of despotic power, giving his mandate to stay the flood of troubles; and, at the same time, the approaching waters of the deep are curling their threatening surges not only to dash the spray upon his feet, but to heave huge billows upon his discrowned head.

The more deeply we study the opening of this drama, the more perfect it is found as a personation of the intense selfishness of irresponsible power. The king sits solitary. Observe, there is no queen to share his throne and to approach him with a wife's counsel, and even the affections of his children are objects of command. Every thing is subordinate—every thing self-centering. The instant he finds his vanity frustrated in a pitiful scheme to extort professions of fondness from his daughters, the silence of his darling child becomes rebellion, and the counsel of a faithful and affectionate subject, treason. The ruling passion is the pride of despotism, and the vengeance of insulted royalty is swift in an indiscriminate destruction. Now, this is very sad—that an old man's heart, a father's heart, should be so hard and so hollow that pride and passion are echoing there as the wind might through the ruins of an ancient Druid temple on some barren British waste. To the eye of a pure moral intelligence, this should be a more deplorable spectacle than that piteous one of the aged king unhoused and unsheltered in the storm. Here it is the moral storm of his own lawless passions—of a vindictive selfishness and a despotic will making havoc in the heart. In the other it is only the thunder, the wind, and the rain—the outer elements beating upon the outer man.

Such is the character of King Lear when first made known to us:—self-willed, irritable, despotic, unnatural, rash in temper and weak in judgment—an object of aversion from the intensity of his cruel selfishness. And yet, beneath all this, there is something which shows that these are the ruins of a noble nature, overgrown, indeed, with all the weeds that rankly luxuriate in the habit of tyranny. The dutiful respect of his courtiers shows that genuine majesty had not wholly degenerated into despotism; and enough is told of what had gone before the opening scenes, to let us know that, in a heart so miserably perverted, there were some gracious affections—the best of them for that faithful child whom he now casts away, "dowered with his curse and strangered with his oath." Cordelia was the darling of the palace —far dearer to him than the hard-fronted Goneril and Regan.

Now, how is this nature to be redeemed? How is human sympathy to be reanimated in a tyrant's heart? What Promethean heat is there to rekindle extinct affections? How shall the barren soil of selfishness be broken up, so that virtuous and gentle emotions may grow there? The mischief wrought by fourscore years of tyranny upon the soul of him that used it, is to be done away. The tragedy teaches the restoration of Lear's moral nature. It is affected in a twofold way—by all the agony that is crowded into the short and stormy twilight of his life, and by the gentle mediation of his injured daughter.

It is this process I am anxious to trace, assuming a familiarity on the part of each one of my hearers with the course of this famous tragedy. The tragic movement begins with the cruel disowning and banishment of Lear's true child, brought about by his disappointment in the miserable device to draw from each of his daughters wordy protestations of filial affection. The hollow hearts of Goneril and Regan are well fitted to utter sounds enough to fill the monarch's craving ears, and their flattery hurries him on in the uncalculating confidence of hearing the sweeter music of Cordelia's voice—for she was the dearest to him—the one of whom he soon after says, even in his angry disappointment—

> "I loved her most and thought to set my rest
> On her kind nursery."

We sympathize with the fond old man's amazement at her answer, and it is hard to suppress a little regret that she could not humour him and yet preserve her sincerity. It is a pity she is forced to speak as she does, and we are half tempted to join in the king's censure when he speaks of her "pride which she calls plainness." But she could not answer otherwise. The truthfulness of her nature instinctively recoiled from the hypocrisy of her sisters to the opposite point of speechless affection. She had just heard language desecrated to the uses of heartless deceit, and the sanctity of her spirit could not suffer the unhallowed thing to touch her lips. More than this, the very form of the question forbade her to speak:

> "What can you say to draw
> A third more opulent than your sisters?"

as if the unpolluted temple of her heart was to be made a place of traffic—as if her dearest and dutiful affections could be bought and bribed and bargained with. Her love had ever been a freewill offering, at once a gift and a duty; and now the parent, in a mood of unthinking, selfish fondness, was seeking to turn it into something for which land and money should be equivalents—it was to be measured out in words and a price paid down for it. All that was left for Cordelia was silence, broken only by the firm reiteration of her simple, respectful answer. When Lear, before the tempest of his anger rises, with a slight admonition, solicits her to speak again, the full heart of his child gives utterance to a few words—few, but with infinitely more truth and love in them than in all the idle echoes that came sounding from the hollow caverns in the hearts of Goneril and Regan:

> "Unhappy that I am, I cannot heave
> My heart into my mouth. I love your majesty
> According to my bond—nor more, nor less."

Cordelia's voice, we are told, "was ever soft, gentle, and low." But it was unintelligible to a mind deluded by flattery; for, after a few questionings, somewhat in the way of remonstrance, the stormy will of a despotic king sweeps away the lingering affections of a father's heart. Cordelia's offence is against her sovereign as well as against her parent—treason as well as filial impiety. In the brief space of a few moments, the turbulent old man casts off a child who never before had offended—the dearest of his daughters—the darling of the household:

> "Thy truth, then, be thy dower.
> For, by the sacred radiance of the sun,
> The mysteries of Hecate, and the night;
> By all the operations of the orbs,
> From whom we do exist and cease to be,
> Here I disclaim all my paternal care,
> Propinquity and property of blood,
> And, as a stranger to my heart and me,
> Hold thee, from this, forever. The barbarous Scythian
> Or he that makes his generation messes
> To gorge his appetite, shall to my bosom
> Be as well neighbour'd, pitied, and relieved,
> As thou, my sometime daughter."

Who does not feel that the angry elements of this deplorable repudiation are passing harmlessly over Lear's innocent child and gathering into a black cloud to burst one day on his own head? With the rash confidence of unchastened power, the king is venturing to set his sovereignty against the mightier sovereignty of nature, and her laws will be avenged. We dread the consequences, not so much for Cordelia as for Lear himself. The fearless interposition of Kent is thrust aside, and the tragedy is begun. Naught can check it, for it is rising with the force and the speed of an ocean's tide upon the Solway sands. The monarch deigns to give a little, a very little, justification of the cruel disowning of his child:

> "I loved her most, and thought to set my rest
> On her kind nursery."

But, on the instant, checking his words, as if it were an

unkingly thing to explain or vindicate any act of his absolute sway, he commands his daughter to avoid his sight:

> "So be my grave my peace as here I give
> Her father's heart from her."

Happy would it have been if the peace of the grave had been nearer at hand; for he little dreamed how much anguish lay in wait for him in the short way he had to travel from his throne to that resting-place. Every thing now savours of absolute dominion—irrational power owning no law but undisciplined will. It is piling up for a more fearful ruin.

It somewhat relieves the pain with which we witness this arbitrary sovereignty wielded against the helpless daughter, to observe that, when, in the full burst of his indignation, Lear casts her away, the bitter irony of the first words was, in reality, a benediction—the infatuated father's unintended blessing:

> "Thy truth, then, be thy dower."

And so, indeed, it was—the dowerless daughter, richer and happier far than her majestic sisters; for Goneril and Regan with all their territories, and the added portion of their plundered sister, with armies at their beck, and all the large effects that troop with majesty, are incarnations of guilty passions and self-tormenting cares. But we feel that the suffering Cordelia will return a ministering spirit.

Lear has now accomplished both his deliberate and his sudden resolves: he has left his throne and he has driven away the daughter who offended him. It only remains for him to spend the remnant of his days without a care, committing himself to the alternate guardianship of the two daughters who had promised so largely. He has quitted the palace, and is housed in the home of his eldest born. When he next appears, there is apparent a want of that majestic bearing which had heretofore given a dignity even to his angry and distempered moods; there is an abrupt impatience, betraying a mind not wholly at ease—something of a desperate effort at joviality. The cares of the kingdom cast aside, he has been seeking to supply the void by the excitement of the chase, and, perhaps, to escape from bitter recollections of his discarded child. On his return from hunting, the first intimation is given that things are already beginning to go wrong. One of his followers suggests that there is an abatement of kindness in the conduct of his daughter. Lear himself, it appears, had felt it; he had been struggling against his own apprehensions —forced, it may be for the first time in all his life, to look for the fault in himself, and even hoping to find it there. The pride of the haughty king is beginning to break. This is the first symptom of that great moral change which is to come over him. The questioning of himself, the willingness to extenuate neglect, and to lay the blame there rather than upon his daughter, shows that he is standing on the threshold of that dark school of adversity in which his heart was to be both chastened and broken. His attendant has harped his fears aright:—"Thou but rememberest me of my own conception. I have perceived a most faint neglect of late, which I have rather blamed on mine own jealous curiosity than as a very pretence and purpose of unkindness. I will look further into it."

The truth is not long to be disguised, for the shameless tongue of Goneril herself announces it. Outraging all decency towards one who was beneath her roof in double trust—her father and her guest—she breaks out in invectives against his followers, mingled with complaints of him. He listens in a kind of dreamy bewilderment—a confused questioning of his own identity and hers. He speaks only a few words, and she resumes her unnatural strain, assailing the virtue and honour of his chosen knights. Lear's royal spirit is roused again; and his first indignant thought, with a fierce exclamation, is, to call his train together, and, on the instant, to quit his daughter's house. Yet, this burst of passion is different from that he poured upon Cordelia, for it is now tempered with sad reflections. Even in the midst of the present provocation, he is wrapt in self-communion. Bitter meditations are interrupted by broken words to Goneril and her imbecile husband, and passionate orders to prepare for departure. You can see, too, in what direction his half-uttered thoughts are travelling—to his own irretrievable rashness—"Age that too late repents;" and to his innocent child, whom he had injuriously driven from him—

"O! most small fault,
How ugly did'st thou in Cordelia show!
Which, like an engine, wrench'd my frame of nature
From the fix'd place—drew from my heart all love
And added to the gall."

If his intellect should afterwards give way beneath the load of woes, he is now, at least, coming to his right heart It is not only turning with forgiveness to his true daughter, but it is also solemnized with self-reproach. It is this which seems to subdue his spirit to a reflective mood, musing at the very time the outrage is done to him:

> "Ingratitude! thou marble-hearted fiend,
> More hideous when thou show'st thee in a child
> Than the sea monster."

There is this subdued tone even in his awful prayer that nature would withhold from his offending daughter a mother's happiness in her offspring, that she may feel

> "How sharper than a serpent's tooth it is
> To have a thankless child."

But his mingled passion and remorse are overmastering him; for, after quitting the presence of Goneril, he rushes back again to give utterance to his overcharged heart by speaking his agony and his anger. His self-command is too weak, and his first relief is a burst of tears. What a strife of emotions is it when a father is forced to speak so to his daughter!

> "Life and death! I am ashamed
> That thou hast power to shake my manhood thus—
> That these hot tears, which break from me perforce,
> Should make thee worth them. Blasts and fogs upon thee!
> The untented woundings of a father's curse
> Pierce every sense about thee. Old fond eyes,
> Beweep this cause again, I'll pluck you out
> And cast you with the waters that you lose
> To temper clay."

The tragedy is now deepening and more hurried Visions of resumed sovereignty—thoughts of taking it again by force—float before Lear's imagination; and, at the departure from Goneril's castle, his broken sentences, convulsive laughter at the wild jests of his faithful follower, the fool—threats—thoughts half-uttered—betray the tumultuous condition of his mind. Among these thoughts is one that shows the sharp moral discipline that is at work upon him—contrition for the wrong done to his true child, which had been growing in his heart, and now, for the first time, is partly spoken. It is to Cordelia alone the words can apply—"I did her wrong." He could not name her.

Lear approaches the dwelling of his second daughter with misgivings of her fidelity. He struggles to suppress them, but they are there. The interview with Regan is a most painful one. In that with Goneril he had assumed the highest tone of his fresh and unchecked anger, and was ready to boast that he had another daughter to look to. But now after Goneril's defection, if Regan, too, prove false, his kingdom becomes desolate. Where can the old man find shelter for his discrowned head? He knows it is his last hope, and his tone is lowered. He strives to prevent this one's misconduct, and yet both his paternal affection and his royal pride recoil from what he feels to be a pitiable degradation—a white-haired father, who had given up all, bending a brow hallowed by eighty years, to beseech in return from a daughter no more than forbearance from cruel and unnatural treatment. Therefore his appeals to her are indirect. He replies to her formal words of welcome with terms of endearment; he tells her of the enormity of Goneril's ingratitude, and of his own wounded spirit; he tells her, too, of her own obligations, and the trust he has in her better nature, and he reminds her of her dead mother:

> "Beloved Regan,
> Thy sister's naught. Oh, Regan, she hath tied
> Sharp-toothed unkindness, like a vulture, here!
> I can scarce speak to thee; thou'lt not believe
> Of how depraved a quality, O Regan!

His emotions overpower his utterance—and what does this speechless agony avail him? Only to bring down one of the worst blows that can be struck on the human heart—when wrongs are passionately complained of to one from whom a sympathy is rightfully due, to find them coldly palliated. Now, would you not have thought that this treatment must call forth another outbreak of parental indignation? But no! Lear's anger turns back only against the first offender with reiterated curses upon Goneril. With Regan he still pleads indirectly by attributing to her a tender-hearted nature, by telling her there is comfort in her eyes and none of the burning fierceness that flamed upon him from Goneril's, and by reminding her of "the offices of nature" and "bond of childhood." He is hoping against hope, and his last hope sickens unto death at the entrance of Goneril herself; for then there flashes upon his mind the horrid belief that his two daughters are confederated against him. Where now does the old man look for help? For the first time, he looks away from earth. Heretofore his pride and his anger have looked up to heaven for the dread purpose of calling down imprecations. Now, his chastened spirit looks up in supplication. Nay, more, as he feels his earthly sympathies perishing around him, there is that sublime effort of imagination by which he identifies his own old age with that of the heavens:

"O heavens!
If you do love old men, if your sweet sway
Allow obedience, if yourselves are old,
Make it your cause; send down and take my part!"

His spirit sank within him at the appearance of Goneril: a deadlier chill seizes upon it at a worse sight:

"O Regan! wilt thou take her by the hand?"

Once his mind seems to be wandering after Cordelia when he speaks of his "dowerless youngest born;" but his remaining pride sweeps the thought away, and there follows that wretched scene in which the helpless old king is bandied by the arguments of his daughters threatening and reasoning about the reduction of his retinue. When Lear speaks in answer—it is a strange utterance—at first, as if he would fain let his thoughts stray from his present misery into a region of abstractions; or, more probably, as if his mind were beginning to lose all law of its own, and were moved only by chance impulses, there is a train of mere speculative reasoning; then a supplication to heaven on behalf of his acknowledged poverty and wretchedness, disturbed, however, by dark infidel doubts that the gods may be the evil destinies to destroy him; then there is a desperate rallying of his mere human energy, fitfully broken with wild and royal threats, vague as the winds that are already heard preparing a rude reception for him on the heath:

"Oh, reason not the need—our basest beggars
Are in the poorest thing superfluous.
Allow not nature more than nature needs,
Man's life is cheap as beasts'. Thou art a lady:
If only to go warm were gorgeous,
Why, nature needs not what thou gorgeous wear'st,

Which scarcely keeps thee warm. But, for true need,—
You heavens give me that patience, patience I need!
You see me here, you gods, a poor old man,
As full of grief as age—wretched in both.
If it be you that stir these daughters' hearts
Against their father, fool me not so much
To bear it tamely; touch me with noble anger.
Oh, let not women's weapons, water-drops,
Stain my man's cheeks!—No, you unnatural hags,
I will have such revenges on you both
That all the world shall———I will do such things,—
What they are, yet I know not; but they shall be
The terrors of the earth. You think I'll weep;
No, I'll not weep.
I have full cause of weeping, but this heart
Shall break into a hundred thousand flaws,
Or ere I'll weep. O fool, I shall go mad!"

Lear is now environed with his thick-thronging afflictions, and the dark presentiment of insanity has entered his mind. The moral tempest has raged its utmost, and the tragic effort is fitly sustained when the aged sufferer, houseless and hopeless, is found wandering over the desolate heath, exposed to the unsparing storm. At the very time that his intellect is becoming unsettled and there is the restlessness of a fevered brain, his thoughts discover a fitful and unwonted strength. Already he has sought to identify by a mighty grasp of the imagination his own old age with that of the heavens themselves, and now he feels in the beatings of the tempests the blows of his daughters:

"I tax not you, you elements, with unkindness,
I never gave you kingdom, called you children;
But yet I call you servile ministers,
That have with two pernicious daughters joined
Your high engender'd battles 'gainst a head,
So old and white as this."

But most impressive is it to trace the effect of this severe chastening upon the king's moral nature. His closest sympathy now is with that humble creature who had been in prosperous days the light-hearted and privileged jester at the royal table, but who clings so faithfully to his master's miseries. Lear's affection for his devoted favourite grows deeper and more sensitive:

> "Poor fool and knave, I have one part in my heart
> That's sorry yet for thee."

His pity for the fool's exposure to the storm and cold, shows a self-forgetfulness which is a new element in Lear's character. When brought to the wretched hovel for shelter, he is solicitous to provide first for the fool; and this sympathy expands with a more comprehensive one for all suffering humanity, accompanied with a self-reproach for having, in his palmy days, taken too little heed of houseless poverty

> "Poor, naked wretches, wheresoe'er you are
> That bide the pelting of this pitiless storm,
> How shall your houseless heads and unfed sides,
> Your loop'd and window'd raggedness, defend you
> From seasons such as these? Take physic, pomp,
> Expose thyself to feel what wretches feel,
> That thou may'st shake the superflux to them
> And show the heavens more just."

Lear's destiny demands a yet lower humiliation. The entanglements of his brain are becoming more perplexed, and you can trace the footsteps of his departing reason. There is coming on, as has been finely said by Mr. Hallam, "that sublime madness, not absurdly sudden as in some tragedies, but in which the strings that keep his reasoning powers together, give way, one after another, with the phrensy of rage and grief. Then it is that we find, what in life may sometimes be seen, the intellectual energies grow stronger in calamity, and especially under wrong. An awful eloquence belongs to unmerited suffering. Thoughts burst out more profound than Lear in his prosperous hour could ever have conceived; inconsequent—for such is the condition of madness—but, in themselves, fragments of coherent truth, the reason of the unreasonable mind."

It is when Lear is brought lowest that his good angel, the lost Cordelia, comes back to minister to him. We first hear of her in that exquisite description—one of the most graphic that Shakspeare ever drew—of her receiving the letters narrating her father's affliction:

"She took them, read them in my presence;
And now and then an ample tear trill'd down
Her delicate cheek; it seem'd she was a queen
Over her passion; who, most rebel-like,
Sought to be king o'er her.
Kent. O, then it moved her?
Gent. Not to a rage; patience and sorrow strove
Who should express her goodliest. You have seen
Sunshine and rain at once; her smiles and tears
Were like a better day. Those happy smiles
That play'd on her ripe lip, seem'd not to know
What guests were in her eyes; which parted thence,
As pearls from diamonds dropp'd. In brief, sorrow
Would be a rarity most beloved, if all
Could so become it.
Kent. Made she no verbal question?
Gent. Faith, once or twice, she heaved the name of father
Pantingly forth, as if it pressed her heart;
Cried, 'Sisters! sisters!—Shame of ladies! sisters!
Kent! father! sisters! What? i' the storm? i' the night?
Let pity not be believed!'—There she shook

> The holy water from her heavenly eyes,
> And clamour moisten'd: then away she started,
> To deal with grief alone."

The turbulence of the tragedy now gives place to gentler emotions. After a tempest so ruinous, there break forth some rays of the pathetic light of sunset. A softer radiance is floating round Cordelia.

But Lear must not pass away from life in the darkness of insanity. The restoration of his mind is as inimitable as its aberration. When he awakes from his sleep of madness he is all gentleness—regenerate by the discipline of adversity and of his phrensy. One of the most beautiful dramatic passages ever composed is that where Cordelia is watching over her sleeping father—praying over him—

> "O you kind gods,
> Cure this great breach in his abused nature.
> The untuned and jarring senses, O, wind up
> Of this child-changed father."

The voice that, in happy days gone by, used to be music in his ears, is heard once more; and it is no wonder that, in his waking bewilderment, Lear answers her question whether he knows her—

> "You are a spirit, I know. When did you die?"

The shrill accents of Goneril and Regan had been the horrid sounds he listened to, and then the stormy noises of an angry sky; but now the melody of Cordelia's voice carries him into the world of spirits. When his daughter beseeches his blessing, his confused recollections begin to shape themselves:

> "Pray, do not mock me:
> I am a very foolish, fond old man,

> Fourscore and upward; and, to deal plainly,
> I fear I am not in my perfect mind.
> Methinks I should know you, and know this man;
> Yet I am doubtful; for I am mainly ignorant
> What place this is; and all the skill I have,
> Remembers not these garments; nor I know not
> Where I did lodge last night: Do not laugh at me;
> For, as I am a man, I think this lady
> To be my child, Cordelia."

That despotic parental fondness which was only tributary to his pride and selfishness is purified, and now Lear looks upon his daughter with a true affection—that happy consciousness so feelingly expressed by the great poet of our times—the consciousness that—

> "There are spun
> Around the heart such tender ties
> That our own children to our eyes
> Are dearer than the sun."*

The happy hours of this recognition are only short moments in the tragedy. The gloom quickly gathers over it. The destiny of the drama demands its tragic ending; something different from a continuance of life with all the ills it is exposed to. There must be no tampering with the solemnities of its close. "Fourscore and upward"—why should Lear linger any longer on the earth? Who

> "Would upon the rack of this tough world
> Stretch him out longer?"

And Cordelia—the earth was too stormy and too wicked a place for one so pure and gentle to dwell upon. Besides, the law of a tragedy so lofty as this—so sublime

* Wordsworth's Ruth. Works, p. 139.

and solemn in its morality—required that she should be not only ministrant to her erring father, but a propitiatory sacrifice. Her last duty was to him; and the pity of it is, that the poor heart-broken old man could not have been spared that last agony of carrying in his arms his dead daughter.

But compare Lear at the beginning of the drama—selfish, irritable, foolish, petulant, despotic, and unnatural—with Lear at the close of it. The chastened spirit—the gentleness of his heart-breaking as he drooped to death over the dead body of his darling Cordelia, and surely we are taught that—"There is in mournful thoughts a power to virtue friendly."

LECTURE II.*

Macbeth.

WHEN I last had the pleasure of meeting you, we were engaged in the consideration of a tragedy in which the chief agency employed was the emotion of pity. It was surely most piteous to contemplate, first, the perversion of Lear's moral nature, and then the accumulation of his agonies; and most piteous of all was it to contemplate the sad sacrifice of the innocent Cordelia. Yet, all this was accompanied with a reconciling principle, found in the reflection that the painful series of afflictions was a process of moral purification. Lear's heart was restored, and Cordelia's filial piety became more beautiful with the glory of martyrdom.

The tragedy of Macbeth is, in these respects, very different. The chastening of the passions, which tragedy is designed to accomplish, is now to be effected by the instrumentality, not of pity, but of terror—terror in the imaginative presence of wicked temptations and of a fearful career of guilt. In the last lecture, I sought to show you how Shakspeare carried Lear along his stormy pil-

* December 13th, 1842.

grimage onward to a better nature; but now we are to trace the downward course of a human soul that has given itself over to the guidance of the spirits of darkness. It is a dramatic story of a temptation followed by guilt, and guilt followed by moral ruin. Nor is it only by showing the awful hauntings of a blood-stained conscience that the emotion of terror is to be awakened. In Lear the tragedy was moved by natural, human influences—the passions of mortal beings only; but in Macbeth other agencies are invoked—the power of witchcraft and all the visionary things that superstition deals with. There is a world of nature and a world above and beyond it; and now both are to be brought together, which can be well accomplished only by a mighty effort of imagination. The natural and the supernatural are to be blended —familiar beings and mysterious are to be associated, as it were, in one living company—things sensible and things fantastic. Without any feeling of incongruity, we are to be made to witness the firm tread of the armed soldier, and the noiseless gliding of ghosts, and the wild motions of witches, flitting and hovering through the air.

To have a just knowledge of the tragedy of Macbeth, we must form a distinct conception of the supernatural atmosphere which envelops the action. The air is lurid and thick with strange and awful creations. Distinct as are all its human interests, the tragedy is set in a shadowy, spectral region of witches—the mysteries of Hecate —ominous dreams and gloomy presentiments—of visions to the open eye of the wakeful guilty, and to the sealed eye of the sleeping—of invisible and mysterious powers in the elements, and of the prophetic sight of distant dynasties of kings—of incantations and of voiceless ghosts rising from fresh graves—blood-boltered visitants from charnel-houses.

Those who have studied the genius of Shakspeare as an artist, are familiar with the significancy of the opening scenes in his dramas—I mean as indicating the general character of the whole play. This is peculiarly manifest in the tragedy of Macbeth. It is scarcely possible to conceive a shorter scene than the first. It contains no more than twelve lines—short and broken—and yet it discloses the supernatural character of the drama, and mysteriously indicates upon whom the powers of darkness are about to employ themselves. This brief scene, which stamps the nature of the play, so far transcends the power of scenic exhibition, that it must be removed from all injurious and low attempts to present it on the stage. It is addressed to the imagination and not to the senses. It cannot be looked at and listened to by the eye and the ear. The scene is a wild and instant appeal to one faculty of the mind, especially by the absence of all description. It is no more than an "open place"—the persons, three witches. No one is looking on to describe them to us, or to express the emotions their presence might create. They are alone, and the only circumstances are "thunder and lightning." No human sight is upon them in their solitude—no human sound is mingling with their speech. It is the dark communion of witches—one speaking to the other, and the only sound that is echoing to their intonations is the thunder, bursting close around them and then passing away in distant reverberations. The only light that falls upon their wild and unearthly forms is the lightning as it flashes from the clouds they are wrapt in. The turmoil and carnage of war are near at hand, and the three witches—kinless—nameless—sexless, too, I may say—the weird women with beards scenting the blood of a battle-field—meet to meet again to seal the deep damnation of their victim. Their fatal intent thus darkly intimated, they answer to mysterious calls of you know not what "Paddock" and "Greymelkin," some of the horrid animals which seem associated with the witches to mark their grossly earthy nature; and, ere their presence has been well conceived, they vanish with wild utterance from them all of the moral confusion and murkiness of a demon's heart:

> "Fair is foul and foul is fair:
> Hover through the fog and filthy air."

In this first short scene of witchcraft, no more than the name of Macbeth is introduced; but, in another scene, he is soon made known to us a soldier, and an adventurous and valiant one. His intrepidity in battle is pointedly presented in the glowing descriptions of those who had just witnessed some of his exploits—first one who had seen him fighting hand to hand a fierce and dangerous rebel against the Scottish king—then one who had seen him breaking through the stout Norweyan ranks. "His praises in the kingdom's great defence," are on the lips of all. He is the brave Macbeth—the noble Macbeth—valour's minion—Bellona's bridegroom—the eagle—the lion in the hour of battle. In setting forth courage as a prominent trait in his character, there is an important purpose which becomes manifest in the contrast with the change his character undergoes. Amid images of death on the field of battle he is undismayed; and the narratives of his companions-in-arms proclaim his exploits of heroic daring. As the interest of the tragedy centres chiefly around the transformation of Macbeth's nature, we should carefully gather all the elements of it which are communicated in the opening scenes. He is a brave soldier, to whom fear is a stranger; and he is dear to his sovereign, not only for his victories, but as a loyal and dutiful subject. This is all that we are told of him, and yet it raises expectations of other and still nobler traits of character; for it has been finely said that—"The field of battle has been the field on which, more almost than on any other, has been manifested the spirit of self-sacrifice and self-devotion. And that war is practically a discipline of self-sacrifice, as well as of self-control, we perpetually see in domestic life; in which hardly any class of men show so much gentleness, so much forbearance, are so regardless of themselves, and so considerate towards others, as those whose hearts have glowed when the trumpet was calling them to battle."*

---

* I have not been able to verify this quotation, though it sounds very much like Archdeacon Hare; and in his favourite De Maistre is to be found a kindred sentiment in eulogy of military character:

"Le métier de la guerre . . . ne tend nullement à dégrader, à rendre féroce ou dur, au moins celui qui l'exerce: au contraire, il tend à le perfectionner. L'homme le plus honnête est ordinairement le militaire honnête, et, pour mon compte, j'ai toujours fait un cas particulier . . . du bon sens militaire. . . . . . Dans le commerce ordinaire de la vie, les militaires sont plus aimables, plus faciles, et souvent même, à ce qu'il m'a paru, plus obligeants que les autres hommes. . . . . . . La religion chez eux se marie à l'honneur d'une manière remarquable. . . . La vertu, la piété même s'allient très-bien avec le courage militaire; loin d'affaiblir le guerrier, elles l'exaltent." Soirées de St. Petersbourg, vol. ii. p. 18

W. B. R.

But the trials to which Macbeth has been exposed have been physical rather than moral dangers; they give no absolute assurance that the trait of character which is proclaimed is any thing more than mere animal courage —a quality common to brutes and to men. Or it may be that courage which is generated in the opinion of the world—a sense of honour. Or, again, he may belong to that common class of characters—men whose course of life is well enough just as long as their impulses chance to be good—just as long as no violent temptation stands in their path; generous when generosity demands no self-sacrifice; dutiful when duty is easy and needs no self-denial, and charitable to error because indifferent to truth. The temptations to which humanity is exposed make it necessary to find a better armour than such negative virtue; and the hero of this tragedy, if only thus armed, will vainly cope with the spiritual powers that are about to wrestle with him.

Before Macbeth appears, we have a further insight into the character of the supernatural beings who are to sway his destiny. The appointed time for their meeting with him is at hand; the thunder of the past storm on that day, which had been "so fair and foul," was yet sounding over the heath, when the witches again meet, hastening together from witchcraft mischief and actually rising to something of sisterly sympathy, as they tell each other their exploits. When you consider the work they have on hand, the sublimity of the harm they are now planning—nothing less than to drag down the soul of a brave and illustrious soldier to perdition—and then listen to the low and gross and comparatively vulgar witchcraft they are exulting over, it is seen what extraordinary, anomalous creations these foul beings are. One of them had been busy "killing swine;" another had been squabbling with a sailor's wife, who refused the witch any of the nuts she was munching. This is surely the lowest caste of witchcraft, but straightway the hag rises from it to the terrific sublimity of a supernatural avenger—a fury of the classic drama. The woman's husband is "a sailor to Aleppo gone;" and upon him the witch, summoning the adverse winds of the sea, threatens to wreak her vengeance:

> "Sleep shall, neither night nor day,
> Hang upon his pent-house lid;
> He shall live a man forbid;
> Weary seven nights nine times nine,
> Shall he dwindle, peak and pine;
> Though his bark cannot be lost,
> Yet it shall be tempest-tost."

The boast of her threatened vengeance is confirmed by the sudden recollection of a trophy gained on some former occasion of mischief on the ocean—"A pilot's thumb, wrecked as homeward he did come." The witches are, indeed, "posters of the sea and land"—vagrant beggars—secret destroyers of the farmer's live-stock—indwellers in the storm of thunder and lightning, with winds and tempests at their command; but what, amid all that is low and grovelling, gives them a strange and terrific sublimity, they are tempters of the conscience. While gloating over the pilot's thumb, they are startled at the sound which signals the approach of Macbeth and his Scottish soldiers. Quickly winding up a charm, and catching somewhat of a solemn demeanour from the magnitude of their malice, they rise suddenly to the full stature of their supernatural strength, and on the blasted heath prepare to proclaim their prophetic salutations. The very first moment Macbeth makes his appearance, the wicked eye is upon him. He has hardly spoken a word to his fellow-soldier Banquo, before it is perceived that their path is stopped by these uncouth appearances. Banquo is the first to speak and to challenge them:

> "What are these,
> So wither'd and so wild in their attire?
> They look not like the inhabitants o'the earth,
> And yet are on't. Live you? or are you aught,
> That man may question? You seem to understand me,
> By each at once her choppy finger laying
> Upon her skinny lips: you should be women,
> And yet your beards forbid me to interpret
> That you are so."

They answer not at Banquo's bidding; but when Macbeth calls on them to speak, demands—"What are you?" at that summons they are quick to answer in the threefold acclaim spoken by one after another—

> "All hail, Macbeth! hail to thee, thane of Glamis.
> All hail, Macbeth! hail to thee, thane of Cawdor.
> All hail, Macbeth! thou shalt be king hereafter."

It is a prophecy—the prophecy is a promise—and the promise is a temptation. From that instant he surrenders himself to a wicked destiny: he is under a fascination he never breaks through till the last hopeless hour of his life. Macbeth's character is further shown by a most instructive contrast with the different mood of Banquo's mind; who, though not listless to the fortune-telling, preserves his self-possession and self-reliance, his open and purer nature not being tempted into communion, as it were, with the mysterious interruptions. The integrity of his spirit is in his words:

> "I' the name of truth,
> Are ye fantastical, or that indeed
> Which outwardly ye show? My noble partner
> Ye greet with present grace, and great prediction
> Of noble having, and of royal hope,
> That he seems rapt withal; to me you speak not:
> If you can look into the seeds of time,
> And say which grain will grow, and which will not,
> Speak then to me, who neither beg, nor fear,
> Your favours nor your hate."

Every thing shows how deep the words of the witches have sunk into the heart of Macbeth. The quiet, martial composure of the soldier was greatly disturbed at the first announcement of the prophecy; for it is then that Banquo says—

> "Good sir, why do you start; and seem to fear
> Things that do sound so fair?"

The commotion of his spirit is shown still more by the impetuous earnestness with which he questions thom for further information:

> "Stay, you imperfect speakers, tell me more:
> By Sinel's death, I know, I am thane of Glamis
> But how of Cawdor?—the thane of Cawdor lives,
> A prosperous gentleman; and to be king
> Stands not within the prospect of belief,
> No more than to be Cawdor. Say, from whence
> You owe this strange intelligence? or why
> Upon this blasted heath you stop our way
> With such prophetic greeting?—Speak, I charge you."

When the witches vanish into the air—what seemed corporeal melting into the wind—his first feeling is, "Would they had stayed!" Banquo thinks of them as "bubbles of the earth," and questions the reality of what had just transpired. But Macbeth, as if seeking encouragement for his thoughts, clinging to the prophecy, repeats what they had promised—"Your children shall be kings;" and thus secures the satisfaction of hearing from human lips the promise to himself, for his companion naturally replies—"You shall be king." Then, as if conscious already of thoughts that could not be looked into, Macbeth turns from the higher to the lower promise:

"And thane of Cawdor too; went it not so?"

On the spot he is soon hailed by the messenger from the king with the new title of Cawdor, the forfeited rank and estate of the rebel thane. This speedy verification of the words of witchcraft greatly deepens the impression on the mind of Macbeth; and, while he is wrapped in meditation, the supernatural influence is driving his thoughts onward to the future—

"Glamis and thane of Cawdor:
The greatest is behind."

Again he turns to Banquo to draw from him other sanction than what his own spirit gave to his yet obscure ambition:

"Do you not hope your children shall be kings,
When those that gave the thane of Cawdor to me,
Promised no less to them?"

But the purer nature of Banquo is already recoiling from the supernatural powers that have crossed their path:

"That, trusted home,
Might yet enkindle you into the crown,
Besides the thane of Cawdor. But 'tis strange:
And oftentimes, to win us to our harm,
The instruments of darkness tell us truths;
Win us with honest trifles, to betray us
In deepest consequence."

Banquo instinctively feels that the promises, glorious as they are, come from powers of evil. His first exclamation, on finding them partly realized, was—

"What can the devil speak true?"

The warning words he addresses to Macbeth are illustrative of Shakspeare's manner of foreshadowing the course of things in his drama, either by admonitions, or misgivings, or presentiments of some kind, which he dispenses as preparations for the future. The warning is wasted on Macbeth. In fact, his career of guilt is begun. He is now not only rapt in solitary musing, but the great temptation is beginning to shape itself into a more definite form. The witches have cast a wicked light upon the crown on Duncan's brow, and it is reflected into the soul of Macbeth to dazzle and to lead him on to his own destruction. His confidence in the event is growing; but his mind, quickened by the agencies that have touched it, is beginning to invent means for the accomplishment of his destiny, and these means, directed to an end thus prompted, are sure to be guilty ones. Indeed, his imagination, in its morbid activity, has already grasped at its worst wickedness. The fancy of murder is the first symptom of the corruption of his conscience, and another sign—a most dangerous one in the career of iniquity—he is beginning to reason about his emotions:

"Two truths are told,
As happy prologues to the swelling act
Of the imperial theme. * * *
This supernatural soliciting
Cannot be ill;—cannot be good.—If ill,
Why hath it given me earnest of success,
Commencing in a truth? I am thane of Cawdor:
If good, why do I yield to that suggestion,
Whose horrid image doth unfix my hair,
And make my seated heart knock at my ribs
Against the use of nature? Present fears
Are less than horrible imaginings:
My thought, whose murder yet is but fantastical,
Shakes so my single state of man, that function
Is smothered in surmise; and nothing is
But what is not."

Macbeth has begun to dally in his mind with conceptions of wicked deeds, not without some convulsion of his better nature, which serves to sustain our sympathy with him. But, in all this process of temptation, amid his impulses and misgivings and agitations, observe there is no fixed principle of virtue in his character. A sense of mere honour may have kept his course of life, thus far, free from reproach; but, doubtless, it is an unsteady and undisciplined conscience which gives to evil suggestions so ready an admittance. He rallies from his agitation, not into the composure which would have been gained by a dismissal from his thoughts of the promises of witchcraft, but by a self-abandonment to his destiny:

"If chance will have me king, why chance may crown me,
Without my stir."

He clings to the temptation, but seeks to commit himself to the uncontrollable tide of fate:

"Come what come may;
Time and the hour runs through the roughest day."

This is the only time the thought enters into the mind of Macbeth, of trusting exclusively to the power of des tiny without co-operation on his own part; and it has furnished a striking illustration of the important principle in human nature, that faith, instead of leading, as has often been theoretically supposed, to diminish exertion, excites, on the contrary, to unwearied efforts. Prompted as Macbeth is, to the possession of the crown by the prediction of the witches, we might have supposed that he would be withheld from the perpetration of crime by the consideration that it must be needless, since it was fated that he must be king. Once, and only once, does such a thought occur to him; and thus has Shakspeare's knowledge of human nature shown that faith—a real faith—whether good or evil, is a principle that leads to action.

This feeble effort of Macbeth's to save his innocence by giving up to destiny his own free agency, is unavailing; for guilty imaginings—thoughts of murder—have begun to vitiate his spirit. Already there is something of the alarm of a conscience fearful that its own wicked musings are betrayed, and he begins to dissemble and prevaricate. He says to Banquo—

> "My dull brain was wrought with things forgotten,"

and proposes to his companion-in-arms candid communion respecting their mysterious adventure. While Banquo keeps his integrity, Macbeth is losing his sense of right and wrong: the poison of a supernatural evil influence is sinking down into his heart, and there is coming forth from the moral murkiness and confusion which begin to prevail there, an echo to the cry heard from the witches at their first appearance:

"Fair is foul and foul is fair."

It is hardly possible to conceive any thing more wild and fantastic and anomalous than the supernatural agencies which have so worked upon the guilty ambition of Macbeth; and it is, therefore, most remarkable that there should be such an air of truthfulness about them. They seem to be, not the phantoms of a gross and absurd superstition, but credible realities, so naturally do they coexist with human passions. This can be explained only by their being typical of something real. Few of us, I presume, are unwilling to believe that there is around us an invisible world, not the less real because we cannot perceive it; and I know of no reason why we may not also believe, that that unseen world has its beings, who are mysteriously ministrant to either the good or the evil of men's lives.* It is no figurative language when we are

* In Chorley's Memorials of Mrs. Hemans, vol. ii. p. 126, she writes from Rydal Mount:—"Have I ever told you how much Mr. Wordsworth's reading and recitation have delighted me? His voice has something quite breezelike in the soft gradations of its swells and falls. How I wish you could have heard it a few evenings since! We had just returned from riding through the deep valley of Grasmere, and were talking of different natural sounds which, in the stillness of the evening, had struck my imagination. 'Perhaps,' I said, 'there may be still deeper and richer music pervading all nature than any which we are permitted to hear.' He answered by reciting those glorious lines of Milton's:

'Millions of spiritual creatures walk the earth
Unseen, both when we wake and when we sleep.
All these with ceaseless praise his works behold

taught that powers of darkness are ceaselessly roaming about to tempt the souls of men; and it is only because our intellects are so materialized, that we are slow to believe what rests upon other proof than the evidence of the senses. The spiritual world is as real or rather more real than the material; and, although we are not yet endowed with faculties to apprehend it, yet, with all its mysteries, it may be close to us and around us. Now, it is one of the functions of the imagination, as Shakspeare himself tells us, "to body forth the forms of things unknown," and "turn them to shapes;" and thus the weird sisters may be regarded as incarnations, not merely of evil suggestions, but of the invisible tempters of mankind—the spiritual enemies, to whose arts humanity is exposed. The tragedy, therefore, is at once an imaginative and most real representation of the career of human frailty yielding to temptation.

The first interview between Duncan and Macbeth shows the progress of the guilty purpose—for the gentle pre-

---

Both day and night: how often from the steep
Of echoing hill or thicket have we heard
Celestial voices to the midnight air
Sole, or responsive each to other's note,
Singing their great Creator? oft in bands
While they keep watch, or nightly rounding walk
With heavenly touch of instrumental sounds
In full harmonic number joined, their songs
Divide the night, and lift our thoughts to heaven.'

And his tones of solemn earnestness, sinking, almost dying away into a murmur of veneration, as if the passage were breathed forth from the heart, I shall never forget; 'the forest leaves seemed stirred with prayer' while those high thoughts were uttered." W. B. R.

sence of the monarch, his confiding kindness, serve only to provoke a more distinct shaping of the "black and deep desires" which Macbeth is revolving in his mind. Thus far his guilt has been instigated only by the witch-craft-temptation, and known only in self-communion. He has been dealing alone with his ambition and his conscience. A new and irresistible power is superadded in the promptings of his wife. The temptation, begun by supernatural utterance, needs now only a wicked human voice to bring it to the consummation.

The character of Lady Macbeth is one of the boldest of Shakspeare's conceptions; but it can here be considered only in its relation to her husband and his guilt. They closely resemble each other in the absence of moral principle, but they differ greatly in this—that she displays a fearful energy of will, a dauntlessness of purpose that is not swayed by any outward or inward influence; while in Macbeth's character, one large element is the philosophic element—the tendency to reflection. It is this musing, meditative habit of mind, and a susceptibility of imagination, which contribute greatly to sustain a sympathy for the character, even after he is involved in criminality. It is hard to help lamenting the ruin of a capacious soul —one whose powers fitted it for better communion than with the dark portion of the spiritual world.

Besides, Lady Macbeth, dwelling in her lonely castle-life, does not, like her husband, feel the secondary motives—the sense of honour, the love of reputation, which are his chief moral principles. She is introduced in the high-wrought fervour excited by her husband's letter, informing her of the prophetic salutation of the witches, and the quick fulfilment of it in part. His confidence in the promises is manifest; and thus the temptation passes on from his heart to hers to kindle there the transport of ambition—the rapturous anticipation of royalty. She sees no obstacle, but what she contemptuously calls the "milk of human kindness" in her husband's nature, and she knows the influence of her own energetic will over his reflective spirit. It is the pride of power, therefore, as well as the lust of ambition, by which she is agitated:

> "Hie thee hither,
> That I may pour my spirits in thine ear;
> And chastise with the valour of my tongue
> All that impedes thee from the golden round,
> Which fate and metaphysical aid doth seem
> To have thee crowned withal."

One thought occupies her mind; one passion fills her heart; and, impelled by supernatural force, it drives her across the bounds of woman's nature. Her fierce excitement becomes more highly wrought by the intelligence of the king's approaching visit, the dread issue of which is already grasped by her quickened thought:

> "The raven himself is hoarse,
> That croaks the fatal entrance of Duncan
> Under my battlements."

Divesting herself of womanly emotions, she calls on the powers of darkness—spirits that attend on schemes of murder—to "stop up the access and passage to remorse," and quell all "compunctious visitings of nature," that she may the better scatter the scruples from her husband's conscience. In the midst of this phrensy of a lawless ambition, Macbeth appears, and nothing can be more rapid or decided than her dealing with him. She meets him with no expression of conjugal affection, no tenderness at his return from the wars, but greets him with his titles, his honours present and promised:

> "Great Glamis, worthy Cawdor!
> Greater than both, by the all-hail hereafter!
> Thy letters have transported me beyond
> This ignorant present; and I feel now
> The future in the instant."

In all Macbeth's intercourse with his wife, there is a certain manliness of affection which contributes in some measure to redeem his character, and sustains a sympathy with him. His manner is distinguished by something of the deferential esteem of chivalry; and, after having seen him entertaining guilty imaginings and dallying with thoughts of murder, we seem to hear the voice of a better nature when, using words that might have been most innocent, he says:

> "My dearest love,
> Duncan comes here to-night."

Thoughts that he had indulged in solitary meditation he withholds from her; but a single question and a single answer betrays the sympathy of their wicked conceptions:

> *Lady Macbeth.* And when goes hence?
> *Macbeth.* To-morrow——as he purposes.

The hesitation is that of a wavering conscience. She knows it from familiarity with his temperament and from the perplexity of his countenance; and she knows it can be swept away by her stronger will looking through all doubts and scruples and fears, to the object which filled her vision:

> "Oh never
> Shall sun that morrow see!
> Your face, my thane, is as a book, where men
> May read strange matters.—To beguile the time,
> Look like the time;—bear welcome in your eye,
> Your hand, your tongue:—look like the innocent flower,
> But be the serpent under it. He that's coming
> Must be provided for: and you shall put
> This night's great business into my despatch;
> Which shall to all our nights and days to come
> Give solely sovereign sway and masterdom."

His feeble answer—

> "We will speak further"—

shows him not quite prepared; but it is a signal not so much of indecision as the vanishing of his doubt, dispelled by the tremendous will of the woman.

From the beginning of the drama, every thing has been growing darker and more threatening; but, as if to give a little respite before it comes to the worst, the sun shines out for a short while in that sweet landscape where Duncan is moving on with sacrificial meekness to his slaughter. When you consider the treacherous and murderous plottings going on between the guilty-seeking pair within the castle, a most solemn contrast may be discovered in the brief colloquy beneath its walls between the pure-hearted Duncan and the equally innocent and noble Banquo. It is the perfection of pathos, as a prelude to the assassination scene; and, indeed, when Shakspeare seeks to impress us with the deepest sense of human character and feeling, the poetic power is in nothing more admirably shown than in the harmony he creates between the material world and the spiritual world in the breast of man. You have here, for instance, the placid temper of the meek monarch—his heart stirred only by affections as pure as the fragrant rural air that lightly touched his brow. You have the unclouded candour of Banquo's heart, and overhead are the blue heavens, which seem to be a reflection of it. Their hearts are touched with the beauty of the earth, air, and sky, and with a sympathy with the cheerful birds that are hovering over their devoted heads.

The same poetic harmony between the immaterial and material world appears in the tempestuous night when the crime is perpetrated—a moral tempest of passions within, and a physical tempest of the elements without. Macbeth's powerful intellect is again busy with reflections and reasonings; but it is not so much the actual guilt he recoils from, or its dread penalty in a life to come, as the retribution in his mortal life. There is something of infidel audacity in his allusion to an hereafter:

> "That but this blow
> Might be the be-all and the end all here,
> But here, upon this bank and shoal of time,—
> We'd jump the life to come. But, in these cases,
> We still have judgment here; that we but teach
> Bloody instructions, which, being taught, return
> To plague the inventor. This even-handed justice
> Commends the ingredients of our poison'd chalice
> To our own lips."

His active mind dwells on subordinate considerations of treason—disloyalty—the breach of trust in murdering his guest—his kinsman—his king—a meek monarch—a train of thought which rises, indeed, to a pitch of wild sublimity in the contemplation of the crime:

> "He's here in double trust:
> First, as I am his kinsman—and his subject,

Strong both against the deed; then, as his host,
Who should against his murderer shut the door,
Not bear the knife myself. Besides, this Duncan
Hath borne his faculties so meek, hath been
So clear in his great office, that his virtues
Will plead like angels, trumpet-tongued, against
The deep damnation of his taking off:
And pity, like a naked new-born babe,
Striding the blast, or heaven's cherubim, hors'd
Upon the sightless couriers of the air,
Shall blow the horrid deed in every eye
That tears shall drown the wind."

At the entrance of his wife he relapses from these agitations of conscience to the more prudential reflections—

"We will proceed no further in this business:
He hath honoured me of late: and I have bought
Golden opinions from all sorts of people,
Which would be worn now in their newest gloss,
Not cast aside so soon."

For an instant he seems innocent, and the wicked purpose cast away; but this cannot safely be inferred merely because the words are used. Indeed, in the study of Shakspeare, a false meaning is often attributed by reading a passage narratively instead of dramatically. The words may express only one of the struggles of a weak conscience and a strong intellect; and the sincerity of them may well be questioned when you reflect on the entire inadequacy of the reasons he assigns in so momentous a question—gratitude to the king and his lately-earned popularity. The one great question, whether he shall be a murderer, he takes no thought of; and this shows the moral condition of his mind. Besides, he has just lamented that he has no spur to prick the sides of his intent, which now he seems to invite by this apparent relinquishment. Lady Macbeth, with a perfect knowledge of her husband's character, treats his expression as a mere flattering of his conscience. She artfully taunts him with indecision, goads him with reproaches, and, as if to awe his spirit by wild exaggerations of her own energy, she breaks out into that terrific boast, that rather than forswear herself, she would pluck the babe from her breast and hideously destroy it.

The guilt deepens, and the supernatural atmosphere thickens at the same time. On the unruly night of the murder, a storm was raging, and, doubtless, the witches were riding on the blast and untying the whirlwinds; for there were

> "Lamentings heard i' the air; strange screams of death,
> And prophesying, with accents terrible,
> Of dire combustion and confused events,
> New-hatch'd to the woful time.
> The obscure bird clamour'd the livelong night;
> Some say the earth was feverous, and did shake."

The whole domain of Macbeth's castle is impregnated with the supernatural atmosphere—visions and dreams and spiritual voices, Banquo's dream of the weird sisters, and the bosom-weight of his gloomy presentiments. Duncan's horses, too—

> "Beauteous and swift, the minions of their race—
> Turn'd wild in nature, broke their stalls, flung out,
> Contending 'gainst obedience, as they would make
> War with mankind."

But more terrible is the tumult in the soul of Macbeth. The intensity of effort powerfully affects the imaginative element in his mind. Where he moves, there is a vision of the air-drawn dagger with gouts of blood upon the blade, the broken sleep of the surfeited grooms, their laughter, their terror, and screams of murder, and their prayers, and the wild curse in the air of eternal wakefulness—all this created or magnified, and distorted through the medium of a murderer's burning brain. The pleadings of conscience had before been hardly audible—he had heard only the suggestions of prudence and expediency; but, at the instant of the murder, the new utterance of a blood-stained conscience strikes into his very soul:

> "Methought I heard a voice cry—'Sleep no more!
> Macbeth does murder sleep, the innocent sleep;
> Sleep, that knits up the ravell'd sleave of care,
> The death of each day's life, sore labour's bath,
> Balm of hurt minds, great nature's second course,
> Chief nourisher in life's feast;' * * *
> Still it cried—'Sleep no more!' to all the house:
> 'Glamis hath murder'd sleep; and therefore Cawdor
> Shall sleep no more, Macbeth shall sleep no more!'"

All the emotions which had been ebbing and flowing in his spirit before the commission of the crime, now rush in one resistless tide. His senses are wound up to a torturing acuteness; one question after another breaks strangely from him. Amid his bewilderment and agony, his constitutional activity of mind assumes a preternatural rapidity. Thoughts and reflections are close crowded in these agitated moments. His wife is confounded by that apostrophe to sleep, which serves to illustrate the mind of Macbeth, and perhaps to show that he had held back the dagger in contemplation of the sweet sleep of the confiding Duncan. He avows his dismay at the thought of what he had done and his inability to look on it again. Fancied voices have alarmed him, and now the simplest sounds strike terror to his soul. The brave man, the soldier, becomes conscious of the change; for, on the knocking at the gate, he exclaims—

"How is't with me, when every noise appals me?"

Nor is it only through one sense that terrors are overwhelming him; he looks upon his hands, and the sorry sight of Duncan's blood upon them "plucks out his eyes." His phrensied imagination, hopeless of any cleansing, sees blood enough there to stain the ocean, to "incarnadine the multitudinous seas." The condition of his feelings is further shown by contrast with the partner of his guilt. She has no thought but of the business on hand: she hears none but natural sounds—the knocking at the gate is precisely known by her, whose senses are not bewildered by fancies; and it strikes a chill to the very heart when, though Duncan's corpse is scarcely cold, we hear her say to her husband—

"The sleeping and the dead
Are but as pictures."

And, after she, too, has dabbled in the murdered man's blood—

"A little water clears us of this deed."

The murderer himself has sunk into a reverie from which with difficulty he is roused by his wife; and then one burst of repentant agony, and the scene is over—perhaps the most appalling scene in all dramatic literature.

Macbeth has worked out his own destiny; he "has it

now, king, Cawdor, Glamis, all, as the weird women promised." Let us now consider the new era of life he has entered on, and see how the presence of one guilty remembrance shall be to him like a triumphant demon in his soul. The more obvious effects of guilt upon his character I need not trace; for they are plain enough to show that fearful truth in the study of human nature, that there is no limit to the hardening of the heart or to the perversion of the understanding. The assassination is quickly followed by the remorseless slaughter of the innocent grooms; and the shedding of blood becomes to him an ordinary means of attaining his ends. The progress of criminality I need not dwell upon; but let me rather seek to trace some of the more recondite influences upon Macbeth's nature.

There is, in one of these scenes, an expression of Banquo's which, simple as it is, I have been deeply impressed with in studying this great work of poetic art. When the death of Duncan is first discovered, and the inmates of the castle are fearfully startled from their slumbers—none but the guilty pair knowing whence the crime came—amid the consternation and panic echoing through the chambers and courts, Banquo is the first to restore some little composure by these simple words:

> "In the great hand of God I stand; and, thence
> Against the undivulged pretence I fight
> Of treasonous malice."

In the darkness of undetected danger—the natural sense of safety destroyed by the presence of secret assassination that is revealed only by the voiceless witness of Duncan's bleeding body—there is a sublimity in this lofty confidence, for it is the strength of an innocent and faithful spirit.

From Banquo, strong in the faith that he is standing in the great hand of God, turn to Macbeth, strong in the possession of his guilt-earned power. He is beset by the torment of new doubts and fears; the restlessness of his conscience makes distant and imaginary evils a present, perpetual, and pressing torture. He envies the murdered dead their repose in the tomb:

> "Better be with the dead,
> Whom we, to gain our place, have sent to peace,
> Than on the torture of the mind to lie
> In restless ecstasy. Duncan is in his grave:
> After life's fitful fever he sleeps well;
> Treason has done his worst; nor steel nor poison,
> Malice domestic, foreign levy, nothing
> Can touch him further!"

The silent rebuke of Banquo's better nature is a growing misery to him, with the added dread that his sceptre is a barren one, to be wrenched from his grasp by an unlineal hand, no son of his succeeding. The anguish of his conscience now travels in this direction:

> "O full of scorpions is my mind, dear wife!
> Thou know'st, that Banquo, and his Fleance, lives."

"There's comfort yet," he thinks, in their destruction; but when his former companion-in-arms is treacherously murdered, a new agony comes upon him—convulsions of a guilty imagination, which calls up, even at a festival, the spectre of the blood-boltered Banquo, glaring and shaking his gory locks at him.

Let it be remembered that I am tracing the career of

no common murderer, whom familiarity with blood might only imbrute, but of one whose capacious intellect is made to feel, more and more, how unreal every thing becomes to a soul that has cast out the spiritual elements of its humanity. Macbeth cannot, as Banquo did, look up to the great hand of God, for to him it can only be the hand of an avenger. His spirit, craving for something more than the support of mere material power, seeks further communion with the witches. He tampers with the "dark and midnight hags," who, with incantations and prophetic sorceries, weave their toils closer and closer around him, and then vanish forever with his curse upon them and upon himself

> "Infected be the air whereon they ride,
> And damn'd all those that trust them!"

Observe, too, that, at the very time the witches have deluded their victim with promises that seem to make "assurance double sure," although he feels that he has taken a bond of destiny, his evil faith actuates him to new works of blood:

> "From this moment,
> The very firstlings of my heart shall be
> The firstlings of my hand. And even now
> To crown my thoughts with acts, be it thought and done:
> The castle of Macduff I will surprise;
> Seize upon Fife; give to the edge o' the sword
> His wife, his babes, and all unfortunate souls
> That trace his line—no boasting like a fool."

The supernatural in the tragedy is now fading fast away; and, ere we come to the catastrophe, we almost forget the witchery of the weird sisters; their malice has been achieved, and then all is left to human vice, human passion, human misery. The high-wrought spirituality of the tragedy has its sublime ending in the "slumbry agitation" of Lady Macbeth,—that terrific, open-eyed sleep-walking, sleep-talking,—and the never-ending misery of the blood-stained hand, with the appalling incoherencies of the hauntings of guilt:

"Out, damned spot! out, I say! . . . Yet who would have thought the old man to have had so much blood in him? . . . The thane of Fife had a wife; where is she now? . . . I tell you yet again, Banquo's buried; he cannot come out of his grave. . . . Here's the smell of blood still: all the perfumes of Arabia will not sweeten this little hand." Her waking imagination had been dull, but now there is a morbid activity of the fancy in sleep. Her force of character, which for a while seemed superhuman, has given way: but still it is in keeping with the character of this strong-willed woman that her remorse is only distantly discovered in her dreams. Darkness seems to have terrors for her, for her attendant says—"She has light by her continually; 'tis her command." The wretched woman perishes a hopeless suicide.

Macbeth is left alone. A deadly heart-sickness is consuming him: it is broken only by a desperate and fitful energy to fire again the soldier's spirit in his heart, which soon sinks into a despondency deeply pathetic:

"This push
Will cheer me ever, or disseat me now.
I have lived long enough: my way of life
Is fallen into the sere the yellow leaf:
And that which should accompany old age,

> As honour, love, obedience, troops of friends,
> I must not look to have; but in their stead,
> Curses, not loud, but deep, mouth-honour, breath
> Which the poor heart would fain deny, but dare not."

He finds that he has been paltered with by the double senses of sorcery. The sea of blood is sweeping him onward, helpless and hopeless; for its red tide has washed out, one by one, the promises which witchcraft had written upon sand.

Throughout this drama, one of its most remarkable impressions is, that we retain, not, indeed, a sympathy, but a pity for the ruin of the hero. It is a feeling wholly different from the unhealthy admiration excited in a vicious school of sentimental romance for its worthless personages. Shakspeare has never suffered the interest in the character of Macbeth to be wholly extinguished, and, appropriately, he gives him the dignity of a soldier's death.

The moral catastrophe is more deeply laid. In the life of man there are two results of goodness and a well-poised faith which, for their impressive beauty, appear to me especially worthy of the deepest reflection: one is, that in a course of existence thus controlled, there is an unbroken continuity; the stream of life flows on in its appointed channel, leaving no ruin behind, and with a sunlight ever before. The past, the present, and the future are blended together in the mind by happy memories—a happy consciousness and the hopefulness of faith. "The thought of past years doth breed perpetual benediction,"* and there is a tranquil looking forward to the future. The

* Wordsworth's Ode on the Intimations of Immortality from Recollections of Early Childhood. Works, p. 387.

other result is, that familiar things are the oftener regarded as symbols of that spiritual world which gives reality to our being—a feeling without which the heart sinks down in dismal and dreary despondency from its sense of hollowness, and with which the heart leaps up with the assurance of its own undying strength. Now, I have referred to these considerations because it is to the very opposite of all this that the soul of Macbeth is brought in the extremity of his career of guilt. It is that condition of mind—the lowest pitch of infidel despair—which looks on life as utterly vain and meaningless. From the innocence of his early days he feels separated by a dread gulf of crime; and, for the future, all is impenetrable darkness. This is the moral catastrophe of the tragedy, and I do not know how I can so well express these opposite conditions to which the soul may be either raised or sunk, than by citing what alone is adequate to express the emotions which accompany them—the language of poetry. The first of them—the exulting joy of a faithful, thoughtful spirit, quickly sensitive to any token which gives assurance of the covenant between things human and divine, and happy in its memory of childhood—has been expressed when a poet exclaimed—

"My heart leaps up when I behold
A rainbow in the sky:
So was it when my life began,
So is it now I am a man,
So be it when I shall grow old,
Or let me die!
The child is father of the man;
And I could wish my days to be
Bound each to each by natural piety."*

* Wordsworth's works, p. 27.

Now, by the side of this, listen to what is almost the last voice that comes from the weary soul of Macbeth :

> "To-morrow, and to-morrow, and to-morrow,
> Creeps in this petty pace from day to day,
> To the last syllable of recorded time ;
> And all our yesterdays have lighted fools
> The way to dusty death. Out, out, brief candle!
> Life's but a walking shadow ; a poor player,
> That struts and frets his hour upon the stage,
> And then is heard no more : it is a tale
> Told by an idiot, full of sound and fury,
> Signifying nothing."

The terrors of the tragedy have subsided into this deeply pathetic strain ; and, hollow as this contemplative melancholy is, it still wins from us enough of sympathy to make us feel that we are standing amid the ruins of a soul which was worthy of a better destiny.

LECTURE III.*

Hamlet.

In passing from the tragedy of Macbeth to that of Hamlet, the transition is a very wide one. Both dramas, indeed, have their supernatural agencies—strange, spiritual things made real to the imagination; and the respective heroes are not unlike in a certain constitutional reflectiveness of mind. In the Scottish usurper, as well as in the young Danish prince, there is a touch of philosophy. But, while in the tragedy of Macbeth there is, I may almost say, a throng of supernatural forms detested and terrific—the witches, with all their train of apparitions, that rose around their cauldron, and the blood-boltered spectre of Banquo—in Hamlet there is one solitary and majestic phantom; and, instead of that lurid, supernatural light which was fitfully breaking upon the former tragedy, we seem to behold now one solemn and awful shadow hanging over the course of the drama. The meditative moods of Macbeth's mind were no more than bubbles, borne onward upon the surface of that rapid and violent tide which hurried the

* December 20th, 1842.

movement of the play; but in Hamlet, the philosophic habit of his intellect is the chief element in the tragedy—the ruling principle which gives to it its gentle and slow progression. Nor is this intellectual character peculiar to the chief person; for, besides the profound and feeling thoughtfulness of Hamlet, you find the insincere and declamatory reasoning of the king, the self-complacent shrewdness of the old politician in Polonius, the fraternal counsels of Laertes, and, in perfect keeping with the predominant tone of the tragedy, the logic of the captious grave-digger—a most thoughtful, reasoning company. In this respect, it seems to me that this drama, more than any other, may be regarded as eminently reflecting the constitution of Shakspeare's mind—as the production in which he incorporated, more largely than any other, the habits of his intellect.

If the question were asked—What personage in the whole range, not only of dramatic literature, but of all fiction, has gained the deepest, the most pleasing, and universal interest?—the answer, I am inclined to believe, which cultivated minds would be most apt to give, would be, The character of Hamlet. Now it would be a very shallow effort were I to seek an explanation of this deep and widespread interest in the outward story of the play, its plot and incidents and catastrophe. The mystery is not to be solved thus; something more inward must be sought to explain it—to show how it is in accordance with our common human-heartedness. Nay, more than this: it is not enough to discover in what respects this poem is illustrative and typical of the mere feelings and thoughts of humanity, for I believe that its sublime philosophy consists in this—that in it we are carried into that region of our spiritual nature which is not peculiar or variable in different human beings, and which is not susceptible of degrees, such as we attribute to intellect or sentiment; it carries us through the domain of passion and thought into that spiritual region where naught is known but what is illimitable and eternal—the human soul. It need not, therefore, cause our wonder that this tragedy has much about it that is mysterious, obscure, and perplexed to critic and to commentator; for it deals with the greatest of all mysteries—that imperishable principle of the personality of each human being—that eternal something which, at our birth, gathers up for a mysterious combination the earthly elements of our bodies, and, after travelling on through the mortal life, scatters those elements at death like the light, lifeless leaves of autumn. Entertaining the thought I do of the tragedy of Hamlet, I find myself approaching it—to say with diffidence would feebly express it, but with a conviction of the greater or less inadequacy of all criticism for the exposition of its sublime imaginings. It is a subject to be thought upon, much rather than talked of.

Let it, however, be remembered that, according to the plan of my course, I am considering these dramas as illustrations of the main subject of tragic poetry. If, in accordance with the definition given by an ancient philosopher, we traced a chastening of the passions by the agency of pity in King Lear, and in Macbeth by the agency rather of terror, we may discover in Hamlet another of the uses of tragedy in showing that mournful thoughts and the sad conflicts of humanity have a power of their own to make known the strength and weakness of the soul—all that lies hid there, and which men rarely become conscious of in the trivial chances of life or in its placid periods. A deeper self-consciousness is awakened from its slumbers by the tumultuous movements of the soul—disappointment, affliction, or anguish. It is thus the hidden energies of the spirit are disclosed, just as the unfelt and unknown strength of a nation is brought into action by the necessities and tribulations of war.

In King Lear we had occasion to study the career of a human spirit under the stern discipline of affliction—a heart palpitating under Promethean torture; for filial ingratitude had "tied sharp-toothed unkindness like a vulture there." In Macbeth we followed the career of a spirit through its yieldings to temptation; but in Hamlet the influences are far more complex. The tragedy is a story of a soul environed by all the agencies which are best fitted to reveal its functions and its aspirations; and the imagination of Shakspeare, after embodying in the character of Hamlet the elements of a susceptible spirit, has gathered around that spirit every influence which could aptly touch it. He has shown this character in the despondency of an unavailing sorrow; another while in the sunshine of a cheerful thoughtfulness; again in the distress of disturbed affections, in the perplexity of obscure and conflicting duties; and again in the solemn awe of a supernatural influence. The observation we have to take is of the starlike light of Hamlet's soul dwelling apart in the region of a lofty self-communion, and moving onward in its path like one of "that host," as it has been finely called, "of white-robed pilgrims that travel along the vault of the nightly sky." We are to observe the light of his life shining, serenely shining, from the large and placid spaces of his own gentle and noble and thoughtful nature, or else struggling with either the mists of earthly sorrow, or the lurid, supernatural reflection that reaches it from the prison-house of the suffering dead. Now, let us inquire, what is the character of Hamlet, before the tragic influences are brought to bear upon it. The first mention of him is of "young Hamlet." He is a prince, the heir-apparent to the throne of Denmark, the son of a most majestic monarch—a father whom he as deeply honoured as he dearly loved; for about that parent there were the grandeur of an heroic warrior and the graceful gentleness of domestic virtue. We are told of the frown that darkened his brow—

> "When, in an angry parle,
> He smote the sledded Polack on the ice,"

and we are also told of the tender affection to his queen, that—

> "He might not beteem the winds of heaven
> Visit her face too roughly"—

a love for her which was "of that dignity that it went hand in hand even with the vow he made to her in marriage." Hamlet was the son, too, of an "all-seeming virtuous mother," the loving wife of his father; and thus he had grown to manhood amid those happy, virtuous household influences that are the best atmosphere for the young heart to live in. To the attractions of manly form and feature, he has added the accomplishments which befit his high birth; and, what is more rare as a princely aim, he has learnt the delights of communion with the recorded wisdom of poets and philosophers. It was not enough for him to be crowned with the pride of expectant royalty, he must also wear the milder glory of scholarship; and how much his heart is in this, is seen when, in the sympathy which common studies engender, he greets his friend Horatio as his "fellow-student." I do not know that there is a character in all the large company of the Shaksperian drama upon whom the poet has, from the exuberance of his imagination, bestowed such abundant and various graciousness. You may observe in Hamlet the princely dignity, and that indescribable and instinctive deference to the feelings of others, which constitutes the gentlemanly spirit; you have the gallant bearing of the soldier, and that meditative composure which philosophy may give.

Nor is it only in these acquirements that the character of Hamlet is arrayed with so much grace: it has a beauty in its large portion of those feelings which, independent of social or intellectual rank, adorn humanity. He clings to Horatio with the steady zeal of a fast friendship, and the deeper susceptibility of his heart is shown in the love for Ophelia, which endured till his destiny demanded the sad sacrifice of it.

Hamlet has just crossed the threshold of manhood, and what more could be added to give him dignity and grace? Young and beautiful, the pride of the palace, and, better still, an indweller in spirit in the palaces of wisdom and learning, elevated by the memories of an heroic ancestry and by noble expectations for the future, and happy, too, in the depth of his affections—this is life in its purest and most serene region of thought and feeling—all is bright and innocent and joyous, but the elements of tragedy are darker.

The first change that comes over a prospect so sunny, the first tragic influence which touches the nature of

Hamlet is the sudden sorrowing for his father. That virtuous freedom from care, which belongs to that period of life spent beneath the paternal roof, and to that period alone, has ceased upon the unexpected ending of his father's life. The object, to which had been devoted all the reverential affection of a nature so thoughtful and sensitive, is suddenly taken away. When Hamlet first appears, you behold the stricken heart of filial piety. Amid the pomp and pageantry of the court he stands a mourner near the throne; and the appeal is a vain one to him, when he is unworthily and unfeelingly entreated to cast his sorrow away:

> "Do not forever with thy vailed lids
> Seek for thy noble father in the dust."

This was, doubtless, the first time the arrow of death had passed so near him; and probably there is no influence on the human spirit comparable to that when separation by death is, for the first time, deeply and really felt. The ending of life is, for the most part, too familiar to be felt: we meet the funeral procession, and it gives us scarce a second thought: we hear of the departure of some one known to us, and we are surprised or sorry, but these are momentary emotions, upon the very surface too. When, for the first time, death invades our own household, perhaps we are too young to heed it: the brief bewilderment of childhood soon gives way to the innocent vanity—the excusable self-importance of the new suit of mourning. But when death for the first time makes itself truly felt—when some sudden separation of what life had closely bound together, startles us to the very centre of our being, there is no greater power to drive the soul into itself in its struggles with that dreary sense of craving after what is gone from our bodily eyes forever—that utter casting down of the heart when the mourner comes back from the fresh grave to the desolate house. The earnestness of life is blunted, and the very sun in the sky shines less brightly than it did before. Pleasant memories are converted into sad associations, and we feel,

> "Where'er we go,
> That there hath past away a glory from the earth."*

Nor is this influence of a genuine grief confined merely to our emotions; it powerfully agitates the intellectual part of man. Let me call it a spiritual rather than a mere intellectual struggle, when the heart in its loneliness is groping after the dead. When the life which animated some familiar form is extinguished—the fire quenched with which the substance of the eye was lighted, we are strangely perplexed, because we are left without the means of apprehending the new life which follows after the mortal life. The bodily elements which used to be known to our senses—things of sight and sound—are left to perish until the soul shall gather them up again; and the dead are, perhaps, separated from the living only so far as this, that the spiritual existence and that mysterious combination of spirit and matter, which we call life, cannot take cognizance of each other. Yet, impenetrable as this barrier is, who can tell how slight it may be! Death may be no more than such a separation: this earth, which has its visible world of living material things, may have also its invisible spiritual world of the

* Wordsworth's Ode on Intimations of Immortality.

myriads of the dead, whose bodies have been commingled with the dust, or whose bones are drifting in the fathomless caverns of the sea. Now, the struggle of a strong and thoughtful grief is to overleap these barriers which are impassable to mortality. Its aspirations would reach beyond the inevitable limits of its materialism; and its intense yearnings after the dead are not to be satisfied by suffering its fancies to travel to the tomb, but strive to follow the imperishable particle which was the very life of what the grave receives. Hopeless as its questionings may be, the soul of the survivor sends them after the disembodied spirit—a process of thought and feeling which has been thus described as from a mourner's own lips:

> "I called on dreams and visions to disclose
> That which is veiled from waking thought; conjured
> Eternity, as men constrain a ghost,
> To appear and answer; to the grave I spake
> Imploringly—looked up, and asked the heavens
> If angels traversed their cerulean floors,
> If fixed or wandering star could tidings yield
> Of the departed spirit—what abode
> It occupies—what consciousness retains
> Of former loves and interests. Then my soul
> Turned inward—to examine of what stuff
> Time's fetters are composed; and life was put
> To inquisition long and profitless
> By pain of heart, now checked and now impelled,
> The intellectual power, through words and things,
> Went sounding on, a dim and perilous way!"*

The active and fine intellect of Hamlet has received what is at once the shock and the impulse of profound grief. His shaping imagination is busy in fashioning the

* Wordsworth's Excursion, b. iii. (Despondency.)

likeness of his dead father's form—now made visible to his "mind's eye," that happy expression which Shakspeare has made so familiar to all who speak our English tongue.* And how dear had that form in life been to his eyes may be known from the enthusiastic admiration he gives utterance to, when, afterwards describing to his mother the picture of her first husband, his own honoured father, he says—

"See, what a grace was seated on this brow:
Hyperion's curls;—the front of Jove himself;
An eye like Mars, to threaten and command;
A station like the herald Mercury,
New-lighted on a heaven-kissing hill;
A combination and a form indeed,
Where every god did seem to set his seal,
To give the world assurance of a man."

From the glowing words of this description, we may perceive how Hamlet's imagination had been filled with

---

* In a private letter written soon after, my brother thus playfully refers to this familiar phrase:

"I have always regarded the 'mind's eye' as eminently and peculiarly a Shakspearian phrase, his originally and nobody else's; but, in a volume of minor Greek poets, looking for something or other, I chanced on the phrase ψυχῆς ὄμμα in some lines by Naumachius; and yet, may be that is the 'soul's eye,' which makes a difference. Pray, who was professor of Greek when Hamlet was a student at Wittenberg? and was the 'Poetæ Minores' one of the text-books in use? What a pity it was not Horatio that used the phrase; for he is so precise and matter-of-fact, that he would certainly have told us where he got it, with, perhaps, a reference; while Hamlet was very much the kind of man to use the phrase, with some little alteration, and say nothing about original authorities—or may be it was a sort of unconscious (S. T. C.) plagiarism." MS. Letter, 28th February, 1845.

W. B. R.

the glorious ideal forms of classic fable; and it is worth noticing, that the very first feeling attributed to him is an anxiety to go back to the calm retreat of his academic life at Wittenberg, to resume that happy communion with the good and wise of all ages which no villainy can betray.

It is not only sorrow that is weighing down the heart of Hamlet. Even the sad seclusion of grief is not allowed to him. He finds himself cheated of his inheritance; and the succession, and the detested paternity that is thrust upon him, inflame ill-suppressed feelings of indignation and resentment. Dark misgivings, too, as we afterwards learn, are flitting across his mind and casting shadows of suspicion too dreadful for him to give utterance to—presentiments of that supernatural revelation which discloses to him the mystery of his father's murder. Worse than all this is the anguish of disappointment in his once-loved mother, the once "most seeming virtuous queen." Memories of his father's deep and honourable love crowd upon his mind. Unable and unwilling to cast away his duty, and perhaps affection, to her, he is agitated by the reluctant conviction that she is unworthy of it; and thus, the sentiment of filial piety, which ought to flow in a placid current, is changed into a broken and fretted tide. Such are the trials that come upon the unprepared spirit of one who had been the happy inmate of a virtuous palace, had breathed the pure atmosphere of domestic love and honour, and whose enthusiasm had been elevated by the heroic associations and trophies of his illustrious father, and not less by ideal visions of truth in the unclouded regions of philosophy. He is suddenly in a situation where sorrows press upon him, which are agonies to such a spirit as his; and yet, see, withal, how graceful a gentleness he maintains! Indeed, from the indecorous tone in which he is addressed both by king and queen, we might believe that his life had been characterized by that scholastic gentleness, which the unworthy might be tempted to presume upon. The king speaks to him, and Hamlet recoils with a play upon words which serves to disguise his deep and disturbed feelings. The queen speaks, and he answers with respect and with reserve; for, while dutifully remembering that she is his mother, he cannot forget that she is his father's fickle and faithless widow. His dearest wish is to withdraw into the recesses of his sorrowing meditations; but he is molested by cold commonplaces on the subject of death, and by reproaches of the fidelity of his grief—a grief so inward and self-communing, that, to confound it with the mere outward customary signs was, indeed, a heartless imputation. The usurper takes up the reproachful strain from the lips of the queen; beginning with empty compliments, and ending with the empty promises of hypocrisy, he tells Hamlet that the filial obligation was discharged by the obsequious sorrow already shown, and that now it was an obstinate condolement—a course of impious stubbornness—an unmanly grief, showing a will most incorrect to heaven—a heart unfortified—a mind impatient—an understanding simple and unschooled—a fault to heaven—a fault against the dead—a fault to nature—to reason most absurd. To this heaping of reproaches of the very kind to wound so sensitive and thoughtful a spirit, Hamlet answers not a word—it is the silence of an almost breaking heart, as he afterwards says—

> "But break my heart, for I must hold my tongue."

These are the first of those conflicts of the heart which disturb Hamlet's nature. There is the double disappointment of his filial piety—the death of his noble father and the moral degradation of his mother: all his gentle propensities, too, are frustrated, his longing for scholastic solitude is thwarted, and his lonely self-communion violated by intrusion. Constraint is on him, and he is forced to dwell amid the unruly revelry of a riotous palace—so changed, too, from what it was—and in the detested presence of all that his spirit is at variance with. Now, the natural consequence of such a state of mind is, a wretched weariness of life, which comes sadly across the young heart when the natural tide of its hopes and affections is suddenly and violently arrested—when misanthropy is forced into a spirit whose native element is love. His first free utterance is when he breaks forth, the very moment he is left alone, in that piteous and incoherent soliloquy, which admirably presents the characteristic condition of his mind—a combination of great intellectual activity with deep moral sensibility manifest in the perpetual commingling of meditations and emotions. A blight has touched his young heart, and not only the palace—his home—but the whole earth is dreary to him: so young, he is already longing after the repose of the grave, and a wish for self-destruction is checked only by a sense of man's duty to the everlasting: he sorrows most of all that he must live. All his pent-up and conflicting feelings are seeking relief at once; and the words that give utterance to them are expressive, at the same time, of his affection and admiration for his departed father, antipathy and contempt for his kinsman, the usurper, and —the worst misery of all—the heart-sickening thoughts of his mother's infidelity.

Throughout this drama, in every soliloquy or speech of Hamlet, you may discover, not only the extraordinary intellectual activity which Shakspeare has given to the character, but also a wonderful susceptibility of sentiment, which is one of its chief charms. I know of no dramatic character in which the processes of thought are so rapid and so complex, and the associations of ideas so quick and various. We seem to feel the depth and purity of Hamlet's spirit the more, when we contemplate the thoughts and feelings which perpetually are speeding so quickly over it, just as to the eye the steadfast firmament has a purer blue and a more measureless height, because of the flying haste of the clouds upon a bright and breezy day; or, rather, to vary the similitude, the pathetic beauty of Hamlet's character impresses us the more from its inimitable variety, like the shifting glory of an autumnal sunset, changing, at each instant changing—the bright foreshadowing of twilight and darkness.

Immediately after the agonized soliloquy, the entrance of Horatio and the gentlemen to whom the ghost had appeared, gives another aspect of Hamlet's character. His deep and painful self-communions are hushed, and it is, indeed, very beautiful to see him at once casting aside all considerations of self in his friendly address to his fellow-student. He will not believe Horatio's avowal of a truant disposition; but, after the momentary diversion of affectionate greeting, his dark thoughts are forced back, first in a painful sense of princely shame that his friend should witness the disgraceful debauchery of the royal household.

Horatio's answer leads on to still more painful thoughts; and yet there is a most attractive grace in the sincerity and pathos with which Hamlet partly opens his heart to his friend:

> *Horatio.* My lord, I came to see your father's funeral.
> *Hamlet.* I pray thee, do not mock me, fellow-student;
> I think it was to see my mother's wedding.

As soon as Horatio replies,

> "Indeed, my lord, it followed hard upon,"

there comes one of those characteristic quick transitions of feeling; for Hamlet, as if conscious of having laid bare too much of his lonely thoughts, even to his friend, rallies with somewhat of a bitter jest—that severe jesting which frequently breaks from him, not forced, but natural to deep and suppressed emotions, which seem to find in it a kind of relief. He tells Horatio that the marriage so speedy after the burial was excellent economy—there was no waste:

> "Thrift, thrift, Horatio! the funeral bak'd meats,
> Did coldly furnish forth the marriage tables."

But he cannot sustain the jesting mood; and he feels, too, that it is a wrong to his friend, for he straightway adds, also addressing him—

> "Would I had met my dearest foe in heaven,
> Or ever I had seen that day, Horatio!"

Again he gives himself up to meditation, and gazes with the "mind's eye" into the invisible world where the spirit of his father dwells. When roused by the account of the apparition, his habitual mental activity is suspended in wonder: there is neither argument nor skeptical distrust, but only the firm resolve to speak to the spectre, if it assume his noble father's person, with the prudential injunction of secresy upon all who had witnessed the mystery. When left alone, the habit of meditation returns and associates the strange intelligence with some of his own unuttered presentiments.

The ghost of the murdered monarch is surely one of the most majestic phantoms that poetic imagination has ever realized. It is an apparition not so much of terror as of awe and solemnity, arrayed with all the impressive associations of the grave, of religion, and of popular superstition. Its movements are stately—the shadow, as it were, of the step of a kingly soldier; the glory of its earthly and warlike majesty is mysteriously mingled with an awful dignity brought from the regions of the dead. It is that fair and warlike form

> "In which the majesty of buried Denmark
> Did sometimes march."

It seems to wear the very armour he had on

> "When he the ambitious Norway combated."

When the soldiers vainly and rashly strike at it with their partisans, they straightway feel—

> "We do it wrong, being so majestical,
> To offer it the show of violence;
> For it is, as the air, invulnerable,
> And our vain blows malicious mockery."

The spectre which most nearly resembles it is the imperial apparition of Cæsar, which awed even the philosophic soul of Brutus before the battle of Philippi.

Now, let us consider how the young philosophy of Hamlet will bear this new and supernatural influence. His presence of mind never forsakes him; for, with all the emotion and amazement and the solemn awe which agitate him, he addresses the phantom of his father with apt questionings: when his attendants become fearfully apprehensive that he may be led away to his destruction, it seems to me that there is a moral sublimity in Hamlet's brief argument for fearlessness—a spiritual fearlessness; and again in the calm expression of his determination, unheeding Horatio's effort to alarm him:

> "Why, what should be the fear?
> I do not set my life at a pin's fee;
> And, for my soul, what can it do to that,
> Being a thing immortal as itself?"

While the ghost speaks, Hamlet's mind is riveted in dutiful attention to words which show his dark misgivings, more than realized in the mysterious disclosure. But the after consequences of such a supernatural visitation are yet greater. In the records of ghost stories, it is said that, "whenever the supernatural character of the apparition has been believed, the effects on the spectator have always been most terrible—convulsion, idiocy, madness, or even death, on the spot."*

The vanishing of the ghost, whose presence had awed Hamlet into a reverential silence, is followed by a burst of language which shows that his intellect is in a state of

* Coleridge's Table Talk, p. 22.

delirious commotion; and the first sign of the disturbance of it has been discovered in the vow "to wipe away from the table of his memory, all trivial fond records, all saws of books, all forms, all pressures past, that youth and observation copied there;" and then, at the very instant, writing down in his tablets the maxim

> "That one may smile, and smile, and be a villain!
> At least, I am sure, it may be so in Denmark."

When his friends rejoin him, the intense excitement of his mind gives way to eccentric jesting. He puts them away from himself and his secret with what seems a strange flippancy—"wild and whirling words," as Horatio calls them. As the tumult of his emotions subsides, his gentle, gentlemanly disposition prompts an apology to Horatio for what looked too like an unworthy trifling with him. The wonted activity of his intellect again appears in what has struck me as the most graceful and thoughtful play upon words I have ever met with. It occurs immediately before the half-sportive allusion to the philosophical studies of himself and his fellow-student. When the ghost is heard speaking from beneath, Horatio exclaims—

> "Oh, day and night but this is wondrous strange!
> *Hamlet.* And therefore as a stranger give it welcome.
> There are more things in heaven and earth, Horatio,
> Than are dreamt of in your philosophy."

Happy would it be, let me add, if, whenever a spiritual mystery is presented to our thoughts, we did not reject it because, transcending our little knowledge, it happens to be "undreamt of in our philosophy;" happy would it be if we did not suffer doubts, and suspicions, and the sophistries of a sensualized skepticism to shut up the avenues of our souls, instead of opening the door wide to give the mystery a stranger's welcome!

Hamlet's character from the time of the interview with the ghost becomes more complicated; and it is a question on which a great deal of comment has been expended, whether his insanity is feigned or real. The difficulties involving the question are of theoretical rather than of practical purport; for they do not seem to affect the poetical impression which the character is intended to make. Indeed, it may be that the interest of the character is rather increased by this very mysteriousness—the obscurity in discriminating between his affected wildness and the actual disturbance of his intellect. These difficulties are owing partly to this—that insanity is of so many degrees, and so multiform, that you can scarce define it: the English language, though not highly esteemed by all for its copiousness, furnishes, it may be, a dozen different words to express the various morbid conditions of the intellect. I, probably, am not wrong in saying that this subject of insanity has often perplexed at least two learned professions, to say nothing of the wisdom of judges and the integrity of jurors. To some charitable minds, enormity of crime is itself an evidence of insanity—of a wrong head as well as a wrong heart; while by others, of sterner judgments, a disordered intellect would not be suffered to plead insanity in bar of justice at an earthly tribunal. Modern philanthropy and science have learnt to classify, for salutary purposes, the inmates of lunatic asylums; but no science has ever attempted the same process for the unhealthy minds that share with the sane ones the business of life.

The difficulty with respect to Hamlet is not so much in forming a just conception of the state of his mind, as in attaching a precise significancy to this word "insanity." At least there need be no such difficulty, were it not oftener caused by the logic of a contracted criticism—the propensity to narrow verbal comment—which will misapprehend the whole drift of a character and destroy the spirit of a drama by dwelling upon detached passages and expressions.

This is fatal to a true appreciation of the dramatic genius of the poet: very much, if I may be allowed to use such an illustration, which I do with entire reverence,—very much in the same way that men often perplex and embarrass their faith—argue it out of their hearts, and tempt themselves into miserable heresies by fastening upon isolated texts, instead of studying the Scriptures with a more docile and catholic spirit than that which trusts to mere logic.

Hamlet mentions to his friends a deliberate purpose of "putting an antic disposition on," and he is seen fulfilling his intention; and hence it is inferred that all his insanity is feigned. On the other hand, there is observed a wildness of demeanour which cannot thus be accounted for; and hence it is inferred that it is real insanity. Now, the human mind is not such a simple machine as this, and Shakspeare knew it too well ever to treat it so. The truth, as well as I can state a matter so abstruse. seems to be this: that, from a combination of influences, the mind of Hamlet was in a state of undue susceptibility of both unnatural excitement and depression; and then further agitated by a supernatural visitation, by which, in his own words, he felt his "disposition horridly shaken with thoughts beyond the reaches of our souls." This visible and audible communion with the dead has so convulsed all the spiritual elements of his nature, that he becomes conscious that the sovereignty of his reason is in jeopardy; and it is this very consciousness—the apprehension of insanity—which suggests to an intellect so active the thought of feigning madness—the device of assuming an antic disposition—which would give him an unwonted freedom, and which might always be controlled by his habitual intellectual strength. It comes, then, to this—that there was disorder in the mind—a disturbance of his intellect, something more than that which he was feigning; but, if this question of insanity involve the question whether his mind ceased to be under the mastery of his will, assuredly there was no such aberration.

In the various allusions to the condition of Hamlet's mind, you may find it variously designated. The queen tenderly speaks of the "transformation" of her son. The king speaks of it as a "melancholy" and a "distemper." Polonius calls it "lunacy." The grave-digger bluntly taks of "Hamlet—he that is mad and sent to England; sent there because he was mad; he shall recover his wits there; or if he do not, it is no great matter; it will not be seen in him there; there the men are as mad as he." But when Ophelia speaks of it, in the simplicity of her opinion, there is not only beauty but truth in the image by which she describes what seems to her the piteous overthrow of a lofty mind:

> "See that noble and most sovereign reason,
> Like sweet bells jangled, out of tune, and harsh."

It is an exquisite similitude of the undefinable condition

of Hamlet's mind: his intellect had lost its harmony, but still there was a wild music in the changes which an untoward destiny was ringing on it.

The scene with Ophelia is one of the most difficult to interpret. There is a natural inclination to refer to real insanity Hamlet's apparent harshness; for there seems to be a rude rejecting of her, which it is hard to reconcile with the truth and gentleness of his natural disposition, and which we cannot quite believe his deep love for her would suffer him to affect. But it must be remembered, that there was a leave-taking before this, which is not dramatically presented, and which, in some respects, is more important. It is only described: it was a silent interview—that silence a better token of his deep feeling than the wild words he afterwards addresses to her. He takes her by the hand; he gazes on her face with

> "Such perusal as he would draw it,"—

perhaps to impress it on his imagination as something dear to his heart, and yet which an awful necessity forces him to banish. A deep and piteous sigh breaks from him; then, without a word spoken, he leaves her—

> "That done, he lets me go.
> And, with his head over his shoulder turned,
> He seem'd to find his way without his eyes,
> For out o' doors he went without their helps,
> And, to the last, bended their light on me."

This was the real leave-taking; and if it be asked why he thus alienated himself from Ophelia, the necessity is to be explained by the fearful responsibility which filled his soul. A voice from the grave was ever in his ears.

The apparition of a loved and honoured father had burst from the prison-house of the dead to lay upon the soul of Hamlet, with supernatural weight, a duty which he felt must absorb his being. What now could he have to do with such a sentiment as love? With all its purity, it could not consort with his solemn charge.

When afterwards Hamlet unexpectedly finds himself again in the presence of Ophelia, all his former affection comes back upon him:

> "Soft you, now!
> The fair Ophelia!—Nymph, in thy orisons
> Be all my sins remember'd."

He had over-calculated his own strength in setting aside his love for her; and of this he becomes conscious when the thought of his one paramount duty quickly returns. Hence, the revulsion of feeling in this painful scene—the desperate energy with which he recovers himself from relapse into an affection, the indulgence of which his destiny can no more admit. His apparent rudeness we must not take too literally—remember it is poetry, and not prose, we are studying now. It is not in reality indifference and heartlessness to Ophelia, but self-reproach of what he sternly condemns as his own weakness, when, with such strange impetuosity, he bids her—"To a nunnery, go"—one moment disclaiming his love, and another acknowledging it—with a wild irony accusing himself of "pride, revenge, ambition—more offences at his beck than he has thoughts to put them in, imagination to give them shape, or time to act them in;" then telling the innocent and artless girl of the vices and frailties, not, indeed, of herself, but of her sex, and warning her that the world is not a safe place for her to abide in :—"Get thee to a nunnery, farewell. . . . To a nunnery, go; and quickly too. Farewell. . . . To a nunnery, go." In confirmation of the view I have taken of this scene, observe that Hamlet's asperity does not wound Ophelia as an injury. Her only feeling is pity—more for the sad calamity of his intellect than for her own dejected hopelessness.

Meditative as is the mind of Hamlet, his nature is too gentle for him to travel on in life a solitary-hearted man. The sense of loneliness is relieved by his friendship for Horatio, to whose manly judgment he could, in consultation, impart his supernatural secret and his dread, though ill-defined, purposes, which it would have been both cruel and useless to tell to one so innocent, so tender, and so artless as the "sweet Ophelia." The friendship of Hamlet and Horatio is one of those—such as may be observed in actual life—founded not only upon sympathies, but upon harmonious contrasts of character—the qualities of one party happily felt as supplying something wanting in the other. Horatio is a man not only of strong, but just and well-regulated, feelings, and especially in intellectual constitution, possessed of sound, practical, common sense, strikingly contrasted with Hamlet's imaginative apprehensiveness—the deep spirit of meditation and overwrought mental activity. The character of Hamlet is overflowing with poetry and philosophy, while Horatio is matter-of-fact and prosaic. Yet, in this very variety, Hamlet, conscious of his own disposition, feels that he has a better friend—a safer counsellor.

Besides this friendship, Hamlet finds relief from the sense of moral desolation, which sickens his heart, in the conscious power of his intellect. It is this, I think, which may explain the abrupt transition from an expression of his dreary feeling to that splendid panegyric upon man:—"I have of late (but wherefore I know not) lost all my mirth, foregone all custom of exercises; and, indeed, it goes so heavily with my disposition, that this goodly frame, the earth, seems to me a sterile promontory; this most excellent canopy, the air, look you, this brave overhanging firmament, this majestical roof, fretted with golden fire—why, it appears no other thing to me than a foul and pestilent congregation of vapours. · What a piece of work is a man! How noble in reason! how infinite in faculty! in form, and moving, how express and admirable! in action, how like an angel! in apprehension, how like a god! the beauty of the world! the paragon of animals! And yet, to me, what is this quintessence of dust?"

The genius of Hamlet is shown not only in such passages interspersed through the ramblings of his antic disposition, but also in his inimitable lonely meditations, such as that most famous of all soliloquies, when, standing on the fancied brink of life—the very tide-mark of "this bank and shoal of time"—he gazes out upon the ocean of eternity, his

> "Soul has sight of that immortal sea,
> Which brought us hither."*

His "mind's eye" is strained almost to blindness in the effort to descry the shores of "that undiscovered country from whose bourne no traveller returns:" and his spirit

* Wordsworth's Ode on the Intimations of Immortality.

falls back again to this earthly life, saddened by thoughts of prosperous iniquity and by his sympathy with suffering humanity, the vision of its wrongs and miseries before "this mortal coil is shuffled off"—

> "The spurns,
> That patient merit of the unworthy takes."

Hamlet's far-reaching mind seeks to fathom the dreams of our afterlife. Indeed, as Charles Lamb, speaking of the impossibility of acting this tragedy, remarks—"Nine parts in ten of what Hamlet does are transactions between himself and his moral sense—effusions of his solitary musings, which he retires to holes and corners and the most sequestered parts of the palace to pour forth; or rather, they are the silent meditations with which his bosom is bursting, reduced to words for the sake of the reader—profound sorrows—light-and-noise-abhorring ruminations, which the tongue scarce dares utter to deaf walls and chambers."*

But the mandate of his father's spirit is not yet fulfilled. The usurper is still on the throne—the incestuous marriage is unbroken. Why is this with one who, at the first intimation given by the ghost, spoke of "sweeping to his revenge with wings as swift as meditation or the thoughts of love"? The chief explanation by the best critics lies in the excessive activity of Hamlet's intellect—disproportionate mental exertion, always busy with its own suggestions and speculations, but flying from the acting point. He is conscious of this himself in some of his self-reproaches:

* Essay on Shakspeare's Tragedies. Prose Works, vol. i. p. 107.

"What is a man,
If his chief good, and market of his time,
Be but to sleep and feed? a beast, no more.
Sure he that made us with such large discourse,
Looking before and after, gave us not
That capability and godlike reason
To fust in us unused. Now, whether it be
Bestial oblivion, or some craven scruple
Of thinking too precisely on the event,—
A thought, which quarter'd, hath but one part wisdom,
And ever three parts coward,—I do not know
Why yet I live to say, 'This thing's to do;'
Sith I have cause, and will, and strength, and means,
To do't."

But this is the exaggeration of self-accusation. Hamlet was brave, yet he was gentle too; and it seems to me that another and, perhaps, chief cause of his inaction, for which sufficient allowance has not been made, was the tenderness of his conscience—the agitation of the moral sense even more than of the intellect:

"Thus conscience does make cowards of us all;
And thus the native hue of resolution
Is sicklied o'er with the pale cast of thought;
And enterprises of great pith and moment,
With this regard, their currents turn awry
And lose the name of action."

It should not be forgotten that when the ghost imposed on Hamlet the duty of vengeance, he said not how, but solemnly charged him—

"Howsoever thou pursu'st this act,
Taint not thy mind, nor let thy soul contrive
Against thy mother aught."

It was the awful duty of blood-shedding to be discharged

righteously, and most natural was it that the duty was entangled in inextricable perplexity.

The tenderness of Hamlet's conscience is shown in his repenting of the chance-killing of Polonius; and afterwards when, eluding the treachery of Rosencrantz and Guildenstern, he sends them to the death they had plotted for him, he makes some little excusing of himself to Horatio:

> "Why, man, they did make love to this employment;
> They are not near my conscience."

And then the thought of putting the king to death comes to his mind with a sense of justice—an act of dutiful vengeance:

> "Is't not perfect conscience
> To quit him with this arm?"

It is his moral doubts which have blunted his purpose—postponing—

> "The important acting of the dread command."

These caused his misgivings that the spectre might be an evil spirit, seeking out his weakness and his melancholy to abuse him to his perdition. He sought, therefore, further assurance of his conscience by means of the play before the king, saying that if his occulted guilt did not there unkennel itself

> "It is a damned ghost that we have seen,
> And my imaginations are as foul
> As Vulcan's stithy."

When once Hamlet has actually drawn his sword to take

the forfeit life of the usurper, he sheathes it again for an expressed reason that sounds almost like a fiendish vengeance—the thought that if the king were killed while praying, his soul, purged and seasoned for the passage, would go to heaven. But surely no one can misapprehend this for the true reason:—it is only a piece of self-deception—an excuse for delay—a palliation for his shrinking from a deed of blood. The soliloquy of the king is the portraiture of a wretched man clinging to his guilt, and therefore helpless in his strivings after contrition. Touching the subjects of mercy and expiation and prayer, it contains one of those vailed and profoundly reverential allusions to Scripture truths and language, which Shakspeare occasionally shadows forth with such a pious reserve:

> "What, if this cursed hand
> Were thicker than itself with brother's blood?
> Is there not rain enough in the sweet heavens,
> To wash it white as snow? Whereto serves mercy,
> But to confront the visage of offence?
> And what's in prayer, but this twofold force,—
> To be forestalled, ere we come to fall,
> Or pardon'd, being down?"

As the play draws to a close, Hamlet seems rather to recede from his purpose than to approach it. It has been truly said of him that he is always perfectly equal to any call of the moment, let it only not be for the future.* He is sent from the kingdom, nothing yet accomplished. Perhaps his absence was to spare him the sad

---

* Coleridge's Literary Remains, (Notes on Hamlet,) vol. ii. p. 229. (Ed. 1836.)

catastrophe of Ophelia's insanity, of which he was the innocent cause. The love he had been forced by higher duties to relinquish, would have come back to her forlorn estate: it did come back at her grave:

> "I loved Ophelia; forty thousand brothers
> Could not, with all their quantity of love,
> Make up my sum."

A most attractive grace continues to be thrown round every movement of Hamlet—spiritual, intellectual, and bodily, in the closing scenes of the tragedy—the thoughtful, playful conversation with the grave-digger, and the gentle moralizing over the relics of mortality—the gentlemanly sporting with the fop—the more than gentlemanly apology to Laertes:

> "Give me your pardon, sir: I have done you wrong:
> But pardon it, as you are a gentleman.
> This presence knows, and you must needs have heard,
> How I am punish'd with a sore distraction.
> What I have done,
> That might your nature, honour, and exception
> Roughly awake, I here proclaim was madness.
> * * * *
> Sir, in this audience,
> Let my disclaiming from a purposed evil
> Free me so far in your most generous thoughts,
> That I have shot my arrow o'er the house,
> And hurt my brother."

One of the latest expressions of Hamlet's habitual thoughtfulness is the beautiful presentiment of his approaching death, when, speaking to Horatio with some confidence of success in the fencing-match, he adds—"But thou would'st not think how ill all's here about my heart: but it's no matter."* This gloominess alarms his friend, and Hamlet tries to shake it off:—"It is but foolery; but it is such a kind of gain-giving as would, perhaps, trouble a woman." Horatio still urges him to postpone the trial at arms, because he is not fit; but Hamlet speaks in a better mood of faith:—"Not a whit, we defy augury; there's a special providence in the fall of a sparrow."

He whose mind had been so active in its purposes—whose heart had beat so quickly to all true impulses—achieves the duty, vaguely commanded by a supernatural voice, only by co-operating with the tumult of an accident, and in the heat of passion. Heretofore, always equal to the present moment, his meditations—meditations of the heart as well as of the intellect—had perpetually carried him into the distant future. Now, the certainty of the poison crowds all the future of his mortal life into a few, short, present instants. Death is in Denmark's palace. The majestic phantom of him who once tenanted the throne, is avenged by the bloody perishing of the guilty. The innocent one is implicated too deeply in the destiny of the tragedy to escape, and Horatio's words are his fitting requiem:

"Now cracks a noble heart. Good-night, sweet prince;
And flights of angels sing thee to thy rest."†

* Coleridge's Literary Remains, (Notes on Hamlet,) vol. ii. p. 234.

† On my brother's manuscript, I find a reference to what he describes as some excellent criticism on Hamlet in the Christian Remembrancer for January, 1849, in an article on the book of Job; and in a private letter written just as he was fresh from the composition of this lecture, he says:—"I have never felt myself so deeply in the heart of Hamlet—my insight into the character clearer than ever before had been given to me." W. B. R.

LECTURE IV.*

Othello.

IN closing my last lecture, I spoke of the subject of this evening's lecture as the deepest of Shakspeare's tragedies. The first impression might be different; for, through the scenes of Othello, there are scattered things which seem to belong to comedy—the pliability of that poor dupe, Roderigo—the sarcastic jests of Iago and his drinking songs, and the tipsiness of Cassio. These are matters which might befit the comic drama, but they are subordinate to what is, I repeat, the deepest of Shakspeare's tragedies. Perhaps, therefore, it is the most remarkable illustration of the power of our great dramatic poet's imagination in blending together, in apt proportions, the tragic and the comic elements—just as in real life you may often find, near each other, things to weep for, and things to smile, or it may be even to laugh, at. The tragedy of Othello is the deepest, because in it the darkest and lowest region of human wickedness is brought to light, because the victim of that wickedness is a most heroic heart, and because, most of all, a being the purest,

* December 27th, 1842.

most innocent, and gentle, is made the sacrifice. It must be very deep when you reflect that in it are combined the destinies of Iago and Othello and Desdemona. Never did poetic creation dive into a cavern so deep, so dark and noisome as the soul of Iago; never did poet's imagination kindle a fiercer fire than flamed from the heart of the frenzied Moor; never did it shine upon a spot so beautiful, so fair, as that loving, meek, and faithful Venetian lady. It is the deepest tragedy, because there is in its course of events less to reconcile the heart to its dismal ending, less to make us willingly, though wofully, acquiesce in the unmerited suffering of the innocent; and, therefore, it is only by justly and strongly conceiving the essential idea of pure tragedy that we can be brought to believe that such a catastrophe was right.

In the tragedy of Othello, the master-spirit is at once set before us—the wicked one who rules the destinies of all on whom he casts his evil eye. Amid the various forms in which the shaping imagination of the poet has fashioned his conceptions of human wickedness, Iago is pre-eminent—the most vicious—the most viciously powerful of all the Shaksperean villains. There is a force of intellect in the character which, divorced as it is from every thing like moral sentiment, is fearful to contemplate. It has the excessive intellectual activity which we had occasion to study in Hamlet, but not, as in that sweet prince, gently wedded to virtuous meditation and kindly sympathies. The consciousness of mental energy in Hamlet spent itself in pure and perpetual musings; while in Iago it delights in annihilating the peace of mind in his happy fellow-beings. There is something of the reflectiveness of Macbeth, but none of his natural tenderness of disposition—none of his apprehensive imagination—none of his fluttering, procrastinating conscience, which needed the outward impulses of a supernatural temptation, and the strong sway of a strong-willed woman to drive him on to guilt. Iago is all-sufficient to himself. He originates his own plans of mischief; he counsels with no one; he needs no help, unless it be for so insignificant a service as to steal a handkerchief, and then he bids his wife perpetrate the theft. Not altogether passionless, his passions are at the absolute command of his intellect: he can, at will, be calm or choleric. Listen as closely as you may, you cannot hear his heart beat. He is one of your stony-hearted philosophers—

> "A reasoning, self-sufficient thing,
> An intellectual all-in-all."*

He knows where his strength lies, and it is his delight to use it; for he plots and intrigues and destroys.

One curious evidence of the power of this character is to be observed in the fact, that the reader himself is often deluded by Iago's sophistries and falsehood, so artfully does he misrepresent them—so vehemently does he vilify. For instance, speaking of Desdemona, he says to Roderigo—"Mark me with what violence she first loved the Moor, but for bragging and telling her fantastical lies!" And not only does this coarse and vulgar perversion of Othello's defence before the senate of his course of love win the weak belief of Iago's dupe, but the reader himself is half disposed to accredit it. Now, it must be remembered that Shakspeare, above all poets, is distin-

---

* Wordsworth's Poet's Epitaph.

guished for this—that he never explains his characters; he creates them, sets them before us in speech and action, and then leaves it to us to find them out—just as in real life we have to study the characters and tempers of actual men and women, and often without rightly knowing them. It is this which most demonstrates the poet's vivid imagination—the intensity of his creative power: it is this which constitutes the self-forgetting intrepidity of the genuine artist, disdaining to be his own commentator, and trusting that some faithful heart will rise from the reverential lowliness of genuine criticism to a just knowledge of his creations. For this confidence we make but a poor return when we interpret a poet's words as literally as the argumentation of prose, and unimaginatively accept for truth the speech that falls from even a villain's tongue. The poems of Shakspeare are dramas, and, therefore, we must not read them as if they were narratives. They are the action, and not the story, of human virtues and vices and passions; and so true to nature are the creations of his genius, that, living mortals, they may be found saying a hundred things in which they are themselves deceived, or in which they would wilfully deceive others. In the study of character, as dramatically portrayed, there can be no more fruitful source of error than to take detached passages without heed to the character of him who speaks. Now, in the tragedy of Othello, unless you carefully adopt this principle as a safeguard, you have to deal with so adroit a villain, so accomplished a sophist, so reckless and insidious a liar in Iago, that he will surely deceive you. No word of his is to be taken on trust—for he owns no obligation to truth, and is instantaneously rapid in fabrication.

It is to this prodigious talent for deception which characterizes Iago that may, I think, be traced an erroneous view in regard to the very germ of the tragedy. It seems to be generally assumed, that Iago's hatred of Othello had its origin in military disappointment—professional pique at Cassio's promotion in preference to him; and that, therefore, this frustrated ambition left behind it the sting of a determined revenge. According to this view, all the tragic consequences followed from Iago's spirit of vengeance; and I do not know but what there is thus insinuated into our minds some secret sympathy with him as an injured man—an approved soldier unfairly dealt with—his services forgotten in the favouritism to a new soldier—

> "Forsooth, a great arithmetician,
> One Michael Cassio, a Florentine."

Now, what is the proof of all this? Nothing, from first scene to last, I believe, but Iago's word. He says so, and therefore it is true, when surely the safer logic would be, that therefore it is false. General as the interpretation has been, that military disappointment was the cause of Iago's animosity against the Moorish chief, I am well persuaded there is nothing to sanction it. I do not believe a word of the story. There is nothing in the intercourse between Othello and Iago and Cassio which looks like it; and, indeed, such an injury was of itself hardly of the kind to imbitter the feelings of such a being as Iago.

But this fiction has found more ready belief from another cause; and that is, the notion that such extremity of wickedness as his is unnatural—that there is not adequate cause for his hatred of Othello, and the havoc he makes of his happiness. The most has therefore been made of this military disappointment, because critics and readers have assumed to think, that otherwise there would be nothing for the superstructure of the tragedy to rest upon. It would be much better if the critic always approached these dramas with a more docile temper, and not with the presumptuous vanity of helping Shakspeare in his interpretations of what is natural. But the great poet-philosopher did not handle his subjects thus timidly. He was no dainty moralist; and in this tragedy it was his purpose to realize one of the most fearful speculations respecting human nature—to show one of the darkest sides of the soul of man—that it is capable of "motive less malignity." This is Coleridge's fit phrase in the description of Iago's villainy.* At least, the incidents which chance to suggest his malignant feelings are so immeasurably disproportionate, that they can scarce be spoken of as causes or motives. In some cases it is clearly apparent, that Iago's reasons are afterthoughts —faint recognitions of the difference between right and wrong—opiates to quiet the few, irregular, and very feeble beatings of a conscience not quite dead. The explanations of his hatred of Othello are not to be credulously received as realities, but to be withstood as the fictions of a quick invention and a wicked spirit—foul things engendered in the pollutions of his heart.

In the science of human nature, it is a fearful truth that there is a temptation to crime in the mere gratification of a pleasurable consciousness of power; that the

* Literary Remains, vol. ii. p. 260. (Notes on Othello.)

mind is tempted to dwell upon guilt, which, thus being taken up into the thoughts, becomes familiar, and then takes possession of our actions. This is the peril of a foul imagination, such as Iago's. It is shallow philosophy to look for outward, instead of inward, motive; and most unsatisfactory is it to be told that the motive to all the misery which Iago worked out was no more than a disappointment in promotion. Such a solution seems only the more to perplex the problem; for, if we must seek for an outward motive, this is, indeed, most insufficient. The true motive was the innate malignity of Iago's heart—the natural antagonism of a base to a noble nature. In this tragedy, Shakspeare has represented one of the most insidious and mysterious temptations that the spirit of man is exposed to—a temptation which, when it triumphs, seems to assimilate humanity, even in its mortal life, to the desperate state of demons. It is the pride of power in its most depraved form: proud of its wicked inventions, and then proud of the conscious strength to achieve them. Perhaps we might in this way trace to its source that strange influence—the contagion or fascination of crime. Some act of depravity is committed, then told in all its appalling details; and, when the public mind becomes thoroughly familiar with the thoughts and emotions thus prompted, a hundred hearts, roused from their sleep of innocence, are impelled, by what almost seems a supernatural influence, to perpetrate their wicked imaginations. The records of crime bear witness to this horrid truth: they show that this mysterious path does exist among the thousand avenues, which the powers of evil have opened, to tempt the soul of man downward. I do not know that philosophy has done much to explain how the will of man is led to this aberration, but there is something analogous to it, and by which, perhaps, it may be illustrated, in an emotion which, probably, has been experienced by most persons—I allude to that singular feeling or impulse, or whatever it may be called, which, on looking down from the edge of any great elevation, seems to be almost a wish to cast oneself into the depth below, and which comes so strongly on some, that they shrink, shuddering, from the spot of danger. This sensation has been described by Shakspeare, with one of his inimitable phrases, in a well-known passage in Hamlet:

> "The very place puts toys of desperation,
> Without more motive, into every brain,
> That looks so many fathoms to the sea,
> And hears it roar beneath."

In like manner the contemplation of crime—the looking down into its deep, dark moral gulf, strangely puts "toys of desperation" in the brain of him who suffers his thoughts and imaginings to dwell too familiarly with guilt. Iago's intellect is habitually busy with the evil suggestions of intense selfishness and native malignity; and his is a strong and active intellect, every movement of which brings along with it a sense of power; and then the inevitable, irresistible, onward course of iniquity is to put these wicked conceptions into action.

The first movement of the tragedy and of the wicked elements of Iago's disposition, seems to be simply this: during an interval of military service, he has insinuated himself into a kind of friendship with a rich young Venetian, whom he flatters with professions of assistance in gaining the hand of Desdemona. Iago is a soldier—a man of adventure; and he has gained an ascendancy over Roderigo for the meanly selfish purpose of using his purse. This mercenary motive, cast in the rank soil of Iago's heart, is the single seed from which springs the harvest of all his atrocity. Unexpectedly, it is discovered that Othello has proved a successful rival in Desdemona's love, and Iago finds it necessary to confirm the assurances he has given of his hatred towards Othello; and then comes the fiction, as I believe it to be, of the wrong done to him by Cassio's promotion. There is on the part of Roderigo an almost immeasurable inferiority of intellect to his companion, but this very inferiority serves an important dramatic purpose, because thus Iago's character is the better developed by his bolder dealings with his dupe. Well assured of his intellectual supremacy, which there was neither force of mind nor of morals to withstand, Iago knows that he is sure of deference to mere power of intellect, even although displayed in a reckless avowal of an absolute want of principle and honour. So completely is Roderigo in his grasp—so absolutely subject to the stronger mind—that Iago talks to him almost as unreservedly as in soliloquy. There is no one to whom he speaks so freely, so fully; no one, indeed, to whom he could have ventured so to open the dark and hollow places of his heart. It is apparently from the pleasureable consciousness of his abundant power of intellect, rather than from the necessity of it, that he goes on arguing and philosophizing with his dupe; and so mighty is the fascination, that Roderigo scarcely flutters under it—he is lost in amazement and admiration at the boldness with which honesty is scoffed at, and the pride of intellectual strength proclaimed. When Roderigo expresses surprise at Iago's reconciling his hatred and service to Othello, he is overwhelmed with the answer—

> "O sir, content you:
> I follow him to serve my turn upon him:
> We cannot all be masters, nor all masters
> Cannot be truly follow'd. You shall mark
> Many a duteous and knee-crooking knave,
> That, doting on his own obsequious bondage,
> Wears out his time, much like his master's ass,
> For nought but provender; and when he's old, cashier'd:
> Whip me such honest knaves. Others there are,
> Who, trimm'd in forms and visages of duty,
> Keep yet their hearts attending on themselves;
> And, throwing but shows of service on their lords,
> Do well thrive by them; and, when they have lined their coats,
> Do themselves homage: these fellows have some soul;
> And such a one do I profess myself.
> For, sir,
> It is as sure as you are Roderigo,
> Were I the Moor, I would not be Iago.
> In following him, I follow but myself:
> Heaven is my judge, not I for love and duty,
> But seeming so, for my peculiar end:
> For when my outward action doth demonstrate
> The native act and figure of my heart
> In compliment extern, 'tis not long after,
> But I will wear my heart upon my sleeve,
> For daws to peck at: I am not what I am."

And when he has thus made sure of Roderigo's absolute submissiveness, observe with what decision he bids him, as to his course against Othello,

> "Make after him, poison his delight;
> Proclaim him in the streets; incense her kinsmen,
> And, though he in a fertile climate dwell,
> Plague him with flies: though that his joy be joy,
> Yet throw such changes of vexation on't,
> As it may lose some colour."

Iago is soon after found by the side of his noble victim. He tells Othello of Roderigo's slanders; and, with blunt professions of love and loyalty, he says how hard it was to refrain from resenting it by stabbing the slanderer—and the calm, placid heroism of the Moor is shown in the simple reply—

"'Tis better as it is."

All attempts to excite or intimidate him are equally ineffectual; for there is an imperturbable dignity when he intimates his lofty birth, his services to the state, and his devotion to a soldier's life, as sufficient security against the angry father's complaints:

"Let him do his spite:
My services, which I have done the seigniory,
Shall out-tongue his complaints. 'Tis yet to know,
(Which, when I know that boasting is an honour,
I shall promulgate,) I fetch my life and being
From men of royal siege; and my demerits
May speak, unbonneted, to as proud a fortune
As this that I have reach'd. For know, Iago,
But that I love the gentle Desdemona,
I would not my unhoused free condition
Put into circumscription and confine
For the sea's worth."

When urged by Iago to retire, the same majestic composure is in his answer:

"Not I: I must be found;
My parts, my title, and my perfect soul
Shall manifest me rightly."

And when the incensed father, with his followers, breaks in upon him to claim his daughter back, amid the tumult of torches hurried hither and thither, and swords drawn by the friends of both, the tranquil and commanding voice of Othello rises above the angry elements:

> "Keep up your bright swords, for the dew will rust them.—
> Good signior, you shall more command with years
> Than with your weapons.
> Hold your hands,
> Both you of my inclining, and the rest.
> Were it my cue to fight, I should have known it
> Without a prompter."

The hero of the tragedy is thus introduced—a man of heroic stamp, an intrepid soldier, honoured for faithful services to the Venetian State; the blood of kings is coursing in his veins, and the royalty of his birth and his martial experience are accompanied with a lofty spirit and a majestic self-command. But he has been first introduced by the ribaldry of Iago, and hence the imagination is unhappily tempted to adopt one of those false impressions, which his filthy fancy delights in giving.

The repulsive notion that Othello was a black*—a coarse-featured African—seems to me directly at variance with the requisitions of both poetry and history; and I cannot but think it is an error which may be traced either to some false critical theory, or else more probably to the too literal interpretation of passages in the play—the unimaginative reading which is fatal so often to the

* Coleridge handles this topic (of Othello's colour) in Literary Remains, vol. ii. p. 256. So in his Table Talk, p. 1: "Othello must not be conceived as a negro, but a high and chivalrous Moorish chief. Shakspeare learned the spirit of the character from the Spanish poetry which was prevalent in England in his time." W. B. R.

spirit of poetry. The hero is styled "Othello *the Moor;*" such is his title and familiar designation throughout. He was one of that adventurous race of men who, striking out from the heart of Arabia, had made conquest of Persia and Syria; and, overturning the ancient sovereignty of Egypt, swept in victory along the whole northern coast of Africa, and, passing thence across the narrow frith of the Mediterranean, scattered the dynasty of the Goths with Roderic at their head. In the most fertile region of Spain they built up an empire which lasted for centuries, and left behind them, for the wonder of remote generations, in the ruins of the Alhambra, a monument of the pomp of Saracenic civilization. Moreover, it was the race that preserved the literature of Greece—its philosophy and science—when Greece itself was prostrate and benighted. Even after the power of the caliphs in their several realms began to decline, the Moors were the chosen and honoured captains of the armies of Christian states. Especially was this the policy of the Venetian Republic, to lessen, it is said, by the employment of mercenary commanders, the danger of domestic intrigue. How true to his nature was it for Othello to stand in conscious pride—the descendant of a race of kings—the representative of the Arabs who had been sovereigns in Europe—his spirit glowing with noble ancestral memories! And, on the other hand, how perfectly consistent it was with the debasing malignity of Iago, and with the petulant disappointment of Roderigo, a foppish Venetian, to be blind to all that ennobled and dignified the Moorish name—to see no distinction between the chivalrous Moor, the chieftain of Christian armies, and the barbarous Ethiop—the despised slave. It was natural that vulgar words should be uttered from the lips of such men, and also that the parental phrensy of Desdemona's father should find relief in the same strain of vituperative misrepresentation—the propensity of a fresh and angry grief to magnify its injury. Such are the authorities which have led to the supposition that Othello was black. In one scene, indeed, he speaks so of himself: but it is when he is in Iago's grasp—when his disordered spirit has begun to give food to his own suspicions. It is when he is "changing with the poison." The agony of doubt has heaved over the lofty, complacent bearing of his happier moments, and his speaking of himself as black is—what is very natural to such condition of mind—a piece of morbid exaggeration, just as when, in the same scene, he describes himself as—

"Declined into the vale of years."

On every account, it is better to clear the fancy of this false conception of Othello's colour—most of all for the sake of our sympathies with the gentle Desdemona; for, if we are brought to believe that this bright, this fair-faced, Venetian lady was wedded to a black, we should almost be tempted to think that the monstrous alliance was fitly blotted out in its fearful catastrophe.

Shakspeare probably took his hero from the Spanish poetry of the times—a Moorish chieftain—one of the dark-complexioned guests, who were familiarly welcome in the houses of the Venetian nobles; and, being cherished for illustrious public services, it was not difficult for the susceptible fancy of a woman to transfigure the shades upon the Moorish brow with the glory of the warrior's spirit. Perhaps, too, it was partly the poet's purpose to show the transforming power of the passion of love—that magic which shows

"Helen's beauty in a brow of Egypt."

The Moorish complexion of Othello—not intended to produce in our minds disgust at Desdemona's choice—is made to serve an important dramatic purpose, in that it greatly ministers to his suspicions of his wife's fidelity. It is the first unprompted argument for doubt—the first suggested by Othello's own thoughts, and, of course, quickly seized on and fomented by Iago. It serves, too, to account for the extreme sensitiveness of Othello's sense of honour—that which is a prime element in his character.

The careless interpretation of this tragedy has usually treated it as Shakspeare's exposition of the passion of *jealousy.** But, in Othello's composition, there is not an element of jealousy. Shakspeare has depicted jealous men in other of his plays, and nothing can be more

* Coleridge was the first to deny the jealousy of Othello, (Literary Remains, vol. ii. p. 258, 266, and Table Talk, p. 1, 39.) Most of the critics have followed him. De Quincey, in a note to his Life and Manners, (Boston ed. p. 79,) says—"Mr. Coleridge has contended, and I think with truth, that the passion of Othello is *not* jealousy. So much I know by report as the result of a lecture which he read at the Royal Institution. His arguments I did not hear. To me it is evident that Othello's state of mind was not that of a degrading, suspicious rivalship; but the state of perfect misery arising out of this dilemma, the most affecting, perhaps, to contemplate of any which can exist, viz., the dire necessity of loving without limit one whom the heart pronounces to be unworthy and irretrievably sunk." To my mind, utterly repugnant as it is to all manner of paradoxical criticism, it seems, after all, that Falstaff *was* a coward, and Othello *was* jealous.
W. B. R.

different from the Moor. Besides, jealousy is a little, a mean passion—something which dwells in small minds, whereas all the passions of Othello are heroic and magnanimous. In his dying words, he was "not easily jealous;" and, indeed, even after Iago has begun to torture his spirit, he, with perfect truth, disclaims the morbid apprehensiveness of jealousy:

> "'Tis not to make me jealous
> To say my wife is fair, feeds well, loves company,
> Is free of speech, sings, plays, and dances well;
> Where virtue is, these are more virtuous:
> Nor from mine own weak merits will I draw
> The smallest fear, or doubt of her revolt;
> For she had eyes and chose me."

Indeed, as if to show how imperturbable Othello is by the impulse of insufficient excitement and irritation, nothing can be more admirable than the unbroken calm he seems to dwell in during the early part of the play—the heroic repose of his spirit—his majestic self-possession, whether under the reproaches heaped upon him by one who is secure from his resentment, or even in the fresh fervour of his love for Desdemona. The military duty which interrupts his bridal days, is placidly welcomed with the cheerfulness of a soldier's spirit of self-sacrifice.

The ship that bears Othello to Cyprus is tossed by a fearful tempest, ominous of the mightier tempest which soon was to heave his heart. When, after the brief interruption of the voyage, he is once more welcomed by his wife, his swelling happiness gives itself freer utterance than he had yet indulged in. There is a sense of joy more than befits a mortal's portion, and therefore it is slightly darkened with what Shakspeare often uses—a presentiment that it can scarce endure—an apprehension sweetly echoed by a faint prayer from the more confiding heart of Desdemona. But the presentiment begins to be fashioned into a threatening reality; for a fiendlike eye is fastened on their bliss, and the heart is chilled by Iago's sneer and his malignant menace:

> "Oh, you are well tuned now!
> But I'll set down the pegs that make the music,
> As honest as I am."

The first indication of the stormy elements, which, by heroic discipline, have been taught to slumber in Othello's heart, is when he finds the midnight tranquillity of Cyprus broken by the drunken brawl which Iago had artfully fomented. This wounds Othello's soldierly pride—his sense of honour; and the hidden fires in his Moorish blood flash for the first time in high indignation at the disgraceful breach of discipline. The scene is note of preparation for the more appalling outbreak of the passions of the Moor.

The way being prepared, Iago's work of destruction is accomplished with frightful rapidity; and probably the most masterly scene in the whole range of dramatic literature is that third scene of the third act, in which, with almost demoniac skill, he annihilates Othello's peace of mind forever. Four or five simple words from Iago's lips—a slight exclamation, half-suppressed, but meant for Othello's ear—and the irretrievable mischief is begun: the poisoned shaft is shot. From that moment the happiness of the Moor is gone. But, throughout this scene, there is nothing of the excitability by inadequate causes, or of the eagerness to snatch at proofs, which are characteristics of jealousy. On the contrary, the efforts of Othello are gigantic against the proofs, but they are forced upon his mind like demonstration: the bitterness of his agony is the unavoidable acquiescence, as, when almost speechlessly, he gives in to the first argument Iago plies him with:

> "She did deceive her father marrying you
> *Othello.* And so she did."

When Iago finds him too much depressed by the first suggestions, he cheers him up with an affected bluntness of honesty and regret, in order that Othello's mind may recover energy enough to move forward to his destruction—by its own force impelled by slight impulses. As when the Moor's disturbed thoughts begin to suggest reasons, such as his sense of the incongruous match, it is instantly seized on by Iago—

> "Ay! there's the point;"

and a hundred-fold aggravated. Othello's mind is now tormented with a morbid activity—the restlessness almost of insanity—first a regret that he had married, and then the misery of his fierce resolve to cast her off:

> "If I do prove her haggard,
> Though that her jesses were my dear heart-strings,
> I'd whistle her off, and let her down the wind,
> To prey at fortune."

When Desdemonda appears, the mere sight of her brings back for a moment his better nature, and there is a desperate struggle to dismiss all doubt:

> "If she be false, O, then, heaven mocks itself!
> I'll not believe it."

But the effort is a vain one, as Iago well knew:

"The Moor already changes with my poison.
Dangerous conceits are, in their natures, poisons,
Which, at the first, are scarce found to distaste;
But, with a little act upon the blood,
Burn like the mines of sulphur.
Not poppy, nor mandragora,
Nor all the drowsy syrups of the world,
Shall ever medicine thee to that sweet sleep
Which thou ow'dst yesterday."

The Moor's doubts have wrought him into a phrensy, and his thoughts, thus strongly impelled, go back to the glory of his martial life, and he feels that it must be obscured by his conjugal indignity. His soldier's spirit sinks within him, and this new sorrow speaks in that plaintive lament, which is heard like the sighing of the wind when its last low sounds are telling of a coming storm:

"O, now, forever
Farewell, the tranquil mind! farewell, content!
Farewell, the plumed troop, and the big wars,
That make ambition virtue! O, farewell!
Farewell, the neighing steed, and the shrill trump,
The spirit-stirring drum, the ear-piercing fife,
The royal banner; and all quality,
Pride, pomp, and circumstance of glorious war!
And, O, you mortal engines, whose rude throats
The immortal Jove's dread clamours counterfeit,
Farewell! Othello's occupation's gone!"

The fiendish Iago, knowing his power, pours the poison into Othello's heart with a bolder hand; and then comes the meditation of revenge—the Moor's outraged honour crying aloud for vengeance. The contending emotions which make this agony are unconquered love and a new-born hate. When the tempter, with hideous hypocrisy, counsels patience—

"Never, Iago.—Like to the Pontic sea,
Whose icy current and compulsive course
Ne'er feels retiring ebb, but keeps due on
To the Propontic and the Hellespont;
Even so my bloody thoughts, with violent pace,
Shall ne'er look back, ne'er ebb to humble love,
Till that a capable and wide revenge
Swallow them up."

His desperation is wrought by the collision of two sovereign passions. He struggles to hate, and yet loves as deeply to the very last. He boasts that his heart is turned to stone, and, at the same time, great streams of love come gushing from it. His suffering sense of honour, too, increases the misery. The conflict of the passions becomes even more tragic in the subsequent interview with the innocent one. Othello's stern heroism breaks into tears, and his bewildered wife seeks to soothe him in the tenderest strain of remonstrance:

"Alas! the heavy day! why do you weep?
Am I the occasion of these tears, my lord?
If haply you my father do suspect
An instrument of this your calling back,
Lay not your blame on me; if you have lost him,
Why I have lost him to."

This calls forth, in a kind of self-communion rather than direct reply, the fullest expression of the anguish that was breaking Othello's heart—a sense of heroic honour fatally wounded, and a deep love blasted by the conviction of impurity:

"Had it pleased heaven
To try me with affliction; had he rain'd
All kinds of sores and shames on my bare head;
Steep'd me in poverty to the very lips;
Given to captivity me and my utmost hopes;
I should have found in some part of my soul
A drop of patience: but, alas! to make me
A fixed figure for the time of scorn
To point his slow unmoving finger at,—
Yet could I bear that too; well, very well;
But there where I have garner'd up my heart;
Where either I must live, or bear no life;
The fountain from the which my current runs,
Or else dries up; to be discarded thence!
Or keep it as a cistern for foul toads
To knot and gender in!
* * * *
O, thou weed,
Who art so lovely fair, and smell'st so sweet,
That the sense aches at thee,—would thou had'st ne'er been born!"

A splendid contrast begins now to be dimly developed between the character of Othello and Desdemona. He has surrendered his generous and confiding spirit to the craft of a subtle intellect; he has suffered himself to be betrayed out of the moral region of faith into the cold atmosphere of doubts and questionings and proofs. The sustaining principle of his nature has perished; for it is against his nature that convictions have overwhelmed him. But Desdemona, trusting to her own pure impulses, still clings to her faith; and, by virtue of it alone, in opposition to all that her senses and her understanding show her, she is wise as well as innocent. She will not believe even what she sees, but, with the most irresistible tenderness of conscious purity, invents excuses for her husband's violence:

> "Something, sure, of state,
> Either from Venice, or some unhatch'd practice
> Made demonstrable here in Cyprus to him,
> Hath puddled his clear spirit; and in such cases,
> Men's natures wrangle with inferior things,
> Though great ones are their object."

She scarcely doubts her husband's righteousness, and only questions her own behaviour. The only complaint she utters is in no higher tone than this:

> "Those that do teach young babes,
> Do it with gentle means and easy tasks;
> He might have chid me so, for in good faith,
> I am a child to chiding."

She seems to have no fear that, come what may,—

> "Though he do shake me off
> To beggarly divorcement,"—

her love can be weakened:

> "Unkindness may do much,
> And his unkindness may defeat my life,
> But never taint my love."

Iago has seen Othello wrought up to the highest pitch of phrensy—wildly crying for blood; but this, he knows, will not answer his devilish purposes. It is necessary yet to work him into the calm resolve of deliberate vengeance—the firmness of a judicial avenger; and the skill with which this is accomplished is fearful to contemplate—to see how he makes Desdemona's attractions, and even virtues, plead against her. When the lingering affection of the Moor still betrays itself, Iago tells him—

> "Nay, you must forget that."

And when, against his darker will, he goes on recounting her graces, he is boldly told—

"She's the worse for all this;"

and Othello, as if reproaching himself for a momentary tenderness, wildly assents—

"O, a thousand, a thousand times!"

The feeling cannot be shaken away—

"And then of so gentle a condition."

This, too, is perverted into proof of guilt:

"Ay, too gentle."

The profound emotion with which assent is wrung from the helpless Moor is, perhaps, the finest touch of pathos in the tragedy:

"Nay, that's certain:
But yet the pity of it, Iago!—
O, Iago, the pity of it, Iago!"

The tumultuous passions which have agitated the agonized Othello, almost subside into a sense of justice—the awful sternness of composure with which he is about to render up an expiation for his injured honour.

The only being whose spotless purity endures is the injured Desdemona. The violent elements rage around her without spoiling her innocence. She shrinks even from the sound of the coarse words that wound her ear, and it is inimitably touching when she appeals to Iago himself:

"Am I that name, Iago?
Iago. What name, fair lady?
Des. Such as she says my lord did say I was."

Desdemona is preserved innocent, for she is a sacrifice—

a victim without blemish—meek and unresisting. It is as such that Othello approaches her to execute her doom:

"It is the cause, it is the cause, my soul,—
Let me not name it to you, you chaste stars!—
It is the cause.—Yet I'll not shed her blood:
Nor scar that whiter skin of hers than snow,
And smooth as monumental alabaster.
Yet she must die."

The fierce Moor is again all tenderness, even in his dire determination. Weeping over Desdemona—his sleeping, unconscious wife, he is impressed with a sacrificial solemnity:

"I must weep,
But they are cruel tears: This sorrow's heavenly;
It strikes where it doth love."

The plot which, by the simplest means, had been entangled so intricately, is unwoven by means as simple. The fall of a handkerchief had been all the machinery* —that handkerchief of which Othello, terrifying the imagination of his wife, told her—

"There's magic in the web of it:
A sibyl, that had number'd in the world
The sun to make two hundred compasses,
In her prophetic fury sew'd the work:
The worms were hallow'd that did breed the silk,
And it was dyed in mummy, which the skilful
Conserved of maidens' hearts,"—

* "Schiller has the material sublime; to produce an effect, he sets you a whole town on fire, and throws infants, with their mothers, into the flames, or locks up a father in an old tower. But Shakspeare drops a handkerchief, and the same or greater effects follow." Coleridge's Table Talk, p. 2. W. B. R.

that handkerchief, the thought of which, in Cassio's hands, recalled by Iago, struck the last hope from Othello's heart:

"Oh, it comes o'er my memory,
As doth the raven o'er the infected house,
Boding to all."

And now the whole truth is revealed to the misguided Othello, by the few words of Emilia:

"O thou dull Moor! that handkerchief thou speak'st of,
I found by fortune, and did give my husband."

The sense of misery and the sense of justice bid Othello most willingly make his own life forfeit to the same hand which had destroyed the innocent one. There only remains a little faint questioning of Iago, "why he hath thus ensnared both soul and body"—a little excusing of himself—

"For nought I did in hate, but all in honour,"—

a little heart-broken pleading for his memory—his soldier's memory for services done to the state, but yet more for his conjugal memory—to be spoken of as

"One that loved not wisely, but too well:
Of one not easily jealous, but, being wrought,
Perplex'd in the extreme; of one whose hand,
Like the base Judean, threw a pearl away
Richer than all his tribe; of one, whose subdued eyes,
Albeit unused to the melting mood,
Drop tears as fast as the Arabian trees
Their medicinal gum."*

* After the delivery of this lecture, it flashed upon me that there is an inimitable and most pathetic beauty in the dying Moor's allusion

This sad tragedy was never meant to give an admonition so superficial as to warn against the evil of jealousy. The moral of Shakspeare's dramas always lies deeper, because they are works of pure imagination—the noblest faculty of the human mind. There may be discovered in this tragedy the loftiest moral that poetry ever shadowed forth—the victory of faith. When Othello was tempted to cast his faith from out his heart, his whole nature was given over to misery and desperation and guilt—he lost the inward spiritual principle which was the very life of his moral being. But Desdemona clung to her faith, and it kept her heart in its perfect integrity and innocence—even through all her sorrows and to the last moment of consciousness on her fearful death-bed. Comparatively, she was happy; for the chief sufferer was the faith-bewildered Othello.

This course of lectures, through which you have so kindly followed me, has comprehended only the subject of *tragic* poetry; and, although King Lear, Macbeth, Hamlet, and Othello afford illustrations as varied as need be desired, yet they have been no more than varieties of terror and pity and sorrow; and, dwelling thus upon sad emotions alone, I have not been without a fear that you

---

to "the *Arabian* trees." What perfect poetic truth it is!—the mind, by one of its almost supernaturally quickened processes, is travelling far back to the land of his birth and the home of his childhood.

It furnishes, too, another proof of Othello's veritable *Moorish* blood.

H. R.

might be craving some relief in having your thoughts so exclusively directed to the dismal side of humanity. Indeed, it would inspire a happy feeling, and finely would it show the universality of the poet's genius, if we could have suddenly turned our attention to the bright side of that world which Shakspeare has created; to delve in the inexhaustible mine of Falstaff's wit, and find the genuine ore of his joyous philosophy and humour; to speed in fancy into the fairy realm of Ariel and Oberon, or to follow the light-hearted Rosalind through the sunny, shady glades of the forest of Arden. But the scope of my course was necessarily confined to "poetry in its deepest earnest," and to trace the moral which tragedy imaginatively teaches—

"That there is often found
In mournful thoughts, and always might be found,
A power to virtue friendly;"

those mournful thoughts not to be spent in luxurious, sentimental dreaminess, but to be taken up into our actions; for, let me say, there is no more insidious temptation than the self-delusion of sentimentality; it is not only worthless as a principle of action, but it may co-exist with a deplorable hardening of the heart.

I have followed the moral teachings of a poet in those tragedies, which serve to show the salutary influences of sorrow; and the lessons of history give further confirmation. For what does history tell of half so much as of suffering? If science teaches that this earth of ours is a glittering planet, the records of history as surely teach, that it rolls on stained with blood and with tears. So has it ever been, and the pages of history which impress us most deeply are its tragedies. In all the annals of the ancient dynasty of Egypt, what is there like that tragic midnight moment, when all the first-born of the land were smitten—"from the first-born of Pharaoh that sat on his throne unto the first-born of the captive that was in the dungeon?" The chronicles of Babylon have perished, and we bear in mind only that tragic hour, when there came forth the fingers of a man, and wrote upon the palace wall the prophecy of an empire's doom. Turn to classic story, and what rises up to the memory more readily than the sacrifice in the tragic pass of Thermopylæ? Come to the annals of our fatherland, and where have they a deeper interest, than when the career of King Charles—him who had been the companion of the loose and profligate Villiers—him who had broken the covenant of the constitution—turned into tragedy, when gloom was gathering over his fortunes, from the day on which the royal standard was raised at Nottingham only to be ominously cast down in a stormy and unruly night, until at length he made a bloody atonement on the scaffold; and, as his corpse was borne to an unnoted grave, with no other funeral rite than silent loyalty, snow fell drearily but purely upon the black pall that covered his coffin?*

Thus it is that history, as well as poetry, shows what has been finely called "the power and divinity of suffering." There is a moral interest in spots sacred to sorrow which grandeur cannot boast of; and a thoughtful traveller has thus expressed the feeling on visiting the palace

* "The king's body was laid in the grave without any words, or other ceremonies than the tears and sighs of a few beholders." Clarendon, b. xi. W. B. R.

of the doges at Venice:—"It is a strange building, with its multitudinous little marble columns and grotesque windows, and the Giant Staircase all glorious of the purest Carrara marble, carved and chiselled into ornaments of the most beautiful minuteness. A splendid palace indeed it is: yet, while my eye wandered in a few minutes over the gorgeous part of the structure, it was long riveted with undiminished interest upon the little round holes close to the level of the sullen canal beneath the Bridge of Sighs: holes which marked the dungeons beneath the level of the canal, where, for years, the victims of that wicked merchant republic were confined. * * *

"And why is it that suffering should have a spell to fix the eye above the power of beauty or of greatness? Is it because the cross is a religion of suffering—a faith of suffering—a privilege of suffering—a perfection arrived at by and through suffering only? Half an hour was enough for the Ducal Palace. I could gaze for hours upon those dungeon-holes, gaze and read there, as in an exhaustless volume, histories on histories of silent, weary suffering, as it filed the soft heart of man away, attenuated his reason into a dull instinct, or cracked the stout heart as you would shiver a flint. * * * * * *

"There is seldom a line of glory written upon the earth's face, but a line of suffering runs parallel with it; and they that read the lustrous syllables of the one, and stoop not to decipher the spotted and worn inscription of the other, get the least half of the lesson earth has to give."*

* Faber's Sights and Thoughts in Foreign Churches and among Foreign Peoples, pp. 285, 288.

To these reflections, let me add what a poet has written to teach that, in this mortal life, we have before us not only the duty of *action*, but the more neglected, yet inevitable, duty of *suffering:*

"Great actions move our admiration, chiefly
Because they carry in themselves an earnest
That we can suffer greatly.
Action is transitory—a step, a blow,
The motion of a muscle—this way or that—
'Tis done, and in the after vacancy
We wonder at ourselves like men betrayed:
Suffering is permanent, obscure, and dark,
And shares the nature of infinity.
Yet through the darkness (infinite though it seem,
And irremovable) gracious openings lie,
By which the soul with patient steps of thought,
Now toiling, wafted now on wings of prayer,
May pass in hope; and, though from mortal bonds
Yet undeliver'd, rise with sure ascent
Even to the fountain-head of peace divine."*

I have, I fear, consumed more than an appropriate portion of your time, and it would, therefore, be ungracious to encroach on it longer; but it would be yet more ungracious not to take one moment more, to say how much I have felt the attention which has been given so kindly to my subject.

* These lines are from Wordsworth, the first ten being from his tragedy, "The Borderers."

THE END.

STEREOTYPED BY L. JOHNSON & CO.
PHILADELPHIA.

www.ingramcontent.com/pod-product-compliance
Lightning Source LLC
LaVergne TN
LVHW020932110826
845150LV00004B/841

9781425552886